THE DECLINE OF
POWER
1915–1964

THE
PALADIN
HISTORY OF ENGLAND

General Editor: Lord Blake
Advisory Editor: Cameron Hazlehurst

Other published titles in this series are

The Formation of England 550–1042 *by* H. P. R. Finberg
Peace, Print and Protestantism 1450–1558 *by* C. S. L. Davies
Reformation and Revolution 1558–1660 *by* Robert Ashton
The Crisis of Imperialism 1865–1915 *by* Richard Shannon

ROBERT BLAKE

THE DECLINE OF POWER
POWER
1915–1964

OXFORD UNIVERSITY PRESS · NEW YORK
1985

Copyright © Robert Blake 1985

Published in Great Britain by Granada Publishing Limited

Published in the United States by Oxford University Press, Inc.
200 Madison Avenue
New York, New York 10016

ISBN 0-19-520480-8

Library of Congress Catalog Number: 85-42751

Library of Congress Cataloging in Publication Data

Blake, Robert, 1916–
The decline of power 1915–1964.
(The Paladin history of England)
Bibliography: P.
Includes Index.
1. Great Britain – Politics and Government – 1910–1936
2. Great Britain – Politics and Government – 1936–1945
3. Great Britain – Politics and Government – 1945–1964
I. Title.   II. Series.
DA576.B53 1985   941.082   85-4909

PRINTING (LAST DIGIT) 9 8 7 6 5 4 3 2 1

Printed in Great Britain by William Clowes Limited,
Beccles and London

CONTENTS

FOREWORD

by Robert Blake

History does not consist of a body of received opinion handed
down by authority from the historiographical equivalent of
the heights of Mount Sinai. It is a subject full of vigour,
controversy, life – and sometimes strife. One of the purposes
of the Paladin History of England is to convey not only what
the authors believe to have happened but also why; to discuss
evidence as well as facts; to give an idea and an evaluation of
the controversies which surround so many episodes and
interpretations of the past.

The last twenty years have seen important changes in the
approach to history and to historical questions. There has
also been much painstaking research which throws new light
on old problems and brings new problems into the field of
discussion. Little of all this has so far got through to the
general reader because it has been, naturally, confined to
specialist journals and monographs. A real need exists for a
series of volumes to inform the wide public interested in the
history of England, and this is what the Paladin volumes are
intended to meet.

All history is in one sense contemporary history. These
volumes inevitably and rightly reflect to some extent the
outlook of those who, whatever their own age, are writing in
the 1980s. But there are in any decade a wide variety of
attitudes and schools of thought. The authors of this series
are not chosen to represent a particular body of doctrine;
conservative, liberal, Marxist – or whatever. They are scho-
lars who are deeply involved in the historical questions of
their particular fields, and who believe that it is possible to put

across something of the challenges, puzzles and excitements of their theme to a large audience in a form which is readable, intelligible and concise.

All historical writing must in some measure be arbitrary as to dates and selective as to area. The dates chosen in this series do not depart far from convention but perhaps just enough to encourage both author and reader to take a fresh view. The decision to make this a history of England, rather than Britain, is quite deliberate. It does not mean omission of the important repercussions of events in Scotland, Ireland, Wales or the countries which later constituted the Empire and the Commonwealth; rather a recognition that, whether for good or ill, the English have been the dominant nation in what Tennyson called 'our rough island-story', and that a widening of the scope would lead to diffuseness and confusion.

Historical writing also has to be selective as to themes. Each author uses his own judgement here, but, although politics, ideas, art and literature must always be central features in any work of general history, economic background, social structure, demography, scientific and technical developments are no less important and must be given proper weight.

All sorts of reasons can be given for reading history, but the best of them has always seemed to me sheer pleasure. It is my hope as editor of this series that this enjoyment will be communicated to a large number of people who might otherwise perhaps have never experienced it.

INTRODUCTION

The previous volume of this series, Richard Shannon's *The Crisis of Imperialism*, ended in May 1915 with the fall of the last purely Liberal government in the history of England. This one takes the story from then to October 1964 when the thirteen years of Conservative rule since 1951 came to an end and Harold Wilson's Labour Party scraped home by a narrow margin. All historiographical divisions by date are to some extent arbitrary, and these are no exceptions. Nevertheless, a historian, even if he is writing the history of the world, has to begin and end somewhere. The dates chosen do perhaps symbolize one feature of the book. It is essentially political history, not economic, technological, social, artistic or cultural. This is not because the author regards these aspects of history as trivial or unimportant – far from it – but because political history which includes the history of war, the continuation of politics by other means, happens to be the subject which interests him most. This volume is therefore mainly concerned with party politics, the constitutional framework within which politicians operated and the events and repercussions of two world wars in terms of Britain's status as a great and imperial power.

When the story outlined in this book begins, Britain was a world power of the first magnitude, the centre of an immense empire spread all over the globe. The retention of that empire depended basically upon sea power, and it was the German naval challenge which was the fundamental reason for Britain declaring war. The Belgian guarantee gave moral colour to the declaration and made it easier for the pacifistically inclined wings of the Liberal and Labour parties to support it, but the violation of Belgian neutrality was not the principal cause of Britain's entry, any more than the German invasion of Poland was the principal cause of the declaration of war in 1939. In both cases what was at issue – or seemed to be – was the survival of Britain as a great imperial power.

In fact, as we can now see, the era of the sea-borne empires was coming to an end. Sea power still mattered. It mattered as late as 1982 when Britain recovered the Falkland Islands. But power, throughout the half-century covered by this book, was shifting from the countries that depended for strength on their navies – Britain above all others – to countries which encompassed the great land masses. The importance of the European 'heartland' and the impending transformation of the balance of power was first perceived by a Briton, Sir Halford Mackinder. His book *Democratic Ideals and Reality*, published in 1919, had little impact in his home country but it was closely studied by General Karl Haushofer, a leading exponent of the school of *Geopolitik* and through him had much influence on Hitler. For a number of technological reasons the future lay with the great continental powers. It was Germany's bid to control the 'heartland' of Europe – the vast territories ruled by Russia – which caused the Second World War. Hitler's failure left the two great continental states, America and Russia, confronting one another, with China an uneasy third in the balance of world power. The era of the sea-borne powers had vanished by the early 1960s. Of all the many changes which occurred during the period, this was the one which affected Britain most profoundly. It is the justification of the title of this book.

MAPS

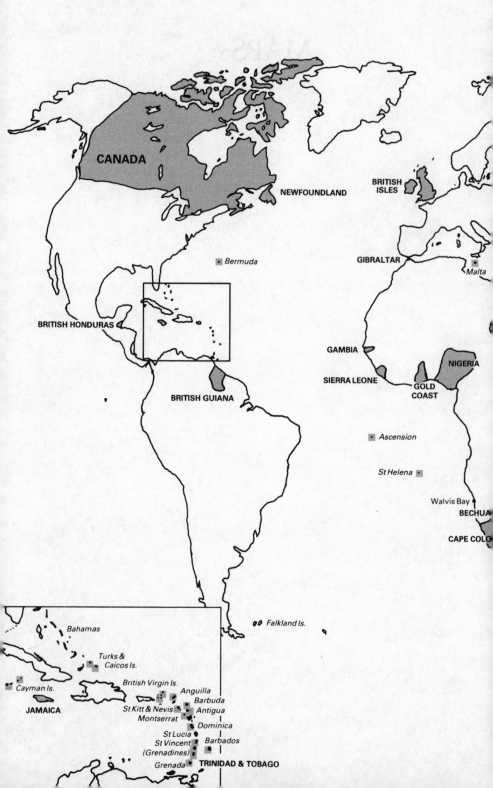

THE BRITISH EMPIRE, 1914

CANADA

NEWFOUNDLAND

BRITISH ISLES

GIBRALTAR

Malta

Bermuda

BRITISH HONDURAS

GAMBIA

SIERRA LEONE

GOLD COAST

NIGERIA

BRITISH GUIANA

Ascension

St Helena

Walvis Bay

BECHUA

CAPE COLO

Bahamas

Turks & Caicos Is.

Cayman Is.

British Virgin Is.

Anguilla

Barbuda

Antigua

St Kitt & Nevis

Montserrat

Dominica

St Lucia

St Vincent

(Grenadines)

Barbados

Grenada

Falkland Is.

JAMAICA

TRINIDAD & TOBAGO

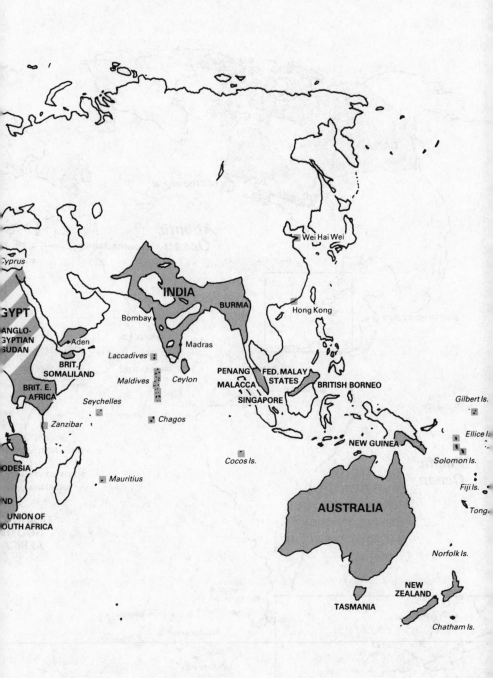

Cyprus

GYPT

ANGLO-
GYPTIAN
SUDAN

Aden

BRIT.
SOMALILAND

BRIT. E.
AFRICA

Zanzibar

ODESIA

ND

UNION OF
OUTH AFRICA

Wei Hai Wei

INDIA

BURMA

Bombay

Madras

Laccadives

Maldives

Ceylon

Hong Kong

PENANG
MALACCA

FED. MALAY
STATES

BRITISH BORNEO

Seychelles

SINGAPORE

Chagos

Cocos Is.

Mauritius

NEW GUINEA

Gilbert Is.

Ellice Is.

Solomon Is.

Fiji Is.

Tong

AUSTRALIA

Norfolk Is.

NEW
ZEALAND

TASMANIA

Chatham Is.

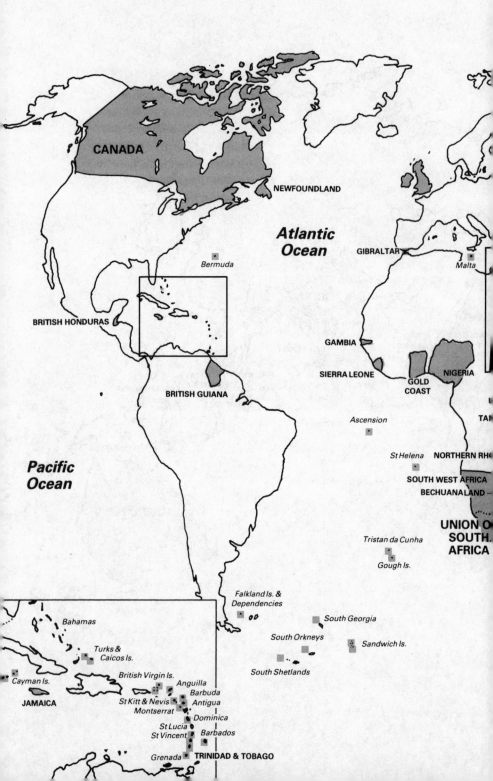

THE BRITISH EMPIRE, 1920

CANADA

NEWFOUNDLAND

Atlantic Ocean

GIBRALTAR

Bermuda

Malta

BRITISH HONDURAS

GAMBIA

SIERRA LEONE

GOLD COAST

NIGERIA

BRITISH GUIANA

TA

Ascension

St Helena

NORTHERN RH

SOUTH WEST AFRICA

BECHUANALAND

Pacific Ocean

UNION O SOUTH. AFRICA

Tristan da Cunha

Gough Is.

Falkland Is. & Dependencies

South Georgia

South Orkneys

Sandwich Is.

South Shetlands

Bahamas

Turks & Caicos Is.

British Virgin Is.

Cayman Is.

JAMAICA

Anguilla

Barbuda

St Kitt & Nevis

Antigua

Montserrat

Dominica

St Lucia

St Vincent

Barbados

Grenada

TRINIDAD & TOBAGO

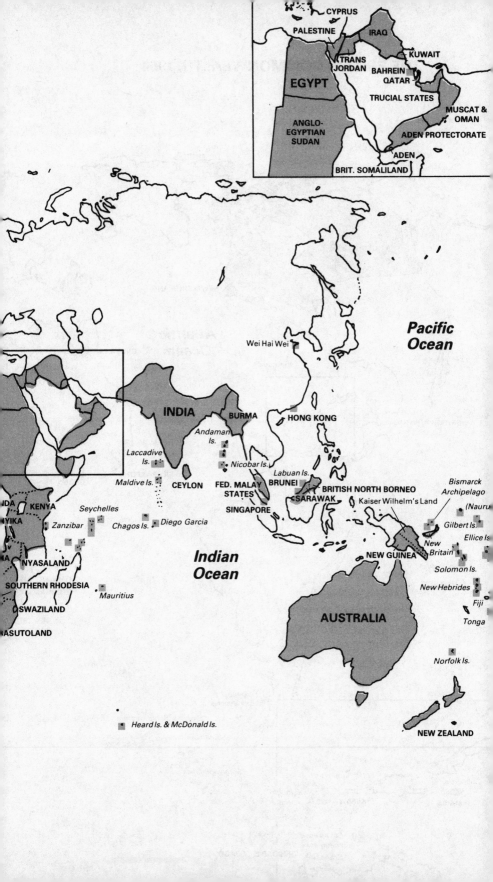

CYPRUS
PALESTINE
IRAQ
KUWAIT
TRANS
JORDAN
BAHREIN
QATAR
EGYPT
TRUCIAL STATES
MUSCAT &
OMAN
ANGLO-
EGYPTIAN
SUDAN
ADEN PROTECTORATE
ADEN
BRIT. SOMALILAND

*Pacific
Ocean*

Wei Hai Wei

INDIA
BURMA
HONG KONG
*Andaman
Is.*
*Laccadive
Is.*
Nicobar Is.
Labuan Is.
BRUNEI
BRITISH NORTH BORNEO
*Bismarck
Archipelago*
Maldive Is.
CEYLON
FED. MALAY
STATES
SARAWAK
Kaiser Wilhelm's Land
(Nauru
SINGAPORE
Gilbert Is.

Seychelles
New
Britain
Ellice Is
KENYA
NYIKA
Zanzibar
Chagos Is.
Diego Garcia
*Indian
Ocean*
NEW GUINEA
Solomon Is.
NYASALAND
New Hebrides
SOUTHERN RHODESIA
Fiji
SWAZILAND
Mauritius
AUSTRALIA
Tonga
ASUTOLAND

Norfolk Is.

Heard Is. & McDonald Is.
NEW ZEALAND

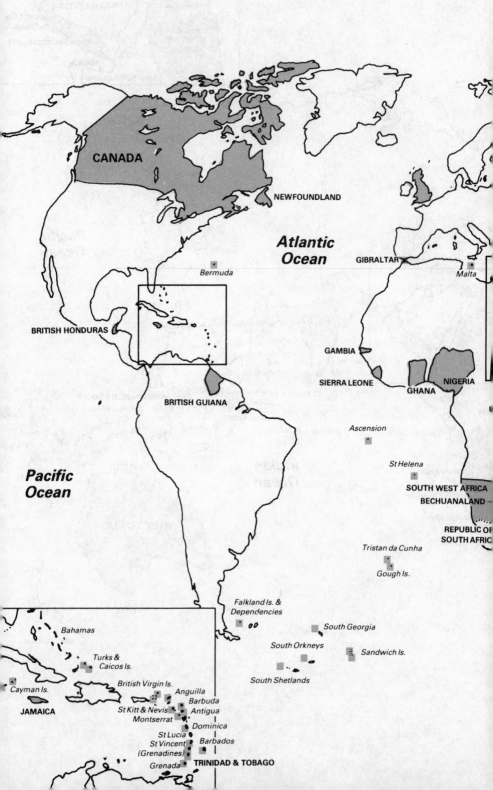

THE BRITISH COMMONWEALTH, 1964

CANADA

NEWFOUNDLAND

Atlantic Ocean

Bermuda

GIBRALTAR

Malta

BRITISH HONDURAS

GAMBIA

SIERRA LEONE

GHANA

NIGERIA

BRITISH GUIANA

Ascension

Pacific Ocean

St Helena

SOUTH WEST AFRICA

BECHUANALAND

REPUBLIC OF SOUTH AFRICA

Tristan da Cunha

Gough Is.

Falkland Is. & Dependencies

South Georgia

South Orkneys

Sandwich Is.

South Shetlands

Bahamas

Turks & Caicos Is.

Cayman Is.

British Virgin Is.

Anguilla

Barbuda

St Kitt & Nevis

Antigua

JAMAICA

Montserrat

Dominica

St Lucia

St Vincent (Grenadines)

Barbados

Grenada

TRINIDAD & TOBAGO

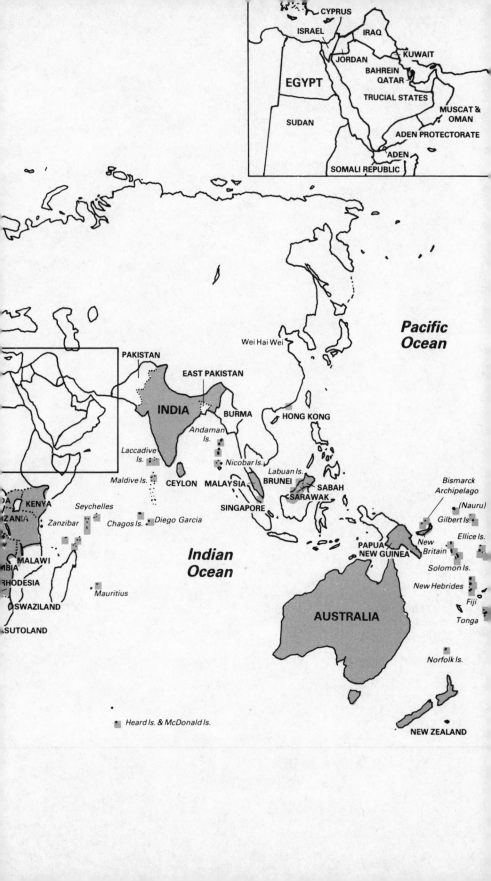

CYPRUS

ISRAEL   IRAQ

JORDAN   KUWAIT

BAHREIN
QATAR

EGYPT   TRUCIAL STATES

MUSCAT &
OMAN

SUDAN   ADEN PROTECTORATE

ADEN

SOMALI REPUBLIC

Pacific
Ocean

Wei Hai Wei

PAKISTAN

EAST PAKISTAN

INDIA   BURMA

HONG KONG

Andaman
Is.

Laccadive
Is.   Nicobar Is.

Labuan Is.

Maldive Is.   CEYLON   MALAYSIA   BRUNEI   SABAH

Bismarck
Archipelago

(Nauru)

SARAWAK

KENYA   SINGAPORE   Gilbert Is.

Seychelles   Ellice Is.

ZANIA   Zanzibar   Chagos Is.   Diego Garcia   PAPUA   New
                                                                                              NEW GUINEA   Britain

MALAWI   Solomon Is.

MBIA   Indian   New Hebrides

RHODESIA   Ocean   Fiji

SWAZILAND   Mauritius   Tonga

SUTOLAND   AUSTRALIA

Norfolk Is.

Heard Is. & McDonald Is.

NEW ZEALAND

Chapter One

THE FIRST WAR COALITION

'The disintegration of the Liberal Party is complete,' wrote Sir Charles Hobhouse, one of the sacked ministers, in his diary on 23 May 1915. 'We shall not return to power for some years and only then because Labour is as broken as ourselves. Lloyd George and his Tory friends will soon get rid of Asquith.'[1] The prediction was partly correct. Asquith was manoeuvred out of office barely over a year and a half later and replaced by Lloyd George with Conservative support. The old Liberal Party disintegrated but Hobhouse was over-optimistic in believing that the divisions of the Labour Party would cause it to reunite. The Liberals never held office on their own again. It was Labour which, for all its disorder, lived to fight another day and become the alternative party of government.

Professor Shannon has mentioned some of the reasons for Asquith's sudden decision to reconstruct his ministry on a coalition basis.[2] The scandal of the shell shortage on the western front, the disasters of the Dardanelles, Lord Fisher's resignation as First Sea Lord, Conservative distrust of Winston Churchill (shared by many Liberals too), combined to make it impossible for Bonar Law, the Conservative leader, to keep his followers in their silent role since August 1914 as a 'patriotic opposition'. The only choice was confrontation or coalition. Much historiographical ink has been spent in disputing which of all these problems determined the issue. There is, however, an even more important point to consider. If Asquith had led from strength he might have been ready to face a reversion to pre-war parliamentary conflict, but in fact his hand was weak. Behind the other causes for his decision lay an even more cogent reason. Under the Parliament Act a general election was due to be held at latest in January 1916. In the existing House Asquith was unlikely to be defeated, even if deserted by Irish and Labour MPs, because more Conservative than Liberal members were on active service, but if he had to go to the polls the prospect was very different. His chances of victory were remote, and in the new circumstances only a coalition could avert a general election.[3]

It is by no means the case that a general election was impracticable in either of the two world wars. The Americans, as their constitution necessitated, held congressional and presidential elections in the Second World War. In fact, in Britain a party concordat resulted, during 1914–18 and again during 1939–45, in the suspension of the Parliament Act, but no such agreement had been reached in May 1915. On separate occasions later both Asquith and Bonar Law mooted the possibility of a dissolution. It was a move that certainly could not be ruled out by political calculators, but at this juncture Asquith had no intention of risking it if he could avoid it.

He had not always viewed the effect of war on his political fortunes with such pessimism. In a curious playlet written for his own amusement only a few weeks earlier he apostrophized himself as he had been in August 1914: 'You were almost a classic example of *Luck* ... above all (at a most critical and fateful moment in your own career) in the sudden outbreak of the Great War.'[4] The war had undoubtedly extricated the Prime Minister and his party from a domestic situation of the greatest difficulty. Apart from a host of other threats, there was a real possibility of civil strife in Ulster. But this stroke of 'luck' depended for success upon another to follow it; a short, sharp, victorious campaign in which Germany was quickly beaten to its knees by the conscript armies of France and Russia and in which Britain played a mainly naval role in support. Asquith would then have been on the top of the wave.

2

Events had not turned out that way. By the summer of 1915 it was clear that the war was going to be a long one, and the longer it lasted the more damaging would be its effect on the Liberals. The values for which the party stood might have survived a rapid war fought by volunteer forces on the basis of 'business as usual'. They could not survive the stresses of stalemate and the necessities of the first 'total' war in modern history. The Liberals had been deeply divided about intervening at all. It was they, not the Conservatives, who needed the moral outrage of the invasion of Belgium to justify hostilities. Even so, two members of the Cabinet resigned. The Conservatives had pressed for intervention from the very beginning on grounds of *realpolitik* and the balance of power.

The Liberals were traditionally the party of freedom of speech, conscience and trade. They were against jingoism, heavy armaments and compulsion. They recognized that some of these ideals would have to be relinquished in war. But the abandonment of them, even temporarily, was painful. Liberals were neither wholehearted nor unanimous about conscription, censorship, the Defence of the Realm Act, severity towards aliens and pacifists, direction of labour and industry. The Conservatives – 'the patriotic party' ever since the duel between Disraeli and Gladstone – had no such misgivings. There were even some of them, who, taking Milner as their political and Kipling as their spiritual mentor, positively welcomed the more draconian aspects of wartime legislation. They regarded many of Britain's pre-war ills as by-products of Liberal 'softness'. Not all went as far as that, but the party would have exploited the patriotic cry to the full in a general election which they would certainly have won easily.

Among the Liberals, Lloyd George had emerged as the leader of those who believed in all-out war. He became aligned with the Conservative 'hawks'. Asquith could not be called a 'dove'. If he had been one, he might, as Professor Shannon suggests, have led 'Liberalism in its natural bent, as Fox and Grey had done in the Revolutionary and Napoleonic

3

Wars and as Campbell-Bannerman had done in 1900'. This would have involved seeking a compromise peace with Germany. Asquith never thought in such terms and he was right. From what we now know about the sort of conditions envisaged by the German government, it is clear that the idea was a delusion. Ironically, it was a former Conservative Foreign Minister, Lord Lansdowne, who took up the cause in 1916 and predictably got nowhere. To say this is not to deny that the world would have been a better place if the great powers had stopped slaughtering each other two years earlier – merely that there was no practical possibility of it happening.

Asquith wished to prosecute the war but he was curiously conservative in his methods while at the same time being much more anti-Conservative in the party sense than Lloyd George. The coalition was thus an uncomfortable affair. The Liberal ministers were on the defensive about their past record and resented the way old colleagues had been unceremoniously discarded, often under Conservative pressure – and in the case of Haldane without even the courtesy of a letter of regret from the Prime Minister. The Conservatives were just as prickly. They distrusted Asquith and hesitated to serve under him at all. The distribution of offices did not help. There were six that mattered in wartime. Of these, four – the premiership, Foreign Office, Exchequer and Munitions – were in the hands of Liberals. The War Office was held by a non-political figure, Kitchener. Only the Admiralty went to a Conservative but since Asquith's choice fell on Balfour who had been driven out of the party leadership in 1911, the arrangement was not calculated to placate Tory *amour propre*. Bonar Law and Austen Chamberlain were respectively fobbed off with the colonies and India.

One consequence of the reconstruction was diffusion in the responsibility for directing the war. The constitutional and administrative problems thus raised were to be an important element in the controversies which led to Asquith's downfall. From August to November 1914 the Cabinet had been the decisive body assuming all the powers of the Committee of Imperial Defence which went into virtual abeyance for the rest of the war. On 25 November a committee of the Cabinet known as the War Council was established. Its powers were never precisely defined. In theory it was subordinate to the Cabinet. In practice its decisions were acted upon and only reported to the Cabinet afterwards by Asquith. But the council met only when Asquith summoned it, and he did not do so regularly. There was a gap of eight weeks between March and May 1915. This was not accidental. It suited Asquith to conduct the war through an informal triumvirate, himself, Kitchener and Churchill.

Kitchener possessed immense authority. Munitions and recruitment came under his aegis as well as military strategy. As the senior serving field-marshal he behaved more like a commander-in-chief than a political minister obliged to take advice from the Army Council. When he visited the western front he wore uniform to the annoyance of Sir John French who saw it as an assertion of rank. His public prestige was enormous and everyone treated him with deference. Yet he had little or no idea what to do with his power. He lacked administrative skill and strategic vision. In the end he was a recruiting poster *et praeterea nihil.* Churchill for rather different reasons also enjoyed great power, a product of that restless questing energy which was to characterize the whole of his life. His weakness which he himself never saw was that the man in the Admiralty whom the public admired was the First Sea Lord, Lord Fisher, and not Churchill who was widely distrusted. When Fisher resigned over Gallipoli, Churchill was doomed.

The rule of the Asquith, Churchill, Kitchener triumvirate was bound to end with the creation of the coalition. Whatever the precise reasons for the fall of the last purely Liberal government, both the shell shortage and Fisher's resignation evidently had *some* connection with it. The removal of munitions to a separate ministry under Lloyd George marked

5

a first step in the break-up of Kitchener's empire, but the old Field-Marshal had too much prestige for his dismissal to be contemplated. He remained at the War Office. Churchill had no such fund of support. The Conservatives made his removal from the Admiralty an absolute condition. He remained on the War Council with the sinecure office of Chancellor of the Duchy of Lancaster, an impotent spectator of events. Fisher, however, did not profit from the change. He put himself out of court by a megalomaniac letter to Asquith demanding 'complete professional charge of the War at sea together with the absolute sole disposition of the Fleet and the appointments of all officers of all ranks whatsoever'.[5]

The war was to be conducted as before by a committee of the Cabinet. The old War Council was rechristened the Dardanelles Committee and in this guise it met for the first time on 7 June, nearly three weeks after the formation of the new government, in order to decide whether to reinforce the Gallipoli operation or cut the losses. Churchill maintained that this decision could have been taken on purely military grounds within forty-eight hours of a crucial telegram from Sir Ian Hamilton on 17 May asking for more troops, and that the delay was fatal. There has been much argument on this point. What is significant, however, from the procedural aspect is that the decision was not finally taken on 7 June but two days later; the delay probably made little difference, but the postponement was a symptom of the malady which now afflicted the conduct of war.

The old War Council and the triumvirate, though in theory supposed to refer back to the Cabinet, had in practice taken decisions which were executed at once. The new Dardanelles Committee was given no such latitude. The Conservatives were not in the mood to delegate any decisions to a committee. Theory now became practice and on 9 June the matter was fought out all over again in full Cabinet. Although the committee's view that reinforcements should be sent to the Dardanelles was endorsed, the episode set a precedent. Throughout Asquith's coalition almost every recommendation of the Dardanelles Committee (called the Cabinet War Committee from 2 November 1915), was rediscussed often at great length by the Cabinet. 'Every military decision,' wrote Churchill, 'had to be carried by the same sort of process of tact, temporizing, and exhaustion which occurs over a clause in a keenly contested Bill in the House of Commons in time of peace.'[6] It was not until Lloyd George became Prime Minister that a more streamlined process was introduced.

It is easy to make a cynical contrast between the setting of the political manoeuvres in London and the daily experiences of those who fought the war. We can see the butlers and footmen silently serving excellent meals; we can hear the pop of the champagne corks and smell the rich cigars with their blue smoke twisting and dissolving against the dark oak panelling. Asquith attended a fashionable wedding on the Saturday afternoon before the crisis, and drove out into the country for his usual weekend, where he had to be sought by Churchill with the news that Fisher's resignation was final. Parliament, clubland, the town houses of the political grandees resounded with the busy hum of intrigue. The war had as yet made little impact on civilian life. It was a far cry to the shadeless torrid shores of Helles and Anzac. There life was grim enough even when a major offensive was not in progress. Men sweltered in the daily increasing heat, assailed by huge black swarms of fat flies which had feasted on rotting corpses; they were half choked by the fearful stench, they were short of water, ridden with disease and dysentery, tormented by lice. They were not short of food, but a diet of greasy bully beef followed by hard biscuits spread with plum and apple jam was not ideal when the temperature was 100 degrees in the shade, if any shade could be found. Such of the troops who thought at all about politics in London could, if they had ever read Dickens, be excused for recalling the passage in *Bleak House* where Lord Boodle says that the choice lies 'between Lord Coodle and Sir Thomas Doodle – supposing it to be impossible for the Duke of Foodle to act with Goodle' . . . and so on.

Yet the contrasts of war have always been like this. The army of the Grand Old Duke of York would not have marched up and down the hill any more efficiently if Pitt had given up port. The troops in the Dardanelles would have been no better off if Asquith had ceased to drink brandy and Bonar Law had abandoned cigars. The politicians manoeuvring for place were not necessarily self-seekers, any more than the men who fought at Suvla Bay were necessarily heroes. The politicians were for the most part patriots who wished to serve their country to the best of their ability in a desperate war; no politician worth his salt will believe that he can do this more effectively out of office than in. Moreover, it was not an affair of Boodle and Foodle; the personalities of those who held the key posts really did matter, and affected the fate of millions of men and women. What was lacking in Asquith's new Cabinet was not a sense of duty or patriotism, but the cohesion which comes from mutual trust. This deficiency was a legacy of the bitter pre-war struggles over the Lloyd George budget, the House of Lords, Ulster and the Marconi scandal. The absence of comparable partisan animosity before 1939 partly explains why coalition came more easily in the Second World War and worked more harmoniously when it came.

2

The year 1915 saw a series of setbacks to the Allies in almost every theatre of war. The greatest of these for Britain was the failure of the Dardanelles Expedition; it had far-reaching effects on British strategical attitudes and it engendered a controversy which has gone on ever since. The removal of Churchill from the Admiralty did not result in the abandonment of the campaign. One can exaggerate his personal role – the more easily because he saw fit in retrospect to take an unnecessary degree of personal responsibility. He had not, originally, been in favour of it at all, preferring an amphibious assault on the north German coast. Asquith, Grey and

Kitchener were keener on Gallipoli than he was, and it was Kitchener who pressed upon a then unwilling Churchill the original plan for an unsupported naval attack. Nor did Churchill have any responsibility for the ensuing military operations. Yet by some strange psychological quirk, as Martin Gilbert says in his great biography, 'Because he was widely accused of having been responsible for the deaths at Gallipoli, he began to defend even those aspects of the attack which he had neither planned nor supported'. This puzzling and perverse 'identification with failure' did him lasting damage.

The Dardanelles Committee, despite the misgivings of Bonar Law and Lloyd George, agreed that a fresh attempt should be made to capture the peninsula. Early in August Hamilton launched a new offensive; it involved a diversionary attack on Suvla Bay where the commanding officer, Sir Frederick Stopford, displayed an ineptitude seldom equalled in the annals of the British army. After disastrous procrastination a desperate struggle for the heights took place. The heat was appalling, the casualties in proportion to numbers involved were immense, and the medical conditions for the wounded were deplorable. The Turks held firm and the offensive was a total failure. Asquith wrote to Kitchener: 'I have read enough to satisfy me that the Generals and Staff engaged in the Suvla part of the business ought to be court martialled and dismissed from the Army.'[7] Stopford was removed and the writing was on the wall for Hamilton.

The anti-Dardanelles party now moved into the ascendant. Led by Bonar Law and Lloyd George they pressed for the liquidation of the enterprise. On 14 October Hamilton was superseded by Sir Charles Monro. He arrived a fortnight later with instructions to report whether to evacuate or reinforce the army in Gallipoli. 'He came, he saw, he capitulated,' wrote Winston Churchill in his memoirs – a neat phrase, but an indefensible judgement. Monro risked his whole career by his response which was hastened by a peremptory message from Kitchener who expected a very different answer, and his recommendation for evacuation was undoubtedly correct. There were no troops available for reinforcement. Two divisions had actually been moved from Gallipoli to Salonika in response to Bulgarian entry into the war on the side of the central powers; and in France the battle of Loos was in full swing. Monro was not, as alleged by the Dardanellians, a block-headed 'Westerner', nor had he made up his mind in advance. His report settled the question despite great anxiety about the possible losses involved. Asquith reconstituted the Dardanelles Committee early in November under the title of the Cabinet War Committee, dropping Churchill who resigned to take command of a battalion in France. Despite a last-minute plea by the Dardanellians for a renewed naval action and despite gloomy prophecies from Curzon – 'hecatombs of the slain' – the army was evacuated from Suvla Bay and Anzac in December and from Helles in January without any losses at all. It was a notable triumph of skilled deception; but, as the generation which saw Dunkirk was to know, wars are not won by evacuations however well arranged.

The campaign had lasted eight and a half months. In the words of its latest historian it 'ended in a tactical draw; regarded strategically, it was a major defeat for the Allies'.[8] Casualty figures are estimates, and particularly uncertain in the case of the Turks whose official figures are certainly too low. The best guess is some 265,000 on the Allies' side, of whom 46,000 were killed or died. Turkish casualties were probably rather higher, around 300,000.[9]

Because of the high hopes and cruel disappointments, the narrow margins between defeat and victory, the theatrical setting and superb scenery, the spectacle of the great ships firing, 'the smell of thyme mixed with the reek of cordite', and also because of a certain self-contained dramatic unity, this disastrous episode in the history of British arms has never been lost to British memory. The extraordinary personalities involved – Kitchener, Churchill, Fisher, even Ian Hamilton himself – have also contributed to its immortality. Rupert

Brooke died on his way to the battle. John Masefield described it in splendid prose. Although the conditions under which men fought were just as terrible as on the western front, the campaign has never quite acquired the sinister aura of the Somme and Passchendaele.

Controversy about it has, however, raged ever since. A Royal Commission under Lord Cromer was appointed in 1916 to investigate the failure. Its evidence was never published, but its findings promulgated early in 1917 were clear and critical: the operation had been ill-conceived and ineptly executed, and the losses were not justified. Churchill came out of it quite well, but Asquith badly. For many years afterwards the majority of informed opinion was hostile to the whole operation, but Churchill's memoirs, and Hamilton's misleadingly described *Gallipoli Diary* did something to redress the balance.[10] Moreover, the issue became confused with another – the merits of the strategy and tactics of the armies in the west. As the public began to learn in the 1920s of the full horrors, hitherto concealed, of trench warfare in France, the conduct of the British and French High Commands came under increasing criticism. The main argument then used for Gallipoli was that the Allies had narrowly failed in a campaign which would have brought munitions to hard-pressed Russia, rallied the Balkan states against the central powers, and led to a victorious mobile war in east central Europe, thus sparing the western Allies the years of deadlock and carnage in France. One can see at once, however, that the two issues are not the same. It is possible to be critical of the way the French and British military leaders fought in the west, without necessarily agreeing that the diversion of substantial forces to Gallipoli from the one front where total disaster could have occurred was a justifiable risk.

The historiographical dispute reflected the wartime dispute between the 'Easterners', led by Lloyd George and Churchill (though they differed on which part of the east to go for), and the 'Westerners' led by Haig and Robertson, backed by Asquith, and of course overwhelmingly supported by the French. Was there 'a way round' which would avoid the confrontation in north-eastern France? Could one bring down Germany by a 'strategy of indirect approach', knocking away the 'props', i.e. the lesser allies which supported her? Gallipoli was the one attempt to do so. The rival historians in the inter-war years emerged with honours roughly even. The memoirs of Churchill and Lloyd George were more eloquent, the *Official History* was more weighty. More recently, however, opinion has tended to come down on the side of the 'Westerners', perhaps because of a second world war which was won only by beating the Germans in the field.

What verdict can be given now? None with confidence for there is no answer to the 'ifs' of history. A more steely commander might have won the day. Hamilton was too 'literary', too detached, too charming, too unwilling to interfere, and above all too anxious to please Kitchener whom he did not badger enough for reinforcements and to whom he reported always in colours of rose. Even so it was very close. A marginal change in the course of events could easily have resulted in the Turks being driven from Gallipoli. Yet one should not forget the converse – an equally marginal change the other way, and the British might have been driven into the sea.

What would have happened if the peninsula had been taken and British warships had gone through to the Golden Horn? It is far from certain that the Turks would have capitulated. Nor, if they had, is it at all obvious where the supplies to rearm Russia would have come from. And even if munitions had been found, would a rearmed Russia really have gained victory without tears – or with fewer tears – on the eastern front? One cannot be sure, but the 'ifs' mount up. Perhaps the answer to Gallipoli and indeed to the whole strategic controversy is given, ironically, by Churchill himself in a letter to Fisher on 4 January 1915. At that time, by a curious inversion of their later roles, the First Sea Lord was pressing for an attack on Turkey while the First Lord was hesitant and doubtful. Churchill wrote: 'I would not begrudge 100,000 men because of the great political effects in the Balkan peninsula: but Germany is the foe, and it is bad war to seek cheaper victories and easier antagonists."[11]

3

In reality the decision for an all-out commitment to the western front had been taken four months before the evacuation of the Dardanelles by Kitchener who only informed the Cabinet afterwards. In August 1915 on his own authority he pledged Britain to a major offensive in support of Joffre. In a sense this was merely the logical result of the pre-war plan to fight on the French left flank, implemented at the outbreak of war. But that commitment had not been regarded, even if it should have been, as inevitable. The War Council on 13 January 1915 resolved that, if there was a stalemate in the west, 'British troops should be despatched to another theatre and another objective'. Gallipoli showed that this was not mere verbiage, and by the early summer there did appear to be stalemate in northern France.

Kitchener, however, believed – and so did Joffre – that Russia might be knocked out completely unless something was done in the west. The German summer eastern offensive had inflicted losses in prisoners and casualties of some 2 million. Kitchener also believed privately that, unless the British Army backed Joffre to the full, a government bent on negotiating a compromise peace would come into power in Paris. He was acutely conscious of the enormous casualties incurred by the French in their offensive in the first few weeks of the war, some 600,000. Few people in Britain knew about these figures but those who did felt continuously uneasy about the reliability of the French Army. On 19 August Kitchener told Sir Douglas Haig whose 1st Army would be the vehicle for any British attack: 'We must . . . do our utmost to help the French even though by so doing we suffered very heavy casualties indeed."[12] Neither Haig nor Sir John French was happy about the sector chosen or the readiness of their troops, but they felt obliged to conform. From then onwards there was no going back. Britain had to fight in France if France was to go on fighting at all. The campaign known as the battle of Loos was launched on 26 September in support of Joffre's offensives in Artois and Champagne. Largely because Sir John French kept the reserves under his own command and sent them up far too late, the British attack failed with some 60,000 casualties to Germany's 20,000. The French attacks on a much larger scale also failed, though the relative casualty lists, 190,000 to 120,000, were not so unfavourable. The onset of bad weather brought the battle to an end in mid-October.

Gallipoli and France were not the only scenes of Allied failure. The Italians, who had entered the war on 24 May on the Allied side, launched a series of offensives against the Austrians on the Isonzo, but got nowhere. In Mesopotamia, General Townshend's force instead of capturing Baghdad was beleaguered at Kut with doubtful prospects of relief. In the Balkans, Bulgaria had entered on the German side, the pro-Allied government of Venizelos in Greece had fallen, and Serbia had been overrun. On the eastern front the Russians had sustained the catastrophic reverse already mentioned, when Falkenhayn's armies broke through at Gorlice.

These setbacks resulted in a major reorganization of the system of command. Those in the know were well aware of Kitchener's deficiencies, but it was still considered too risky to sack him. Asquith resolved instead to enhance the powers of the Chief of the Imperial General Staff. That office until October 1915 had been held by a nonentity, General Wolfe Murray (described as 'Sheep' Murray by Churchill). He was confusingly succeeded by another Murray, Sir Archibald, who also carried little weight. Now in December Asquith decided to bring Sir William Robertson, French's Chief of Staff, back to Whitehall to replace Sir Archibald Murray. Robertson, who had risen from the ranks, was one of the ablest and most formidable officers in the British Army. At the same time, Sir John French, who had done himself no good by trying to put the blame on Haig for the handling of the reserves at Loos, was removed, given a peerage and made Commander-in-Chief of Home Forces. Haig succeeded him in France. He and Robertson worked closely together and did much to prime Asquith; they were determined that the CIGS should replace the War Secretary as principal military adviser to the government with direct access to the War Committee. The new terms were put in writing and accepted reluctantly by Kitchener. From May to December 1915 Kitchener and Churchill (who was still vociferous despite loss of executive office) had fought a losing battle against Bonar Law and Lloyd George, the principal issue being Gallipoli versus the western front. Asquith acted as a sort of umpire. Now a new element was injected. Throughout 1916 control lay with Asquith, Robertson and Haig. The change represented a triumph for 'Westerners' against 'Easterners'. The failure of the Dardanelles expedition was a fatal blow to those who believed in a strategy of indirect approach or, as their opponents said, 'side-shows'. Haig and Robertson were convinced that the war could be won only by defeating the German Army in the field, which meant in France. Despite attempts at diversion, their view prevailed. Whether or not they were right has been a matter of controversy ever since.

Before considering events in the west we should not forget 'the forgotten war' – the campaign known colloquially as 'Mespot'. Mesopotamia (modern Iraq) constituted one of the predominantly Arab provinces of the vast sprawling empire of the Ottoman Turks. Both this and the later campaign in Palestine had an historical importance greater than their influence on the war or the numbers involved. They were the origins of the last great extension of the British Empire – an extension which was to have significant effects on foreign and defence policy during the inter-war years and indeed beyond. The encirclement of General Townshend's force at Kut stemmed from an imprudent addition to a prudent strategic purpose – the protection of British oil interests in the Persian Gulf. The changeover from coal to oil firing made this vital for the navy. Although the oilfields and refinery were in neutral territory, no one doubted that, if they could, the Turks certainly would cut the pipeline from southern Persia to Abadan. It therefore made good sense for the government of India to send a division (mixed British and Indian) to seize the Turkish port of Basra in November 1914, and it also made good sense to capture two key approaches further up the two vast rivers, Tigris and Euphrates, which converged in the Persian Gulf and constituted both the sole means of communication and the source of drinking water in that desolate land. In the high summer of 1915 Generals Townshend and Gorringe by brilliant amphibious offensives captured Amara on the Tigris and Nasariyeh on the Euphrates.

The oilfields were now amply secured, and General Nixon, the Commander-in-Chief, would have been well advised to leave it at that. He was at the end of a long and very incompetently managed supply line and he ought to have realized that he had so far only encountered inferior troops – Arab levies officered by Turks. But there is always some sort of argument for going on when the enemy is in retreat. The glittering prize of Baghdad – more glittering in prospect than reality – beckoned to Lord Hardinge, Viceroy of India, and to Nixon himself. At least it would be reasonable to advance another 120 miles to Kut-al-Amara which commanded an important water link between the two rivers, and then consider what to do next. On 20 August, with the hesitant assent of Austen Chamberlain at the India Office, the advance was authorized. It was a fatal decision.

In respect of climate, terrain and inhabitants alike, Mesopotamia was one of the most disagreeable countries in the world. It was absolutely flat and there was a perpetual mirage. For much of the summer it was flooded but, since the floods came not from rain but from distant melting snow, there was no relief from the heat which was intense, up to 120 degrees or more in the shade. It was impossible to sleep after 5 A.M. The only consolation was that the heat reduced even the myriads of insects to temporary torpor. In late September the floods subsided, but it was still very hot and a furious wind would at any moment produce blinding dust storms. In the autumn the temperature could drop 50 degrees at night, and in winter, which was quite cold, sudden rain storms could convert the desert into gluey mud. There was a shortage of medical supplies, and comforts alleged in the press to be plentiful, such as spine protectors, ice, mineral waters and fresh vegetables, were non-existent. Heat-stroke, sun-stroke, enteric dysentery and scurvy were endemic. The local inhabitants, whom the British were supposed to be 'liberating', were of a piece with the country. The Marsh Arabs were a nation of robbers, cut-throats and corpse-despoilers who followed the flanks of the rival armies like packs of jackal, marginally assisting whichever side seemed to be winning. Into this dismal place, one of the hottest and unhealthiest on earth, Britain was to throw in the end some half a million men engaging about a tenth of that number of Turks.

Townshend captured Kut on 28 September. He was reluctant to go on without reinforcements, but Nixon insisted. In late November at Ctesiphon, some twenty-two miles from Baghdad, he met for the first time a force of real Turks in equal numbers and well dug in. He lost 4,500 casualties and retreated to Kut. The plight of the wounded both there and on the way back to Basra was appalling and the Crimean-type conditions later publicized in an official report caused a major scandal. Again overruled by Nixon, Townshend stayed in Kut to face a siege. All efforts at relief failed. Starved into submission he surrendered on 27 April 1916. There had been no comparable episode since Cornwallis at Yorktown. It was a blow to public morale in Britain. It would have been a greater blow if people had suspected the fate of the prisoners. The Turks of that time had an acute sense of hierarchy, but were barbarians at heart. Townshend was given every comfort. The 400 British and Indian officers had a bad time by normal standards, but most of them survived. The troops, however, suffered atrocious hardships, the mildest of which were the homosexual attentions of their guards forced on the

17

younger men by threats and beating. They were marched for day after day in scorching heat. They were robbed, starved, flogged, left to die or clubbed to death. Of the 2,600 British Other Ranks, seventy per cent were killed or died and the same fate befell 2,500 out of 9,300 Indians.

The shock of Kut forced Whitehall to take over from India and to stop the campaign being run on a shoestring. The supply line was reorganized, railways and roads built, river steamers multiplied. Reinforcements were poured in. By the autumn of 1916 the new Commander-in-Chief, General Maude, had 150,000 men under his command and was poised to attack as soon as the order came. He was to do this with great success, but the humiliation of Kut has produced an almost traumatic oblivion about this strange campaign – the least known of all the 'side-shows' of war.

Chapter Two

THE SOMME AND JUTLAND

I

The war on the western front was unlike any before or since. After the race to the sea which ended in stalemate in November 1914, there was no chance of an outflanking movement by either side. The only possibility of success was to break through the enemy 'line' – a word which conceals more than it reveals. One sees a black line on the maps looking rather like a flattened S tilted to the left, running on a south-east to north-west axis from the frontier of neutral Switzerland to a point on the Belgian coast between Dunkirk and Nieuport. But large parts of it were regarded by both sides as hopeless places for launching an attack, for example the mountainous area full of deep valleys and forests south of Verdun, the similar terrain between the Aisne and the Oise, and the flooded land north of Ypres. In those sections of the inverted S the word 'line' is perhaps appropriate. But in the areas where fighting raged it is not. One has to envisage a belt some ten miles or more wide. It was described by Valentine Fleming (father of Peter, the explorer, and Ian of James Bond fame) in a vivid letter to Winston Churchill:

[It] is positively littered with the bodies of men and scarified with their rude graves; in which farms, villages and cottages are shapeless heaps of blackened masonry; in which fields, roads and trees are pitted and torn by shells and disfigured by dead horses, cattle, sheep and goats scattered in every attitude of repulsive distortion and dismemberment. Day and night ... are made hideous by the incessant crash and whistle and roar of every sort of projectile, by sinister columns of smoke and flame, by the cries of wounded men . . .

Along this terrain of death stretch more or less parallel to each other lines of trenches, some 200, some 1,000 yards apart . . . In these trenches crouch lines of men in brown or grey or blue, coated with mud, unshaven, hollow-eyed with the continued strain, unable to reply to the everlasting rain of shells hurled at them from 3, 4 or 5 miles away and positively welcoming an infantry attack from one side or the other as a chance of meeting and matching themselves against *human* assailants and not against invisible, irresistible machines.[1]

The sense of being caught up in some vast impersonal disaster is a persistently recurrent theme in the literature and memoirs of the time. It was enhanced because in this unlike in almost every previous war, the South African war being an exception, one scarcely ever *saw* the enemy. Despite the emphasis in training on the use of the bayonet, man-to-man conflict was extremely rare. The invisibility of the foe was itself a result of the mechanization to which Valentine Fleming referred. Barbed wire, a comparatively recent American invention designed to keep in cattle, the machine-gun which was another American invention and artillery used on a scale never approached in the past, enforced a form of trench warfare unique in history. To appear above the ground in daylight near the enemy line was suicide.

Normally there were three lines of trenches – the front line, the support line and the reserve line – each separated by several hundred yards. These were the 'firing' trenches. They were six to eight feet deep and five feet wide with a parapet of sandbags two or three feet above ground level on the enemy side. There was a 'fire step' two feet or so above the bottom of the trench. Here the defenders were supposed to stand and shoot at the oncoming enemy. The trenches usually zig-zagged to avoid the danger of enfilade fire if the enemy captured a section. Barbed wire in great rusty rolls which gave the front, as one observer noted, an appearance of everlasting autumn, was placed far enough away to prevent the attackers from lobbing grenades on to the occupants. The three lines were connected by communication trenches, and it was along these, normally at night, that the troops were relieved. The front line could be anything from fifty yards (in exceptional cases) to a mile from the German line. In between was no man's land – a wilderness of wire, shell craters, corpses and debris of every sort. Into this were pushed more or less perpendicularly from the front line, shallower trenches known as 'saps'. Designed to provide forward observation posts and machine-gun positions, they were not manned continuously and were often evacuated at night. Behind the reserve line of trenches were the guns, and the great preliminary objective of every offensive, Allied or German, was to reach the gun line. For the war was essentially an artillery war; it has been reckoned that seventy per cent of all the casualties came from shells, compared with thirty per cent from bullets.

The first forty miles from the sea until just north of Ypres were held by the Belgians. The area was flooded and serious hostilities were impossible. The next ninety miles to the river Ancre were held by the British, the rest by the French. The British forces were thickly concentrated in two areas. One was the Ypres salient in Flanders, the other round the river Somme in Picardy. The infantry – some 800 battalions of 1,000 each – operated on a relief system. There were four stages. A battalion occupied its 'sectors' of the front line for a week – or sometimes less. (A 'sector' was about 300 yards in width and was held by a company.) The battalion would then move back to the support line and to the reserve line for similar periods, followed by a week of 'rest', out of shelling distance, usually in the area of Poperinge behind the Ypres salient or Amiens behind the Somme. The battalion would then move up again through the labyrinthine communication trenches to the front line and repeat the cycle.

Unless there was an offensive in progress – and on most of

the front for most of the time there was not – the day in the
trenches followed a regular routine. It began about an hour
before dawn with 'stand to' when everyone was on the alert
for enemy attack. 'Dawn has never recovered from what the
Great War did to it,' writes Paul Fussell in his remarkable
book, *The Great War and Modern Memory*, alluding to the new
and sinister associations of that traditionally romantic and
'poetical' hour. If nothing happened, the troops spent their
time cooking, sleeping, writing letters, cleaning weapons and
learning to endure shellfire. The day ended with another
'stand to' at sunset – not that an attack was expected then,
rather it was an opportunity to catch enemy patrols, working
parties, ration parties, etc., which had set out too early. For it
was after dark that the real work began of digging saps,
repairing wire, revetting trench walls, and reinforcing parapets. Moreover, supplies of every sort, ammunition, food,
weapons, had to be brought up by night and the same applied
to the process of relief and rotation of the front line units
themselves. Then there were night patrols and raiding
parties. And the night ended with the dawn 'stand to' once
again.

British trenches compared badly with those of the French
and even worse with the enemy's. The Germans were
basically on the defensive (though Verdun was to be a
disagreeable reminder that they could attack too), and they
made themselves as comfortable as possible since they were
there to stay. The 'luxury' of their trenches astonished British
troops who captured some sections in the battle of the
Somme. Their dugouts, clean, dry and reasonably sanitary,
were often as much as thirty feet deep with bunks, cupboards,
boarded walls and electric light. By contrast the British
trenches had an appearance of squalid improvisation – partly
a product of the 'offensive spirit' which was orthodox military
doctrine and dictated that they were temporary jumping-off
places for 'the great breakthrough'. The trenches were all the
more unpleasant because the level of the water table in both
the Somme and the Ypres areas was especially high where the

British lines ran. Duckboards with a sump below for drainage were a necessity in every trench, but the water often rose to thigh level or higher and only a lucky few had adequate waders. Mud was the word engraved on the hearts of those who fought and suffered in these dismal campaigns. Old hands argued whether that of Ypres or the Somme was worse. Both were terrible, and those who knew their Milton must often have thought of 'that Serbonian bog where armies whole have sunk'.

According to one calculation there were 6,000 miles of trenches on the British front alone. It is strange to think of this semi-subterranean world with its turnover of millions of young men who saw little but brown earth walls, crumbling or sodden, and a narrow slice of enigmatic ever-changing sky. Apart from the fear of death or mutilation, the worst feature of the front was the stench of decaying corpses, human or animal, supplemented by that of poison gas. One could smell the front a mile or more away. It was not only the dead bodies in no man's land. The trenches themselves were partly faced in their walls and parapets by these fearful fragmenting reminders of mortality, and were filled with the rats that fed on them – large, black, bold and fierce. Another odious feature of trench life was the ubiquitous louse which infested clothing and, despite all efforts, was virtually uneliminable. The slang phrase, 'lousy with' meaning 'full of' – e.g. 'Oxford is lousy with tourists' – significantly dates from 1915. Rotting corpses, huge rats, verminous clothes, fear, stink, mud, filth, cold and wet – these were to be the principal memories of those who fought in this seemingly interminable war.

Although many previous wars lasted much longer, none has given quite the same impression of going on for ever. This sense of endlessness emerges again and again from the writings published or unpublished, contemporary or retro-spective, of the participants. R. H. Mottram in *The Spanish Farm*, one of the great novels of the war, makes a gloomy officer calculate that at the rate of progress up to the summer of 1917, it would take the Allied armies 180 years to reach the

Rhine. Another feature which differentiated this from nearly every other war in British history was the ease with which the transition could be made from the squalor of the front to the comforts of home. In the Second World War Britain was itself a part of the theatre of operations, suffering from the blackout, rationing, austerity and bombing. Moreover, the troops for the most part were fighting far away and got little home leave. In the Great War by contrast, civilian life remained till a late stage remarkably normal and there was regular leave from a front only seventy miles away; one could breakfast in the trenches and, if able to afford it, dine that night at the Café Royal. The cross-Channel boats were efficient, the post arrived on time bringing hampers which were seldom spoiled in transit. Belgian and French newspaper boys sold the *Daily Mail* at the entrance to the communication trenches.

This proximity of civilian to military life did not bridge the gulf of incomprehension that lay between the two. Paradoxically it may have widened it. How could one explain what the western front was really like to parents, sisters, wives, fiancées living in all the normality of peacetime? And what was the point of doing so? A tacit conspiracy of silence enveloped the reality of war, and it was certainly not illuminated by the war correspondents who saw little of battle anyway, and deemed it their duty, even if censorship had not existed, to keep what they did see to themselves. It was to be many years beyond Armistice Day before the British public began to learn something of what lay behind the stylized language of official communiqués and the fatuous double-speak of the journalists.

2

The offensive in Picardy, usually called the battle of the Somme, opened on 1 July 1916. It was Britain's principal military effort of the year. The broad strategy of which it was a part had been settled on 5 December 1915 at the Confer-

ence of Chantilly attended by the principal Allied Comman-
ders-in-Chief or their representatives. The plan was to
launch simultaneous major offensives on the Russian, Italian
and Western fronts. The date was not precisely fixed, but
there was agreement that it could not be before the summer,
by which time, it was hoped, sufficient ammunition would be
accumulated and the new Kitchener armies adequately
trained. Haig would have preferred to attack further north in
Flanders, but one of the many fateful implications of the
Continental strategy agreed in the 'military conversations' of
1906 was that the British High Command had to conform
with the French plans. The British Army was on a voluntary
basis till January 1916 and was much smaller than the French
conscript forces. A large part of France was in the hands of
the enemy. In these circumstances Joffre was certain to call
the tune.

Joffre plumped for the Somme for a bad reason; he
believed – unjustly – that a joint attack launched from the
point where the British and French lines came together was
the only way of ensuring British cooperation. His original
plan involved using twenty-five British divisions north, and
the same number of French divisions south of the river. But
on 21 February 1916 the Germans started a major offensive
at Verdun which sucked in ever increasing numbers of
French divisions for many months. It was ultimately contained, but the plans for the Somme were thrown into
disarray. In the end the French attacked on a smaller front
with only five divisions, but their gunnery and assault techniques were better than those of their allies.

The Somme was thus a predominantly British affair. Its
effects were to condition much of Britain's later history in war
and peace; for the first two days (1 and 2 July) saw one of the
greatest disasters in British military experience. On the first
day alone there were nearly 60,000 casualties of whom
21,000 were dead – or 'missing'. It was a disaster to a
particular and unprecedented sort of army – the patriotic,
enthusiastic volunteers who enlisted in Kitchener's 'New

Army'. Despite Haig's hopes they were not in fact properly trained by the beginning of July. The staff doctrine – probably right – was that they lacked the skill to adopt the French pattern of assault (itself far from a recipe for success): short, sharp rushes by mobile groups taking advantage of shell craters and other cover, and supporting each other by fire. Instead it was decided that the British 'waves' should move at a slow walk in four lines at intervals of fifty to a hundred yards behind each other towards the allocated sections of the German line – about a mile to each British division. The first 'wave' would take the front line trenches, the second the support trenches – and so on.

These plans presupposed a preliminary bombardment so devastating and, after the troops went 'over the top', a barrage (i.e. a moving curtain of artillery fire) so effective that the German defences and defenders would be obliterated. Nothing of the sort occurred. One million, out of the 1.5 million shells fired, were shrapnel – principally because at that stage of the war British factories were geared to produce little else. A hail of bullets could not cut the German wire or kill its subterranean defenders. The high explosive shells with the heavy casing needed to avoid bursting in the gun barrel were also far less effective than their weight suggested. They exploded on impact throwing up huge fountains of earth and metal, but did little damage and the amount of explosive was relatively small. Thirty tons of them descended on every square mile bombarded during the nine-day run-up to 1 July. This sounds a lot, but in Normandy in 1944 the figure was 800 tons – mostly bombs with a far thinner casing and higher explosive; and yet plenty of Germans survived to fire at the Allied tank columns.[2]

The barrage too was relatively unsuccessful. Fifteen months later British gunners could lay down a 'creeping barrage' so accurately that men could advance behind this lethal, thunderous, swirling cloud as close as twenty-five yards away, while it moved at their own pace towards the enemy line. In 1916 the operation was far too chancy. The barrage 'lifted' in pre-programmed jerks of several hundred yards and the troops prudently waited till the next jerk before moving. In theory the 'programme' could be changed by orders from the forward observation officers who moved up with the attacking troops. In practice this was impossible. Telephone wires laid hastily by hand over the surface of no man's land behind the advancing infantry were soon cut by a curtain of fire from the German artillery whose communications with their own front line were largely undamaged and who wrought at least as much damage on the attack as the machine-gunners. The barrage would often rumble on irrevocably into the middle distance leaving the troops to face German strong points still not eliminated. The difficulty of knowing what was happening after the assault waves disappeared into the dust and smoke is a feature of the battle which cannot be overemphasized. It largely explains the ignorance of GHQ. Haig reckoned that there were 40,000 casualties in two days – bad enough, but far short of the true and terrible figure.

After the barrage lifted, the battle was largely a race between the attackers across no man's land and the defenders up their scaling ladders, the goal being the machine-gun emplacements on the German parapets. Since on that sweltering summer day each British soldier carried 66 lb of equipment, half his own weight (Liddell Hart comments that even army mules were expected to carry only a third of theirs), and was instructed to walk at a slow pace in line, the 'race' was one which the defenders usually won. The attack began at 7.30 A.M. It ought to have begun at dawn, but the French, whose artillery power was much greater, insisted on the later time for observation purposes. The result was a fiasco. Although the French attained their objectives, largely because they were far more experienced but also because the Germans had not expected them to attack at all, the British gained little ground and suffered enormous losses.

The 'battle' did not end until November amidst mud, cold and rain. Territorially Allied gains were negligible. But that is not the whole story. The untried amateur army did manage to learn from experience; casualties continued to be heavy, but not on the scale of 1 July. Moreover, it is too often forgotten that the Germans also suffered immense losses; the campaign was one of counter-attack as well as attack. At the end, the German Army was as exhausted as its opponents. The numerical balance of casualties has been one of perpetual dispute ever since. The British, according to the *Official History*, suffered in round numbers 420,000, the French 300,000, the Germans 680,000. Winston Churchill reckoned, however, that the Anglo-French losses amounted to 894,000 compared to a German figure of 538,000. Each side had an axe to grind. However, Sir Charles Oman, who did not, estimated in a reply to Churchill's *World Crisis 1911–18*, lower, but roughly equal losses on both sides, around 560,000. There will never be any way of settling the matter. The German official figures on which Churchill argued are known to have been deliberately underestimated for purposes of morale, but it is impossible to say by how much. Bomb damage in the Second World War destroyed a great deal of the evidence in both London and Berlin. Perhaps it does not greatly matter. The casualties on both sides were enormous but neither had any intention of giving up.

3

The other famous and equally indecisive battle of 1916 occurred at sea a month before the Somme. This was Jutland on 31 May/1 June (known to the Germans as the battle of the Skagerrak). The encounter took place in the North Sea some seventy-five miles from the north-west coast of the continental peninsula of Denmark. It has caused as much controversy as the Dardanelles, the Somme or Passchendaele. Far fewer lives were lost, but the prestige of the Royal Navy was at stake; the Senior Service with its unbroken tradition of success from Trafalgar onwards found itself in retrospect very much on the defensive; the sailors of the day were perhaps more articulate than the soldiers and the resultant literature is enormous.

The complications of describing any naval battle are very great. Professor Marder, whose account is probably the most authoritative of all, takes more than 250 pages together with sixteen charts to explain the course of events.[3] Jutland was the first and last full-scale battleship encounter of the 1914–18 war, fought within sight, by guns and torpedoes. Nor has there been anything quite like it since. By 1919 the air dominated events at sea. Most of the vital naval battles of the Second World War were fought by aircraft over vast distances between the combatant ships whose crews never set eyes on each other (an unusual exception being the sinking of the *Scharnhorst* by Admiral Fraser in December 1943). But Jutland was a contest in which the rival navies could, however dimly through mist, spray, smoke and gathering twilight, see their opponents and shoot accordingly.

There was no chance of Admiral Scheer's High Seas Fleet voluntarily seeking an engagement with the British Grand Fleet. The latter's superiority was overwhelming.[4] Britain possessed by the eve of Jutland a total of thirty-three dreadnoughts compared with Germany's total of eighteen. The actual force under Jellicoe's command on 30 May 1916 included twenty-eight dreadnoughts and nine battle cruisers, whereas Scheer sailed with only sixteen dreadnoughts and five battle cruisers. The British Grand Fleet enjoyed comparable superiority in lighter craft including destroyers. The speed of the two dreadnought fleets was roughly the same, but Jellicoe had an advantage of which he was not aware; Scheer unwisely took with him at Jutland a squadron of pre-dreadnoughts whose maximum speed was 18 knots. Since he could not abandon these in battle, the Grand Fleet had an effective lead of 1.5 to 2 knots. In terms of weight of broadside Jellicoe possessed a crushing advantage of 332,360 lb against 134,216, almost two and a half to one.

This superiority was offset to some extent by certain German advantages and certain British deficiencies. The

German range finders were more accurate and their gunnery technique was more effective. The armour plating of their ships was thicker especially against torpedo attacks, and the much larger number of watertight compartments below water level made German ships almost unsinkable. It is, however, a myth that British armour was ineffective, though widely believed. Throughout the whole battle there is only one clear instance of even a fragment of a projectile penetrating the vital parts of any British capital ship. Nevertheless, British ships did suffer from two serious defects not appreciated at the time. Their armour-piercing shells were weak compared with their opponents', and their gun magazines were not properly protected against flash from bursting enemy shells – a danger enhanced by the use of an oversensitive propellant. German chemists had taken much trouble to make theirs shockproof and to keep the ignition point as high as possible. A further precaution taken on German ships was to store the charges in zinc containers, whereas the British used silk bags which provided no protection at all.

The failure of Verdun and the increasing severity of the blockade determined the German government to try and break or at least weaken the stranglehold of the British Navy. Scheer's broad plan was to station some eighteen submarines off the naval bases from Rosyth to the Orkneys and to lure the Grand Fleet into disastrous losses. He decided on 30 May to send his battle cruisers under Admiral Hipper from Wilhelmshaven up the Danish coast. He thus hoped to bring out the British battle cruisers under Admiral Beatty. What was left of them after the U-boats had done their work would be drawn by Hipper towards Scheer's dreadnoughts and annihilated. Jellicoe's dreadnoughts might follow, but they too would suffer heavy losses from the U-boats on leaving the Orkneys, and in any case Scheer would be near enough to his own base to escape.

The German fleet left in the early hours of 31 May – Hipper at 1 A.M., Scheer an hour and a half later. The Admiralty was aware of German movements well before they occurred, since the German signals were regularly intercepted and deciphered. Jellicoe was warned at noon on 30 May that the High Seas Fleet would put to sea in little over twelve hours' time. At 10.30 P.M. that night, two and a half hours before Hipper left the Jade, the Grand Fleet, including twenty-four dreadnoughts and three battle cruisers, was heading from Scapa Flow for an agreed rendezvous (if positions sixty-nine miles apart could be thus described) with Beatty's force ninety miles west of the entrance to the Skagerrak. Beatty himself, with six battle cruisers and four dreadnoughts, cleared the Forth half an hour later. If Beatty had not spotted enemy ships by 2 P.M. the next day he was to turn north, cover the sixty-nine-miles gap and join Jellicoe.

Scheer's U-boats failed completely. They did not sink a single ship and they were equally unsuccessful as scouts, providing no information of value. The Grand Fleet headed unscathed for its rendezvous. Jellicoe was, however, gravely misled on a vital matter. Owing to lack of cooperation between 'Room 40', the secret intelligence department of the Admiralty largely manned by clever civilian code-breakers, and the Operations Division which looked down on them with professional naval contempt, he was told at 12.48 P.M. on 31 May that Scheer's flagship had been at Wilhelmshaven at 11.10 A.M. In fact Scheer had left nearly nine hours earlier, and the error was the fault of Rear-Admiral Jackson, Director of the Operations Division. Jellicoe accordingly felt no need to hurry. Within three hours Beatty sighted Hipper's battle cruisers, and Jellicoe thereafter was understandably reluctant to believe anything from Whitehall.

Soon after 2 P.M. Beatty turned north according to orders having seen no sign of the enemy, but one of his scouts at 2.20 P.M. reported the presence of enemy cruisers to the south-east. Beatty at once swung in that direction to cut them off from their base. At 3.30 he sighted Hipper's cruisers fourteen miles away in line ahead steaming north-west. Hipper promptly turned round to draw Beatty towards Scheer. Beatty formed into line of battle, and at 3.45 P.M. the two Admirals on roughly parallel courses opened fire at a range of 15,000 yards almost simultaneously. Beatty's four dreadnoughts, owing to a signalling error, did not enter the fray for another twenty minutes, but with an advantage of six to five in battle cruisers he was bound to engage the enemy. The battle opened with two disasters. Hipper had the advantage of seeing the British ships silhouetted against the western sky, and the north-west breeze which blew his funnel and cordite smoke away to the leeward blew Beatty's across his own field of vision. Just after four o'clock the *Indefatigable* was hit and exploded; there were only two survivors. At 4.26 the *Queen Mary* suffered the same fate, breaking in two and disappearing under a cloud of smoke a thousand feet high; there were twenty survivors. It was at this moment that Beatty on the bridge of his flagship, the *Lion*, made to his Flag-Captain (later Admiral Lord Chatfield) one of those observations which echo along the corridors of history: 'There seems to be something wrong with our bloody ships today.' We now know what was wrong. The loss of both was almost certainly caused by the flash of an exploding shell into the gun magazines. A quarter of a century later the same disaster occurred to the battle cruiser *Hood*, inflicted by the *Bismarck* west of Iceland in the arctic dawn of 24 May 1941 when all but three of the *Hood*'s crew of 1,500 perished. There is a terrible all-or-nothingness about naval battles.

Beatty, however, was still justifiably confident that he could polish off Hipper. His four dreadnoughts were now in action and he had no cause to suspect the approach of Scheer. But at 4.30 P.M. Commodore Goodenough, 'scouting' two or three miles ahead in the light cruiser *Southampton*, spotted first smoke, then masts and finally the outlines of Scheer's sixteen dreadnoughts and six pre-dreadnoughts, about eight miles to his south-east steaming north. Beatty on getting the news at once saw that he must do to Scheer what Hipper had been trying to do to him. He turned about and headed north to draw the German dreadnoughts towards Jellicoe.

The 'run to the north' was successful in that Beatty

inflicted more damage than he received and brought his pursuers within reach of the Grand Fleet. But in the process he exhibited what was to be one of the weaknesses of British naval technique throughout the battle – failure to pass on information. Despite repeated requests he sent no message to Jellicoe between 4.45 and 6.06 P.M. Moreover, the first message was unluckily garbled in transmission and gave the impression that the whole High Seas Fleet was out – eighteen dreadnoughts and ten pre-dreadnoughts. This was not a very great disparity in force, and the message certainly influenced Jellicoe's later conduct for, owing to poor visibility, he never saw more than two or three of Scheer's ships at any one time, and so had no means of knowing that the information was wrong.

By six o'clock the most critical moment of the whole war was coming near. To understand it one must know something of the naval tactics of the day. It was generally agreed that the approach to a battle should be in divisions or columns steaming parallel in line ahead (six columns of four in Jellicoe's case) in order to present the minimum target to torpedoes; but, for the battle itself the whole fleet should 'deploy' into a single line ahead with the enemy 'abeam' so that the maximum broadside would be brought upon him. Ideally one would seek to 'cross his "T"', as the phrase was, i.e. put one's line at right angles in front of his line of advance so that he could fire only with the forward turrets of his leading ships while they were exposed to the full broadsides of the cross of the 'T'. But this would be a stroke of luck. The battle was more likely to be fought by hard pounding between two fleets steaming in line on roughly parallel courses. Given time and good visibility the Grand Fleet was bound to win such a contest.

Jellicoe knew that Scheer had deployed, but though he could hear gunfire he could not yet see the German fleet, and it was vital for him to know its distance, its bearing (i.e. direction from him) and its course as soon as possible in order to decide when and how to deploy. His six columns (he himself led the lefthand of the two centre divisions) were steaming south-east. Although it was in theory possible to deploy on one of the centre columns – and Churchill argues the case in his Jutland chapters in *World Crisis 1911–18* – this was not a practical option if only because it had never been practised. The choice was between the starboard (or western) wing column and the port (or eastern). In each case the procedure was fairly simple. The column chosen to lead would go ahead on its existing course, and the others in succession would each make two right-angled turns, first in the direction of the leading column and then back again in order to follow behind it. The flagship would thus be in the middle of the line – which was agreed to be the best place – and would signal the appropriate course when the line had been formed. It was essential to carry out the manoeuvre before Scheer came within range. A fleet, even though superior, was highly vulnerable if caught in parallel columns or in the act of deployment. On the other hand, premature deployment might mean losing the chance of a decisive engagement altogether. No wonder Jellicoe, waiting for information, irritably remarked: 'I wish someone would tell me who is firing and what they are firing at.'

When at last he got a reliable situation report it was disconcerting. He had assumed from such meagre information as he had so far received that Scheer was straight ahead of him, but the latest message correctly put the German battle fleet on his starboard bow, i.e. much further west than he had believed. This made the choice of a port or starboard deployment far more difficult. Since the two fleets were approaching obliquely and there was a gap of nearly five miles between Jellicoe's two outer wings, his eastern column was much further from the enemy than the western column. Deployment on the latter would bring Jellicoe's line at least 4,000 yards nearer to Scheer and thus enable him to engage the enemy sooner – an important consideration, given the lateness of the hour and the approach of dusk. On the other hand, he ran the risk of coming into range too soon and being caught by Scheer's guns in the act of deployment – which could be fatal. Deployment on the eastern or port column would take him away from the enemy, but it would enable him to cross Scheer's 'T' and put himself between the enemy and his eastern bases. It would also give him the advantage of the light, for he would be firing west and south. Scheer's battleships would be silhouetted against a bright if hazy western sky, whereas Jellicoe's were almost invisible to the east and north-east.

Jellicoe on the bridge of the *Iron Duke* had to make up his mind without delay. The rival fleets were approaching at high speed – about half a mile a minute. Visibility remained uncertain, as it had been throughout the afternoon, and was made worse by Beatty's ships steaming across his front to take up position in the van. The noise of gunfire grew nearer. Deployment in whichever direction would take nearly twenty minutes, and the order once given was irreversible.

On no occasion in the years covered by this history did a more crucial decision have to be taken in a shorter time by a single man. The defeat of the Grand Fleet would have knocked Britain out of the war with consequences of vast significance for the country and the world. There was no comparable moment in the Second World War. As Churchill, critical in some ways of Jellicoe, wrote: 'Jellicoe was the only man on either side who could lose the war in a single afternoon.' At 6.14 P.M. he received a further signal confirming the position of the German fleet. One minute later he gave the momentous order to deploy to port.

Despite some eloquent criticism Jellicoe was right. If deployment to starboard had gone awry he might have lost enough battleships in a few minutes to alter the whole balance of power in the North Sea. Even if it had been achieved successfully and he had engaged Scheer ten minutes earlier, there was nothing to stop the German Admiral executing then, as he did later, the sudden about-turn, under cover of a smoke screen and torpedo attack, which extricated him from the battle. Scheer himself always believed that a British deployment to starboard would have played into his hands. As things went, he received the shock of his life when he encountered the entire British fleet ahead of him across his line of advance in a great arc from north-west to north-east blazing away from the murk at his own clearly silhouetted ships. There was no option but to flee, and at 6.33 P.M. Scheer gave the order, though not before inflicting yet another blow on the British when the flagship of the 3rd Battle Cruiser Squadron, the *Invincible*, exploded with the loss of Admiral Hood and over a thousand men.

The story need not be pursued in detail. Scheer successfully disengaged amid smoke and mist to the west. The neat diagrams of naval historians tend to make one forget the fog of war. Jellicoe now set course to the south to cut off Scheer from his base. The German Admiral some half hour later turned back to the east and, whether by accident or design, headed for the centre of the Grand Fleet. His 'T' was again crossed, and again he had to turn about in order to escape catastrophe. Darkness soon fell. A series of indeterminate night engagements fought mainly by destroyers ensued. What really mattered was for Jellicoe to prevent Scheer reaching safety before dawn. He wrongly guessed that Scheer would head for the Ems, but a series of vital Admiralty intercepts, which would have shown that he was heading south-east for Horns Reef were, apart from one, never passed on to Jellicoe. Had he seen all of them or even a few he would have realized what was happening. Equally blameworthy were his own ships engaged in night action astern of him. Some were well aware of the presence of German battleships, but not a single report reached the *Iron Duke*. This failure, endemic in the navy at that time, accounted for Jellicoe steaming on southwards in the belief that Scheer was to his north-west when in fact the German Admiral had crossed his course astern and was rapidly reaching safety. By dawn on 1 June the High Seas Fleet was out of danger and when Jellicoe learned of this at 3.30 A.M. he had no option but to return to base.

Like that of the Somme the balance sheet of Jutland has

been a subject of perennial dispute. On the material side there can be no argument. The British lost fourteen ships with a total tonnage of 111,000. The German figures were eleven and 62,000. In terms of casualties, too, the British were the losers, 6,784 compared with 3,058. In terms of ships ready to continue fighting the story is different. Eight British compared with ten German capital ships were damaged; in proportionate terms this was a heavy debit for the High Seas Fleet. At the end of the day Jellicoe had twenty-four dreadnoughts and battle cruisers ready to take to sea again at once, whereas Scheer had only ten. The German Admiral might order champagne to be served on the conning bridge of his flagship as he put into the Jade at noon on 1 June, but privately he knew that Jutland was not a victory in the only sense that mattered. Jellicoe still commanded the sea.

Nevertheless, British opinion was not satisfied. The battle had shown up the Royal Navy's technology as inferior to the German. These defects were, it is true, soon recognized and remedied. Comparisons suggest that, if Jutland had been exactly repeated in 1918, six German capital ships would have been sunk, but this was not a thought which could console anyone in 1916. A bitter controversy also arose over tactics, the verve of Beatty being contrasted with the caution of Jellicoe. There is little reason to believe that Jellicoe was over-prudent or to suppose that, if Beatty had been Commander-in-Chief, he would have annihilated Scheer. Critics forget that where fleets are of roughly equal speed, it is virtually impossible to bring to action an enemy determined to avoid it. Nelson was a commander of genius, but there would have been no Trafalgar if Villeneuve had behaved like Scheer.

Chapter Three

THE SECOND WAR
COALITION

I

Throughout 1916 Asquith's coalition moved from crisis to crisis. It finally fell, unregretted, at the end of the year. The early months were convulsed by a series of intense disputes about conscription. It seems strange that this obvious measure had not been enacted earlier. But a hard core of Liberals bitterly opposed it and the Conservatives at first hesitated because Kitchener, who certainly could not be accused of being a Liberal, remained surprisingly wedded to the voluntary system. He changed his mind by the end of 1915. Eventually a limited measure was passed, obliging single men of eighteen to forty-one to 'attest' – i.e. agree to serve when called upon – but even that caused Sir John Simon to resign, and three other Liberal ministers nearly followed him. The great wartime issue of freedom against organization could not have been more stark. Clearly, matters would not be left at that. Lloyd George was a strong conscriptionist. So too was Bonar Law, though he hesitated to break up the government until an Army Council memorandum convinced him that universal conscription was vital. Asquith introduced the Bill on 2 May. No one resigned and only thirty-seven MPs voted against it.

Meanwhile, momentous events occurred in Ireland, which have cast a long shadow from that day to this. On 22 April Sir Roger Casement, a renegade British subject, was landed by a U-boat in Kerry. On the same day the navy seized a vessel packed with German arms off the Irish coast. Two days later on Easter Monday a rebellion broke out in Dublin. Sinn Fein forces seized a number of public buildings, and P. H. Pearse proclaimed himself President of the Irish Republic. The rising was quelled only after a week of fighting. There were considerable casualties on both sides and a large part of the city centre went up in flames. Several of the captured leaders were court-martialled and shot. Casement was later prosecuted and hanged. He had in fact landed in Ireland to stop the rebellion but his treasonable conduct in Germany was indisputable.

The Easter Rebellion was at first repudiated by many Irishmen. Whether it would have remained discredited if the dead rebels had not furnished the blood of martyrdom can never be proved. Perhaps clemency might have paid dividends, but at the height of a desperate war it would have been indeed quixotic to spare the lives of those who had led a rebellion in the full knowledge of the consequences. Whatever the 'might-have-beens', the executions did in fact give Sinn Fein that legend, inspiration and emotion which are the stuff of almost every nationalist movement. Modern Eire dates from Easter Monday 1916.

The danger of Sinn Fein pre-empting the moderate Nationalists was obvious. To avoid it Lloyd George was deputed to negotiate with Redmond and Carson a plan for the suspended Home Rule Bill to come into force at once, the six Ulster counties being excluded till the end of the war. As so often he was too clever by half, and neither the northern nor southern Irish leader felt they had been fairly treated. Moreover, he was stirring a hornets' nest. The Conservative diehards were furious, and, although Bonar Law at first acquiesced, he jibbed at the preservation of a hundred Westminster MPs for an overrepresented Ireland. Why should they be able to settle 'British' domestic issues, even the colour of a British government, *after* getting Home Rule? The argument, familiar much later in the context of Scottish devolution, proved conclusive. Redmond would not give way and the issue was shelved early in July. The government's precarious unity survived.

Before this there occurred the most important change in the Cabinet since its formation in May 1915. On 5 June, the cruiser *Hampshire*, conveying Kitchener on a mission to Russia, struck a mine off the Orkneys. He was drowned along with his staff and most of the crew. The War Office was now vacant and the obvious claimants were Bonar Law and Lloyd George. They discussed the matter with each other, not very cordially, and agreed on Lloyd George. Asquith reluctantly acquiesced; he had no choice, but Lloyd George was now a more formidable rival than ever and the alliance developing between him and Bonar Law, uneasy and intermittent though it was, boded no good for the Prime Minister's own position. Six months later it was to be fatal.

The second half of 1916 brought increasing dissatisfaction with the progress of the war. There was the Somme with its huge casualties directly affecting for the first time a high proportion of British families. There was Jutland. There was the renewed U-boat campaign of the autumn which took a heavy toll of merchant shipping. Tsarist Russia's last great effort – General Brusilov's breakthrough in Galicia, which seemed the only gleam of light that summer – petered out with heavy losses. Its superficial success brought Romania into the war on the Allied side on 27 August, but Austro–German forces rapidly overran the country entering Bucharest on 6 December and securing valuable resources of grain and oil for the central powers.

All this began to rub off on the government. Disenchantment with Asquith's style and method grew in Parliament, the press and other areas of informed opinion. Until the summer there had been little criticism. He had many qualities – clarity of mind, 'unflappability', patience, integrity. He was a firm 'Westerner' and he was respected by the top soldiers and sailors. Prime Minister for a longer continuous period than anyone since Lord Liverpool, he seemed almost indispensable – a symbol indeed of national unity. But he was getting tired, and the death in action of his beloved elder son, Raymond, in September was a grievous blow. Moreover, like other Prime Ministers who have managed successfully in peace – the younger Pitt, Lord Aberdeen, Neville Chamberlain – his temperament was not suited to the demands of war. He was conservative in all matters concerning his office. He regarded the popular newspapers with a dislike which was reciprocated; he made no concessions to Lord Northcliffe who as owner of *The Times* and the *Daily Mail* could speak to both 'the classes' and 'the masses', and who controlled half the circulation of the London press in an era when radio was unknown. In wartime, a friend told Asquith, it is not only necessary to be active, it is necessary to seem active. Asquith, the antithesis of a showman, refused to seem active. He had another foible that did not go unnoticed. Haig, who liked him, might write in his diary after Asquith's fall: 'I am personally very fond of poor old Squiff. He had a hard time and even when "exhilarated" had much more capacity and brain power than any of the others.' But there were those who took a less tolerant view of 'exhilaration'. At the opposite extreme was Churchill. He was no teetotaller, but he had a grievance. He wrote bitterly to his brother in the summer: 'Asquith reigns sodden, supine and supreme.'

By November a number of influential figures were convinced that the government could not go on as it was. Milner, widely respected in Conservative circles as a great proconsul, was one. Carson was another. Since his resignation he had been using his destructive genius to lead the informal opposition in Parliament. At times he seemed to be vying with Bonar Law for the 'soul' of the Conservative Party. Northcliffe, who operated quite independently, was a third. All three believed that Asquith should go. But they did not oppose Robertson and Haig or the policy of concentration on the western front. They wanted to get rid of Asquith because they thought he did not give the soldiers a sufficiently free hand. Lloyd George too was a strong advocate of change, but he did not wish to oust Asquith. Chafing under the restrictions of the Kitchener–Robertson treaty, which he had hoped but failed to remove, he wanted to have a say in strategy. He was a confirmed 'Easterner' still, and he deeply distrusted the tactics of Haig and his commanders even in terms of a 'Western' strategy. If he could acquire a position which would at least give him some control over the generals he did not mind if Asquith stayed on as Prime Minister. Indeed he regarded him as an asset.

Milner, Carson and Northcliffe could not have brought Asquith down on their own, even if they had been in agreement. The essential ingredient of any compound sufficiently explosive to do this was Bonar Law, and at the beginning of November he was not on cordial terms with any of the others. The catalyst was another newspaper proprietor, Sir Max Aitken, MP, owner of the *Daily Express* (not in those days, however, a paper of any significance). He was a self-made Canadian millionaire and, though much younger, an intimate friend of Bonar Law who was himself of Canadian birth. By a remarkable combination of charm, persuasion, manoeuvre and cajolery, he brought Lloyd George, Bonar Law and Carson together during the second half of November. The proposal which they decided to put to Asquith was a change in the 'decision-making process' – the creation of a War Council, small in number (the final version was three), sitting from day to day with real powers to act and with Lloyd George as chairman. The Prime Minister was not to be a member, the excuse being that he would be too busy with other things (no one said what), but he would be entitled to call in any decision to which he objected and refer it to the Cabinet as a whole.

There was a genuine administrative point here, and Asquith ought to have changed the 1915 system long before. But the real issue was personal. It was a transparent device to sidestep the Prime Minister and vest the only area of government business that mattered in a triumvirate consisting of Lloyd George who was his chief Liberal rival, Bonar Law for whom he had little respect, and Carson who was one of his sharpest critics. Asquith saw what was intended quickly enough and, when Lloyd George put it to him on 1 December, he gave a polite but firm refusal. He had no objection to some measure of reorganization, but he insisted on the Prime Minister being chairman of the War Council. If personalities could be ignored, Asquith was right. The arrangement was a constitutional absurdity. Personalities, however, were what the crisis was all about. If Asquith insisted that the Prime Minister must be chairman of the War Council, Lloyd George and Bonar Law were going to insist that the Prime Minister must not be Asquith.

In the end they got their way. After five days of complicated manoeuvres which would take as many pages to recount as it took hours to occur (the volume of literature on the subject is already vast), Asquith resigned on 6 December and Lloyd George became Prime Minister. The episode caused lasting resentment in the Liberal Party and almost all the Liberal ministers followed Asquith. It was the origin of a split which was never healed while both the rivals were alive. Inevitably, the new government was predominantly Conservative.

Lloyd George at once dropped his original proposals for reorganization. Nothing more was heard of the impossibility of the Prime Minister being chairman of the War Council. That problem and the relationship of the council with the Cabinet were solved by merging them into a 'War Cabinet'. It consisted of Lloyd George, Bonar Law who became Chancellor of the Exchequer, Arthur Henderson who represented Labour, Curzon and Milner who was a last minute substitute for Carson. The two latter gave a high independent tone to the Cabinet for, though respected by the Conservatives, they did not in any sense depend on the party. Full ministerial and constitutional responsibility lay with the War Cabinet and with that body alone. Carson as First Lord of the Admiralty, Robertson as Chief of Staff, and Balfour whose acceptance of the Foreign Office had staggered Asquith and greatly eased Lloyd George's path, had the right to attend when their business was being discussed. Other ministers came only if summoned. Sir Maurice Hankey, Secretary to the former War Committee became Secretary to the Cabinet, a new office. For the first time there was a regular agenda and minutes were recorded – innovations which became permanent features of the constitution.

Lloyd George's position was in some ways weak and paradoxical. He could claim no 'mandate'. He had risen to power through a process obscure to Parliament, to the public – and in some details even to historians. He was an 'Easterner' helped into office by 'Westerners'. Since Asquith retained the Liberal leadership, organization and funds, he was a Prime Minister without a party. He was a Liberal whose principal support came from Conservatives and was far from whole-hearted. Yet he had important assets. He soon forged a genuine friendship with Bonar Law, described by Stanley Baldwin as 'the most perfect partnership in political history'. He had eloquence, energy, ebullience, gaiety, resourcefulness and a deep disrespect for establishments of every kind. He was a fresh wind blowing through Whitehall. And he was not Asquith.

2

Lloyd George was at last unfettered, anyway in theory; but in practice he was not going to find it easy to escape the commitment made by Kitchener in August 1915. It is true that the War Cabinet – particularly the 'Imperial War Cabinet' which was the same body enlarged by the dominion Prime Ministers when they were in London – was sympathetic. 'Eastern' strategy was in one sense better than 'Western' for the empire. Milner and Curzon were imperially minded. The dominion Prime Ministers did not want anything like Milner's Federal Empire, but they were highly critical of the squandering, as they saw it, of dominion lives in France by the British High Command and on this point struck up an alliance with Lloyd George. But even the most empire-minded person had to face the dilemma of British policy ably analysed by Michael Howard.[1] How was a great industrialized military state like Germany to be prevented from wrecking the empire by advancing right across Asia to India unless its strength was tied down in the west? The problem became even graver with the gradual disintegration of Russia after the revolution of March 1917.

Moreover, the War Cabinet was not typical of general British opinion. By the end of 1916 'Western' strategy had acquired an almost irreversible momentum of its own. The military establishment was solidly behind it – even a maverick like Sir Henry Wilson was not an 'Easterner'. The Asquithian Liberals agreed with them. The press too was universally pro-'Western'. Against these forces Lloyd George could do little. He did remove the ban that had existed since the end of 1915 on offensive operations in the Middle East, authorizing advances up the Tigris and into Palestine. The results of the latter were not seen till the end of the year. The former brought an immediate gain – General Maude's capture in March 1917 of Baghdad known engagingly by the troops as the 'City of Haroun-Al-Rothschild'. But their expectations of the pleasures of *The Thousand and One Nights* were to be disappointed. One could not even get a glass of beer in the place. These campaigns did not of course mean a strategic switch from west to east, nor was Lloyd George ever able to achieve it. The most he could do was to try to make his particular views prevail within the general framework of a 'Western' strategy. His first attempt had unhappy results.

Haig and Joffre on 15 November 1916 at the Conference of Chantilly had agreed on a plan for 1917 involving a renewed offensive on the Somme early in February with the British taking the main burden. In December, however, a political crisis similar to that in London erupted in Paris. Briand, the French Prime Minister, quicker off the mark than Asquith, reconstructed his government into a 'war cabinet', and for good measure sacked his Commander-in-Chief. Joffre's successor, General Nivelle, hero of Verdun, had great charm and spoke perfect English. He captivated Lloyd George and he convinced politicians in both countries that he had the secret of success. The soldiers were not so sure.

Nivelle's proposal was to attack in great force on the Aisne in April. The British role was to be subsidiary – a diversionary attack by Allenby's 3rd Army at Arras seventy-five miles north-west. Lloyd George disliked 'Western' offensives of any sort, but this one had the advantage of laying the burden on the apparently willing French, and he saw an opportunity. With the connivance of Briand and Nivelle he resolved to curb Haig by putting the British Army under French command. At the Conference of Calais on 26 February 1917, called ostensibly to discuss transport, his proposal was sprung on Haig and Robertson without previous warning. In its original form it would have sidetracked Haig entirely, leaving him with responsibility only for administration while Nivelle would have had direct command of the separate British armies, through a British Chief of Staff – and Sir Henry Wilson was the name proposed. Haig and Robertson were horrified and protested so strongly that the plan was modified. Haig was now to come under Nivelle only for the duration of the actual offensive and retain command of his armies with the right of appeal to the Cabinet. But neither he nor Robertson ever forgave Lloyd George. It was the origin of a mutual mistrust which bedevilled their relations for the rest of the war.

Nor was Lloyd George's confidence in Nivelle justified. The British attack in snow and sleet at Arras on 9 April met with a limited degree of success including the Canadian capture of Vimy Ridge. Nivelle's offensive launched a week later was a fiasco. In two days his armies suffered 100,000 casualties and advanced 600 yards. The French soldiers had now had enough. There were widespread mutinies and desertions. Nivelle was replaced by the cautious Pétain who restored order after one month and twenty-three executions (not a large number in the circumstances), chiefly by tact, attention to grievances and the unspoken message that there would be no more offensives.

A major strategic problem now faced the War Cabinet. Was the British Army also to stay on the defensive for the rest of the year? Or should it, as Haig urged, launch a major attack to roll up the German right flank, and seize the Belgian coast with its U-boat bases? There were powerful arguments both ways. The Allies were passing through a desperate period of the war. The U-boat campaign in the last four months of 1916, even in its 'restricted' form, had already doubled the average monthly losses in Allied and neutral merchant shipping from 75,000 to 158,000 tons. The Admiralty seemed powerless even then. On hearing a list of losses Balfour was heard to murmur: 'It is very tiresome. These Germans are intolerable.' The number of U-boats in service rose during 1916 from 58 to 140. The situation became even worse when, in February 1917, the German government made the campaign 'unrestricted'. The decision to torpedo at sight raised Allied and neutral losses to the terrifying figure of 852,000 tons in April. It also brought America into the war on 6 April, but Germany could ignore that threat if losses on this scale continued; Britain would be starved out before America could make any difference. In fact April was the nadir. The turning point was the initiative of the convoy system in May, largely at Lloyd George's insistence, though it is a myth that he did it single-handed. Nor could it have been introduced much earlier if only because of the shortage of destroyers. By August 1917 monthly losses were down to 200,000 tons, and the worst was over.

This was not self-evident on 20 June when the decision to allow Haig to attack in the west was taken. Jellicoe, now First Sea Lord, was very pessimistic, and did not appreciate that the Germans in fact made little use of Belgian ports for U-boats. Haig's main argument, however, was that 'the German was now nearly at his last resources' and that an offensive could 'effect great results ... which will make final victory more assured and which may even bring it within reach this year'. He was also influenced by the state of the French forces, informed as he had been about the mutinies in strictest confidence by Pétain; he did not pass this on to the War Cabinet, but the prevention of a German attack on the

47

French sector was certainly a consideration in his mind. Lloyd George did all he could to dissuade Haig. If there was to be any offensive he preferred to reinforce the Italian front. The War Cabinet was divided, but in the end felt it could not overrule the Commander-in-Chief. On 31 July after ten days' bombardment the third battle of Ypres began. It is known to posterity as Passchendaele.

The campaign has been the subject of perpetual dispute ever since. It achieved none of Haig's declared objectives, and at last became bogged down (literally) on 10 November with the capture of Passchendaele. Conditions were appalling. Men fought in a quagmire produced partly by perpetual rain which, it is both alleged and denied, was predictable, and partly by the effect of the bombardment on the dykes built to prevent flooding. The grey weeping skies, the continuous downpour, the ubiquitous, unfathomable mud left a scar in the national memory. There is a nightmare quality about Passchendaele which nothing will erase. Haig could and perhaps should have cried off after the failure of his first blow, 31 July to 2 August. He certainly ought to have called it a day after taking the main ridge east of Ypres on 4 October. Yet one has to remember that, heavy though British casualties were, enemy losses were not much less. The Germans had to endure the same fearful conditions. To them too it was a nightmare experience. It is easy to forget that in the trench warfare on the western front the defenders suffered almost as heavily as the attackers, and one cannot measure the result only by miles lost or gained. It is not certain which side was weakened most. Had there been no Passchendaele, would the British have been better placed to resist the offensive of March 1918 or the Germans to exploit their early successes? No clear answer ever has been – perhaps ever can be – given to this question. Nor to another: did Passchendaele avert a German offensive against the demoralized French Army?

Long before the end Lloyd George became convinced that the campaign was a disaster; he was determined that there should be no repetition. The striking but transient success of

General Byng's tanks at Cambrai on 20 November – the first large-scale use of a weapon destined to transform the art of war – merely confirmed his opinion of British generalship; if Passchendaele had not occurred Byng might have had the reserves to exploit his initial breakthrough. The Prime Minister's difficulty was that he still dared not get rid of the Haig–Robertson partnership. His problem was how to avoid taking their advice without provoking their resignations. The Calais Conference had been the first round in his fight with the military hierarchy, and he had lost it. He now prepared for a second round. His approach was to be even more circuitous than it had been at Calais.

Meanwhile, one gleam of light shone out in the gathering gloom of autumn. This was General Allenby's capture of Jerusalem, the opening stage in the second of the two 'side-shows' which were to shape the post-war empire (Mesopotamia being the first). Allenby, nicknamed 'the Bull', was one of the most remarkable generals of the war. With his thick neck, florid complexion and explosive temper – officers were known to faint in his presence – he seemed a caricature of the archetypal military man. In fact he was nothing of the sort. It is true that he was doctrinally a 'Westerner', though he did not much like Haig or approve of his tactics, especially the prolonged artillery bombardments which heralded every attack. It is also true that when he was asked to take command of the Egyptian Expeditionary Force sweating lethargically amidst the flies and heat of the Sinai desert opposite the Turkish Gaza Line, he felt at first that he was taking a step down. But he was cheered by the enthusiasm of Lloyd George who presented him with Sir George Adam Smith's *Historical Geography of the Holy Land* (typically Allenby already had a copy) and he resolved to accept the challenge.

Behind his exterior, Allenby, though not quick, was highly intelligent, very thoughtful and extremely well read. He took an avid interest in the fauna, flora, topography and history of the area. What other general would have discovered that Richard Coeur de Lion failed to take Jerusalem because he chose the malarial season for his advance, or investigated the reasons for the ophthalmia which blinded so many of Napoleon's soldiers in Egypt in 1798–1801, or studied in the original Greek Strabo's account of the ancient route through the Sinai desert? And what other commander-in-chief would have put up with the exhibitionism of T. E. Lawrence 'of Arabia' – a mere major posturing in Arab clothes?

Allenby, to the surprise of his staff, saw that there was real use to be made of this eccentric figure. Lawrence's part in the Arab Revolt in the Hejaz begun by Hussein Sherif of Mecca in June 1916 and his single-handed capture of Akaba may have been moves towards his unrealistic goal of creating an Arab state based on Damascus under Hussein's son, Feisal. Allenby did not care. The politicians would sort out the post-war partition of the Ottoman Empire. An Arab guerrilla campaign led by Lawrence and directed against the thousand-mile railway from Damascus to Medina would tie down a disproportionate number of Turks and disrupt their communications. The distortions and omissions discovered by later critics in Lawrence's own account of his role should not blind one to the fact that nearly everyone personally involved regarded it as a highly important element in British success during 1917 and 1918.

Allenby, though almost broken by the death of his only son in France, launched his attack late in October after elaborate preparation and deception. The German commander of the Turkish forces expected an attack along the coast, whereas Allenby put his whole weight against their left flank at Beersheba. It was completely successful, and there seemed a real chance of taking Jerusalem. At this juncture the British government made an important announcement whose full consequences they could scarcely have foreseen. It took the form of an open letter on 9 November from the Foreign Secretary to Lord Rothschild, the leader of English Jewry. The Balfour Declaration stated that the government favoured 'the establishment in Palestine of a national home for the Jewish people'.

The final stages of the advance on Jerusalem were not easy going. The weather broke, and the Turks put up a stiff resistance in rain, cold and mist, but on 8 December the Old City was evacuated. On 11 December, a chilly but bright day, Allenby entered on foot by the Jaffa Gate. He stood on the steps of the citadel and listened to his own proclamation read in many languages, declaring the end of Turkish rule and the inviolability of the sacred places of the three great religions. It was 401 years since the Turks had taken Jerusalem from the Mamelukes, and more than seven centuries since the end of the crusader kingdom, the last period of Christian rule. No wonder that the event was one that appealed to the imagination of the world.

3

By the end of 1917 the German High Command no longer had to worry about its eastern front. The October Revolution, one of the most disastrous events in twentieth-century history, harbinger of the first totalitarian state and of untold misery to the Russian and many other peoples, took Russia finally out of the war. The Germans now had a chance, if a slender one. Faced with the tightening grip of the British blockade and the prospect next year of large-scale American intervention, Ludendorff resolved to strike as soon and as hard as he could in the west. At the beginning of 1917 the Allies had enjoyed a numerical advantage of nearly three to two. A year later the Germans had 192 divisions to the Allies' 173. It was now or never.

In these circumstances Haig needed all the troops he could get. The imminence of a major German offensive was obvious. There were substantial reserves available in Britain, and Haig's armies were dangerously depleted after some 400,000 casualties during the Passchendaele campaign. Lloyd George knew all this, but he took an extraordinary decision. Fearing that Haig might try to renew the offensive in Flanders and feeling too weak to overrule or dismiss him, the Prime Minister, during the winter of 1917–18, deliberately starved the Commander-in-Chief of men, so that a renewed offensive could not plausibly be even suggested. The historiography of the First World War is – or until recently was – divided between 'Haigites' and 'Georgeites', but few of the latter have found this aspect of Lloyd George's policy defensible. He risked losing the war altogether – a risk which nearly became a reality when Ludendorff opened his spring offensive in March.

A Prime Minister who has lost confidence to this extent in a commander-in-chief ought to dismiss him. No doubt there would have been a major political row if Lloyd George had got rid of Haig. The press would have been eloquent. The Asquithians would have been up in arms and would have had a good deal of support from the Unionists. Many of them regarded Haig's presence as a guarantee against the vagaries of a Prime Minister whom they never really trusted. Law warned Lloyd George against removing Haig. But, even if dismissal was too much of a political risk, Lloyd George could certainly have overruled any proposal by Haig for a fresh offensive. After all, the War Cabinet had the ultimate responsibility, and it came close to vetoing the first Passchendaele. It could certainly have vetoed a second, and Haig would not have resigned.

The relationship between the civil and military power was always uneasy in the First World War and the problem remained unsolved to the end, but this episode was the high point of mutual mistrust. It is hard to believe that Lloyd George was not seeing turnip ghosts; his enemies were less united and less powerful than he thought. This was shown when Robertson resigned as CIGS in February 1918. Lloyd George and Clemenceau (the new French Prime Minister) had decided to convert a shadowy body called the Allied Supreme War Council from a sort of 'think-tank' into one with executive powers over a newly proposed Anglo-French 'general reserve'. The British military representative on that body was Sir Henry Wilson whom Robertson and Haig detested. Robertson rigidly saw the change as a backstairs way of providing Lloyd George with an alternative source of military advice over which the CIGS had no control. He insisted that the CIGS or his deputy must also be the military representative. At the same time an article appeared by Colonel Repington, military correspondent of the *Morning Post*, denouncing the proposed change. It was clearly based on confidential information widely believed to stem from General Sir Frederick Maurice, one of Robertson's principal aides in the War Office.

Lloyd George hit back. He presented Robertson with an ultimatum; he could either remain CIGS, but with powers reduced to those prevailing before December 1915; or he could be military representative; he could not be both. At the same time the Attorney-General prosecuted Repington under the Official Secrets Act. Robertson at once resigned, and Lloyd George appointed Wilson in his place – a shrewd move since Wilson was a strong, almost virulent Unionist whereas Robertson had never got on well with the party. There was an uproar and Lord Derby, the War Minister, proffered his resignation too, though not very enthusiastically; but Lloyd George had no difficulty in riding the storm.

In his memoirs he purports to see in these events the hand of a 'military junta' seeking to overthrow the government and substitute one that would be a puppet of the army. This is nonsense. The top British generals, apart from Wilson himself ironically, were essentially non-political. Haig, whose attitude was awaited by the War Cabinet with some trepidation, did not like the new arrangement, but he was prepared to work under it. If he and Derby had resigned, the government might have tottered, though it probably would have survived. In fact Haig had no intention of resigning and he tried to persuade Robertson and Derby to withdraw, in the case of the latter successfully. He probably did as much as anyone to cool the agitation. If there was a 'military junta' Haig clearly did not belong to it.

There was to be one last episode in the struggle between

the soldiers – or, rather, some soldiers – and the government. On 7 May, 1918 when Ludendorff's offensive seemed to threaten the whole position of the British Army, General Maurice, recently retired from the War Office, wrote a sensational letter to the press. He impugned the truth of statements in the House by Bonar Law about the extension of the British front and by Lloyd George about manpower. The latter was the important one, for the Prime Minister had claimed that the army on the western front was stronger in January 1918 than it had been in January 1917. Maurice was raising the question hitherto not publicly ventilated of Lloyd George's deliberate refusal to reinforce Haig. This was a challenge and the government at first decided to hold a confidential judicial inquiry. Asquith demanded a Select Committee instead. The press was now in full cry, and it looked as if the Asquithians might be joined by the Unionist backbenchers led by Carson who had resigned in July 1917 from the Admiralty and was back in his old role as an oppositionist: Lloyd George and Bonar Law now decided to drop the inquiry altogether, state their case in the House and make Asquith's motion an issue of confidence. As far as the debate went, they were totally vindicated. Carson was not prepared to challenge the existence of the government, and Asquith was beaten by 293 votes to 106.

There is an ironic footnote to the affair. Bonar Law's veracity was beyond dispute, and on that score Maurice was shown to be simply wrong, but the real issue was Lloyd George's. He made great play of the fact that his figures were provided by Maurice's own department. This was true, but what Lloyd George did not say was that they had been discovered to be wrong and a correction, which would have confirmed Maurice's charge, had been sent to Lloyd George in ample time. He was not lying. The red box containing the amended version was found unopened a few days after the debate by J. T. Davies, his principal private secretary, and Frances Stevenson, another secretary (also his mistress and later his second wife). Davies put the document in the fire observing: 'Only you and I, Frances, know of the existence of this paper.'[2]

Ludendorff opened his offensive on 21 March with an attack by sixty-three divisions on the forty-three-mile sector between Arras in the north and La Fere in the south. The northern third of the line was strongly held by Byng's 3rd Army and Arras never fell, but the southern two-thirds was only thinly defended by Gough's 5th Army. The Germans broke through and within a week their 18th Army had reached Montidier forty miles from the original front line. By 5 April they were within fifteen miles of Amiens, the most important railway centre in northern France, but the momentum then died away. There had been nothing like it since the autumn of 1914. Eighty thousand prisoners were captured and nearly 1,000 guns. Gough paid the penalty. Removed on 4 April, at the government's insistence not Haig's, he was the only army commander to receive neither a peerage nor a grant of money at the end of the war.

Meanwhile, an important change had occurred in the chain of command. Haig had always been opposed to Lloyd George's panacea of unity under a French generalissimo, but he was abruptly converted, not on its abstract merits, but because Pétain, when called upon for reinforcements, sent only nine divisions and significantly stated that, if the Germans penetrated any further, he would have to fall back on Paris and use his main reserves to cover the capital, at the cost of losing contact with the British. Haig regarded this defeatism as fatal. He urged Wilson and Milner, who had replaced Derby at the War Office, to come to France at once, and on 26 March at the Conference of Doullens, Foch was given command of all the forces on the western front. Foch had his defects, but he was a fighter. It was an *ad hominem* solution to an *ad hominem* problem.

Ludendorff's second attack took place on 9 April on the sector between Hollebeke in the north (a few miles south of Ypres) and the La Bassé canal in the south. By nightfall next day he had broken through on a twenty-four-mile front. On the 12th, Haig issued one of the most famous orders of the day in British military history: 'There is no other course open to us but to fight it out. Every position must be held to the last man ... With our backs to the wall and believing in the justice of our cause, each one of us must fight on to the end.' The attack did not penetrate as far as its predecessor – little more than ten miles; but the objective, the railway junction of Hazbrouck, was much nearer than Amiens. The Germans were only five miles away on 29–30 April when this attempt too faded out.

The last of Ludendorff's major attacks was made after nearly a month's delay on 27 May – against a sector held partly by the British and partly by the French on the Aisne, where Nivelle had launched his ill-fated offensive the previous year. The Germans advanced some thirty miles capturing Soissons and reaching the Marne, but once again the impetus was lost. They got near enough to terrify Paris by bombarding the city with a gigantic gun called Big Bertha which had a range of over sixty miles, and they took 65,000 prisoners along with valuable supplies, but victory still eluded them. There was one significant feature of the battle of the Aisne. The Americans made their first attack in the war on 28 May when the 28th Regiment of their 1st Division captured the village of Catigny. On 6 June the American 2nd Division made a counter-attack at Belleau. These were not in themselves episodes of any great importance but they were portents for the future. America had declared war more than a year earlier, but the build-up of her forces in France had been slow and laborious, even apart from the problem of shipping them across the Atlantic. By 1 May 1918 there were some 430,000 American soldiers in France, but except for one division, the 1st, they were a collection of men with no organized structure. By June there was a second division, but it was not till August that the American 1st Army came into being. General Pershing, Commander-in-Chief, was determined not to allow his troops to be scattered under other commands for a moment longer than necessary. Meanwhile,

individual divisions fought with great courage though inevit-
ably with heavy losses due to inexperience. They played no
serious part in Haig's August offensive, but they were to make
a major contribution in the last two months of the war at the
battles of St Mihiel in September and Meuse-Argonne in
October which were almost exclusively American operations.
The latter cost them 117,000 casualties. From March to
October 1918 1.75 million American soldiers landed in
France. But it remains an interesting comment on the
American war effort that the army of the greatest industrial
nation in the world depended up to the end on British and
French manufacturers for all its artillery, all its tanks and half
its aircraft – a startling contrast with what happened in the war
of 1939–45.

Ludendorff's May offensive was not quite the end of the
German effort. On 9 June a relatively minor attack at
Compiegne came to nothing, and on 15 July his last serious
attack was launched on either side of Rheims only to be halted
three days later by what is sometimes called Foch's 'counter-
stroke', although in fact Foch had intended to launch an
offensive that day irrespective of any German action.

Foch's offensive was indecisive. The truth, as Haig frequently observed in his diary, was that the French troops were
not in a condition to fight effectively. It was the British who
counted. Ludendorff saw this and his strategy was above all
else aimed at eliminating Haig's armies. On 8 August came the
turning point in the struggle on the western front subsequently
described by Ludendorff as 'the black day of the German
Army in the history of the war'. Haig launched a brilliantly
successful offensive east of Amiens, which took the enemy
completely by surprise. Designed mainly to free that vital
centre it did not effect a startling penetration – only twelve
miles all told – nor did it inflict startling losses; some 21,000
prisoners were not a lot compared with Ludendorff's 'bag'.
What it did achieve was that essential objective of every war, to
convince one's opponent that there is no hope of him winning.

In spite of all that has been written about the Ludendorff

offensive, two puzzles remain. Neither side had made any real impression on the other in the frustrating siege warfare of the previous three and a half years. Why did Ludendorff's armies at last achieve a breakthrough and why, having done so, did they everywhere grind to a halt before their principal objectives? There was an element of luck in the attacks. Those on 21 March, 9 April and 27 May were by a curious chance in each case launched under the protection of a blanket of mist. Oddly enough Haig was to have the same asset on 8 August. Ludendorff certainly profited, anyway at first, from Lloyd George's policy over reinforcements, though this was quickly reversed. Between 21 March and August half a million men were despatched across the Channel. Finally, he exploited on a tactical level the element of surprise more effectively – for example a brief intense bombardment instead of the conventional prolonged prelude – than any previous commander. It is fair to say that Haig with his massive and unexpected tank attack (Rawlinson launched some 450 on 8 August), also showed an awareness of surprise which contrasted with his tactics at the Somme and Passchendaele.

As for Ludendorff's failure to reach his objectives, the answer is partly that he did not adhere to his own policy of following the line of least resistance. In practice he could not escape from Clausewitz's doctrine of attacking the enemy's main force. For example, if he had not expended so many divisions on Arras, he might easily have captured Amiens. The other reason is a surprising one. Perhaps military historians have not sufficiently investigated the effect of alcohol on war, though it is of course widely known that 'Dutch courage' was often needed to inspire men 'going over the top'. The Germans, now far behind the British front line, not only found lavish supplies of food, clothing and footwear (by the standards of blockaded Germany), but also great quantities of drink; there is evidence that wine and looting brought the advance to a complete standstill on several occasions during the drive for Amiens and also during the Rheims offensive in the heart of the champagne country.

Years of privation had led to scenes of drunkenness and gluttony which the officers could not control and in which they themselves sometimes participated.

August 8 was the prelude to a series of highly successful attacks by Haig. These have been curiously disregarded by later historians. Indeed the breast-beating English tendency – and it is essentially English, not Scottish or Welsh – to dwell on defeats and disaster, makes it quite a puzzle for a later generation to understand how the war was ever won. There is no space or need to describe the details. By 30 October the Allies had not only recovered all the ground lost in Ludendorff's offensive, but had advanced many miles beyond the old front line of 21 March. The Allies in effect means the British. Foch was generalissimo, the exhausted French armies played some part, and the American forces, still relatively small, fought with courage, though America's real contribution was her future threat; but the truth remains that this was essentially a British battle shaped by a British commander subordinate to a Frenchman only in name and only because of the defeatism of another Frenchman.

These facts are little recognized. No doubt Haig's responsibility for the Somme and Passchendaele is one reason, and the two most eloquent memoir writers, Churchill and Lloyd George, were anti-'Western'. Lloyd George in particular was not going to admit that the battles which won the war had been won by someone whom he would have gladly dismissed, following a strategy which he had strongly opposed. But posterity does not see everything through Lloyd George's eyes, or even Churchill's. There must be more than that to this wilful occlusion. Perhaps it is one of the symptoms, even causes, of the decline of empire.

The collapse of the central powers occurred sooner than most people expected. As late as the end of September it was assumed that the war would not end till 1919. Although Ludendorff gave up hope of victory after Haig's August offensive, the last straw for him was an event not in France, but in an almost forgotten area of war. This was the stagnant malarial theatre of Salonika where an Anglo-French force of half a million had done nothing at all since landing there some three years earlier. An Allied offensive was unexpectedly launched on 15 September, and Bulgaria capitulated only a fortnight later. On receiving the news Ludendorff had a fit. He collapsed foaming at the mouth and when he recovered he insisted that the Chancellor must negotiate a general armistice. It was a premature decision, for the German armies were by no means beaten yet in the west, and a few days later Ludendorff himself recognized the fact, but it was too late. The news of his collapse had become widely known among those who governed Germany and their despondency was enhanced by the disasters which now struck their principal allies.

Allenby moving north from Jerusalem destroyed the Turkish forces at Megiddo in September and was approaching Aleppo when the Ottoman Empire capitulated on 31 October. In Italy the Italian, British and French forces on the Piave where they had been driven in 1917 by the defeat of Caporetto were thrusting in late October towards Vittorio Veneto. On 4 November Austria asked for an armistice. Militarily the Germans could have prolonged the war into 1919, but the blockade and the knowledge that there were 2 million American troops now in Europe turned the scales. A revolution swept the country. The fleet mutinied and the Kaiser fled to Holland. The Armistice was signed at 5 A.M. on 11 November; it came into force at 11 A.M. – the eleventh hour of the eleventh day of the eleventh month. The Great War had at last ended.

Chapter Four

THE SECOND COALITION
IN PEACE

I

It is easy to assume that during 'total' war nothing happens
except war. This was not true of England in either of the two
great conflicts which afflicted the twentieth century. The
passage of the fourth great Reform Bill in the first and the
publication of the Beveridge Report in the second were not
alone in having important effects on the course of later
domestic history. The Representation of the People Act was
passed on 5 February 1918. Despite subsequent changes it
has constituted the basic framework of the British Parliamentary system ever since. It also had a significant, though ill-
appreciated influence on the post-war fortunes of all three
major political parties. Yet until recently, unlike its predecessors of 1832, 1867 and 1884, it has received little
attention from historians. As a result many people have a
vague impression that for practical purposes something akin
to adult male suffrage already existed before 1914 and that all
the Act did was to tidy up the male vote while adding a limited
number of female voters to the register.

In reality the pre-war franchise, though based on seven
different qualifications, came nowhere near to manhood
suffrage. The Act of 1918 which established it for the first
time added 5 million to the existing figure of 8 million male
voters. As for women, by enfranchising those aged thirty or
more, who were on the local government register or whose
husbands were on it, the Act added another 8.4 million to the
electorate. The total thus rose from 8 million to 21.4 million
– the biggest single jump in the history of electoral change.

The Act also brought about a major redistribution of seats and entirely redrew the electoral map of Britain.

Its passage during wartime occurred because under the Act of 1911, Parliament was due to expire on 31 December 1915. The French faced with a similar situation passed a simple law abrogating elections till the end of hostilities. There was little chance of a measure like that getting through in Britain. Asquith hoped that the coalition which he formed in May of that year would extract from Parliament an electoral moratorium for the duration of the war. He was far too optimistic. It was not till December that he obtained at the very last moment a postponement of the crucial date – and then only for one year. An election was therefore on the horizon throughout his premiership and, unless something was done, it would be fought on the March 1914 register. This was not only becoming rapidly obsolete with each year that passed, but it excluded almost all members of the armed services. The victims of this omission were probably those who cared least, but everyone else considered it outrageous. The Cabinet therefore dared not ask for a second prolongation of Parliament without proposing amendments to the register, but any amendments were bound to stir up the controversies which had culminated in the collapse of Asquith's Franchise Bill in 1913. They could easily break up the coalition and precipitate the very election which it was Asquith's object to avoid.

In the summer of 1916 the Prime Minister faced a major crisis. He put forward two Bills, one to prolong Parliament till 31 May 1917, the other to deal with the 1914 register. The first got through, but the second foundered in a storm of controversy. In desperation he suggested vaguely that the House might 'see if we cannot work out by general agreement some scheme . . . ' Whether from exhaustion or the difficulty of lunging at a target of cotton wool, the House accepted the suggestion. It was the origin of the famous Speaker's Conference. A cross between a select committee and a widely composed body of the Royal Commission type, the conference consisted of thirty-two members of both Houses balanced on strict party lines. It was thus named because a suitable judicial figure could not be found, and the Speaker, Sir James Lowther, agreed with reluctance to preside instead. A Speaker's Conference has subsequently become the established way of ventilating electoral change, but the origin of this respectable constitutional device was not careful consideration, but expediency grasped by a tottering government to save itself from a collapse which was destined to occur in any case within a few weeks. However, British constitutional innovations have often been the result of accident rather than design; they are not necessarily the worse for that.

The conference was an unexpected success. It owed much to Lowther's tact and skill, but he could not have produced an almost unanimous report if the bases for a compromise had not existed. Liberals and Labour had long advocated manhood suffrage. The Conservatives were bound to gain by the inevitable redistribution of seats, and, although they would have preferred a purely service franchise, manhood suffrage alarmed them less than it had because of their naïve and by no means justified faith in the pro-Conservative effect of military service on the unenfranchised male. Moreover, they were able to retain a modified plural vote – one extra (instead of a limitless number) *either* for occupation of business premises in another constituency *or* for possession of a university degree – not both. Discontented Radicals had to wait another thirty years for the abolition of this *douceur* to the Conservatives, but they were consoled because elections would now all take place on the same day – which at least made the business vote less easy to exercise.

It was not, however, certain that Lloyd George would act on the report at all. Legislation meant forgoing the important option of an early dissolution. A Bill was sure to be slow and further time would be taken in the preparation of a new register. Meanwhile, barring some extraordinary crisis, he could hardly dissolve on the old one. Yet he was by no means averse to an early election. Unlike Asquith he was almost certain to win it, and he needed a mandate as war leader to

63

consolidate his young and still shaky government. On the other hand, it would make him even more dependent on the Conservatives and it would mean the loss of a major Reform Bill which was basically a Liberal measure. He hesitated for several weeks, but the prospect of the expiry of Parliament on 31 May made a decision imperative. With the report in his hands he could not ask for a further postponement unless he also dealt with the franchise. On 26 March he took the plunge and decided to bring in a Bill.

Based on the report of the conference it took as long to get through as the most pessimistic prophet could have predicted, and it was not placed on the Statute Book till February 1918 nearly eleven months later. The principal point which the report had left open was the age at which qualified women would get the vote – thirty or thirty-five? Parliament chose the lower age, partly through a miscalculation by Walter Long, the minister involved, about numbers which turned out to be much higher than expected. It is sometimes suggested that women got the vote because their wartime work converted the doubters. There is little to support the theory. As Martin Pugh points out, war emphasized the traditional differences rather than the newly found equalities between the sexes – the male as warrior, the female as bearer of his children. Earl Grey wanted to give an extra vote to men and women who had produced four children – 'they have rendered a service to the State without which the State could not exist'.[1] He was a well known crank and his idea did not catch on, but, clearly, recognition of the part played by women in factories, hospitals and auxiliary branches of the services can hardly have been the reason for creating a franchise which restricted the vote to women over thirty with a property qualification. The truth is more likely to be that the report of the conference merely elicited the frustrated latent majority for some sort of female suffrage, which had always existed in the 1910 Parliament.

Two important recommendations were rejected by Parliament. The conference had come down unanimously in favour of an experiment in proportional representation – the Single

Transferable Vote limited to three-member constituencies. By a majority it also favoured the Alternative Vote in single-member seats. The latter was a Radical panacea to prevent the Conservatives getting in on a minority vote in constituencies where the majority was split between Liberal and Labour. It passed the Commons, but the Lords rejected it, and, for fear of losing the Bill altogether, the Commons did not insist.

Proportional representation on the other hand was regarded as a safeguard for the Conservatives. The 'landslide' of 1906, when the Liberals and their allies gained a vast majority in the House on the strength of fifty-five per cent of the vote against the Conservatives' forty-three per cent, could not occur under a system of proportional representation. Yet the Conservative MPs rejected the proffered boon on no less than three occasions by enough votes to swamp the narrow favourable majorities in the other three parties. The Lords, however, were keen supporters and passed an amendment which would have given proportional representation to almost the whole country – not simply to a few three-member boroughs. When this went back to the Lower House the Conservatives still voted against it, but by a much smaller margin than before: 96 to 61. The Liberals, however, perhaps because anything from the Lords was suspect, now came down heavily on the same side by 111 to 43. They thus missed the chance to insert a provision which would certainly have postponed and might have arrested the post-war decline of their electoral fortunes. The party has been kicking its collective self ever since. And Britain has bumbled along to this day with what is virtually a unicameral, sovereign legislature elected on the first-past-the-post system – the least fair, most arbitrary and least 'democratic' of all methods of election in the democratic world.

As soon as the Bill became law Lloyd George turned his mind to a general election. Like everyone else he assumed that the war would go on into 1919 or even 1920. When the new register was ready – autumn at the earliest – he planned

65

to appeal to the country at a suitable moment for a mandate to carry on as war leader. The unexpected speed of the German collapse made an election urgent. Whatever Bonar Law might perfectly sincerely say to him, Lloyd George knew that his indispensability to the Conservatives would diminish with every month after the end of the war, as they became aware that they could win without him. In July 1918 the Lloyd Georgeite Whip, F. E. Guest, had discussed with Sir George Younger, his Conservative opposite number, a possible bargain under which 150 of Lloyd George's Liberal supporters would be given a free run at the coming general election presumed to take place while the war was still going on.

The arrangement presupposed a split with Asquith whose supporters would have no such immunity, but it was evidently not final or at any rate the imminence of peace produced second thoughts on both sides. On 24 September Lloyd George through an intermediary invited Asquith to join the government as Lord Chancellor and to nominate two principal secretaries of state and six under-secretaries. Asquith, however, refused. On the Unionist side as late as 5 October Bonar Law in a letter to Balfour expressed some misgivings about continuing the coalition though on balance coming down in favour. It was not till the day after the Armistice that, in reply to a formal offer by Lloyd George ten days earlier, he clinched the deal. Even at that late stage Lloyd George, with Bonar Law's agreement, renewed the offer of the Lord Chancellorship to Asquith, though it is hard to see how this could have been squared with the Guest–Younger bargain. Asquith solved the problem (if it was one) by again refusing. On 14 November the issue was further clarified by Labour withdrawing from the coalition and expelling those who, led by G. N. Barnes, stayed behind. The lines were now drawn for the election. Candidates who had the coalition's imprimatur received it in the form of a joint letter from Lloyd George and Bonar Law immortalized by Asquith as 'the coupon' – a reference to the bit of paper which had to be cut out of a wartime ration book to show entitlement to this or that quantity of meat, sugar or tea.

Both the timing and style of the 'Coupon' election have received much criticism, mostly retrospective, but some of it contemporary. It was said to be premature and unduly rushed. The King urged Lloyd George to postpone an appeal to the public until passions were less inflamed. The Asquithian Liberals took the same line, and many later historians have endorsed it. Such criticism is unrealistic. Parliament would never have consented to yet another prolongation; it had already exceeded its constitutional span by three years; hostilities had ceased and the entire electoral system had been recast. Lloyd George had his private reasons for a quick election, but he could not have postponed it even if he had wished.

A more plausible charge is the atmosphere of vindictive chauvinism in which the campaign was conducted and which is alleged to have coloured the whole peace settlement. But it is hard to blame the leaders for this. Analysis of their speeches, particularly those of Lloyd George and Bonar Law, does not confirm the charge that they exploited national hysteria. They were careful to avoid endorsing the absurd figures claimed by various pundits to be extractable as reparations from Germany, and they made no rash pledges. They were not to blame for the virulent propaganda of Lord Northcliffe who was furious at Lloyd George's refusal of his absurd demand to be a delegate at the Peace Conference. He whipped up passions in a campaign directed against the government because of its alleged softness and secret pro-Germanism. Some candidates were carried away into making ridiculous promises. G. N. Barnes, a Labour coalitionist, was for hanging the Kaiser; and, although Sir Eric Geddes did not use the often quoted words about squeezing the German lemon 'till the pips squeak', he did say: 'We will get everything out of her [Germany] that you can squeeze out of a lemon and a bit more.' It was certainly not a dignified election, but Keynes's mordant account in *The Economic Consequences of the Peace* – a book which did lasting harm – was a travesty, and there is no reason to believe that the election had much effect on the peace settlement, or that postponement would have made any great difference.

Polling day was 14 December and the count took place a fortnight later because of the service vote. In spite of all the efforts to ensure that soldiers had the vote, it was the ordinary civilian population which determined the result. There were some 3.9 million service voters on the new register, of whom, owing to technical difficulties for which Lloyd George unfairly blamed and dismissed Hayes-Fisher, the relevant minister, only 2.7 million received ballot papers. Yet only a third of these actually returned them. The historian can but speculate about the war-engendered cynicism which may have lain behind these simple figures. The result was a turnout of fifty-seven per cent – the lowest in any British general election during the twentieth century.

The coalition won a crushing victory with 474 members in the new House, of which 338 were Conservatives and 136 Lloyd Georgeite Liberals. It was a major rebuff to Northcliffe and did something to deflate the myth of press omnipotence. Labour fielded 388 candidates and won 59 seats. Tarred with the brush of Bolshevism and pacifism – unjustly in most cases – they did well to be the largest anti-government party and therefore become the 'official' opposition. But their principal leaders, Henderson, MacDonald and Snowden were defeated and they elected as leader William Adamson, a Scottish miner who was replaced in 1921 by J. R. Clynes. Only 26 of the 253 Asquithian Liberal candidates were successful, and Asquith himself lost his seat. His place was temporarily taken by Sir Donald Maclean. The old Irish Nationalist party of Redmond (now dead) was almost obliterated. Had they been more percipient about proportional representation they might have made a respectable showing – some 25 members. Instead they got only seven. The 73 Sinn Feiners who replaced them repudiated Westminster and refused to take their seats. And so the old Irish Party – that colourful, witty, rhetorical obstructive band – departed from the parliamentary theatre which they had amused, enlivened and infuriated for nearly 120 years. As was said long ago in a reverse context, it was the end of an old song.

Much of the political pattern of the next quarter of a century can be discerned in the electoral results of 1918. It was essentially a Conservative victory – they would have done even better but for the coupons allocated to Lloyd George – and the Conservatives were to be the dominant party till 1945. They were helped by redistribution which may have given them up to thirty extra seats, by the disappearance of the southern Irish members which removed some eighty regular opponents, and probably by the women's vote, however much Conservatives themselves deplored it. One cannot be sure of this but, if modern public opinion polls can be interpreted retrospectively, more women tend to vote Conservative than for the other parties. If this is true the Conservatives were probably further strengthened by the Act of 1928 which gave women the vote on the same basis as men.

The future of the anti-Conservative parties was similarly foreshadowed. Labour's 1918 constitution had two main features; it specifically declared for the first time that its objective was socialism, though in a muted and non-specific form, and formally laid down what had long been true practically, that the trades union representatives, 'the block vote', would dominate the National Executive. The second feature was more important than the first, but both were symptoms and causes of the abandonment of any alliance with the Liberals. The 1918 Act, by creating a franchise in which the industrial working class had an indisputable majority, gave Labour a new source of electoral support which had not existed in the 1910 elections, and in the rising strength of the trades unions the party had a highly effective semi-authoritarian mass organization. It was logical to drop the electoral truce (as they had in June 1918), abandon any alliance with the Liberals, break with the coalition and fight as an independent party.

As for the Liberals, their history of division was also foreshadowed. The 136 Lloyd Georgeites for the most part were only in on Tory sufferance except in Wales. The Asquithians who controlled the party funds and organization were eventually united with them under Asquith, though not for long, but they never became more than a third party. The new mass electorate, concerned as it was with trade-union solidarity, wage claims and class conflict, was unlikely to be attracted by the party of free enterprise and free trade even if the fragmentation caused by Asquith's fall, the Maurice debate and the 'Coupon' election had never occurred. It was not a matter of the Liberals losing votes which they once commanded to the Conservatives and to Labour because of inadequacies in their ideology or dissension in their own ranks. There is no evidence that their old supporters deserted them to any substantial extent. What they failed to do was to make sufficient inroads into the vast new addition to the electorate.

Lloyd George's government contained few surprises. The only unexpected feature was the continuation of the small Cabinet established in December 1916. This was accidental. Austen Chamberlain, who was the new Chancellor of the Exchequer, displayed great indignation when Lloyd George informed him that he was not to be a member of the Cabinet. The Prime Minister surprisingly replied that he did not intend to have a Cabinet at all; it was impossible while he, Bonar Law, Balfour and Barnes were at the Paris Peace Conference; they could not refer everything back to London. Chamberlain was adamant that he would not be Chancellor without a seat in the Cabinet. Lloyd George was equally determined not to have the full Cabinet which, he said, would be forced on him because of other ministerial claims if he gave way to Chamberlain. Bonar Law characteristically produced a compromise. Chamberlain happened to be already a member of the War Cabinet. Why not continue that body in being and shelve the wider problem till the peace treaties had been signed? And so the small War Cabinet remained in being for another ten months.

Bonar Law ceased to be Chancellor, but had his hands full as Leader of the House from which Lloyd George absented himself more and more. Curzon as Lord President took on the section of foreign policy not affected by the Paris negotiations. He became Foreign Secretary in October 1919, changing places with Balfour. Of the other leading Conservatives, Walter Long became First Lord of the Admiralty and Milner Colonial Secretary. F. E. Smith, elevated to the peerage as Lord Birkenhead, was a controversial appointment for the Woolsack and disapproved of by the King. Of the Liberals, Edwin Montagu as Secretary for India was to be a source of trouble and Churchill as Secretary for War and Air a subject of criticism both on personal grounds and for the combination of the two posts. H. A. L. Fisher was a successful President of the Board of Education.

2

The Prime Minister's immediate preoccupation was the peace settlement. With Woodrow Wilson and Clemenceau he was one of the 'Big Three' who shaped the Versailles Treaty. It is not necessary to add to the vast literature on that subject except to repeat the warning against taking Keynes's account too seriously. The economic clauses of the treaty were absurd, but it is important to remember that in the end they were never enforced. Keynes is severe on the indefiniteness of Germany's reparation obligations, but French pressure for a draconian levy would undoubtedly have made any specific figure far too high. Lloyd George and Bonar Law were not being unreasonable in pressing for the sum to be settled in two years' time, when as they hoped passions would be cooler, by a Reparations Commission on which America, Britain, Italy, France and Belgium would be represented. America was likely to have the chair, and in any case the first three countries could outvote France and its Belgian satellite in favour of moderation and realism. What could not have been predicted in 1919 was that America would refuse to ratify the treaty and would withdraw from the commission; France would successfully claim the chair and thus have a casting vote which turned out to be exercised by the ex-President, Raymond Poincaré, one of the narrowest, bitterest and most chauvinistic of French statesmen.

On the political side Lloyd George again used his influence for moderation. Clemenceau and Foch wished to create an autonomous republic on the left bank of the Rhine and to retain indefinitely the four bridgeheads over the river provided under the Armistice terms. Lloyd George, aided by President Wilson, managed to substitute for this the demilitarization of the Rhineland, including both the whole of the left bank and a zone of thirty miles on the right; the occupation of the left bank by Allied forces for fifteen years; and – most important of all – a mutual security guarantee by the USA, Britain and France, which was tantamount to a military alliance. Here again American withdrawal was disastrous. The validity of the guarantee depended on all three nations signing. Parliament ratified the treaty, but early in 1920 Wilson failed to secure the needed two-thirds majority in the Senate, and Britain then also withdrew. Legally the government was within its rights, but politically its action was a major blunder. France inevitably felt let down. The French search for security became even more intense and their policy towards Germany even more intransigent.

The Versailles Treaty has been much abused, but, by and large, it was a reasonable settlement. The League of Nations, discredited later and weakened from the start by American refusal to join, offered at least some hope of peacefully deciding international disputes. Wilson's often denounced principle of national self-determination simply echoed Gladstone's appeal for 'nations rightly struggling to be free'. It was recognition of what had been the strongest political force in western Europe since the fifteenth century, and in eastern Europe since the revolutions of 1848; nationalism was to play the same part in Asia and Africa during the next sixty years. After 1918 more people were living under governments of their own nationality (if not choice) than ever before and still more do so today. Whether they were or are any the happier is an unanswerable question. Exceptions, like the German minorities left in Czechoslovakia and the Polish corridor, or the Germans of the old Austro-Hungarian Empire forbidden to join the German Republic, were almost inevitable (after all Germany had lost the war), but it is not true, as is often alleged, that their existence led to the Second World War. Minority grievances were pretexts not causes of Hitler's aggression.

The weakness of the new Europe was the lack of a balance of power. This was the result of something unpredicted and unpredictable – the almost simultaneous collapse in 1918 of the Hohenzollern, Romanov and Habsburg Empires. The latter being the negation of self-determination could never be reassembled, but the others – great monolingual blocs – would revive sooner or later under new management. When they did, the weakness of the numerous states which filled the temporary vacuum between Germany and Russia from the Baltic to Bulgaria would become all too clear. Meanwhile France in her endless search for security could find no great power as an ally after the withdrawal of America and Britain from the security pact. She sought instead military alliances with countries like Czechoslovakia, Yugoslavia and Poland, while at the same time pursuing a rigidly repressive policy towards Germany.

Lloyd George saw the problem. His solution, propounded first in his Fontainebleau Memorandum of 25 March 1919, was a non-vindictive approach towards Germany in order to draw her into the comity of nations and away from Soviet Russia. He did not despair even of bringing Russia into the 'Concert of Europe' and insisted, contrary to Churchill's wish, on liquidating as quickly as possible the British commitments to various anti-Bolshevik armies, which had been undertaken to keep Russia in the war after the October Revolution of 1917. With the purpose of reconciling Germany, satisfying France and settling the unfinished business of Versailles, a series of international conferences was convened – no less than twenty-three before the fall of the coalition in October 1922. Mostly held in pleasure resorts, they provided an agreeable forum for the Prime Minister with his entourage of aides, secretaries, toadies and satellites, but these meaningless gyrations led nowhere. France never deviated from its hard line. Anglo-French relations deteriorated throughout Lloyd George's time, and got no better after his departure. The nadir was perhaps reached in August 1922 when a sub-committee of the Committee of Imperial Defence argued, with apparent seriousness, the case for an air strike force as a counter to the possible threat of a French air attack. True they left the political risk to be decided by the government, but it is remarkable that the argument could be used at all.

The settlement with Turkey proved even more troublesome for the coalition than the treaty with Germany. In the end it caused Lloyd George's downfall, although many other matters also contributed. The non-Turkish areas were divided into British and French 'mandates' – in effect colonies. The French took Syria and the Lebanon where they were supposed to have certain traditional religious and cultural interests. This meant evicting Feisal, one of the sons of the Hashemite Sherif of Mecca who had raised the Arab Revolt in 1915; Feisal had believed – though whether he had any reason to do so is disputable – that he would obtain Damascus. French troops forced him out in July 1920. The British received the areas they had fought over – Palestine and Mesopotamia. The latter, called Iraq with its capital at Baghdad, was awarded as a consolation prize to Feisal who was placed on the throne in August 1921. In September the following year Transjordan was detached from Palestine and given to Feisal's brother Abdullah. His descendants still rule in Amman, but the Iraqi monarchy came to a bloody end in

1958. Both were in effect client kingdoms under British military protection which turned out to be remarkably economical thanks to judicious use of the Royal Air Force. But the Kingdom of the Hejaz (the Sherifdom of Mecca) from which both originated did not last long. Abandoned by Britain, Hussein's domain was conquered in 1925 by Ibn Saud of the Nejd and incorporated into Saudi Arabia. It has been ruled from Riyadh ever since – a victory for the anti-Hashemite anti-Lawrence faction within the British–Indian establishment.

The area of the globe coloured pink was thus vastly increased. With the addition of the British mandate over German East Africa, rechristened as Tanganyika (modern Tanzania), and the South African mandate over German South West Africa (now called Namibia), the empire had never covered more territory. But it had also never faced graver problems. National self-determination was in the end to be as damaging to it as to the rule of the Habsburgs or the Sultan. This was already evident from the attitude of the white self-governing dominions. It was to manifest itself in violent form first in Britain's oldest colony, Ireland; and next in her youngest, Palestine.

Before one considers these developments, the situation in Turkey needs to be examined. It was one thing to partition the non-Turkish areas of the old Sultanate. The Turks were reconciled to their loss. It was quite another to annex parts of the heartland of Ottoman Turkey itself. The Italians, under the Treaty of London, were allocated Adalia and Smyrna, and the French under the Sykes-Picot Agreement could have had Cilicia in addition to Syria. These claims provoked a nationalist revolution in Turkey under an army officer, Mustafa Kemal, who in 1920 set up an alternative government at Ankara. He began a 'war of liberation' which prompted the Italians to withdraw altogether and the French to drop their claim to Cilicia.

Kemal now threatened the British forces of occupation on the Asiatic side of the Straits. Lloyd George, with the uncertain support of France, decided to bring in the Greeks who had a shadowy claim on Smyrna and the adjacent coast because of their co-nationals living there. Greece, under the leadership of Venizelos, a statesman of more charm than prudence, stepped in where Italy feared to tread and launched a major offensive against Kemal, which had considerable initial success, though in the end it was to be disastrous both for Greece and Lloyd George. Meanwhile the Treaty of Sèvres was concluded with the Sultan on 10 August 1920. The French and British mandates were confirmed. The Straits and the Dardanelles were demilitarized and internationalized. Greece received Eastern Thrace, Gallipoli, the Aegean islands and the right to administer Smyrna for five years with a plebiscite to be held at the end. Since the Sultan was a mere puppet left on the throne only because of the India Office's unwarranted fear of offending Muslim sentiment, the settlement depended on the Greeks defeating Kemal. For the moment it looked as if they would and the British government turned its eyes elsewhere.

At home the euphoria greeting the end of the war was short-lived. The Prime Minister might talk of making 'Britain a fit country for heroes to live in', but it soon became clear that the country was very much the same as it always had been. There was muddle and discontent about demobilization. Widespread unemployment had been anticipated, and the scheme adopted gave priority to 'key personnel' in industry on the grounds that their release was essential to create jobs. But these were just the people who had been most recently called up. The principle of 'last in first out' infuriated the troops. There were demonstrations and mutinies. Churchill rapidly reversed the scheme and he saw to it that there was no repetition after the Second World War. This was not the only trouble in a dismal winter. To the discomfort of shivering round an inadequate grate owing to the shortage of coal, there was added the last of the great plagues. 'Spanish influenza', as it was called, swept the world. It took a toll of lives mainly in Africa and Asia which is believed to have exceeded the deaths in the Great War. Its effects were less acute in Europe, but bad enough; in England and Wales during the winter and spring of 1918–19, 150,000 deaths were recorded. It was particularly lethal to children (though not always fatal; the author contracted it at the age of two), and to an exhausted nation it seemed the last straw.

Labour unrest was another feature of the aftermath of the war. In January 1919 the Clydeside seemed about to erupt into a general strike. It was a political, rather than industrial demand for a forty-hour week to absorb the unemployment erroneously expected from demobilization. The government, after a clash between strikers and police at which the Riot Act was read – possibly for the last time in British history – sent in troops to 'occupy' Glasgow on 1 February. The strike ended ten days later. If it now seems an overreaction, one should remember that episodes like the hoisting of the red flag and its concomitant rhetoric appeared to much of the public as harbingers of revolution. Many of the attitudes in politics, journalism and literature of the 1920s are otherwise inexplicable. The prospect of the Russian experience being repeated in England was as big a bogy to the established order as the French Revolution had been to their forebears 120 years earlier. The Labour Party rigidly refused every request from the British Communist Party, formed in 1920, to become an affiliated branch, but Labour could not easily escape being tarred with that embarrassing brush.

The accusation seemed the more plausible when a year later the trades unions made the most powerful, purely political intervention in their history. A war was being waged between the USSR and Poland. On 10 May the dockers refused to load a ship, the *Jolly George*, suspected of conveying munitions for the Poles. The government took no action, but early in August when a Soviet counter-offensive had reached the gates of Warsaw Lloyd George, in response to Polish pleas, decided to intervene. The TUC warned him that there would be a general strike if he did. The Prime Minister felt obliged to back down, and his face was saved only by an unexpected Polish victory which resulted in the compromise Treaty of Riga and nineteen years of peace before the Russians took their revenge. But the episode, together with the naïve admiration for all things Russian displayed by a generation of left-wing intellectuals, was to be a potent Conservative weapon for many years to come. Nor was it without justification. The Labour Research Department, at the instance of G. D. H. Cole, one of the best known socialist intellectuals, in September 1921 accepted a grant of £6,000 per annum from the Russian government to finance an inquiry into capitalist industry. The more sober elements of the Labour establishment were appalled.

The unemployment predicted from all quarters did not occur as quickly as expected. The immediate aftermath of the war saw an inflationary boom which lasted until April 1920 and gradually collapsed thereafter. The consequences of the boom were more significant than was recognized at the time. The old industries – cotton, coal, shipbuilding, iron and steel – which were to be the most vulnerable in the inter-war years, expanded beyond their viable capacity. Their temporary success encouraged a general mood of nostalgia for the pre-war economy and a rebellion against the carry-over of governmental wartime regulations. There was, to use a phrase from the late 1940s, a 'bonfire of controls' and an end to talk of 'reconstruction' which had been so fashionable during the last years of the war that a Ministry of Reconstruction was actually set up in July 1917 under Christopher Addison. The psychological effect of the boom and the ensuing slump was to encourage the belief that 1913–14 represented 'normality' and that all one needed to do was to wait for its return. The later decision to go back to the gold standard at pre-war parity was another sign.

There had been a strong movement at the end of the war – and not only in the Labour Party – for the permanent nationalization of coal, transport and electricity, all of which for wartime reasons were under temporary governmental control. Nothing came of it in the new mood prevailing. The

Sankey Commission on the Coal Industry resulted during 1919 in no less than seven different reports, and although a bare majority of the thirteen members favoured nationalization, the government not unreasonably regarded it as insufficient. The miners felt betrayed and the owners were furious that a body set up by a predominantly Conservative administration should have come out with such socialistic recommendations. Both sides dug in their toes. Labour relations in the coal mines, partly because of the shelving of the Sankey recommendations, were worse than in any other industry between the wars. Not surprisingly, nationalization plans for transport and electricity were as abortive as for coal. The Ministry of Transport under a Bill introduced in 1919 would have had the power to take over by Order-in-Council any undertaking connected with transport or electricity – a remarkable foreshadowing of Labour's programme after 1945. The most that Parliament would concede in 1919 was the establishment of the Electricity Commissioners with certain regulatory powers and the compulsory amalgamation of the railway companies into the four groups which were to operate from 1923 till the whole system was taken over by the state a quarter of a century later – the Great Western, the Southern, the London Midland and Scottish and the London and North-Eastern.

One important non-event took place in March 1920 – Lloyd George's failure to secure 'fusion', i.e. amalgamation of the coalition Liberals with the Conservative Party. The question came to a head because of poor cooperation in by-elections and the apparent revival of the 'official' Liberals with the recent return of Asquith and Simon to Parliament. A round-robin urging the creation of a 'single united party' was presented to Lloyd George and Bonar Law on 2 March. The Prime Minister saw it as a lifeline. Bonar Law was less enthusiastic but was prepared to put it to his followers. Lloyd George, however, found the response of his Liberal ministerial colleagues so hostile that he decided to drop the matter. The attitude of the Liberal ministers is the more

79

surprising since they seemed to be the ones who would gain most by amalgamation. If they hoped for a reunion with the Asquithians they were under a delusion. Asquith announced a few days later that Liberal headquarters would oppose coalition Liberals even if nominated by their constituency associations, and in May the National Liberal Federation pronounced anathema on the coalitionists. In retrospect the defeat of 'fusion' can be regarded as the 'point of no return' for the Lloyd George coalition.

Lloyd George's position as a Prime Minister depending on an alien majority party which accepted him only half-heartedly now became more precarious than ever. Asquith, like Peel after 1846, retained control of the party 'machine'. He bitterly resented the way in which he had been ousted but he never seems to have contemplated any serious attempt to reunite the party. His intellectual powers were now fast failing. Yet his prestige and the continued adherence of the old Liberal establishment kept him as a co-equal rival to Lloyd George. The latter, repudiated by the Asquithians and foiled over fusion, could not, like an American president, rely on appealing over the heads of the parliamentarians to the people. To be a populist it is necessary to remain popular. The most 'presidential' of all British Prime Ministers, he did not have the resources of the American constitution. He had to find a parliamentary base or perish. In the end he perished.

Chapter Five

THE FALL OF LLOYD GEORGE

I

The British Empire began to decline as soon as it reached its territorial peak. In March 1919 riots and sabotage erupted in Egypt. They were suppressed but it was deemed wise in 1922 to concede 'independence', a status which left foreign policy in British hands and a British force to guard the Suez Canal. In April a series of disturbances occurred in India, particularly in the Punjab, culminating in a disorder in Amritsar crushed with reckless ruthlessness by the local military commander, Brigadier-General Dyer. Five Englishmen had already been killed and a woman missionary gravely assaulted when a crowd assembled on 13 April to listen to inflammatory oratory in the sunken square called the Jallianwallah Bagh near the famous golden temple. Ample warning had been given that such assemblies were illegal but nothing can excuse Dyer's order to his Gurkha troops to shoot indiscriminately into the mob. It was six minutes before the cease-fire was given. The official figure for casualties was 379 dead and 1,200 wounded. It may have been many more. The episode was a decisive turning point in British–Indian relations.

A Commission of Inquiry was set up by Edwin Montagu, Secretary for India, a Liberal and a Jew, whose alien appearance provoked the latent anti-Semitism of certain elements in the Conservative Party. The commission condemned Dyer who admitted to acting *in terrorem*. Churchill insisted on his dismissal, but any good done in Indian eyes was destroyed by the high Tories in England, who raised £26,000 for Dyer. A bitter debate took place in the House of

Commons over a year later on 8 July 1920. Montagu, who denounced 'the ascendancy of one race over another' and spoke, according to Lloyd George's informant, in a 'Yiddish ... screaming tone' provoked a deadly reply from Carson who described the 'breaking' of Dyer as 'un-English'. Amritsar became a symbol of alien tyranny and a source of martyrology. It killed the compromise solution of 'dyarchy' (i.e. joint British and Indian rule in the provinces, some areas of government being reserved for the Indians others for the British), even as Easter Week in Dublin killed Gladstonian Home Rule.

It was Ireland where the decline of empire began soonest. Eight centuries of English rule in its oldest colony had failed to produce the change from government by force to government by authority, which is the hallmark of legitimacy. Why did the English, endlessly tormented by the 'Irish problem', cling on to this alien and resentful island? The reason was partly strategic, partly the existence in northern Ireland of a Scottish 'plantation' which, having driven out the original inhabitants some 300 years earlier, constituted a Protestant enclave in a Catholic island. The religious labels might be regarded as 'tribal' or 'racial', but, whatever their exact meaning, they represented atavistic hostility. The Protestants of the north were determined not to be governed from Dublin. 'Ulster will fight and Ulster will be right' – this slogan, exploited by Lord Randolph Churchill in the 1880s, was no less of a threat thirty years later, and one of the most important politicians of the day, Bonar Law, himself an Ulsterman, had assumed Lord Randolph's mantle.

Asquith's Home Rule Act of 1914 gave Ireland a devolved Parliament with limited powers which, however, extended to the whole island. It was suspended for the war. The election of 1918 gave complete victory in the south to the Sinn Fein party committed to republican separatism. Those of the seventy-three elected who were not in prison proclaimed themselves to be the Irish Legislature. Meeting as the Dáil Éireann at the Dublin Mansion House on 21 January 1919, they declared independence – and war on England – electing Eamon de Valera as President and Arthur Griffith as Vice-President. Both were behind bars, but Michael Collins, President of the Irish Republican Brotherhood, Director of Intelligence for the Irish Republican Army and the ablest military leader on the Republican side, engineered de Valera's escape from Lincoln prison, while Griffith was released soon afterwards by a British amnesty. On the same day that the Dáil met, 'war' or 'rebellion' began with the capture by the Irish Volunteers of a load of gelignite intended for a quarry at Soloheadbeg near Tipperary. Two members of the Royal Irish Constabulary were killed. It was the start of a campaign by the IRA against the British military and civil authorities, which was waged with increasing brutality by both sides for the next two and a half years.

It was against this background that a new Irish Home Rule Bill was prepared. Even Bonar Law agreed that Home Rule on the old Gladstonian model could no longer be denied to the south, but he was strongly opposed to dominion status – an issue which divided Conservatives from most Liberals; and he was adamant against Ulster coming under a Dublin legislature.

The Government of Ireland Bill, introduced on 30 March 1920 created Gladstonian 'parliaments' for the south and north to be elected on 24 May 1921, with limited powers excluding defence, foreign policy and finance. This was the system under which the six counties of the north were to be governed till Edward Heath suspended the Stormont Parliament in 1972. There was also provision for a Council of Ireland to which, if north and south agreed, something near dominion status would be granted; but it was a dead letter from the start. Sinn Fein regarded the Bill with contempt and declared their intention to treat the elections under its provisions as elections to the Dáil, even as they had in 1918.

The story of the Irish revolt is one of great complexity and much obscurity. To take only one example it is still not clear exactly what lay behind the terrible events of 'Bloody Sunday'

(21 November 1920) when fourteen British officers and civilians were dragged from their beds in various Dublin hotels early in the morning and shot by IRA terrorists, some of them in front of their wives – an atrocity followed by a counter-atrocity the same afternoon when twelve people in a football crowd at Croke Park were shot by the Black and Tans. Many documents have vanished or been destroyed, and a substantial part of the relevant War Office papers are banned from research for 100 years till 2022. A thick varnish of gossip, myth and legend covers the course of events. The best account is by Charles Townshend, one of the few writers not influenced by emotion, chauvinism or guilt.[1] The British government was understandably at sea in coping with the novel problem of how to defeat a clandestine enemy moved by relentless idealism utterly foreign to English ideas of compromise, and using methods of murder and intimidation to which there had been no parallel in imperial history.

The coalition government took the line that negotiation was out of the question until order had been restored. Success might have been achieved by an early declaration of martial law and press censorship in the twenty-six counties, together with unity of command over an adequate army and police force, and a proper coordination of intelligence services – the most important of all weapons in waging a campaign of counter-insurgency. Not one of these requirements was met.

Martial law, cynically called 'partial law', was half-heartedly enforced – and only in the eight south-western counties. It was never proclaimed in Dublin. Until the summer of 1921, when at last substantial reinforcements arrived from England, troops in the eight counties numbered less than half those employed in Northern Ireland during the emergency of the 1970s. The command of the army and police was at no stage unified, nor was there any proper coordination of their intelligence services. The Royal Irish Constabulary remained independent, and the recruitment of ex-servicemen at 10s. (50p) a day – the so-called 'Black and Tans' – at the end of

1919 was a major error. The name originally stemmed from
their uniforms, a mixture of khaki and the dark green of the
RIC, but it came to be applied specifically to non-Irish
recruits after a group of them went on an alcoholic rampage
in Limerick on 28 April 1920, 'Black and Tans' being the
name of a local pack of hounds. These undisciplined irregu-
lars shot, burned, and drank, through much of southern
Ireland. Their brutality did not even have the compensation
of effectiveness, and they were regarded by the military with
contempt. To say this is not to condone the atrocities
committed by the IRA. It was a grim, cruel, treacherous war
as guerrilla wars always are, but a parliamentary democracy
which believes in freedom under the law cannot successfully
behave like a totalitarian despotism. It is possible for a liberal
regime to defeat a guerrilla campaign, but the process needs
disciplined forces with a clear directive from a government
which has public opinion behind it.

2

By the early summer of 1921 the government was approaching the parting of the ways – either all-out war or a move
towards compromise. At this juncture an important change
occurred in the Cabinet. On 17 May Lloyd George with tears
in his eyes announced the resignation of Bonar Law on
grounds of ill health. His successor as Lord Privy Seal and
Leader of the House was Austen Chamberlain who was also
elected Leader of the Conservative Party. The change did the
coalition no good. Bonar Law was better liked, better at
dealing with the House and better at coping with Lloyd
George than his warm-hearted, loyal but outwardly stiff and
formal successor. Law was far readier than Chamberlain to
tell Lloyd George what the Conservative Party would or
would not stand, and he was a more popular figure with the
rank and file. He was also more deeply committed on the
Irish question and less open to persuasion. His ill health was
genuine. He did not resign *pour mieux sauter*, but he kept his

seat, and it was obvious that, when he recovered, he would, whether he wished or not, be a potential focus for Conservative discontent.

In spite of the incompetence of the RIC there were signs by now that the British forces were beginning to get the upper hand. The army had acquired something of the capacity for secrecy, mobility and surprise which characterized the IRA. In March and April, it made substantial captures of arms in Dublin and elsewhere, which the rebels could ill afford. The government's first instinct was to exploit these successes. In less than a month (14 June to 7 July) the Irish command was reinforced by one-third. Collins's often quoted remark after the signing of the treaty in December – 'You had us dead beat. We could not have lasted another three weeks' – was an exaggeration. Nevertheless, he genuinely believed that the IRA could not survive if the struggle was prolonged for several months in the new circumstances, and he may well have been right.

On the other hand, the Cabinet had good reason for seeking a compromise. Under the Act of 1920 if, as everyone expected, the southern Irish Parliament after the elections in May failed to muster more than half its members when formally opened on 28 June, Home Rule would lapse in the south, and crown colony rule, with the certainty of extended coercion, would take its place. This was bound to be embarrassing, especially as an imperial conference had been convened to sit in London during June. The elections on 24 May produced the anticipated result. In the north the Unionists won forty out of fifty-two seats, Craig became the first Prime Minister, and the King agreed to open the Belfast Parliament on 22 June. In the south Sinn Fein made its predicted clean sweep (apart from the four seats for that Protestant fortress, Trinity College, Dublin), and again treated the election as constituting the Dáil.

Crown colony rule with full coercion and military reinforcement could well have brought victory, but no one was confident and the soldiers gave ambiguous answers. Lunching with the King, General Smuts, in England for the Imperial Conference, suggested that the opening of the Belfast Parliament might be an opportunity for an appeal for peace. He also saw Lloyd George who agreed and submitted to a willing monarch the draft of just such a speech. The occasion, the contents and the deep emotion of the speaker's delivery caused a sensation. It is often described as the 'catalyst' which brought about a compromise peace, for it was promptly followed by Lloyd George's overture to de Valera for tripartite discussions with Craig, and these did lead first to a truce and then, after many a tortuous twist and turn, eventually to the treaty of 6 December 1921. Professor Lyons, however, shrewdly observes that its effect was essentially confined to Britain where it may have made people rethink the situation. The supporters of Sinn Fein were not likely to be placated by 'a royal declaration delivered in Belfast, of all places, and, of all occasions at the opening of a parliament which set the seal on the partition of their country'.[2]

Lloyd George's overture was what mattered. For the first time neither constitutional preconditions nor the surrender of arms was demanded. Moreover, the IRA, if by no means 'dead beat', was badly in need of a respite. There was a further reason for anyone with a tincture of realism in his outlook to respond to the offer. Nationalists wanted then – and still do – a united Republican Ireland, but the battle was also one for British public opinion. This is a mysterious and unquantifiable entity – in the end perhaps only what politicians think it is, an impression derived from their letters, the media, gossip, conversation, general 'hunch'. Britain had the physical force to crush the rebellion, and, although by the summer of 1921 public opinion was sick of slaughter and ready for a reasonable settlement with the south, it would not, in the words of Dr Townshend, 'support Republican intransigence against a fair constitutional offer – and its idea of fairness did not include "the coercion of Ulster" into a United Ireland'.[3]

This was to be the key to the seemingly interminable discussions which followed – this and the age-old fear for British security. The first determined the government's position on Ulster, the second its refusal to concede separatism even for the south, and its insistence on dominion status, the oath of loyalty and the retention of naval bases. The prolonged parley began on 11 October. The Cabinet was represented by some of its ablest figures, the Prime Minister, Birkenhead, Churchill, among others. The principal Irish 'envoys plenipotentiary' were Griffith and Collins. Ominously, de Valera did not come. Still more ominously, it was never clear whether the envoys had the power to sign on their own responsibility.

The naval bases caused little trouble, though logically they should have been the greatest obstacle of all, since they made neutrality in war – the true test of independence – impossible. (In the event they were handed back to Eire in April 1938 as the result of a much publicized deal by Neville Chamberlain with de Valera.) But this was not the only unreal feature of the negotiations. Lloyd George somehow persuaded Griffith that if the envoys would agree to the oath of allegiance he would pull Ulster into an acceptable settlement. He even said he would resign if he failed. He did fail and he did not resign. It is surprising that Griffith believed him. Craig having got his own legislature would never have consented to any modification. Even if he could have been overruled, there was the threat posed by Bonar Law. He was now fully recovered in health. When in November he learned that Lloyd George had suggested to Craig that, subject to numerous 'safeguards', Ulster should come under an 'All- Ireland Parliament', he privately told the Prime Minister that he would come out in open opposition unless the plan was dropped. Lloyd George dropped it like a hot brick.

December 6 was the date fixed as the deadline for these protracted negotiations, though, as Professor Lyons observes, it is not at all clear why that date was chosen nor why the deadline could not have been postponed. Lloyd George on the evening of 5 December presented an ultimatum – dominion status and the oath, or a renewal of hostilities. He had two letters prepared, one of which he said must reach Craig in Belfast next morning. It must go by special train from Euston at ten o'clock and thence by destroyer from Holyhead. The first letter announced that the Sinn Fein representatives had accepted dominion status, the second that they had opted out of the empire. 'If I send this letter,' said Lloyd George, 'it is war, and war within three days. Which letter shall I send?' Griffith and Collins had seen de Valera on 3 December, but their instructions were still obscure. Incredibly they made no attempt to telephone Dublin. Such was the tension that everyone seems to have forgotten this method of communication. After all, Lloyd George could perfectly well have rung up Craig next morning instead of insisting on an epistolary deadline that night.

The Irish envoys decided for dominion status, and the treaty was finally signed in the early hours of the morning. Collins still believed that the IRA could not sustain a new campaign. Both he and Griffith accepted Lloyd George's promise of a Boundary Commission to redraw the Ulster frontier. They hoped – and Lloyd George encouraged their hope – that the commission would allocate such substantial areas to the south that the residue would not be economically viable and would have to join a united Ireland. Lloyd George kept his word and set up the commission, but the result of its deliberations was to be very different from that expected by the Sinn Fein representatives, though what Lloyd George expected only Lloyd George knew.

The treaty did not bring peace to Ireland. De Valera and his supporters repudiated it, but they were narrowly defeated in the Dáil. Michael Collins became Prime Minister of the Provisional Government and Griffith President in place of de Valera. Civil war broke out in April 1922 between the two factions. Led by a Republican fanatic, Rory O'Connor, an armed force seized the Four Courts, centre of Dublin's legal administration. Collins's efforts to crush it seemed half-hearted. In London, on 22 June, Sir Henry Wilson, now an Ulster Unionist MP, was shot down outside his house in Eaton Place in broad daylight by two Sinn Fein assassins who were caught and later executed. The crime caused a sensation unparalleled till the murders of Airey Neave and Lord Mountbatten nearly 60 years later.

It was assumed in Whitehall and Westminster that this was the work of the Republicans. On 26 June Churchill made a speech in the Commons in the strongest language calling on Collins to crush O'Connor, or else . . . The coalition ministers were under attack – and not just from the diehards. Bonar Law said: 'I agree with the Treaty, but I confess, had I seen what the position would have been today, I doubt whether I would have voted for it.' Collins now took action and launched an assault on the Four Courts which went up in flames lighted by its occupiers whose leader was later shot. Collins was killed in an ambush on 22 August, predeceased by Griffith ten days earlier from a heart attack. Generous tributes were paid in Britain to both. Many years later it was revealed that Collins had given the order to murder Wilson – without telling Griffith who would have been horrified, had he known. The Provisional government in the end defeated the Republicans, and Ireland temporarily faded from the English scene. On 6 December 1922 with palpable lack of enthusiasm Bonar Law, now Prime Minister, introduced the Bill creating the Irish Free State.

Sinn Fein had won a qualified victory, but the qualifications were important: after the treaty Ireland was neither unified, independent nor republican. Britain had successfully insisted in the South on dominion status which at that time seemed a more subordinate position than it later became under the Statute of Westminster of 1931. In the North there was an *ignis fatuus* for Southern aspirations. Belatedly set up in 1924 the Boundary Commission recommended trivial exchanges of territory. The Free State Prime Minister, Cosgrave, brought discussion to an end by refusing to concede an acre of the South under any circumstances, whatever the *quid pro quo*. The boundary after ten years of dispute since 1914 remained unchanged. It is still unchanged today.

The Irish rebellion had both long- and short-term effects on English history. Over the next half-century the revolt came to be a precedent and parallel in the minds of both rulers and ruled in Palestine, India, Malaysia, Cyprus and Africa. The lessons, analogies and warnings, whether or not they were correctly learned or applied, were constantly in the thoughts alike of those who wished to disrupt or to preserve the British Empire. The short-term effect was on the fortunes of the coalition. The settlement consolidated the hostility of the diehards and it implanted doubts in the mind of the one man able to bring down the government – Bonar Law, who had blocked successfully, but, as he may have thought luckily and narrowly, Lloyd George's attempt to bring Ulster into an 'All-Ireland Parliament'.

3

At first the coalition leaders believed that the Irish treaty would be an electoral winner. Birkenhead and Lloyd George pressed for an election early in 1922. Chamberlain had doubts, quickly confirmed by the party's chairman, the great brewer Sir George Younger, who published on 11 January a letter to all Conservative associations, which quashed the plan. Publicly he declared that no election should be held till trade was revived, public expenditure cut and the House of Lords reformed. This last question was an important one with Conservatives at the time, though usually ignored by historians.[4] The preamble to the Act of 1911 had invited reform of the composition of the House with the corollary of the restoration of some of its powers, and the Cabinet had given specific pledges in the matter. Younger was saying that the coalition should continue but not for very long. If it failed to reform the Lords its uselessness would be proved. If it succeeded its usefulness would have ended.

Government economy was easier. The collectivism engendered by the state's role in war quickly withered when war ended. 'Why if men and women, all classes and all parties, are able to work together like a mighty machine to produce *destruction*, can they not work together for another five years to produce *abundance?*' asked Churchill in an election speech in 1918. Why indeed? Perhaps the task presupposes an omnicompetent state which a free society simply cannot tolerate in peace. The Second World War was more 'total' than the first and followed by a positively collectivist government. Yet appeals to 'work together' were sounding very hollow by 1950.

After the First World War most Conservatives and many coalition Liberals were instinctively anti-collectivist. Of ministers only Christopher Addison (Health which included Housing) and H. A. L. Fisher (Education) were strongly on the other side, though the Prime Minister backed them – up to a point. But in 1919 income tax actually went up from five to six shillings (25p to 30p) where it stayed for three years. This and the inflation of 1920 produced an uproar. 'Homes fit for heroes' became the 'Housing Scandal' – with some justice since council houses which had on average cost £838 to build in 1921 were down to £371 two years later – and Addison resigned. Fisher, whose Act of 1918 and other reforms were costing by 1921 ten times his original estimate, soon found his budget drastically reduced. The press took up the cause of economy. Lord Rothermere's Anti-Waste League began to win by-elections. 'Squandermania' became the cry of the hour, and cartoons appeared of two fictitious bureaucrats called Dilly and Dally.

Bowing to the gale the new Chancellor, Horne, told the departments to produce cuts of £175 million in the estimates which for the 1921 budget had been £1,136 million (the budget of 1913 was under £200 million). The departments came back with reductions of only £75 million. In August 1921 Lloyd George set up an independent committee to obtain cuts of another £100 million. The chairman was Sir

Eric Geddes who had in the past headed the Admiralty and
the Ministry of Transport – experiences that evidently soured
him. His committee recommended a cut of £21 million in the
estimates of the former and the total abolition of the latter,
along with several other departments. The three reports of
the committee appeared in February 1922 and were collec-
tively known as the 'Geddes Axe'.

The protests from Whitehall generally and the Admiralty
in particular made the government pause. In the end the
departments survived and the £100 million cut was reduced
to £64 million. Nevertheless, the 1922 budget remains from
then till now the most striking example of reduction of public
expenditure in a single year – a fall of over twelve per cent.
Income tax came down from six shillings to five (30p to 25p)
and the excise duty on tea was lowered by a third. It was the
first post-war budget to fall below £1,000 million.

An election in early 1922 might have saved the coalition.
After that almost everything that could go wrong did. Bonar
Law refusing an offer of the Foreign Office in January
remained a potential threat. On 24 February Younger, acting
on his own initiative, publicly declared against a second
'Coupon' election. Birkenhead gibed at the cabin boy taking
charge of the ship in a storm, and Lloyd George referred to a
'second-rate brewer', but the favourable Conservative reaction boded no good for the coalition. At the end of February
Lloyd George offered to make way for Austen Chamberlain
who with characteristic loyalty – and timorousness – declined.
The 'Geddes Axe' alienated the Liberal social reformers
without placating the anti-squandermaniacs who regarded it
as too little and too late. On 9 March Montagu resigned after
publishing a telegram from the government of India con-
demning British foreign policy as too pro-Greek. The Conservatives who detested Montagu and were anti-Greek
should have been pleased, but they regarded the episode as a
further sign that the government was in a mess.

Lloyd George now resolved to restore his waning prestige.
He would deal with reform of the House of Lords and he

would bring off a major coup at the European Conference in Geneva on 10 April. This was to be the last of his 'circuses' and it was a failure. The plan was to revive international trade by settling the reparations problems, bringing Soviet Russia back into the 'Concert of Europe' and restoring 'normal' economic relations. Success in foreign policy is not usually a vote winner but on this occasion it might have given a boost to the stagnant British economy, reducing unemployment which had been 690,000 at the end of 1920 and stood at 1.5 million in the spring of 1922. Lloyd George was resourceful and brilliant as ever, but the conference which finally sank into the sands on 19 May got nowhere. Poincaré, the new French Prime Minister, cold, legalistic and obdurate, refused to attend personally and ordained that there should be no concession over reparations. The Germans and Russians, fearing with some justification that Lloyd George intended to play them off against each other, concluded a treaty (Rapallo) to forestall him. Russia remained unrecognized. France headed for the futile occupation of the Ruhr in 1923, and Lloyd George returned to London with nothing to show.

Events continued to go against the government. Reform of the House of Lords foundered on the rocks of coalition Liberal opposition. The outbreak of civil war in Ireland and the assassination of Sir Henry Wilson suggested that the treaty, far from settling the Irish question, had merely exported murder to London. In June there was a damaging debate on the swollen number of personal staff employed at public expense by Lloyd George – the so-called 'Garden Suburb' because they worked in temporary huts in the garden of 10 Downing Street. The more respectable members like Phillip Kerr (Lord Lothian) had got out by now but there were some dubious figures among the residue and replacements. This was followed on 17 July by an even more damaging debate on the 'Honours Scandal'. It was sparked off by the announcement of peerages for three questionable characters – among them Sir Joseph Robinson, one of the most disreputable of all the Rand millionaires. The South

African government publicly announced that it had not been consulted, and Sir Joseph in the end withdrew.

For many years past, both of the major parties when in office had given, and in opposition had promised, honours to contributors to party funds. But they had been careful about names, and those chosen were usually not only respectable but noted for some sort of public service as well. What distinguished Lloyd George was that he operated on an unparalleled scale with unprecedented blatancy and a remarkable disregard for character. His situation was admittedly unique – a Prime Minister with no party base. Fusion with the Conservatives had failed in 1920 and in the same year he had been excommunicated by the Asquithians. The construction of a new party machine could not be achieved without funds. Although the coalition Liberals did not formally constitute themselves as a separate party till January 1922, under the title of 'National Liberals',[5] Lloyd George began to raise money long before that. The Conservatives could obtain at least some of their requirements from rich ideological sympathizers. The Labour Party's funds came from the trades unions also on ideological grounds, aided by the 'contracting-out' clause of the Act of 1906. The Asquithians were hard up but they too had some wealthy supporters and a certain accumulation from the past. There were, however, few if any ideological reasons for supporting the National Liberal party, without a *quid pro quo*.

The full truth about Lloyd George's practices – or rather those of his agents – will probably never be known, but there is no reason to doubt that honours were sold on a regular tariff to Liberals and Conservatives alike, some of the latter being people who would never have figured on the Central Office list. This was in itself infuriating to the Conservatives for, although the two parties had quite separate funds, the Honours List was one and indivisible, so that the public had no means of knowing who had recommended whom. And even if a Conservative nominee was perfectly reputable why should Lloyd George be the beneficiary. 'This is poaching on our preserves with a vengeance,' wrote Sir George Younger of one recommendation. At least one highly disreputable 'broker', Maundy Gregory, was involved and many of the people honoured were very shady characters. Cardiff became known as the 'City of Dreadful Knights'. Sir Joseph Robinson's peerage was last of a long line of discreditable nominations. Lloyd George survived the debate, but was forced to concede a commission of inquiry.

The honours scandal did Lloyd George great damage – more even than the Marconi scandal. The Conservative buccaneers, like Birkenhead and Horne, may not have minded much, but what Disraeli called the 'respectability' of the party was deeply offended. It was a serious factor in the break-up of the coalition, and it at once prompted a delegation of junior ministers on the eve of the recess to wait on Austen Chamberlain and his Conservative Cabinet colleagues with the request that a victory at the next general election would mean a Conservative Prime Minister whether or not as the head of a coalition. It was Chamberlain's last chance, for Lloyd George would probably have stepped down, but he muddled it away allowing Birkenhead to give them an arrogant 'wigging' and saying he would make up his mind during the recess.

There was a second damaging aspect of the Lloyd George fund though it emerged only later. The traditional parties put their funds either in the hands of trustees or at least vested them in someone other than the party leader. This was not a complete safeguard. The Conservative Treasurer, Lord Farquhar, went off his head late in 1922, refused to sign cheques for election expenses and eventually had to be dismissed by Bonar Law. Thereafter cheques could be signed by more than one officer. Lloyd George kept a degree of personal hold over his fund as unprecedented as the method by which he raised it. This was to cause great annoyance when attempts were made after 1923 to reunite the Liberal Party. He refused to relax his personal control and secured a high legal opinion that he was free to gamble the money away at Monte Carlo if he wanted to.

There were two other groups now gunning for the coalition.

One was the diehards – Lord Salisbury's 'Free Conservatives'. Its implacable opposition dated from a motion of no-
confidence in the government's Irish policy on 31 October
1921. Some forty-two members signed one or both of two
manifestos in 1922. Many of them held views of primeval
obscurantism, but Salisbury, a cut above the rest, used the
respectable argument that the working class would come to
see – if they had not already seen – the coalition as a cynical
capitalist bargain to keep Labour out and, in reaction, would
sooner or later put Labour in. Numerically the diehards were
no threat but they sharpened every controversy, rubbed salt in
every wound and caused much trouble by running candidates
at by-elections.

The other group was the 'agricultural' members who sat for
constituencies which depended on the farmers' vote. Their
grievance was the repeal of the Agriculture Act of 1920. This
had guaranteed minimum prices for various products and
seemed a clear sign that the policy of *laissez-faire* which had
almost ruined English agriculture during the last forty years
was at an end. The post-war agricultural boom, however,
collapsed soon after the passing of the Act. The price of a
quarter of wheat which had been 86s 4d (£4.32) in 1920
tumbled to 49s (£2.45) in 1921. Faced with the cry of
'squandermania' and a bill of some £20 million, the government ratted and in 1921 repealed the guarantees. It has been
argued that failure to help the farmers was 'probably the
coalition's biggest single mistake'. The agricultural MPs were
respected moderates who had nothing in common with the
diehards. Most of them, some forty or fifty, voted against the
coalition at the Carlton Club on 19 October, and it may well be
symbolic, as Mr John Ramsden suggests, that one of their
leading figures, Captain E. G. Pretyman, proposed both the
motion in support of Chamberlain as leader in May 1921 and
the motion that brought him down seventeen months later.[6]

4

The immediate cause of the coalition's fall lay in foreign not home affairs. On 26 August the Turks suddenly reversed the military situation in Anatolia and routed the Greek forces. They swept into Smyrna burning a large part of the city and massacring a great many Greeks. They then turned north towards the neutral 'Zone of the Straits' created by the Treaty of Sèvres and guarded, after the Greek débâcle, only by minor Allied detachments at Chanak and Ismid on the Asiatic side of the Dardanelles and the Bosphorus. Lloyd George, Churchill and a small group of ministers believed that Kemal intended to invade European Turkey. On 15 September they sent telegrams drafted by Churchill saying that they would 'oppose by every means any infraction of the neutral zones by the Turks or any attempt to cross to the European shore'. Unfortunately this document issued on 16 September appeared in the Canadian, Australian and New Zealand press before the telegrams to the Prime Ministers had been decoded. Canada and Australia returned dusty answers, South Africa none at all. Only New Zealand and Newfoundland (still a separate dominion) replied favourably. On 18 September the French and Italians who had their own reasons for concluding a peace with Kemal withdrew their contingents from the Zone of the Straits. Britain seemed to stand almost alone.

These developments startled the press and a public wholly unprepared for what appeared imminent war. 'Not a single Dominion soldier,' said the *Daily Mail* on 18 September, 'should be allowed to lose his life in order that Mr Churchill may make a new Gallipoli', and three days later its headline was: 'GET OUT OF CHANAK'. On 23 September a small detachment of Turkish troops came within sight of the British lines but made no attempt to attack. On the same day Curzon, who had not been involved in the Cabinet discussion of 15 September, issued from Paris along with Poincaré and the Italian ambassador a joint note in which they looked 'with favour' on the Kemalist claim to European Turkey and suggested a peace conference. This gave Kemal all he wanted and should have ended the crisis. He was not going to attack even an isolated Britain if he could get his way without war. The Cabinet, however, persisted in regarding an attack as imminent. On 29 September they ordered General Harrington who commanded the British force to present an ultimatum to the Turks to withdraw from Chanak. Luckily Harrington had a cool head. He made no reply to the impatient Cabinet for thirty-six hours. When he did he urged caution and delay. In the end no ultimatum was sent. Harrington parleyed with the Turks at Mudania and a pact was made to respect the neutral Zone till peace had been signed.

It is a myth that British firmness halted an aggressor, and that the alleged consequential fall of the government was an unfortunate warning to politicians, which set the country on the road to appeasement. There was no aggression to halt, and there is little evidence that Chanak played any part in the thinking of the thirties. It certainly damaged the coalition. Liberal supporters were alarmed at the sudden prospect of war. So were Conservatives, with the additional objection that it would be on the wrong side. With a strange amnesia about the recent past they regarded the Turks as 'gentlemen' and natural allies. Forgetting Kut and the Armenians they remembered the Crimea and the Congress of Berlin.

There was an even more damaging charge. Many believed as Baldwin did, that Lloyd George, Churchill and Birkenhead wanted a war in order to hold a coalition 'Khaki' election. There is some evidence that both Churchill and Lloyd George were sorry when peace prevailed, and it may be significant that the day when the Cabinet first plumped for an early dissolution was 17 September.[7] The avowed reason, however, was to get it over before the Conservative conference on 15 November, which was likely to carry anti-coalition resolutions. The party managers were horrified. It is remarkable that a leader who on a vital point of tactics was opposed by his chairman, his chief whip and his principal agent, should not have paused. Opposition, however, only made Austen Chamberlain more obdurate. The plan as in January was to 'bounce' the Conservative Party into a coalition election but with the difference this time that Chamberlain was in favour.

The decision was not finally ratified until 10 October, but it at once set all the alarm bells going in the Conservative Party and the ensuing month was one of hectic intrigue and manoeuvre. The key figure was Bonar Law, the only politician of prime ministerial calibre outside the coalition. On 7 October he published an important letter in *The Times* repeated by Beaverbrook in the *Daily Express*. He endorsed the government's 'stand' at Chanak but by implication criticized the policy which made it necessary. He used words which were to be often quoted: 'We cannot act as the policemen of the world. The financial and social condition of this country makes that impossible.' He was at once bombarded with letters adjuring him to take a lead against the coalition. His friends urged him on. Beaverbrook was among the foremost. Sir Samuel Hoare, an able up-and-coming backbencher, later to hold high office, organized support among Conservative MPs. Another active backbencher was J. C. C. Davidson, friend of both Law and Baldwin, a mole-like figure destined to have much influence on the Conservative Party. The editor of *The Times*, Wickham Steed, who for the fleeting period between Lord Northcliffe's death and Lord Astor's purchase was in sole control, also detested Lloyd George. Then there was Baldwin, the only Conservative Cabinet minister clearly hostile to the coalition, although, very late in the day, both Curzon and the Minister of Agriculture, Griffith Boscawen, came out against it too.

Bonar Law did not respond at first to these pleas. Hamlet himself could scarcely have been more irresolute. Sunk in a lethargic depression, receiving a train of callers as he smoked incessantly in the rather frowsty study of his house in Onslow Gardens he would say neither yes nor no. Meanwhile Chamberlain, aware of the groundswell of discontent, decided to take the war into the enemy's camp. At very short notice, given that it was still the recess, he summoned on 16 October a meeting of Conservative MPs at the Carlton Club three days later at 11 A.M. If they did not toe the line he would resign. The date was chosen because the result of a by-election at Newport was due that morning. An independent Conservative was standing against a coalition Liberal and a Socialist. It was confidently expected that he would split the anti-Socialist vote and let Labour in.

Law now had to make up his mind and, whether influenced by Beaverbrook or Mary Law, his sister whose political judgement he greatly respected, he decided, after much havering, on the very eve of the meeting to speak at the Carlton Club. Chamberlain's plan blew up in his face. At the Newport election the independent Conservative won easily. At the meeting Law spoke clearly, though not vehemently, against the coalition. A motion to fight the next election as an independent party with its own leader and programme was carried on a card vote by 187 votes to 87.[8] Austen Chamberlain at once resigned the leadership, and in the afternoon Lloyd George resigned the premiership. The coalition had ended.

Chapter Six

ELECTION FEVER

I

Bonar Law refused to take office till he had been formally elected party leader four days later on 23 October – a precedent followed by no subsequent Conservative Prime Minister, though in similar circumstances it probably would be today.[1] He had little difficulty in forming an administration. Curzon continued in the Foreign Office. Baldwin, who had spoken with particular force at the Carlton Club against Lloyd George, accepted the Exchequer, though it was first offered to Reginald McKenna. Although described by Churchill as 'the second eleven', a ministry with three Fellows of All Souls and most of the politicians who were to govern Britain for the next eighteen years can hardly be called mediocre. Nor was it, as Lloyd George charged, reactionary. The only diehard was Lord Salisbury, and many of the Cabinet belonged to the centre or left of the party.

It was undeniably aristocratic, though the number of peers, seven out of sixteen, was not in itself very unusual. Baldwin had six in 1924, and so did Neville Chamberlain in 1937. But Bonar Law appointed a duke, two marquesses and an earl, including the heads of three of the oldest and grandest territorial families in England – the Cavendishes, the Cecils and the Stanleys. It was certainly a government of the establishment, rich and respectable; but though perhaps slightly humdrum and rather inexperienced, it was neither obscurantist nor incompetent.

Law promptly dissolved Parliament and the election held on 15 November vindicated the rebellion – if an election ever vindicates anything. Law himself was pessimistic as always, but many others also believed that the multiplicity of parties – Conservatives, Independent Conservatives, Labour, National Liberals, Asquithian Liberals, Liberals without prefix, Independents, Constitutionalists, Communists, etc. – would produce an indecisive result. It has been calculated that there were seventy-eight different permutations of contestants in the 615 seats. Seldom has there been a more confused election. The Conservative programme consisted largely of a list of things they were *not* going to do – including one that was to have later repercussions, a promise not to introduce tariffs before another election. Their slogan was 'Tranquillity' and it seemed to work. The press was strongly on their side. Perhaps the electorate really was weary of excitement and crises. Perhaps the closing paragraph of Law's manifesto declaring that 'the nation's first need ... is in every walk of life to get on with its own work with the minimum of interference at home and disturbance abroad' struck a chord.

In such a chaotic election, agreed figures are difficult to ascertain. The best reckoning is that the Conservatives (including certain independents) won 346 seats giving them a majority of 77 over all the rest combined, Labour 142, Liberals 117 divided more or less evenly between supporters of Lloyd George and Asquith. The Conservatives obtained about 5.5 million votes, Labour 4.2 million (compared with 2.3 million in 1918) and the Liberals 4.1 million. The Conservatives secured just over thirty-eight per cent of the popular vote, the same proportion as in 1923 and 1929 when they lost, but they fielded a larger number of candidates in both those years, and fewer Unionist seats were uncontested.

Labour had made a great gain in votes and seats, and most of their leading figures were back, including Ramsay MacDonald whom the party voted into the chairmanship (i.e. leadership) in place of J. R. Clynes by a narrow majority. He was a more charismatic figure and, for all his vanity and weaknesses, the only plausible choice. The parliamentary party had become rather less of a trade-union pressure group than before, with up to a third of its members from the 'middle class'. The Liberals were bitterly divided. The principal coalitionists, apart from Lloyd George, lost their seats – Churchill at Dundee (stricken with appendicitis), Hamar Greenwood, Edwin Montagu, F. E. Guest, and others. Asquith was happy 'to gloat over the corpses which have been left on the battlefield', as he wrote to a friend.

Bonar Law's 'style' was as different as possible from Lloyd George's. He had clear views about the limits of government action. Unemployment, for example, would go down only when prosperity had been revived by reducing taxes. In Lloyd George's day 10 Downing Street was always in the limelight. Every deputation or delegation found its way there. By contrast, when some unemployed hunger marchers demanded an interview Bonar Law refused; they were, he said, merely wasting their shoe leather, in any case it was a matter for the Minister of Labour, not him.

Then there was the 'Garden Suburb'. J. C. C. Davidson, now Law's parliamentary private secretary, was given orders 'to clean up Number Ten'. The 'Garden Suburb' was promptly disbanded. There was some danger that the Cabinet Secretariat might go too, but it had proved its indispensability. Davidson cut its numbers from 129 to 37 but the organization itself survived, its efficiency unimpaired. Honours were another contrast. Law refused to issue a New Year's list until the Royal Commission, forced on Lloyd George in July, had reported. When it did in February 1923 he nominated a small number of unimpeachably respectable persons. The ex-coalitionists cannot have been pleased that Younger, made a Viscount, was one of them.

The main problems for the new government were external. Curzon had the task of picking up the pieces after Chanak and negotiating an Allied settlement with Kemal. Here again there was a contrast with the old order. Restoration of the Foreign Office to its proper role was one of the few positive features of Law's election manifesto. Curzon, no longer plagued by the intrigues behind his back of Garden Suburbanites directed by a presidential Prime Minister, achieved his finest hour. At the Conference of Lausanne he played a weak hand with great skill. Although on 4 February 1923 he temporarily broke off negotiations on some minor points, he had gained the substance. His victory was ratified when the Conference was renewed. The Treaty of Lausanne signed on 24 July was the only Allied post-war treaty to stand the test of time. Moreover, he so effectively demolished the Turkish claim on oil-rich Mosul that it was referred to arbitration by the League of Nations, which Curzon believed would – and in fact did in 1926 – award it to Iraq in the British sphere of influence.

The second major problem was German reparations. Law himself dealt with this, for Curzon's interest in financial matters was, as his biographer observes, limited to his own income. The problem was insoluble, because the French were not concerned with solving it. Poincaré was using German default as an excuse to occupy the Ruhr and set up the Rhineland republic which Foch had demanded in 1919 but which Clemenceau had relinquished in return for an Anglo-American security pact. The pact had never been signed but this was no justification for reverting to a policy which had never made sense. Poincaré, whom Law like most people who dealt with him greatly disliked, remained obdurate. A final effort in Paris on 6 January failed to move him. French troops entered the Ruhr, the Germans passively resisted, inflation rocketed and the central European economy collapsed into chaos. There was a bonus for Britain in the form of a short-lived boom in coal exports, thanks to the standstill on the Ruhr, but the *rupture cordiale*, as it was called, did nothing but harm in the long run.

The third great problem – and it nearly brought the government to premature collapse – was the funding of the American debt, nearly £1,000 million owed by Britain. Law, who had lost two sons in the war, believed strongly that this was not an ordinary commercial transaction but part of a joint wartime effort. He also believed that Britain, owed four times that amount by other countries, should be called upon to repay only to the extent that her own debtors repaid her. He considered that the annual payment should not exceed £25 million. Baldwin and Montagu Norman, Governor of the Bank of England, departed late in December to Washington to settle within those limits. The American attitude was unsympathetic. The lowest offer was £34 million for ten years and £40 million thereafter, with no concession about Britain's debtors. Baldwin telegraphed it to Law who promptly recalled him. It is not true that Baldwin, as alleged by some historians,[2] accepted the offer without reference to the Cabinet, but he certainly believed that no better could be got, and when he met reporters at Southampton on 19 January, the terms having leaked to the press, he unwisely said they showed 'an immense advance in American opinion'.

He defended them to the Cabinet that day, while apologizing for his blunder. Law strongly opposed the terms. The others, apart from Novar and Lloyd Graeme, felt that they now had no option but to accept. Law, whose health had been declining ever since he became Prime Minister, said he would resign rather than agree. The Cabinet adjourned till next day when there appeared a letter in *The Times* signed 'Colonial' reiterating most of Law's arguments. Those who suspected him as author were right – a unique episode in prime ministerial history. By thus relieving his feelings he perhaps helped himself to climb down. A deputation saw him that morning and he agreed to stay, though his relations with Baldwin were never again the same. On the merits of the debt settlement he was right. Countries which stuck out longer got better terms. But Law had gone back to politics to preserve the unity of the party. He could not let it break up less than four months later.

2

Law had intended to retire after a year. He hoped that by then the party wounds would be healed and he could hand on

to Austen Chamberlain, but there was little sign of reconciliation. An indirect offer by Law to Chamberlain in April to
return to the fold with the prospect of the reversion to the
premiership in November was rebuffed. Law was now a sick
man and he wanted to resign. His voice was failing and he
was suffering acute pain, taking up to ten aspirins a day for
relief. On his return via Paris from an ineffectual sea cruise
he was examined on 17 May by his doctor, Lord Horder, who
diagnosed inoperable cancer of the throat. Law was never
told what his illness was, but those who were, Beaverbrook
among others, and had been hitherto pressing him to stay
now encouraged him to retire. He returned to London and
sent a letter of resignation to the King on 20 May, feeling too
ill to say goodbye in person.

Who was to succeed him? The ex-coalitionists had ruled
themselves out, and the choice lay between Curzon and
Baldwin. Curzon was cleverer, better known, more experienced, more distinguished; but his rococo grandeur put off
some people, he could be curiously prickly over petty personal matters, as Law had good reason to know, and he was a
peer – not an insurmountable obstacle but a handicap when
Labour was unrepresented in the Lords. Baldwin was an
easier character but he had been in the Cabinet for barely two
years. He was liked in the House, and his budget knocking 6d
(2½p) off income tax had gone down well, but the American
debt settlement had done him no good. He did not look like a
Prime Minister.

The choice would nowadays be made by an intra-party
election, subsequently endorsed by the Crown; but the
Conservatives did not design the machinery for this until
1965, at the behest of Sir Alec Douglas-Home. In 1923, as in
1957 and 1963, the Crown had a genuine option. The
monarch could consult anyone or no one, but was likely to pay
particular attention to the opinion of the outgoing Prime
Minister. Sick, tired, divided in mind about the succession,
Law convinced himself that he need not give advice. He did
not see how Curzon could be passed over in favour of

Baldwin, a relative tyro. Yet he would not take the personal responsibility of recommending Curzon. He did not 'refuse' to give advice, as is sometimes said. He merely indicated that he would prefer not to, and his wish was respected.

Curzon *was* passed over and Baldwin became Prime Minister. The backstairs intrigue which contributed to this decision was not revealed to history until 1955.[3] It is now clear that there was a pro-Baldwin conspiracy, probably unknown to Baldwin himself, and that the plotters who included both Davidson and Colonel Waterhouse, Law's private secretary, contrived to mislead the King about the opinion of the retiring Prime Minister. One cannot say that the deception was decisive though it was certainly discreditable. There was a genuine argument against a peer becoming Prime Minister – and, of all peers, Curzon. Balfour, who had nothing to do with the plot, put the case strongly when consulted by the King's private secretary. The choice of Curzon would have caused uproar in the Labour Party and any vote by Conservative MPs would have been heavily pro-Baldwin.

Whatever the reasons for the King's decision, it was right. Curzon, apart from the peerage question, would not have been a good Prime Minister. Baldwin who, as was said, 'is not so simple as he looks' made blunders but he guided his country and his party with urbane skill for fourteen years. He was a far more appropriate successor to Law than Curzon in the era of the new Conservatism. Law died six months later. He had not been a great Prime Minister and never would have been, even if time had been granted, but he was a notable party leader. The survival of the Conservatives through the war and its chaotic aftermath as a more or less united party – the ex-coalitionists were soon to return – owed more to him than to any other single person.

Curzon, after the first shock of disappointment, displayed magnanimity. He continued as Foreign Secretary and he proposed Baldwin for the leadership of the party. Hoping, as Bonar Law had, to get McKenna who was ill, as Chancellor,

Baldwin doubled the Exchequer with the premiership – a combination last made by Gladstone in 1880 and before that by Peel in 1834. McKenna recovered but could not find a seat. At the end of August Baldwin appointed Neville Chamberlain – the 'late beginner' of his famous family and the only one who in the end got to the 'top of the greasy pole'. Chancellor 1923, Minister of Health 1924–9, Chancellor again 1931–7, Chamberlain, described by Churchill as the 'Pack horse of our great affairs', was Baldwin's indispensable support, bound to him by a common and ineradicable hatred of Lloyd George.

Nothing of note happened during the next few months. Then in November Baldwin announced one of the strangest decisions in recent political history. Although he was under no obligation to go to the country till 1927, he told an astonished public on 13 November that he would hold an election on 6 December to obtain a mandate for protection, which, he said, was the only remedy for unemployment. Law had promised not to bring in tariffs till after another general election. This was a quite categorical pledge, and so Baldwin could not introduce them in the existing parliament. But he might have played for time. When he put the question to a sceptical cabinet on 23 October he said he was prepared 'to take the verdict of the country in six months'. However, his much applauded speech at the party conference two days later precipitated events. It is difficult to argue that a change in policy is vital, and, in the same breath, say that you need several months to convert the public. The timing was left open by the Cabinet on 9 November. Three days later Baldwin advised the King who agreed only with great reluctance to dissolve Parliament.

The ensuing election was a Conservative disaster. Protection had long been the creed of the now ageing bright young men of the party but its appeal was based on Joseph Chamberlain's objective of 'Imperial Unity' which presupposed a preferential tariff in favour of empire food imports. Baldwin, fearing the cry of 'stomach taxes', repudiated this idea, but he did not convince the public, and at the same time he lost the support of the imperialist press proprietors, Rothermere and Beaverbrook who were highly critical throughout the election. The press in general was hostile and puzzled. The Liberal Party, with Asquith taking first place to Lloyd George's second, rallied into short-lived unity under the tattered but not yet faded banner of free trade. Labour, firmly avoiding any semblance of alliance with the Liberals, denounced protection as a capitalist ploy which would make the poor poorer.

The Conservatives obtained roughly the same number and percentage of votes as in 1922, but since they fielded fifty-four more candidates, and fewer Conservative seats were uncontested, the statistics mask the real decline. They won only 258 seats. Liberal and Labour voting figures were also very similar to those of 1922, but Labour went up in seats to 191 and Liberals to 158. There was no love lost between the two anti-Conservative parties. The battle for protection was no less bitter than the battle for the leadership of the 'progressive cause'. The Conservatives lost the first, the Liberals the second. Labour did not exactly win either of these battles. Nevertheless there was something appropriate in the final upshot being a minority Labour government.

Why did Baldwin dissolve? Various subtle explanations are given: he wanted to go with a view to returning all the stronger after his opponents had made a hash of things. This is very unlikely. No Prime Minister except under necessity ever chooses to hold an election which he expects to lose. Did he fear that Lloyd George would pre-empt him over protection to secure the allegiance of the ex-coalitionists? This story though widely repeated is a later invention. There is little to show that Lloyd George had such a plan and no contemporary evidence that Baldwin believed so, whatever he said afterwards. It is more likely that he genuinely thought that protection was the answer to unemployment and simply miscalculated the reaction of the voters, underestimating the confusion which would be caused in a divided party faced with a sudden election whose timing was very difficult to justify even to the party faithfuls. All the same one should avoid hindsight. Defeat was not self-evident. On the eve of the poll the Central Office predicted an overall majority of eighty-seven.

3

The ambiguous result caused the clubs, the country houses, and the press to hum with speculation about various possible political permutations to avoid the calamity of a Labour government. Baldwin wished to resign at once on the ground that, whatever else the vote meant, it was a repudiation of protection. The King, however, pressed him to meet Parliament, which is surely the correct constitutional procedure after an election when the government party is still the largest one even though it does not possess an absolute majority in the House. The situation in 1929 (see below Chapter Seven) was not the same. Baldwin gave way, possibly influenced by the knowledge that a group of malcontents headed by Birkenhead were trying to oust him. On 18 December Asquith announced that the Liberals would not join any combination to keep Labour out. A Labour government, he said, 'could hardly be tried in safer circumstances'. On 17 January 1924 Clynes moved an amendment to the King's speech carried by seventy-two votes. Baldwin, who shared Asquith's opinion, resigned next day and Ramsay MacDonald became the first Labour Prime Minister. On 11 February under strong pressure from Derby, 'uncrowned King of Lancashire' – a bastion of free trade – Baldwin, addressing a party meeting, formally repudiated protection until there was clear evidence that the public had changed its mind.

There had been an argument in the Labour Party about taking office without a majority, but refusal would have been a denial of all MacDonald's strategy. Since his return in 1922 he had two objectives – to show that Labour could be a 'constitutional' party capable of managing a 'mixed economy', and to drive the Liberals off the middle-ground. If Labour now refused, Asquith and his colleagues would occupy the government front bench, relegating Labour to seats on the same side below the gangway. When the Liberals were defeated, as they soon would be, they would be entitled to the opposition front bench, and Labour would lose its great gain of 1922. Parliamentary *placement* is more important than one might think.

MacDonald was the first Prime Minister never to have held cabinet office before. Indeed, only two members of his government had, Arthur Henderson and Haldane who, rather surprisingly accepted the Woolsack – perhaps getting his own back on Asquith for his treatment in 1915. He instructed his colleagues in etiquette. MacDonald must always be addressed as 'Prime Minister', others by surname or office – never Christian name. There was, however, one innovation. J. H. Thomas set a precedent by smoking at his first meeting. No one rebuked him and others followed suit.

The great problem was the Foreign Office. Nobody seemed very suitable and MacDonald whose chief interest was in foreign policy took it himself, the first and last person to do so since Lord Salisbury. Philip Snowden, a prominent member of the ILP and an expert on finance, was the obvious Chancellor of the Exchequer. Henderson was another problem. His claims to high office were very strong but he had lost his seat and MacDonald tactlessly suggested that he should take charge of the party machine as there was sure to be an early election. The suggestion was ill-received. MacDonald then gave him the Home Office and he was soon returned at a by-election, but the episode rankled. The other key appointments were: J. H. Thomas, General Secretary of the National Union of Railwaymen, to the Colonial Office, Clynes as Lord Privy Seal and Leader of the House, and John Wheatley, an able self-made Roman Catholic businessman who represented the left-wing of the party, to the Ministry of Health.

Then there was the House of Lords. Despite pledges to abolish it, a 'constitutional' government had to make respectable appearance there. Lord Parmoor, an Asquith creation converted to Labour, became Lord President and Leader of the House; Sidney Olivier, a distinguished Colonial Servant took a peerage and the India Office; Lord Chelmsford, a life-long Conservative and an ex-Viceroy of India, accepted the Admiralty. The government looked very respectable – an impression confirmed by the presence of Sir Charles Trevelyan, a great Northumbrian landowner, at the Board of Education, and Arthur Ponsonby, son of Queen Victoria's private secretary, as Under-Secretary at the Foreign Office. True, it was the first Cabinet to have no Etonians but it contained eight products of famous independent schools, including two Harrovians and two Wykehamists.

The panic at the very thought of Labour in office soon died away. There was minor friction with the King over court dress, but this was soon solved, and the ministers fitted easily into their new roles. MacDonald made it clear that he was not going to bring forward provocative legislation and 'ride for a fall', also that he would not resign except on a vote of censure or an issue which he regarded as one of confidence. An orthodox budget which reduced both direct and indirect taxation gave Snowden's reputation a boost, and for the next few months things went as smoothly as could be expected for a minority government which refused to make any agreement with the only party that could keep it in power. The Liberals found this attitude hard to understand, but it was logical. MacDonald deeply disliked Lloyd George and resented Asquith's patronizing manner, but the question was not one of personalities. It was essential to eliminate the Liberals as rivals for the moderate anti-Conservative vote. Labour's minority status gave cast-iron reasons for not enacting the panaceas of the far left, but it was equally important to have no truck with the Liberal Party. For different reasons the Conservatives were equally anti-Liberal. Their great object was to stop the march of Labour. One answer was a Conservative–Liberal alliance, but that had failed. Whether for personal or political reasons, or both, did not matter.

Baldwin would never revive it. His object too was to eliminate the Liberals. Just as Labour sought to recruit their left wing so the Conservatives aimed to recruit their right.

MacDonald scored one notable success in foreign affairs. The French agreed to the Dawes Plan – an American device to stabilize the German economy and put reparations on a rational basis – with the corollary of withdrawing their troops from the Ruhr. The Prime Minister played a major part in the negotiations which were concluded on 16 August, helped by growing French consciousness of the futility of the occupation and by the opportune fall of Poincaré – at a crucial moment early in May. But the other great question in foreign policy during 1924 indirectly proved fatal. This was the Russian treaty. MacDonald recognized Soviet Russia almost as soon as he took office. He hoped to negotiate a settlement of the main differences. After much hard bargaining the Russians agreed to sign a commercial treaty and to compensate expropriated British interests, but on condition that the British made them a loan of £30 million, of which they promised to spend two-thirds in Britain. The Conservatives determined to oppose this tooth and nail when it came up after the summer recess, and there was every sign that many Liberals would too.

MacDonald was already running into trouble. In March he had accepted from an old friend, Alexander Grant, the self-made biscuit king of McVitie and Price, the loan of a Daimler car and chauffeur, and of shares of £40,000 from which he was to draw the dividends during his premiership. In April he recommended Grant for a baronetcy. The honour was fully warranted on grounds of public service. There is little doubt that neither MacDonald nor Grant linked the two transactions, but MacDonald's naïvety in the aftermath of the honours scandal is scarcely credible. The facts emerged in the press in mid-September, and the cry of 'biscuits' by hecklers at meetings during the October general election was painful for a proud and sensitive man.

The Russian treaty would almost certainly have brought

down the government, had not an even more embarrassing question supervened. This was the Campbell Case. John Campbell, editor of the official organ of the Communist Party, the *Workers' Weekly*, published on 25 July an article which could be regarded as incitement to soldiers to mutiny. The Attorney-General, Sir Patrick Hastings, instructed the Public Prosecutor to bring proceedings, but left-wing Socialists regarded the words used – 'let it be known that neither in the class war nor in a military war, will you turn your guns on your fellow workers' – as just the sort of thing they were saying themselves. Campbell, moreover, had an exceptionally gallant war record for which he had been decorated. The matter came to the Cabinet on 6 August. The Cabinet is not entitled to require the withdrawal of a prosecution, but the Attorney-General is entitled to consult the Cabinet and to withdraw it, if he thinks fit. This was what happened. MacDonald, however, in reply to a parliamentary question on 30 September when Parliament reassembled, denied that he had ever been consulted at all.

This was untrue and known to be so by a good many people. The Conservatives put down a motion of censure for 8 October. The Liberals put down an amendment asking for a select committee to inquire into the affair. MacDonald declared that he would regard that too as an issue of confidence. He had to make an embarrassing personal statement about his earlier answer, explaining not very convincingly how he had come to mislead the House. At the end of the debate the Conservatives voted for the Liberal amendment and against their own motion. Defeated by 394 to 198 MacDonald next day asked the King for a dissolution. It would not have been granted if either Baldwin or Asquith had been willing to take office. They were not, and the King, again very reluctantly, agreed to the third general election in under two years – to be held on 29 October.

It was an election that the Conservatives were almost certain to win – and they did. Labour would be defending itself against a highly circumstantial charge of political inter-

ference with justice and the accusation that MacDonald was
the political lackey of Soviet Russia. The Liberals were in
disarray. The split between Asquith and Lloyd George had
only been papered over. The official machine was desperately
short of money. Lloyd George kept a firm hold on his famous
fund and merely disbursed a measly £50,000 for the campaign. The Liberals could not field more than 340 candidates
and entered an election for the first time with no possibility of
winning it. The Conservatives were united, thanks to the
adroit tactics of Baldwin. Protection had brought Austen
Chamberlain and his friends back into the fold, but the
dropping of it did not drive them out. On the contrary it
added to Conservative strength by bringing in Churchill who
had always been anti-tariff and had been out of the House
since 1922. He now stood for the safe seat of Epping as an
independent 'Constitutionalist' with full support from the
Conservative Central Office.

The campaign was conducted by all three parties with
intemperate virulence in the constituencies, though Baldwin,
MacDonald and Asquith were more moderate than their
supporters. The Russian treaties in particular caused some
ludicrous charges. Four days before the poll, excitement was
heightened by the publication of the 'Zinoviev letter'. It
purported to be from the President of the Communist
International to the British Communist Party, giving advice
and instruction on subversive activity especially in the armed
forces. The full story is one of labyrinthine complexity. The
letter was a White Russian forgery, but neither the Foreign
Office which had its copy a fortnight earlier, nor the Conservative Central Office, which was aware of its contents and
may have passed on another copy to the *Daily Mail*, knew this.
The impression gained by the public was that a document,
very damaging to the credibility of the government's Russian
policy, would have been suppressed till after the election if
events had not forced the Prime Minister's hand.

The 'Red letter' became one of the great pieces of Labour
demonology, like the 'bankers' ramp' in 1931 – an excuse for

attributing defeat to a plot and not to the party's deficiencies. Its effect on the election cannot be quantified. We know little enough why people vote as they do today, let alone in the 1920s. The Zinoviev letter probably gave the Conservatives a bigger victory than they would have otherwise had, but it did not in itself give them victory. The likelihood is that they won, partly because of MacDonald's general policy towards Russia, partly because of a Conservative programme more detailed and enlightened over social reform than anything before and partly, perhaps principally, because of the appeal for 'stability' – the elimination of the three-party system which had produced three elections in two years. The electorate was voting for the 'tranquillity' promised by Bonar Law, thrown away by Baldwin a year later and now again on offer.

Whatever the correct explanation, the Conservatives won the biggest single-party victory in the twentieth century, bigger even than the Liberal triumph of 1906 (the elections of 1931 and 1935 were fought on a coalition basis). The turnout was the highest (76.6 per cent) in the inter-war years, and 2 million more people voted than in the previous election. Labour actually increased their vote by a million but lost forty seats, their score being 151. The Conservative vote went up by nearly 2.5 million (48.3 per cent of those voting – over 50 per cent if one allows for unopposed returns), and they won 419 seats. The Liberals were slaughtered, winning only forty seats (with a popular vote of 2.9 million compared with nearly 4.2 million in 1923). Asquith who lost his seat had been manoeuvred – or had manoeuvred himself – into appearing first as the maker and then as the unmaker of the Labour government. It is difficult to see quite what else he could have done, but a large question mark now hung over the whole future of the Liberal Party.

Chapter Seven

BALDWIN'S SECOND INNINGS

I

Baldwin had no programme but he had a purpose. Like Disraeli he wished to project a new picture of the Conservative Party, not too detailed – Monet rather than Frith – and above all emollient and sympathetic. Baldwin was described by Lord Boothby as 'the nicest' of all the men in high office that he ever met. He was invariably courteous to his opponents. He never sneered and he was never sarcastic, though he could hit back hard at people he regarded as malignant like Lords Rothermere and Beaverbrook. He wished to soften class conflicts, unify England – he seldom talked about Britain – and do for the Conservative Party what Disraeli, whom he greatly admired, had tried to do half a century earlier. His concentration on England and the English spirit was compatible with being personally rather un-English, again like Disraeli and also like his first cousin, Rudyard Kipling. Behind his stolid façade there was intuition, impetuousness and imagination; possibly they stemmed from Celtic forebears on his mother's side of the family, as perhaps also did his long memory of personal feuds. This trait, added to an element of English puritanism, gave him undying dislike and distrust of Lloyd George. He could see the corruption, the duplicity, the amorality – sale of honours, and a mistress in Downing Street – but never the genius, the flair and the achievement.

Baldwin was determined to queer Lloyd George's pitch for good and all; his niceness did not prevent him from being an astute politician. Sensing that the Liberal Party was on its way out he saw that Lloyd George could be a threat only if he managed to re-create the alliance with the ex-coalitionists. He gave the Foreign Office to their leader, Austen Chamberlain. Swallowing his dislike of Churchill's bumptiousness and Birkenhead's bibosity he offered the Exchequer to the former and the India Office to the latter. Neither of them was particularly suited to his department, and Churchill's appointment caused astonishment. Baldwin only offered it after Neville Chamberlain had preferred the Ministry of Health, but the choice conveniently symbolized the abandonment of protection, while neutralizing a potential critic. Baldwin, however, drew the line at Sir Robert Horne, a womanizing bachelor nightclub devotee, whom he once described as 'that rare phenomenon, a Scotch cad'. He offered him the Ministry of Labour, but in such a way that refusal was certain. After the death of Curzon a few months later he brought back Balfour as Lord President and thus completed the reconciliation of the party.

Churchill's first budget, introduced on 28 April 1925, was the most important of the decade, apart from Horne's three years before. He reduced income tax from 4s 6d (22½p) to 4s (20p), brought in a new contributory pension scheme devised by Neville Chamberlain for widows, orphans and the old, and – most important of all – announced the return to the gold standard at the old parity of $4.86 to the pound. He did this only after much discussion and some misgivings, but the City, the Treasury, the Bank of England and the economists of academe favoured it. McKenna, Keynes and Hubert Henderson were the principal dissentients, but McKenna admitted that in Churchill's place he could not have resisted. There is now a general, though not universal, opinion that the decision was wrong and contributed to the depression of British industry while other industrial countries were enjoying a boom. The critics made two points: first, the conditions in the nineteenth century, when London was the sole financial centre of the world and Britain a creditor nation based on a trade surplus, no longer applied; New York and other cities had become rivals with different views, and London depended on short-term loans to operate the system; second – and more serious – the rate was wrong, overvaluing the pound by some ten per cent and handicapping exports. On the other hand, imports of food and raw materials became cheaper, and it can be argued that British industry was trying to export outdated products which would have sold no better if prices had been lower.

Both before and after the budget, Churchill was involved in a major battle with the Admiralty represented forcibly by the First Sea Lord, Beatty, and by his political head, W. C. Bridgeman, who had been one of Baldwin's keen supporters in the succession crisis of 1923. It was the most serious internal crisis during Baldwin's second administration, but J. C. C. Davidson's attempt in his memoirs to blow it up into an attempted coup by the 'old gang', i.e. the ex-coalitionists, to oust Baldwin reflects the author's paranoia rather than reality. There was after all a genuine argument that the Admiralty was pitching its claims too high at a time when no naval enemy was even on the horizon. Churchill always pressed with enthusiastic extremism the case for whatever department he headed – the Admiralty itself in the past, the Treasury now. This was why he was such a maddening colleague and why the premiership, which has no department, was the only office that really suited his genius.

None of this warrants the theory of a coup, though Davidson may have persuaded Baldwin. It is more likely that Baldwin's decision to back the Admiralty, though with a slight amount of face-saving for Churchill, was taken because he thought the Chancellor had gone too far and because he felt he could not hold the party together if the whole Board of Admiralty resigned. Whatever the reasons, the navy got its way over its principal demand – seven cruisers to be laid down by 1927 – at the cost of some minor economies and postponements.

2

These inter-departmental disputes took place largely behind closed doors. The principal public problem was the deterioration of the coal industry, which led directly to the General Strike, the one turbulent episode in Baldwin's otherwise placid administration. Coal-mining was the symbol and epitome of Britain's declining industries. In 1913 it employed over a million men, about one in ten of the working population. Wages were higher than in any other major occupation, expansion was continuous, and coal, though nowhere near to textiles, was the second largest contributor to British exports.

All this changed after 1918. Fuel economy in industry, new sources of energy like oil and hydro-electricity, the collapse of important foreign markets, such as Russia through ravage and revolution, sharply diminished a demand which never recovered in the inter-war years. There was a world surplus of coal. British mining was not inefficient, but it lagged behind, as old industries do. In 1927 the Ruhr extracted eighty per cent of its coal by machinery compared with Britain's twenty-five per cent. This long-term decline was masked first by the post-war boom and then, after a brief slump in 1920–21 by the export boost resulting from the American coal strike of 1922 and the French occupation of the Ruhr next year. The adverse figures of 1924 and 1925 came, therefore, as a shock to owners and miners alike.

The Miners' Federation was the most militant of trades unions. The Mining Association which represented the coal-owners was the most obstinate of employers' bodies. A long history of venomous dispute overshadowed their relations. On 30 June the owners gave notice to end existing wage agreements and introduce longer hours and lower pay – the only way, they said, to cut prices. If these were refused there would be a lock-out on 31 July. The General Council of the TUC pressed the government to subsidize the industry, pending an inquiry into ways of making it more profitable. The Cabinet at first refused. The TUC then threatened an embargo on all movement of coal, and the Cabinet went into reverse. At the last moment they gave a subsidy for nine months and set up a Royal Commission under Sir Herbert Samuel.

'Red Friday', as it came to be called, in contrast to 'Black Friday' in 1921, looked like a push-over for the TUC, and was bitterly criticized by Conservatives and Liberals. Later it came to be regarded as a tactical move to give time to prepare against a general strike. Different ministers had different motives. Revival of plans laid down earlier and put on ice by the MacDonald government played some part, and much was done to meet the coming crisis. But there was also genuine fear of the consequences of a stoppage and hope that an inquiry might produce acceptable proposals for 'reorganizing' the industry. The Samuel Commission reported on 11 March 1926 and made such proposals, but it was emphatic that wage reductions must come first. The government accepted the report and left the owners and the federation to work out the details.

The miners refused. 'Not a penny off the pay, not a minute on the day' was the slogan of their left-wing secretary, A. J. Cook. The subsidy ended on 30 April and the lock-out began next day. Simultaneously a special trade-union conference approved plans for a general strike, and the miners authorized – though in ambiguous terms – the TUC's Industrial Committee to negotiate with the government. The Cabinet was ready to seek a formula within the Samuel Report, but refused to be coerced into continuing the subsidy by the threat of a general strike.

Negotiations proceeded during 1 and 2 May. The Cabinet broke them off soon after midnight on 2 May, after learning that the compositors of the *Daily Mail* had refused to set up an editorial endorsing a government advertisement for volunteers to cope with the emergency. Their action was treated as the start of the General Strike itself. In fact it was a purely local affair unauthorized by the TUC or even the union involved (NATSOPA). The TUC repudiated it but their own strike notices had already gone out. This may have been a piece of brinkmanship but there was no going back now by either side. The government refused to negotiate till the strike notices had been withdrawn. Elected by a huge majority it was bound to see the General Strike as a political threat to the whole basis of parliamentary democracy. The TUC did not intend this at all. They thought they were merely trying to pressurize the government into suspending the owners' lock-out by the grant of a temporary subsidy. They were ready to see miners' wages lowered, as long as the government agreed to impose the Samuel Report on the owners too. The TUC leaders were half-hearted and reluctant, the government was well organized and tough.

The rank and file of the unions displayed remarkable solidarity, but so did everyone else. The two nations confronted one another, peacefully it is true, but uncompromisingly, and the middle class was as determined as the organized working class. The motor car had changed the transport situation and a rail stoppage was not as serious as it would have been before the war. Volunteers drove lorries, buses, even locomotives – thus realizing many a boyhood dream. There was little violence, and, except in the mining areas, little bitterness. The printers' strike stopped the *Daily Herald* as well as the 'capitalist' press and so damaged the TUC more than the government which was able to communicate via the *British Gazette* – a rumbustious official right-wing organ brought out by Churchill. When it became clear that the Cabinet would not negotiate on the coal industry the TUC leaders sought a way out. There is little evidence that they were influenced by Sir John Simon's celebrated – and incorrect – claim that the General Strike was illegal, but they grasped at a new formula produced by Herbert Samuel who had returned from San Vigilio where he was writing a book on 'what is wrong with the world'. Samuel, careful to deny any authority from the government, suggested the creation of a National Wages Board to enforce reductions, but only after the other proposals in his report had been implemented. The TUC accepted his proposal and on 12 May unconditionally called off the General Strike, hoping perhaps that Samuel really had more authority than he claimed and that public opinion would bring about a settlement on those lines.

The miners, however – a strange tribal world insulated geographically and mentally from most of Britain – fought on to the bitter end of total defeat by the owners six months later. They repudiated the TUC's acceptance of the Samuel formula and thus released Baldwin who, now that the General Strike was over, had promised to operate the report but only if both sides would agree. He was even ready to give a temporary subsidy. The obduracy of the miners thus threw away whatever slight gain the General Strike might have brought them.

The General Strike had less effect on industrial relations than might have been expected or some historians allege. The allegation presupposes a militant union challenge to constitutional government, whose defeat led to a change of heart. There was in fact no challenge intended, and the change away from the militancy of the immediate post-war years had begun before the General Strike. Its continuation thereafter was helped by circumstances. The retail price index fell steadily from 117 (1938: 100) in 1922, the first 'normal' post-war year, to 101 in 1930, but wages, except in the case of the miners, were virtually unchanged. After 1930 RPI fell even more sharply reaching a low of 90 in 1933 and 1934. Attempts to lower wages or, as in 1931, unemployment benefits, which seem outrageous to a generation brought up on perpetual inflation, have to be seen against that background. The preservation of money wages at a constant level in most occupations during the second half of the 1920s conceals a marked improvement in the working-class standard of living.

One consequence of the strike was the Trades Disputes Act of May 1927. This is often presented as a vindictive measure which cut across Baldwin's role as a conciliator and which he ought not to have allowed. The Bill certainly did not achieve what the Cabinet committee that presided over its prolonged gestation had hoped – 'command the support of the great mass of public opinion, including that of the moderate trade unionist, and ... not be capable of being represented as having a party character'. If it had remained in its original form with clauses prohibiting sympathetic strikes and those 'calculated to coerce the government', giving safeguards to non-strikers, making strike ballots obligatory and mildly reforming the law on picketing, it might have had some appeal to the 'moderate' trade unionist. Even the clauses debarring civil servants from affiliation with the TUC and forbidding local authorities to insist on union membership for their employees caused little opposition. But the bill in its final form, while omitting the items about strike ballots and picketing, contained a new and contentious provision: unions were forbidden in future to charge a 'political' subscription to their members other than to those who positively 'contracted-in', whereas hitherto they could do so to anyone who had not 'contracted-out'.

On grounds of moral and political justice the government's case was overwhelming and confirmed by an immediate drop of a third in political contributions. The change had been on the Conservative agenda since 1906 and was at one time an election promise in 1924, though dropped in the final manifesto. Baldwin could not have vetoed it. All the same, it looked vindictive, and it had nothing to do with the General Strike. Labour opposed it furiously and it was the first measure since 1921 to be carried by the closure. Baldwin had used all his eloquence in 1925 to defeat a private member's bill on similar lines when he movingly appealed for 'peace in our time'. The contrast was not forgotten.

3

The two ministers who most effectively promoted the social reform aspect of the 'new Conservatism' were Neville Chamberlain and Churchill. Oddly, they were also the two most disliked by Labour – Churchill because of his attitude to Russia and his management of the *British Gazette*, Chamberlain because of his abrasive manner and his suppression of 'Poplarism'. The word referred to the London borough council of Poplar which in 1921, led by George Lansbury, refused to pay its share of the expenses of the London County Council, with the result that some thirty councillors were sent to prison. Later the name was applied to any defiance of central government by Labour-dominated local authorities. Chamberlain in 1926 put through an act giving him the power to suspend councils and boards of guardians – the bodies that administered poor relief – if they paid wages or benefits above the level laid down by the Ministry of Health, often aggravating the offence by doing it with borrowed money.

Chamberlain's assertion of the law did not signify any hostility to local government as such. On the contrary, he wished to reform and strengthen it. Like his father, Joseph, he probably knew more about the subject than anyone else in national politics. In 1928 he decided to do for the poor law what Balfour had done for education. He abolished the boards of guardians thus bringing the last of the functions hitherto administered by *ad hoc* elected bodies under the control of the local authorities. In England and Wales the sixty-two counties operating partly directly on the public and partly through rural and urban district councils, together with the eighty-four county boroughs operating directly, became the effective authorities under the supervision of the Minister of Health for a wider range of activities than ever before or since – education, poor law, planning, welfare, public health, slum clearance, highways, police, local transport, gas, water, electricity. It was the high point of their activity. After the Second World War, gas, electricity and water were nationalized – and much of health administration was hived off too. Mr A. J. P. Taylor points out that in Britain after 1928 the citizen had less contact with central government administrators than almost anywhere in Europe. The Post Office, the employment exchanges, tax authorities, and law courts were the only major exceptions. Nearly everything else was a matter for the town hall or the county council offices.

Paradoxically, local government in England was less independent than on the continent. It received two-fifths of its revenue from the government – the figure in 1979 was two-thirds – and the Ministry of Health exercised a powerful control. In Europe local authorities dealt with fewer functions, but had a freer hand with those that were left to them. A Lord Mayor of Birmingham could no longer make a national name for himself as Joseph Chamberlain had in the 1870s. A Mayor of Lyons still could – and did. English local authorities became instruments of national policy and have been ever since. *De jure* the English system of government looked loose and decentralized. *De facto* it was one of the strongest and most centralized in the free world.

In this respect there was another paradoxical contrast between appearance and reality. The older writers on the constitution, like A. V. Dicey, said that the 'rule of law', the Common Law, was the great safeguard, along with an independent judiciary, against the encroachment of executive power. They contrasted it favourably with the *droit administratif* of Europe. In reality the rights of the individual were better protected in France than in England where the judges, during the First World War and onwards to beyond the end of the Second, tended to interpret most questions in favour of the executive. It was not till the 1960s that Lord Denning began to reverse this trend. For half a century, despite the protests of Lord Hewart (Lord Chief Justice 1922–40) in his famous book, *The New Despotism* (1929), the government had almost as little to fear from the judiciary as in the reign of Henry VIII.

4

Foreign policy during Baldwin's second administration was curiously unreal – a matter of phrases and gestures rather than achievements. Ramsay MacDonald's Geneva Protocol was rejected as an answer to the problem of security because it involved obligations too wide ranging for the dominions. The famous Russian treaty disappeared without trace, and after the police in 1927 had raided Arcos, Russia's London trading organization suspected of espionage, diplomatic relations were broken off. The question of security was dealt with by the Locarno Pact of non-aggression between France and Germany, guaranteed by Britain and Italy. Presumably the guarantors were to intervene by force if Germany invaded France or vice versa. No inter-staff conversations were possible in such unpredictable conditions. The treaty effectively precluded Britain from military collaboration with France and it entailed complete dissociation from the various French alliances with eastern Europe. Austen Chamberlain said that the Polish corridor was something for which 'no British government ever will or ever can risk the bones of a British grenadier'. The pact made little sense but did no particular harm while Germany was disarmed and the French had no appetite for another occupation of the Ruhr. However, it all seemed a great affair at the time, and Austen Chamberlain was given the Garter.

There was much talk about disarmament. People believed that armaments caused the fear of war instead of seeing that it was the fear of war which led to armaments. None of this got very far. There was the meaningless Kellog Pact in 1927 renouncing the use of war and signed by nearly all the nations in the world; Anglo-French discussions and the naval conference of 1927 between Britain, America and Japan – boycotted by France and Italy – were abortive. MacDonald made their failure one of the counts against the government in the election of 1929, alleging that Chamberlain was too favourable to France, the chief obstacle to disarmament. There was not much substance in the charge, and British expenditure on defence fell from £119 million in 1925 to £103 million in 1932, not because of pacts or treaties but because successive governments wanted to economize and there was no enemy in sight. Nobody could seriously envisage war with America or France. Germany was disarmed, Russia was in a state of enigmatic confusion and Japan was friendly. In 1919 Lloyd George had told the heads of the armed services to plan on the assumption that there would be no war within the next ten years. The 'Ten Year Rule' lasted till 1932. Much condemned in retrospect the policy was sensible enough in the circumstances of the time.

The only cloud on the horizon to which the Admiralty applied its most powerful telescope was Japan, however friendly. The Japanese Navy could dominate the Far East including India, if the British had no base for capital ships east of Malta. The Admiralty pressed for the creation of one at Singapore. Yet the danger did not seem very great, and Churchill wrote in December 1924: 'A war with Japan! But why should there be a war with Japan? I do not believe there is the slightest chance of it in our lifetime.' Churchill did not carry the day in his own party and the fortification of Singapore was one of the few defence questions treated on party political lines. It was begun at Jellicoe's suggestion in the early 1920s, discontinued by Labour in 1924, renewed by the Conservatives, though without great enthusiasm in 1926, stopped again by Labour in 1929, and begun again in 1933. Since it was a naval affair, the defence was thought of solely in terms of an attack from the sea – a decision which proved disastrous when the Japanese troops captured it from the land in 1941.

Baldwin's government had one important achievement to its credit – the rationalization and definition of relations between Britain and the dominions. The pressure came largely from Mackenzie King, Prime Minister of Canada, who erroneously believed that the Governor-General's refusal to grant him a dissolution in September 1925 was an example of 'colonial' treatment. In fact Lord Byng acted independently, though perhaps unwisely, and consulted neither the Crown nor the British government. There was also pressure from other dominion Prime Ministers, especially Hertzog for South Africa and Cosgrave for the Irish Free State, to define the constitutional position, because of the Chanak incident and the questions raised by the abortive Geneva Protocol and by Locarno. The Imperial Conference of 1926 discussed the matter and Balfour's subtle mind was invoked to produce the celebrated definition of Britain and the dominions as 'autonomous Communities within the British Empire, equal in status, in no way subordinate one to another in any aspect of their domestic or internal affairs, though united by a common allegiance to the Crown, and freely associated as members of the British Commonwealth of Nations'. This formula was made into law by the Statute of Westminster in 1931.

What did it mean? In effect the dominions, i.e. Canada, Australia, New Zealand, South Africa and the Irish Free State, became for all practical purposes independent sovereign states. Most vital test of all – they could not be bound by a British declaration of war. Dominion allegiance to the Crown became purely symbolic, and any rights reserved to the British Parliament, for example the process of amending the Canadian constitution, remained only because the dominion concerned wanted them to remain, not because Westminster wished to assert them. Governor-Generals were appointed on the advice of dominion Cabinets, and were constitutional monarchs in their own right. The British Empire was thus divided into two different juridical systems, and the change was marked by the creation of a new Secretaryship of State for the Dominions, though Amery, the Colonial Secretary, held the two offices together. The rest of the British Empire including India, which remained as it had been under a separate department, continued to be governed ultimately from London. Even the Viceroy of India, though more powerful in some respects than a colonial governor, in the end had to obey the decrees of Whitehall, but Edward Wood (later Lord Halifax) who as Lord Irwin became Viceroy in 1926 was convinced that India must be given dominion status – and sooner rather than later.

There was one anomaly in the system little noticed at the time but destined to have uncomfortable consequences forty years later. Southern Rhodesia had been governed from 1890 to 1923 by the last of the chartered companies. In that year the white settlers were allowed to choose by a referendum between joining South Africa, where Smuts would have welcomed an English-speaking fifth province of the Union, or becoming a crown colony with 'responsible government'. To the irritation of the Colonial Office the settlers chose the latter, and Southern Rhodesia became a curious hybrid between a dominion and an ordinary crown colony – self-governing for almost all practical purposes in internal affairs but subject to Whitehall for external policy. The anomaly was emphasized by the decision in 1926 to put Southern Rhodesia under the Dominion Office rather than the Colonial Office. If the country had been a 'real' dominion Britain could have wiped her hands of the racial problem as she did with South Africa. If it had been a 'real' crown colony, Britain could have effectively prevented a declaration of independence. As events turned out many years later she got the worst of both worlds – responsibility without power.

5

A general election had to be held before the end of 1929 and, after some hesitation, Baldwin chose 30 May for the date. It would be on a new franchise. In 1924 Baldwin had promised to equalize the male and female qualifications. Joynson Hicks in 1925 ratified this pledge, speaking on a private member's Bill, but it is a myth that he accidentally 'bounced' the government into the Equal Franchise Act of 1928. The Cabinet was certainly split but it is hard to see how equalization could have been avoided, and the suggestion, made by some compromisers, of twenty-five instead of twenty-one as the voting age was not practical politics. The Act of 1928 added over 5 million women to the electorate. The effect on the election of the 'flapper vote' cannot be estimated but there is no reason to believe that it damaged the Conservatives, despite the claims of its diehard opponents.

The opposition parties entered upon the election campaign in better trim than could have been guessed two years earlier. Labour had been stimulated by the abolition of 'contracting-out' into organizing its party machinery, and the loss of funds proved far less damaging than expected. MacDonald's aloofness from the General Strike enhanced his prestige after its failure. The party's divisions had been largely healed, and a series of by-election victories boded well for the next major battle. The Liberals too had recovered. The General Strike produced a final split between Asquith (now Earl of Oxford and Asquith) and Lloyd George whose attitude to it seemed equivocal and whose articles in the press inordinately pessimistic. It was a foolish matter on which to pick a quarrel and in the ensuing exchange of published letters Lloyd George won easily. On 12 June Asquith had a stroke. On 15 October he resigned the leadership: he died fourteen months later in February 1928. For some reason he has come to be called 'the last of the Romans'. It is not clear why.

Lloyd George was bound to win. He had the advantage of years, funds and health. From the end of 1926 he was in total control of the party for the first time in his life. He applied himself with all his immense energy to its rehabilitation, despite a letter in *The Times* by Lord Rosebery, as from the tomb, describing himself as an 'Old Fogey' and wondering about the source of the electoral fund: 'It surely cannot be the sale of the Royal Honours? If that were so there would be nothing in the worst times of Charles II or Sir Robert Walpole to equal it.' Undeterred, Lloyd George recruited paid speakers, keen investigators, bright intellectuals and clever propagandists. Pamphlets and leaflets appeared thick as autumnal leaves, and no less than three weekly papers were set up or taken over in order to put across Lloyd George's message. And the message was undoubtedly one that ought to have been heeded. His economists, Keynes, Hubert Henderson, Seebohm Rowntree, E. D. Simon, made much better sense than Montagu Norman or the Treasury officials.

By the time that the election was imminent several substantial books had come out of the Lloyd George machine, but the most famous which appeared less than three months before polling day was a pamphlet called *We Can Conquer Unemployment*, advocating public works, especially road development, to be financed by a loan of £145 million. The Conservatives denounced it as financially profligate. Labour alternated between saying that it had been their idea first and then that it was totally impracticable. Later MacDonald took a better electoral line, dismissing the pamphlet as a typical Lloyd George gimmick. This was a shrewd blow. Unemployment was the great question of the day. If the voters had voted only on the merits of his proposals Lloyd George ought to have won. But they voted also on the merits of the proposer. He was not trusted and never had been since the heady aftermath of the war.

The Conservative slogan based on recent traffic notices was 'Safety First' – not very inspiring nor greatly helped by Sir Waldron Smithers' dotty song 'Stanley Boy' based on a well known ditty of the day. 'Tranquillity' had worked in 1922 and something very like it in 1924, but perhaps one can be too tranquil. 'The snores of the Treasury Bench reverberate throughout the land,' said a rebellious backbencher. MacDonald attacked the government's foreign policy but a more serious liability was its domestic enactments. The Conservatives had a very respectable record but social reform in the short run usually offends more people than it pleases. The government made a major error by deferring local government reorganization until 1928 in order to combine it with Churchill's plan for derating industrial premises. The object was to reduce industrial costs and stimulate employment. The immediate effect, because of an inadequate Treasury grant to fill the gap, was to raise domestic rates, and the new assessments arrived in the householder's letterbox only a few weeks before the election.

Despite very adverse by-election figures Baldwin was encouraged by the Central Office to expect a narrow overall majority. His election tour seemed to be a great success. But Lloyd George and MacDonald received similar ovations. It was the last clear three-cornered election. Each party put up over 500 candidates. The Conservatives with over 8.6 million votes won 260 seats. Labour with 267,000 fewer votes, won, by a quirk of the electoral system, 28 more seats, a score of 288 but their position was precarious, for they won many on a split vote and by tiny majorities. The Liberals received 5.3 million votes and 59 seats – only 19 more than in 1924. They had put up more candidates than at any election since 1906 and their programme was better thought-out than that of any other party in the inter-war years, but their defeat was overwhelming and conclusive, even though they possessed for a fleeting period that double-edged weapon, the balance of power. The revival of the three party system was short-lived. At the next 'normal' election six years later the Liberal vote was down to 1.5 million and the party won only twenty seats.

Chapter Eight

THE ECONOMIC CRISIS

I

Baldwin resigned after three days to avoid being manoeuvred into a Conservative–Liberal alliance. MacDonald took office on 5 June and met Parliament three weeks later. Baldwin emphasized his hostility to the Liberals by moving an anti-free trade amendment to the Address. MacDonald's government as in 1924 was formed without Liberal aid. Twelve of his ministers had been members in 1924, five of them in the same offices. Henderson now became Foreign Secretary. MacDonald preferred Thomas but Henderson insisted that it was the Foreign Office or nothing. The episode enhanced the ill feeling of 1924. Thomas became Lord Privy Seal with special responsibility for employment. His second-in-command, the Chancellor of the Duchy of Lancaster, was a rich recent recruit from the Conservatives, Oswald Mosley, 6th Baronet, a brilliant orator, young, impetuous, impatient – destined to be the Lord Randolph Churchill of the Labour Party. Lord Sankey who had recommended coal nationalization in 1919 became Lord Chancellor, and Margaret Bondfield, Minister of Labour, was the first woman to enter the Cabinet. The most notable omission was Wheatley, one of the successes of 1924 – debarred by a financial scandal. The worst appointment was Tom Shaw to the War Office. When one of his civil servants sought ratification for some urgent action over riots in Palestine, Shaw's private secretary relayed a telephoned reply: 'Mr Tom Shaw is a pacifist and does not wish to have anything to do with war or military operations.'

When MacDonald took office there were few signs of the economic blizzard that impended. The condition of the nation was described by one of the leading economists of the day as one of 'suppressed boom'. Unemployment figures were falling slightly. It was the foreign scene that appeared to need attention. Like most Prime Ministers MacDonald welcomed escape from the humdrum of home. Leaving Henderson to deal with Europe and the League he visited America in October, the first British Prime Minister to do so. His object was to restore good relations and prepare the way for a major naval disarmament conference. At that time the Conservatives, suspicious of American hostility to the empire, tended to be more anti-American than Labour, still nostalgic for Wilsonianism long after Wilson had vanished. MacDonald got on admirably with the Republican President Hoover, although he had naturally hoped that his Democratic rival, Al Smith, would win the 1928 election. He took the chair at the London Naval Conference of January to April 1930 which achieved agreement that the American, British, Japanese ratio of 5:5:3 in capital ships should apply to cruisers, destroyers and submarines also. There were many untied loose ends and a Franco-Italian deadlock was never broken, but to the British public the conference seemed quite an achievement.

In Europe also conciliation went ahead. Henderson in Geneva was as successful as MacDonald in London – not wholly to MacDonald's pleasure. He had better relations than the Prime Minister with the French who remembered his whole-hearted support in the war, and he was trusted by the Germans. The Young Plan for German reparations and the evacuation of the Rhineland by Allied troops in 1930, five years before the deadline, attested to his diplomacy, along with the summoning of a world disarmament conference for February 1932.

The vital problem at home seemed at this time to be the question of the 'hard core' million or so victims of 'structural' unemployment – a result of the long-term decline in the profitability of the older industries, textiles, coal-mining, shipbuilding, etc. In the summer of 1929 MacDonald set up the Committee on Finance and Industry under the chairmanship of Lord Macmillan, an eminent Law Lord, to investigate. It contained among others, McKenna, Keynes and Ernest Bevin. It took evidence from many eminent figures including members of the committee itself. It did not report till early in July 1931. At the beginning of 1930 MacDonald made an innovation for which he is seldom given enough credit – the setting up of the Economic Advisory Council, a sort of 'think-tank' to provide him with alternative advice from that of the Treasury. Keynes and Bevin were also members of this body. One of the secretaries was Hubert Henderson who can be said to be the first person, independent of the Treasury, to be economic adviser to a Prime Minister.

MacDonald's tactical problem was relations with the Liberals. As in 1924 he began by treating them with aloof contempt for the first six months. He could do this while his own electoral prospects were good, but in October Wall Street crashed. The repercussions affected the world economy with unprecedented devastation. By the end of the year a major slump had obviously begun. Unemployment in January 1930 at 1,533,000 was only up by 100,000 from the corresponding date in 1929, but then it escalated – 1,731,000 in March and a million more in December. 'Structural' unemployment had been overtaken by something even more threatening. By-elections began to go strongly against the government from January 1930 onwards.

MacDonald had to reconsider his attitude to the Liberals. The idea of a deal was repugnant to him. His distrust of Lloyd George equalled Baldwin's. One of his main purposes for the last seven years had been the elimination of the Liberal Party. A bargain with them for electoral survival meant electoral reform – proportional representation or the alternative vote – and this would preserve the three-party system which he, like Baldwin, wished to destroy. He had agreed to set up in December 1929 an all-party conference under the chairmanship of Lord Ullswater, a former Speaker, to consider the law about elections. Its Liberal members pressed for an elaborate arrangement dividing the country partly into multi-member constituencies based on proportional representation and partly into single-member constituencies based on the alternative vote. MacDonald saw Lloyd George on 19 May and offered the alternative vote only. Perhaps to his relief the Labour National Executive next day turned down even that – though it was not to be the end of the story.

Meanwhile there had been an important conflict within the government about economic policy. Sir Oswald Mosley on 23 January 1930 submitted a controversial memorandum to the Cabinet on unemployment. He advocated a new administrative system largely by-passing the Treasury, and – more important – a major programme of public works, mainly roads, to be financed by a loan of £200 million. This was a leaf from the Liberal book and it was warmly approved by Keynes. The Cabinet referred it to a committee headed by Snowden, which brooded on the subject for three months of rising unemployment and then issued on 1 May a report turning down every one of Mosley's suggestions. The Cabinet neither accepted nor rejected this counter-blast but, rather surprisingly, referred it to yet another committee – a seeming rebuff to Snowden.

By this time Mosley's patience was exhausted. After two meetings with the new committee his resignation was made public on 21 May, coincidentally the day of the announcement that the National Executive had rejected electoral reform – a double rebuff to the Liberals who would have largely supported Mosley's policy. MacDonald tried to placate them by inter-party talks which began on 26 June. Baldwin, who was also invited, refused because MacDonald ruled out 'safe-guarding' (really protection) which was now becoming the Conservative panacea. The discussions with the Liberals despite their being given access to relevant official papers were conducted in an atmosphere of mistrust and bore little fruit.

Before the talks began MacDonald decided on a ministerial reshuffle announced on 5 June. Thomas, whose incapacity in the economic field had been abundantly demonstrated, went to the Dominion Office, and was replaced by Vernon Hartshorn. More significantly, a group of ministers was set up to deal with unemployment headed by the Prime Minister, with Hartshorn as deputy. Mosley had plenty of support in the party. MacDonald's new role helped to disarm criticism for the moment but it put him in the firing line if he failed to find a solution.

For many years after the Second World War it seemed almost self-evident that the way to meet a depression was to spend one's way out of it. The alarming inflation of the 1970s, however, has made it easier now to understand the resistance which this idea encountered in 1930. People were obsessed by the currency collapses in central Europe less than ten years before. 'Keynesianism', they believed, would be inflationary, and they were in a sense right. There was, however, a further aspect of the argument. It is easy in retrospect to see the controversy in a far clearer form than was actually the case at the time. The Keynesian revolution was by no means a simple affair, spelt out in a specific set of documents, nor was Keynes himself always consistent. For example, he was for a long while a free trader and was converted only late in the day to import duties.

Yet a policy of public works to stimulate demand and create purchasing power logically entailed protection although for different reasons from those of the protectionists. In the absence of tariffs it was impossible to create greater demand without at the same time stimulating imports; and there would be no counter-balancing rise in exports since nearly every other country by this time had surrounded itself by a tariff barrier. Free trade in these circumstances would have produced balance of payment problems of the kind that have plagued Britain from 1945 onwards. The policies of the parties were full of contradictions. Liberals believed in 'Keynesianism' but could no more give up free trade than the clergy could abandon the Creed. The Conservatives favoured protection, but also low taxes, Treasury economy and minimal state intervention.

The attitude of the Labour Party was equally confused. The accepted view was that capitalism was 'bad' and must be replaced by 'socialism' which was 'good' but never clearly defined. Meanwhile, since a minority government could not carry socialism, the Labour Cabinet had better make capitalism work and soften its hardships as far as possible. The best way to make it work was to follow its own rules as laid down by the high priests of the Treasury and Bank of England. Thus, paradoxically, the operation of the capitalist system was examined least critically by those who hoped to abolish it altogether. This was one reason why most Labour supporters were free traders. Orthodox capitalists still regarded protection as a heresy.

There was also the idea that tariffs were a plot to deprive the masses of cheap food. In a general way Labour felt they were there to guard the interests of 'our people' – the wage-earning class. But they were also aware that this class was anything but homogeneous. Tariffs might give jobs to the unemployed but would put up the cost of living for those in work. Quotas and restrictions in the coal industry would keep up miners' wages but make it more costly to heat the poor man's home. These conflicts of interest could be multiplied many times over.

Labour thus was divided and bewildered. It would be wrong to suppose that Snowden had his own way completely. MacDonald, though sceptical about a big loan as recommended by Mosley and Keynes, was not against a measure of investment in public works. At first he had the Ministry of Transport on his side and the trunk road programme was increased on 5 June from £13.5 million to £21 million. The total of approved public works which stood at £70 million in February 1930 had doubled by September. These were big amounts by contemporary standards but not enough to make much difference to the mounting unemployment figures. The Liberal proposal for a loan to spend another £145 million during the next two years on further road construction foundered. The Treasury was naturally against it, but the conclusive argument now came from the Ministry of Transport whose consulting engineer, Sir Henry Maybury, convinced even the Liberals that it was technically impossible. He was probably right about the practicalities of the first year, though he certainly underestimated what could have been done after that. Right or wrong his arguments won the day. Public works, contrary to much mythology, were defeated by an engineer and not by some anonymous Treasury official who had read the classics at Oxford.

The Keynes–Mosley approach had been blocked. There remained import duties. MacDonald was feeling his way in this direction but he did not press his case at all strongly. The question came to a head in the autumn over the ratification of the 'tariff truce'. This was an agreement, made in September 1929 before the crisis, among eleven countries, including the UK, not to increase tariffs before April 1931. It was subject to ratification by November 1930. William Graham, President of the Board of Trade, and Snowden strongly pressed for ratification. MacDonald disliked it but could not effectively fight it without questioning what Graham called the 'free trade policy of the movement'. He cut the crucial Cabinet meeting on 29 August which supported Snowden. The matter could be reopened in April but for eight months of economic deterioration tariffs were ruled out as a remedy.

MacDonald had made no progress at all and he approached the autumn with mounting pessimism enhanced by the spectacular tragedy of the airship R101, which on 5 October crashed into a hill near Beauvais on the first leg of a test flight to India. Almost all on board were killed including one of his closest friends, the Air Minister, Lord Thomson.

Parliament resumed on 28 October. MacDonald had a month earlier struck a somewhat shadowy bargain with Lloyd

George. The Cabinet minutes contain no reference to such a sensitive subject but Hankey, the secretary, filed a separate paper on the matter. In return for electoral reform Lloyd George would do his best to keep the government afloat for the next two years – in particular he would not oppose the second reading of a Bill to modify the Trades Dispute Act of 1927. The arrangement was secret and tentative, but the King's Speech contained references to both measures though without details. In fact electoral reform now meant the alternative vote which Liberals and Labour accepted as a compromise, and after much prodding the Labour National Executive and the Parliamentary Labour Party agreed to this in mid-December. The bargain made sense politically. By-elections had gone even worse for the Liberals than Labour. Despite the feuds among the Conservatives an early general election seemed certain to result in MacDonald's defeat.

The autumn saw one of those waves of 'coalition-mania' which every now and then sweep England at times of national despondency – or rather sweep the clubs, newspapers, the weeklies and the media. The deepening economic depression along with a 'hung' Parliament gave rise to much speculation at select dinner parties about possible combinations. There is an obscure passage in MacDonald's diary in November suggesting that he played with the idea of a national government and made a tentative suggestion to Baldwin with whom he was discussing the name of the next Viceroy of India. Baldwin turned it down: 'He said protection made that impossible and I agreed.'[1] MacDonald who was by nature suspicious believed at the time that there was a Labour cabal to oust him from the leadership. His belief, whether or not well founded, probably made him temporarily receptive to the idea of some reshuffle of political cards. To see the episode as evidence of a long-term plan realized nine months later is fanciful. When the crisis of August 1931 came he showed extreme reluctance to head a national government, and only did so at the very last moment and in circumstances quite unpredictable in November 1930.

Otherwise the year ended with little of significance to record. There was a round table conference about India, which produced no result. There was an imperial conference which provoked Snowden into an even more obdurate declaration for free trade. The divisions in the Cabinet showed no sign of being healed. Yet there were one or two glimpses of light on the horizon. The Lib–Lab 'pact' – though never openly described as such – worked remarkably well. The second readings of the Electoral and Trades Disputes Bills went through early in the New Year. True, the Liberals at the end of February moved a wrecking amendment to the latter in committee and it had to be withdrawn, not entirely to the regret of some members of the Cabinet. But in general the Liberals kept the government in office, and the Electoral Bill was carried in the Commons. The Lords, however, used their power of delay, and electoral reform, along with much else, was to founder in the deluge of the 1931 election. By March 1931 – a month in which unemployment for the first time since 1929 actually fell slightly – MacDonald could feel some reason for optimism.

2

Although the Conservatives seemed to be odds-on favourites for the next election their internal relations were anything but harmonious. From his defeat till the crisis of August 1931 Baldwin was under continuous attack. He survived, thanks to the divisions of his opponents and the reluctant loyalty of Neville Chamberlain, his only possible supplanter, but it was a narrow escape. The story is too often told in terms of a man of honour defeating the wiles of unscrupulous usurpers. Baldwin was honourable but there was good reason for the narrowness of his escape. He had lost two elections out of three, one from impetuousness, the other from apathy – or so his critics claimed. Ousted from office he was a feeble performer on the opposition front bench, too ready to accept the government's point of view. A defeated party wants a run for its money, not a master of hounds who seems to be as often as not on the side of the fox.

The election result weakened him in another way. The younger MPs who supported his social reformist outlook tended to have constituencies in the north, and this was where the Conservatives lost most ground. Harold Macmillan was defeated in Durham, and there were many similar setbacks. The diehards, based on the south – some fifty or sixty MPs – held their ground and were proportionately stronger in a parliamentary party of 260 than in one of 400. The Indian connection was similarly strengthened. The 1929 Parliament contained fifty-two members who had been officers in the army, the Colonial or the Indian Civil Service. If they had not all actually served in India they had the 'Anglo-Indian' attitude, and many more members were connected by blood or friendship with the same world. Since Baldwin's views on India were well to the left of his party's, his leadership was clearly at risk. The tariff reformers, who partly overlapped with the diehards and the Anglo-Indians, were also now much more assertive. They had hoped that Baldwin, in spite of his free trade pledge, would introduce protection by 'safe-guarding' so many areas of industry that tariffs would be almost universal. They had underestimated his honesty and perhaps the power of the free trade faction led by Churchill. Now that they were in opposition they were no longer inhibited, and they had the support of the two greatest newspaper owners of the day, Lords Beaverbrook and Rothermere. India and protection were to be the principal political bones of contention in the ensuing battle.

Baldwin's opponents began, however, with an attack on the party's central organization, especially its chairman, J. C. C. Davidson who owed his position solely to Baldwin's patronage. Skilled in subterranean intrigue but otherwise a mediocrity, he was unpopular, prickly and suspicious. He was silently sacrificed by Baldwin in May 1930 and replaced by Neville Chamberlain. This was a clever move for it made Baldwin's chief rival his effective prisoner.

The first policy problem which came up was the question of dominion status for India. Baldwin simplistically believed that the 'success' of the Irish Treaty pointed the way for India. The success may have been questionable and the analogy dubious, but the argument seemed persuasive. Baldwin had long been determined not to play the Indian card in the way that his predecessors had played the Orange card. It might win votes but it would make a peaceful settlement hopeless. He sent out Lord Irwin, who had the same views, as Viceroy in 1926, and in 1927 appointed the Commission on Indian Constitutional Reform headed by Sir John Simon. India, enshrining as it did for one of the most influential sections of Tory society a whole way of life, was an emotive issue. The *Morning Post* still printed a page of Indian news in which the whites were described as 'Indians' and the Indians as 'natives'. Baldwin ran a big risk when on 31 October 1929 he refused to dissociate himself from Irwin's declaration that his long-term aim was dominion status. 'Indian' rebelliousness led by Churchill simmered on throughout 1930. Early in 1931 he resigned from the shadow Cabinet. Churchill was on his way out for another reason. If India simmered, protection boiled over. As the party moved inexorably away from free trade Churchill who had crossed the floor of the House on that very question in 1904 became increasingly uneasy. His estrangement from the Conservative leadership was to have important consequences for the history of the party and the country.

The great battle over tariffs between the press barons and Baldwin has been retrospectively oversimplified. Like most of such struggles its edges were more blurred, its motives more confused and its results less clear cut than they seem with hindsight. Although Rothermere backed Beaverbrook's Empire Crusade launched on 10 December 1929, their attitudes were not identical. The crusade was for 'Empire Free Trade' – an ingenious Beaverbrookian phrase based on the premise that the public would accept protection only if it was called free trade. It was a repeat of Joseph Chamberlain's

Tariff Reform, mainly concerned with the dominions – above all, Canada; and it meant taxes on foreign imported food stuffs with rebates and preferences for the empire. Rothermere, however, shared his late brother Lord North-cliffe's dislike of 'stomach taxes'. He was an insular pro-tectionist – in this respect like Baldwin, though his relations with the Conservative leader were even worse than Beaver-brook's. Rothermere was an out-and-out diehard on India which Beaverbrook regarded as a distraction. At the same time, though holding views of extreme illiberality, he called himself a Liberal. Neville Chamberlain and the Conservative establishment considered him irreconcilable whereas there was some hope in Beaverbrook who at least remained a member of the Conservative Party. At one stage, though not for long, Baldwin even addressed him as 'Dear Max', but he hated him as much as he hated Rothermere, and he was soon back to the more congenial 'Dear Lord Beaverbrook' and 'Yours faithfully'.

On 18 February 1930 Beaverbrook turned the crusade into the United Empire Party and threatened to run candidates of his own. After various moves and counter-moves the matter was put to the first major test at a by-election in South Paddington where the United Empire candidate, Vice-Admi-ral Taylor, on 31 October defeated the official Conservative by 941 votes – a result which effectively neutralized a heavy victory by Baldwin at a party meeting the previous day. Baldwin's leadership was now under fire, though many of those who shot at him did not wish their aim to be directed by the press lords. Matters came to a crisis in February–March 1931. Beaverbrook decided in January to fight every by-election he could – a questionable tactic since it was likely to make the anti-Baldwinites, however fervent, hesitate before splitting the Conservative vote. However, at East Islington on 19 February the United Empire candidate pushed the official Conservative into third place, and on 19 March a crucial by-election was due in the cast-iron Tory seat of St George's Westminster. There was no Liberal or Labour candidate and the local party could not find a pro-Baldwin man willing to fight the Beaverbrook–Rothermere nominee, an obscure industrialist called Sir Ernest Petter. At this juncture Sir Robert Topping, the Principal Agent, handed Neville Chamberlain a memorandum on party feeling which was said to be strongly in favour of a new leader. On 1 March Chamberlain showed it to Baldwin – with some embarrassment, for he was himself the obvious successor, but also with the private conviction that Baldwin ought to go.

Baldwin's first instinct was to resign, and Geoffrey Dawson, editor of *The Times*, actually had a leader set up, headed 'Mr Baldwin withdraws'. His second instinct, fortified on 2 March by Bridgeman, one of the few survivors of the pro-Baldwin group of 1923, and by Davidson, was to announce that he would himself fight St George's. Chamberlain was horrified when Baldwin told him: 'S. B., you can't do that.' 'Why not?' 'Think of the effect on your successor.' Baldwin curtly replied: 'I don't give a damn about my successor.'

He was in the end dissuaded from personally contesting the seat but he resolved to fight back. Alfred Duff Cooper courageously gave up his safe candidature for Winchester and agreed to stand for St George's. Two days before the poll Baldwin at a public meeting made his famous attack on the press lords, using a phrase borrowed from his cousin, Rudyard Kipling: 'What the proprietorship of these papers is aiming at is power, and power without responsibility – the prerogative of the harlot through the ages.' A listening Tory agent buried his head in his hands and murmured 'Bang goes the harlot vote'. But all was well. Perhaps they were otherwise occupied. Duff Cooper won with a majority of 5,710. It was the most dramatic by-election in modern times.

3

The Labour government's prospects, though brighter than they had seemed during the previous year, became clouded during the early months of 1931 by the mounting deficit in the unemployment insurance fund, and the increasing burden of 'transitional benefits'. There were three varieties of unemployment pay: insurance benefits, paid from the fund, to those who had made not less than thirty contributions in the last two years; 'transitional benefits' paid by the Exchequer to those who had either made eight contributions during the last two years or thirty since first entering the scheme; and finally public assistance, the old Poor Law administered by local authorities. The burden of all three naturally rose with the rise in unemployment. Snowden regarded the effect on the budget with much alarm. The unemployment insurance fund was running more and more into debt. Its borrowing power of £50 million could be increased only by Parliament and the necessary resolutions inevitably caused a parliamentary row. The figure was raised to £60 million in August 1930, but the price was a sub-committee of the Economic Advisory Council to inquire into abuses of the system. Despite being chaired by G. D. H. Cole the sub-committee condemned it as an 'unjustifiable burden' on the Exchequer. In October MacDonald set up a Royal Commission to examine the whole question. In November the government asked to raise the figure to £70 million. The Liberals agreed but insisted that the Royal Commission should produce a series of interim reports and accelerate its consideration of transitional benefits which, estimated at £10.5 million for 1930, had actually cost £20 million, and were calculated to be £30 million for 1931.

Early in February the Conservatives moved a vote of censure against the government for its 'policy of continuous addition to the public expenditure'. The Liberals tabled an amendment calling for an independent committee to advise the Chancellor on the best way to achieve 'all possible and legitimate reductions in the national expenditure consistent with the efficiency of the services'. As the price of survival MacDonald decided to accept the amendment, for which the Conservatives also voted. A month later the committee was set up under the chairmanship of Sir George May, former secretary of the Prudential Assurance Company. It was a time-bomb that was to blow up in the face of the government nearly five months later at the worst of all possible moments.

Meanwhile, the economists' committee of the Economic Advisory Council chaired by Keynes had in October 1930 produced a report for the Cabinet on the depression, which advocated reform of unemployment insurance, balancing of the budget without extra direct taxation, public works, and a temporary revenue tariff. The latter remedy was very much after MacDonald's heart and there were signs that the most intransigent obstacle might be removed. Snowden who had already indicated a wish to go to the House of Lords as Colonial Secretary was laid low by a prostate operation. Visiting him in hospital before the budget, MacDonald noted: 'Uncanny impish aspect like that of a being a thousand years old looking young for his age.' The budget on which Snowden was singularly uninformative even to the Prime Minister contained a proposal for a land tax which nearly brought the government down, though eventually the Chancellor gave way. Clearly this was likely to be his last budget, and, with his elevation the principal barrier to a revenue tariff would go. Moreover, the party seemed more united than it had been for a long while. In February Mosley and his closest followers resigned the Labour Whip. This final breach, followed a few days later by Trevelyan's resignation from the Cabinet on a different issue, had the effect of consolidating the loyalty of the great majority.

Whatever gleams of hope on the horizon there may have been in the early summer of 1930 were abruptly extinguished by a series of disasters in Europe. In May the great Austrian bank, the Kreditanstalt, failed, setting in motion a domino effect which first shattered Germany's tottering credit, then destroyed the Labour government and finally drove Britain off the gold standard. The process was expedited by the obduracy of the French over reparations. With the connivance of Henderson they misled MacDonald at a crucial moment, though one may doubt whether anything could have saved the situation by then. 'Again and again, be it said,' wrote MacDonald, 'France is the enemy' – a sentiment which must have been re-echoed by many a Prime Minister from that day to this.

The nature of the crisis is often misunderstood. It was not a matter of budget deficits or adverse trade balances, except insofar as the latter caused the Bank of England to seek short-term loans at high interest rates in order to prevent loss of gold. The basic trouble was that for many years London had been lending 'long' and borrowing 'short'. The lending had been largely for the laudable (and profitable) purpose of financing post-war reconstruction in central Europe. The collapse in Austria made these loans impossible to recover and obliged the German banks to declare a moratorium on their international debts. London bankers with their foreign loans frozen were at the mercy of 'hot' money depositors who had no reason to keep their money in Britain if they had any doubts about sterling. In theory Britain could have done what Germany did – block foreign funds and introduce exchange control. But this would have been financial heresy in the City and would have wrecked London as a world financial centre. The only remedy, though in reality it was irrelevant, seemed to be a balanced budget which, it was believed, would restore confidence in the pound.

MacDonald had not at first appreciated how weak Britain's own position was. On 13 July 1931 the German banks suspended cash payments. Two days later the Bank of England endured heavy losses and by the end of the month a quarter of its reserves had been used up. At this juncture the May Report was issued. Nothing could have been more damaging to the pound. The committee prophesied a budget deficit of £120 million and recommended stringent cuts in expenditure of £97 million including a reduction of £67 million in unemployment pay. The report was published on 31 July, the same day that Parliament went into its summer recess, and the government made no statement of policy to mitigate the damage inevitably done in the international financial world already highly doubtful whether the gold standard could be preserved.

During the first week of August, MacDonald on holiday at Lossiemouth received two sharply contrasting pieces of advice. Keynes had been asked for his views on the May Report. He replied on 5 August that they were not fit for publication or even circulation to the EAC. He considered the report hidebound and foolish. The existing gold parity could not now be preserved. His solution was to call on the empire countries, and perhaps on South America, Asia and central Europe to adhere to a new currency which 'might be a gold unit obtained by devaluing existing units by not less than twenty-five per cent'. On 8 August MacDonald was given counsel of a very different nature. Snowden pressed for an urgent meeting of the Cabinet Economy Committee enclosing a letter from Sir Ernest Harvey, acting Governor of the Bank of England. The international financial world, Harvey said, was increasingly uneasy about the pound. The trade balance had got worse and the reports of the Macmillan and May Committees – the Labour government was bedevilled by committees – made it essential to produce a balanced budget. Major economies were necessary in order to preserve the existing parity which the Treasury, the Bank and the whole of the City regarded as sacrosanct – a view shared by most economists including some who were by inclination Keynesians.

It was inherently improbable that MacDonald would accept Keynes's diagnosis. He was not a man of original mind. Prime Ministers seldom are. To go against the orthodoxy of the entire establishment was simply not in his nature. He was patriotically convinced that the existing gold parity must be preserved. Throughout the ensuing political battle no one in the Cabinet dissented from that view, and the same went for almost the whole of the Parliamentary Labour Party. The dispute was about the nature and extent of the cuts needed to restore foreign confidence, not about the desirability of the objective. Devaluation was regarded by nearly all politicians of whatever party as a major disaster. They turned out to be wrong but this should not blind us to the unanimity with which they judged the situation.

Snowden's letter brought MacDonald back to London on Monday, 10 August. Next day Harvey with his colleague, Sir Edward Peacock, repeated his written warning, adding that without drastic action the situation could not be held for more than a fortnight. They asked to put the position to the leaders of the other parties and MacDonald agreed. Returning respectively from Aix, Perthshire and Norfolk, Baldwin, Chamberlain and Samuel were back in London by 13 August and saw the bankers and the Prime Minister that day. These meetings openly reported in the press were later stigmatized as 'secret consultations' by the anti-MacDonald ministers in the Cabinet. Meanwhile, the Economy Committee had held its first meeting on 12 August. It was to hold three more in the next six days (13, 17 and 18 August). The Treasury, outdoing even the May Committee, estimated that, unless current policies were changed, the budget deficit next year would be not £120 million but £170 million. After much tortured argument the committee decided to recommend the Cabinet to increase taxation by £89 million and cut expenditure by £78.5 million. This fell just short of balancing the budget but presumably was considered to be near enough. The cut was to be achieved principally by a reduction of £48.5 million in unemployment pay – the Treasury had pressed for £67 million – and the rest was to be made up by cuts in teachers' salaries, and in pay for the police and the armed forces. The actual rates of unemployment benefit were not lowered. The reduction was to be achieved by higher contributions, by shortening the benefit period to twenty-six weeks and by unloading £20 million of 'transitional benefits' on to the ratepayer. These proposals were made at a time of falling prices (see page 124).

The exact status of the committee's report to the Cabinet became the subject of much recrimination. Henderson who was to be the leading dissident, along with Graham, and who wished later to repudiate any association with cuts in the 'dole' claimed that it was only a 'preliminary examination' and that he was committed to nothing till he had seen 'the complete picture'. The acting Cabinet secretary pointed out that no such reservations were made at the time and that the report was unanimous. Professor Marquand, MacDonald's biographer, adds that it is hard to see what else could be needed to complete the picture. Henderson may have had mental reservations, but if so he failed to articulate them.

On 19 August the report was presented to the full Cabinet which sat with short intervals from 11 A.M. to 10.30 P.M. Much of the time was spent on discussing a revenue tariff either as a substitute for or addition to the committee's tax proposals. The opposition of the Chancellor was, however, decisive. The other contentious issue was unemployment benefit, especially the proposal to put 'transitional benefit' on the rates. The Cabinet turned it down for the time being and set up a sub-committee to consider other ways of reducing the cost of unemployment. MacDonald and Snowden were authorized to confer with the opposition leaders next morning, for the combined opposition of Conservatives and Liberals would be fatal. Chamberlain and Hoare represented the Conservatives, Baldwin characteristically having returned to Aix, while Samuel and Maclean represented the Liberals, since Lloyd George was ill. MacDonald presented them with a provisional programme – cuts of £78.5 million and increased taxation of £89 million. Chamberlain's reaction was that the tax increases were too high and the cuts too low; they should not be less than the £97 million recommended by the May Report which had assumed a deficit of £50 million less than the £170 million now predicted by the Treasury. Both he and Samuel were convinced that a cut in the rate of unemployment benefit was essential. Snowden agreed, observing that the rise in benefits and fall in prices had made the unemployed thirty-six per cent better off than seven years earlier.

The opposition leaders agreed to confer with their

colleagues. Meanwhile MacDonald on the same day had further meetings which made his political problem even more intractable. The first, with the Consultative Committee of the Parliamentary Party, was inconclusive. The second was with the National Executive and the General Council of the TUC. The latter expressed the strongest opposition to any cuts in benefit. The Cabinet met again at 8.30 P.M. The sub-committee on unemployment pay had predictably failed to discover a painless path to economy, and its deliberations still left some £19–20 million to be found somehow. MacDonald told the Cabinet that this would not do and that even the £78.5 million proposed by the Economy Committee was regarded as insufficient by the opposition leaders. At 9.30 P.M. the Cabinet adjourned for the Economy Committee to meet a deputation from the TUC including Walter Citrine and Ernest Bevin. They wholly repudiated the policy which the Cabinet was pursuing. There should be no reductions in unemployment pay; contributions should be replaced by a graduated levy on profits, incomes and earnings; new taxation should be introduced on unearned incomes; and the sinking fund should be suspended. The policy had many advantages as a long-term remedy. It was not dictated solely by working-class interest, though opposition to a cut in the dole naturally had much class feeling behind it. But, whatever their general merit, the proposals could not meet the government's imme-diate problem.

Bevin was prepared to meet it by devaluation. In an addendum to the Macmillan Report he preferred devaluation to deflation. The report of the General Council of the TUC on the financial situation in August took the same line – not surprisingly, as Bevin had drafted it. The deputation which met the Economy Committee on 20 August did not, however, argue for devaluation. The argument was still confined to the means of preserving the existing exchange rate. The most that Bevin did was to express well justified scepticism about Snowden's dire warnings of the consequences of going off the gold standard.

Yet even if the TUC's delegation had come out in favour of devaluation they would have got nowhere. The Cabinet, though split on methods and amounts, was united on the need to save the pound. It was clear that foreign confidence in sterling could only be preserved, if at all, not merely by the balancing of the budget but by balancing it in a particular way – by reduced expenditure rather than increased taxation. Moreover, on top of an imminent financial crisis – the bankers' fortnight was nearly up – there emerged a major internal political crisis. The government could not survive a united opposition onslaught. Chamberlain and Samuel would certainly not accept anything less than the £78.5 million cut provisionally proposed but not yet agreed by the Cabinet, and an essential part of it was a saving of £43.5 million in unemployment insurance.

MacDonald had a moment of doubt after the interview with the TUC delegation. 'Are we to go on?' he noted in his diary, adding, 'Henderson never showed his ignorance and vanity more painfully.' Henderson was basically a TUC man imbued with that deep sense of 'brotherhood' so incomprehensible to non-trade unionists. MacDonald and Snowden had come into the Labour Party by a different route. Henderson had gone along reluctantly with the Economy Committee's proposals till the TUC delegation made its counter-attack. He now went over to the other side. MacDonald, however, after sleeping on the events of 20 August, decided to fight. 'If we yield now to the TUC,' he wrote, 'we shall never be able to call our bodies or souls or intelligences our own.' He persuaded the Cabinet next day (Friday, 21 August) to reject the TUC's alternative plan but he could not get them to accept the Economy Committee's cut of £43.5 million in unemployment insurance. The most they would go to was £22 million, which meant a total reduction of £56 million compared with the committee's £78.5 million.

Harvey and Peacock, informed by MacDonald that afternoon, replied that it was not enough. Moreover, they had some new and alarming news: the pound could not last more than four days unless Britain obtained large credits from New York and Paris. The problem of a vague general lack of confidence in sterling was thus abruptly transformed into the very specific problem of obtaining at short notice a major international loan. MacDonald then saw the opposition leaders, Chamberlain and Hoare for the Conservatives, Samuel and Maclean for the Liberals. They at once declared that £56 million was inadequate – they had been told twenty-four hours earlier that the figure would be £78 million – and said that if this proposal was final they would eject the government at the first opportunity. At a further meeting early next day (22 August) they reiterated their view, observing that the crash would come before Parliament could meet, that it was MacDonald's job to avert it and that if he would take the necessary steps they would give him all support in his present or a reconstructed Cabinet.

If MacDonald had been the avid coalition-maker of Labour mythology he would have jumped at this chance to 'betray' the party and dish his dissidents. On the contrary, he did everything he could during that blazing hot weekend of 22 and 23 August to persuade the Cabinet to remain in office and acquiesce in cuts to which even Henderson and his followers had no alternative remedy; they merely said in effect that if it had to be done it must be done by others – an attitude which exasperated both MacDonald and Snowden. There were alternative long-term policies as adumbrated by Bevin and Citrine. There were other ways of balancing the budget, e.g. heavier taxes and lower cuts. But at this stage there was only one way of getting foreign credits – a reduction of expenditure by at least £78 million of which £42 million or so must be found from unemployment benefit. In practice this could only be by a ten per cent reduction in rates. Nothing less would satisfy the opposition leaders and, unless they were satisfied, New York would not lend the money. Even if they were, the loan was by no means a foregone conclusion.

It is not surprising that conflicting accounts of what

happened, not only that weekend but during the previous ten days, have survived to perplex the historian. The recollections of twenty people, some of them elderly, all of them tired, with tempers frayed, arguing amidst clouds of tobacco smoke for hour after hour in a heat-wave, are not likely to be consistent or reliable. Proposals and counter-proposals, amendments, formulae drafted and then abandoned, floated across the Cabinet room table. It must have been hard to remember what one had said oneself the previous day or even a few hours earlier, let alone what others said. The Cabinet record inevitably gives only a part of the story. The reminiscences written by ex-ministers after the break-up of the government have to be treated with scepticism. MacDonald, however, kept a day-to-day diary and his biographer's account based partly on a critical use of it and first published in 1977, is as reliable as anything we are likely to get.

At the Cabinet meeting on the morning of 22 August MacDonald reported his conversations with the bankers and the opposition and implored the Cabinet to accept the additional £20 million of economies in unemployment benefit. They refused, but grudgingly allowed MacDonald to find out whether, if they did agree, £20 million would satisfy the opposition. MacDonald saw Chamberlain and Samuel and received the answer that this depended on the attitude of the financial authorities who would have to raise the loan. At the afternoon Cabinet MacDonald secured permission to authorize Harvey to discuss the matter with George L. Harrison, Chairman of the Federal Reserve Bank, and with J. P. Morgan and Co., the British government's American bankers. This would take time and the Cabinet would meet at 7 P.M. next day to take a final decision on the proposed economies.

Meanwhile, the King returned by the night train from Balmoral, and Baldwin left Aix for London. MacDonald saw the King at 10.30 on Sunday, 23 August. According to MacDonald's diary, the King, after hearing the facts and of the possibility of the Cabinet resigning, told him that he

157

(MacDonald) was the only man who could pull the country through. He said that he would see the opposition leaders and advise them strongly to support him. MacDonald's diary thus suggests that the traditional view that the King's attitude was determined by the advice of Samuel whom he saw alone at 12.30 and who certainly did argue for a national government needs to be modified – also that the absence of Baldwin, who could not be found till the afternoon and who was much less coalition-minded, was not especially significant. MacDonald's diary also makes it clear that he personally did not at this stage think a coalition to be feasible and told the King so. If the Cabinet broke up he had every intention of going out too.

It was not, however, by any means certain that the Cabinet would break up. Both the King and the opposition leaders regarded acceptance of the cuts by the existing government as much the most desirable solution – any other as second best. The Cabinet met at 7 P.M. but had to wait till after nine o'clock for the arrival of Harrison's telegram which MacDonald read out. It was non-committal, offering at best a short-term loan of $100 million to $150 million and significantly asking at the end, to the indignation of some ministers, whether the full programme of cuts 'will have the sincere approval and support of the Bank of England and the City generally'. MacDonald consulted Harvey who was waiting outside and conveyed his view to the Cabinet that the programme would suffice and would bring the necessary City support to reassure New York.

The moment for decision had come. MacDonald used all his eloquence to persuade ministers that, in the words of the Cabinet minute, 'a scheme which inflicted reductions and burdens in almost every other direction but made no appreciable cut in Unemployment Insurance Benefit would alienate much party support and lose the Party their moral prestige which was one of their greatest assets'. His opponents did not dispute that the pound must be preserved and could not dispute that acquiescence in the cuts was now the only way to do so. They simply had the 'gut reaction' that they never could assent to this blow to the unity of 'the movement', this betrayal of working-class solidarity. MacDonald carried the day but by the narrowest of margins – eleven to nine. And it was clear that some of the nine would resign. MacDonald announced that he would at once see the King, and the ministers put their resignations in his hands. He would advise the King to consult next day with Baldwin, Samuel and himself. He left for Buckingham Palace at 10.10. The King strongly urged him not to resign and agreed to the conference next day. MacDonald returned at 10.40 to Downing Street, said that he had told the King they could not go on as a united Cabinet and that the conference would take place on Monday. After the ministers had gone he talked to Baldwin, Chamberlain and Samuel. The two latter urged him not to resign. Baldwin said nothing. The impression gained by the opposition leaders was that MacDonald had finally decided to throw in his hand.

MacDonald's diary, however, suggests that he had not in fact closed the door. Just what went on in his mind that night no one can say, but he took, or half took, a far-reaching decision. When the King next morning pressed him to remain and when Baldwin and Samuel offered to serve under him he agreed to remain in office as head of a national government to last for a few weeks and tide over the crisis. It would be a government of individuals and it would implement the cuts agreed upon by the majority of the Labour ministers. There would then be an election fought not by the government but by the parties which would revert to their ordinary roles. MacDonald returned to Downing Street and announced the decision to the Cabinet who agreed that their resignations should now be submitted formally to the King. A few polite remarks were uttered and the Cabinet recorded its appreciation of MacDonald's 'great kindness, consideration and courtesy when presiding over its meetings'.

An acrid cloud of mythology and misunderstanding has shrouded the events of the crisis of 1931. It is as well to remember some of the things that did *not* happen. There was no long-matured 'plot' on MacDonald's part to put himself at the head of a national government. To deduce it from casual stories relating to a different context or from MacDonald's preference for the company of Lady Londonderry to that of Mrs Sidney Webb is absurd. No proof has ever been produced, and all the evidence attests to MacDonald's extreme reluctance to take the step.

It is not true that the battle in the Cabinet turned on a conflict between Treasury orthodoxy and enlightened Keynesianism. On the contrary the opponents of the larger cuts were just as convinced of the need to balance the budget and save the pound as MacDonald and Snowden. Still less is it right to convey the impression, as both Sir Ivor Jennings and Harold Laski have in their writings, that the majority of the Cabinet repudiated the cuts. The majority, admittedly a narrow one, voted in favour, however reluctantly – a point of some importance later.

Nor is it true that either the King or MacDonald acted 'unconstitutionally'. The word is usually suspect, being too often merely a term of abuse for an action which the user dislikes on other grounds. The King could have accepted MacDonald's resignation and invited Baldwin to form a government (the suggestion made in some quarters that he should have invited Henderson is ridiculous). MacDonald could have insisted on resigning – whether or not retaining the leadership of the Labour Party – despite pressure from the King to remain. It can be argued that these might have been wiser decisions – though not very plausibly. But they would not have been any more or less 'constitutional' than the course adopted. To say, as Laski did, 'Mr MacDonald was as much the personal choice of George V as Lord Bute was the personal choice of George III' is a travesty. Without the support of the opposition leaders, which meant support of a majority of the House, the King could not – and never would – have pressed MacDonald to form a national government. As for alleged 'unconstitutionality' on MacDonald's part, the charge in the end depends on the assumption that only a leader of a party can accept the premiership. Setting aside the fact that MacDonald was still leader of his party, one can simply reply that the appointments of Lloyd George in 1916 and Winston Churchill in 1940 show that this doctrine is no part of the British constitution.

Finally, the crisis was not brought on by a 'bankers' ramp'. If it is a 'ramp' to decline to lend money to a dubious debtor except on conditions which safeguard the creditor's interests, then no doubt the word is applicable, but this is not its usual meaning. If it was, it could be applied to almost any loan transaction.

Chapter Nine

THE NATIONAL GOVERNMENT

I

By the late afternoon of Tuesday, 25 August 1931 the new Cabinet had been formed. There were only ten members – the smallest peacetime Cabinet since Disraeli's in 1874. The four Labour ministers, MacDonald, Snowden, Sankey and Thomas retained their posts. There were four Conservatives; Baldwin (Lord President), Chamberlain (Health), Cunliffe-Lister (Board of Trade), Hoare (India). The Liberals had two places, both near the top of the tree: Lord Reading and Herbert Samuel being respectively Foreign and Home Secretaries. The Conservatives had only twenty-one out of forty-six ministerial posts despite their preponderance in the House. MacDonald made little effort to secure support from the Labour Party. 'Strange eerie feeling,' he noted when the new ministers were sworn in. 'We are like marooned sailors on a dreary island.' Whether from exhaustion or resentment he seemed indifferent to his old supporters. He cut the crucial meeting of the parliamentary party on 28 August, which elected Henderson as leader and adopted the full Bevin/Citrine policy. This was a repudiation not merely of the £78 million economy programme accepted by a narrow majority of the Cabinet but of the £56 million which had been accepted by the minority too. However, on the same day at similar party meetings the Liberals with one dissentient and the Conservatives unanimously declared their support for the new government.[1]

On 8 September Parliament reassembled. The short session that followed was terminated by dissolution on 7

October. It was one of acrimony and recrimination. The New National Economy Bill enacted the cuts agreed by the majority of the Labour Cabinet. In the original Bill all public employees suffered a reduction of ten per cent except the police who got off with five per cent and school-teachers who for some reason had their salaries sliced by fifteen per cent. The measure was fiercely contested. In the end it was agreed that no one should lose more than ten per cent. MacDonald hit hard and his opponents hit back even harder. Cabinet secrets often in a highly garbled form were revealed with reckless intemperance. 'The first Labour Government was destroyed by a Red Letter, the second by a Bankers' Order,' declared Hugh Dalton. The 'plot' theory and the 'bankers' ramp' were countered by accusations of 'funk' and desertion of posts in the hour of peril. It was a bitter struggle in which each side had cause for grievance.

The change of government did not save the pound. Keynes had been right when he told MacDonald early in August that the case was hopeless. A loan of £80 million was negotiated on 28 August, but the reserves continued to slip away. No one could lose by selling sterling: it was not going to go up, whatever happened. British loans to Germany remained frozen and foreign depositors were as worried as ever about their money. The final blow to confidence came when the navy – that symbol of British prestige – 'mutinied' at Invergordon on 15 September. It was a mild sort of mutiny but the fact remains that the men on the lower deck refused to obey orders as a protest against reductions in pay which were announced on the radio before any official communication had been made to them and which in some cases amounted to more than ten per cent. Discipline was soon restored but the Board of Admiralty quickly withdrew any cuts above ten per cent. The run on the pound began to accelerate. Between 16 and 18 September the Bank of England lost £43 million. This time there was no hope of a loan and the government decided that there was no option but to go off gold. On 21 September 1931 the Gold Standard

(Amendment) Bill was passed through all its stages. The pound fell at once from $4.86 to $3.80. After sinking to $3.23 it rose to fluctuate around $3.40. The economic situation at once improved. Many other countries including the dominions, Scandinavia and Japan followed Britain's example, but the principal European countries did not, and British exports received a boost. The gold standard countries raised their tariffs, but Britain riposted by abandoning free trade, thus preserving the improvement in balance of payments. By April 1932 the crisis was over, and the foundation of a boom which reached its height in 1937 had been laid.

From the end of August onwards the date of the next general election was the principal topic of political discussion. MacDonald's new government had been formed on the assumption that it would simply carry the necessary legislation to deal with the emergency and balance the budget. Thereafter it would bow itself out and MacDonald would retire, leaving the parties to go to the polls on their appropriate platforms. It was a government of 'individuals' not a coalition of parties, and it was not expected to last. But the virulence with which Labour repudiated its policies, although the majority of the late Cabinet had supported them, gave MacDonald second thoughts. He had not expected such a storm. The result of a three-cornered political fight under the rules of the first-past-the-post system was unpredictable as the examples of 1922, 1923 and 1929 showed: and a Labour victory or a deadlock would be fatal to the pound. On 5 September he wrote to Baldwin wondering whether the national government should not go on rather longer than planned. The furious scenes in Parliament enhanced his doubts about an election. And when could one say that the emergency was over? The new budget and the economies did not end it, witness the fresh run on sterling and the abandonment of the gold standard, which of course gave Labour a powerful debating point. Now that the pound was 'floating' it could be argued that a 'sound' government was even more necessary and a general election even more dangerous than ever. The Liberals who had their own reasons for regarding an appeal to the electorate with apprehension endorsed this attitude.

The argument could, however, be stood on its head. It was equally plausible to maintain that the economy would recover only if there was a government which had a clear majority and the prospect of years rather than months in office. The Conservatives wanted an early election in order to enact tariffs – their favourite panacea. This brought them up against Samuel but an unexpected development occurred on 15 September when Sir John Simon, at odds for some time with the party leadership, came out publicly in favour of an emergency tariff and persuaded twenty-nine Liberal MPs to support him. On 3 October he announced the creation of a breakaway group, the Liberal National Party which repudiated the leadership of Lloyd George and Samuel. Conservative pressure for an election mounted. They reckoned that they could probably win it on their own. If MacDonald was Prime Minister the result was a certainty. They were further persuaded by a Labour argument which had been imprudently publicized by Graham in an article in the *Daily Express* on 31 August. Assuming wrongly that the national government could not hold an election till after the budget of April 1932 he gloated over the likely decline of Conservative support. The voters, he said, had a short memory. They would soon forget about August 1931 and would be influenced by the disasters which he confidently predicted for the ensuing six months.

MacDonald drifted amidst these shifting currents and uncertain breezes. He did not wish to battle against his old friends of the 'Movement' to which he still belonged. Ought he to proffer his resignation? The King, stern voice of duty, said he would not accept it. On 29 September MacDonald, along with the Labour members who still served under him, was expelled from the Labour Party, against the advice of Henderson. It cannot have come as a shock, but the sudden crystallization of a fluid situation shook him badly. He decided on an early election. The Cabinet after endless haggling agreed that there should be a very general manifesto signed by the Prime Minister with each party putting forward its own views. Many Conservatives hoped that Samuel would resign. He nearly did, and he was strongly urged to do so from the other side of the fence by the invalid Lloyd George who bitterly opposed an election. The Liberals were thus divided three ways: Simonites who soon became merged with the Conservatives; Samuelites from whom the modern Liberal Party derives its descent; and Lloyd Georgeites, a tiny group who belonged or were related to the Welsh Wizard's family – a sad and petulant ending to a great tradition.

None of this affected the election. Parliament was dissolved on 7 October 1931 and polling day was announced for 27 October. There can be little doubt, despite the non-existence of psephologists in those days, that MacDonald's reluctant lead was a major element in the ensuing landslide. Then, as often before and since, MPs were not a guide to public sentiment. The electorate was scared, and rallied to a man who, as it seemed, had sacrificed party for country. No Prime Minister in all British history has ever gained a greater majority.

The results were on any view astonishing. The various government parties won 14.5 million votes to Labour's 6.6 million. The Conservatives had 471 seats, the Simonites 35, the Samuelites 33, MacDonald's National Labour group amounted to 13. The Labour Party was slaughtered, winning only 46 seats. Lloyd George's family group won four seats and the old ILP got six. George Lansbury alone survived among the ex-ministers who had repudiated MacDonald and he was at once elected leader of the now exiguous official opposition. Labour statistically was back to 1918.

The Conservatives constituted over eighty-five per cent of the national government's support in the House of Commons. Proportionately this was not much more than before the election (seventy-five per cent) but they now had an overwhelming absolute majority and no longer depended on Liberals and national Labour. Although MacDonald, doubtful and depressed despite the destruction of his enemies, saw himself as a Conservative prisoner, he possessed enough of the residual power of his office to give the Cabinet a national flavour. Only eleven out of twenty were Conservatives. Baldwin was Lord President, and none of the others had key positions except Neville Chamberlain whom MacDonald reluctantly accepted for the Exchequer. Notable Conservative omissions were Leo Amery whom MacDonald disliked for his fanaticism over tariffs, Winston Churchill who had put himself out of court over India and Austen Chamberlain who waived his claim. Three of the four national Labour ministers held the same posts as before, including Sankey on the Woolsack. Snowden, who did not contest his seat, went to the House of Lords as Lord Privy Seal. There were three Samuelites and two Simonites, the leaders being respectively Home and Foreign Secretaries.

MacDonald was wrong if he seriously hoped to keep Neville Chamberlain at the Ministry of Health. The Conservative party had fought the election principally on the tariff question and Chamberlain had tariff reform in his blood. Baldwin did not press for much but he could not fail to insist on the second man in his party becoming Chancellor. MacDonald was lukewarm on free trade and lukewarm on tariffs, but he was most anxious to keep his government 'national' and not to lose the Samuelites. He could not block the Import Duties Bill enacting a ten per cent tariff and carried in February 1932; but, thanks to the ingenuity of Lord Hailsham, Secretary of State for War, a formula was found allowing the dissident Liberal free traders to 'agree to differ', thus abrogating the usual role of Cabinet collective responsibility. The Conservatives who had hoped that Samuel would resign were disappointed, for he was greatly disliked (Sir Robert Vansittart quoted to Baldwin the old song: 'It ain't exactly what 'e sez. It's the nasty way 'e sez it'), but they did not have to wait long. In July and August an imperial economic conference was held in Ottawa. Baldwin aided by Chamberlain led the British delegation. After protracted and bitter haggling imperial preference of a sort was agreed. Neville Chamberlain saw in it the realization of his father's ideal of empire unity, although in fact dominion nationalism, finally institutionalized in the Statute of Westminster which had been passed only a few months earlier, was beyond the point of no return. The days when the workshop of the world supplied manufactured goods to her colonies in return for raw materials and food had long vanished. The dominions now wanted to protect their own industries and the British their own agriculture. But Ottawa, though essentially a symbolic arrangement, drove out the Liberal free traders – perhaps just because it was symbolic. Snowden went with them and vented his spleen against MacDonald in a series of sour and sneering speeches. Economic historians have debated ever since, without any clear verdict, the effect of tariffs on the British economy. The answer is probably very little.

Meanwhile, in April 1932, Neville Chamberlain had introduced the first of his six budgets – a number surpassed only by Lloyd George in the twentieth century. Snowden's emergency budget of the previous September had raised income tax from 4s 6d (22½p) to 5s (25p). Chamberlain did not change it but made further cuts in expenditure, including police pay which was now reduced by the full ten per cent. His most notable economy was achieved by the conversion, on a basis that was voluntary but reinforced by patriotic appeals, of nearly £2,000 million of War Loan from five per cent to three and a half per cent. Only a handful of stock holders took their money and invested it elsewhere.[2] There was an immediate saving of £23 million p.a. and, by 1936, as a result of further reductions in interest rates, the taxpayer had been relieved of an annual sum varyingly estimated between £86 million and £131 million. These measures had a mildly inflationary effect, and so contributed to economic recovery, although they were adopted more in the spirit of Scrooge than Keynes and their main object was to help the taxpayer.

In 1934 income tax was lowered to 4s 6d (22½p). At the same time an effort was made to reverse the economies of 1931. Unemployment benefit was brought back to its pre-crisis level, and the reductions in public sector pay were halved. Chamberlain announced that *Great Expectations* had succeeded *Bleak House.* A year later the full figures for public salaries were restored. Unemployment which had reached a peak of just under 3 million in January 1933 fell steadily to 1.7 million by January 1937, though its incidence was extremely uneven. In South Wales, Scotland and the north of England there was little improvement, but in the Midlands and the south the scene was very different; in Coventry the percentage of insured workers unemployed in 1934 was 5.1 per cent, in Jarrow it was 67.8 per cent. By 1935 industrial production was up to 110 (1929: 100) and in 1937 it reached 124. Although average wages had fallen by three per cent, the cost of living had fallen by thirteen per cent. The government had been forced into devaluation and a managed currency; it had drifted into cheap money; it had consciously espoused tariff reform. These were major changes from the policies of the 1920s. How much they contributed to the prosperity of the economy is anyone's guess. If they did, it was by accident rather than by design. It is just as likely that the revival was a cyclical phenomenon which would have occurred anyway, as happened in most of the industrial countries of the world despite a diversity of policies or non-policies.

MacDonald never became the complete puppet Prime Minister that his bitter Labour enemies liked to depict. Even after the Samuelite secession he was able to keep the Conservatives from securing the share of offices to which their numbers would have entitled them, if the Cabinet had been composed on the basis of proportionality. They now had thirteen out of nineteen. Baldwin doubled the offices of Lord President and Lord Privy Seal – not an arduous task since both were sinecures. Two Samuelites were replaced by a Conservative and a Simonite. A third, Sir Donald Maclean (father of the Communist spy), had died in July and was succeeded by the Conservative Lord Irwin whose term as Viceroy of India had ended.

Nevertheless, the Liberal resignations were a blow to MacDonald. It was just plausible to talk of a national government when two of the three political parties which had traditions and organizations of their own supported it. It was no longer plausible after September 1932. The Liberal nationals were indistinguishable from the Conservatives. As for national Labour, it denoted not a party but a small group of MacDonald's personal adherents. The Prime Minister had a fairly free hand over foreign policy which was his speciality. The Foreign Secretary, Simon, resembled the proverbial Dr Fell, whom people did not like though why they could not tell. He was not going to get Conservative support in a clash with the Prime Minister. On India too MacDonald had his way at the second Round Table Conference ending in December 1931. He was able to declare that the commitment to an all-India federation would not be affected by a review of the system of provincial devolution, even though the latter would be enacted first.

There were, however, many matters on which MacDonald lost. The secession of the Samuelites was itself one. He would have preferred a compromise on tariffs but could not block the results of Ottawa. Then he was obliged in 1933 to accept Neville Chamberlain's proposal to tax the cooperative societies, although this touched a sensitive Labour nerve and could be regarded by enemies as the betrayal of a personal pledge at the election. He had also to give up the land tax clauses of Snowden's last budget. They were on the statute book but had not been activated and were not likely to be by a national government. None the less, their repeal in 1934 was a symbolic Conservative repudiation of Labour policies, bound to embarrass a Prime Minister who still tried to think of himself as Labour.

2

The Cabinet of 1931–5 faced two major external problems and a minor one. These were first the inter-related issues of disarmament, the League and international relations; secondly India; thirdly Ireland. The government got nowhere on the first of these. From 1931 onwards authoritarian nationalism, whether described as fascism, communism or some other 'ism', moved more and more into the ascendancy in Japan, Italy, Germany and Russia. Its appeal in Britain was very small. Mosley, who finally broke with the Labour Party in February 1931 and formed his 'New Party', lost every one of the twenty-five seats contested at the general election. Thenceforth, ambitious, impatient and angry he moved ever nearer to what his biographer describes as 'that abyss where dark spirits, unknown to Westminster, luxuriated in an underworld of fantasy and frustration and from which, once drawn in, there could be no escape unless society itself exploded'.[3] Society did not explode and the British Union of Fascists formally inaugurated on 1 October 1932 never cut much ice. Society also failed to explode in America or France, although both Jacques Doriot's Parti Populaire Français and Colonel de la Rocque's Parti Social Français made some headway.

Russia, Italy and Japan had been under one party or authoritarian rule for several years. Germany in 1931 was still a parliamentary democracy but its stability was very doubtful. Both Germany and Japan were more seriously hit by the economic crisis than any of the other major powers, and Japan, determined to riposte to a Chinese boycott of her goods, was the country that first broke the League Covenant by invading Manchuria in September 1931 and setting up the puppet state of Manchukuo in March 1932. At the end of January 1932 a second Japanese force based on the inter-national settlement at Shanghai marched into the suburb of Chapei which went up in flames. There were strong argu-

171

ments for restoring order in an area of banditry, chaos and confusion, where the Chinese government's writ no longer ran but the incursion into Chapei was indefensible. In any case, however, Britain and France, the only powers that mattered in the League, were in no position to take action even if they had wanted to at the height of a world financial crisis. Much futile huffing and puffing ensued. In February 1933 Japan gave notice to leave the League. The episode was invested later with a somewhat spurious significance. It is a myth that Japan could have been brought to heel by an Anglo-American blockade, that Britain let America down by refusing to cooperate and that 'collective security' was thus pusillanimously abandoned. Britain's navy was weak, Singapore was still unfortified, and America never had the slightest intention of jeopardizing her share in Japanese trade. The only difference between London and Washington was whether to make a mild protest or a strong one. Since no action was intended anyway, MacDonald's preference for mildness had something to be said for it.

A more serious problem was Germany. On 2 February 1932 the long promised Disarmament Conference began in Geneva, the culmination of years of work by the Preparatory Commission, itself a product of the alleged 'obligation' incurred by the victors at Versailles to disarm to the level imposed on Germany in 1919. MacDonald reflected much British opinion across the parties in regarding this as a great occasion. Within two years it was as dead as the most inanimate doornail. The French demanded 'security' to avoid yet another German invasion, and argued either for an 'international police force' or the preservation of Germany's military inferiority. Much ingenuity was spent on 'qualitative' disarmament – the reduction of weapons claimed to be 'aggressive' – but no one could decide on a definition. All this took place against a background of the visible disintegration of the Weimar Republic, and the rising chauvinism of the Nazi movement. Brüning, the last peace-minded German Chancellor, fell in May 1932. After a series of obscure and convulsive intrigues accompanied by riots, intimidation and violence, Hitler became Chancellor on 30 January 1933. On 14 October Germany withdrew from the conference and from the League. In the course of only two years the basic assumptions on which Britain conducted her diplomacy had been irretrievably destroyed.

The second major problem was India. The Government of India Act of 1919 had envisaged a constitutional inquiry ten years later. Baldwin, deeply conscious of what he believed to be the lessons of the Irish experience, brought it forward and set up a Commission in 1927 under the Chairmanship of Sir John Simon. Baldwin unwisely agreed that the commission should be drawn only from the two Houses of Parliament, thus excluding any Indian members. The gigantic report which appeared in June 1930 was naturally ill-received in the sub-continent. Even before it came out the Viceroy on 31 October 1929 had proclaimed the government's intention to be the attainment of dominion status. The Simon Report favoured the replacement of dyarchy by complete local self-government subject to emergency powers being retained by the Governor. On the more important problem of central government Simon was obscure, indefinite and ambiguous. There was no mention of dominion status.

To make further progress MacDonald set up an India constitutional conference, known soon as the Round Table Conference. This opened on 12 November 1930 and consisted of sixteen representatives from the British Parliament, sixteen from the princely states and fifty-seven from British India. It was boycotted by Gandhi's Congress Party. Its main achievement was to put federalism, hitherto regarded as a distant possibility, high on to the agenda of constitutional reform. The problem was to produce a central government which could meet the needs of some 560 semi-feudal states in separate treaty relationship with the Crown and those of British India divided into eleven provinces themselves often sharply split on 'communal' i.e. religious, caste or racial lines. The final session of the first of the three meetings of the

Round Table Conference took place on 19 January 1931. MacDonald committed his government in general terms to a wide measure of provincial self-government and to a central executive responsible to a federal legislature. It was Churchill's attack on this plan in the House followed by Baldwin's defence that finally caused his resignation from the Shadow Cabinet on 27 January.

Churchill now engaged in a campaign against concession to India, which lasted over four years and did him great harm. At the beginning, however, he believed that he spoke for a majority of his party. No one can be sure that he was wrong. Baldwin was very unpopular at the time, and his famous counter-blast to the press lords still lay ahead. Gandhi's behaviour infuriated most Britons, and Churchill struck a responsive chord when he referred to 'this malignant subversive fanatic'. Many Conservatives recognized that in the long run it was Britain's task to hand over power, but how long was the run? When it came to the test, the white man – especially if he happened to be a Conservative white man – was curiously reluctant to lay down his burden. However, by the time the Round Table Conference was reconvened on 7 September, after an interval to test Indian opinion, the situation was very different. There was a national government in office and the new Secretary for India, Sir Samuel Hoare who stood on the left of the party, had a clear-cut objective and, though not very likeable, was an able debater and administrator. The Conservative leadership was committed to a liberal line on India, Baldwin's prestige was now much higher and the Conservative dissentients were less inclined to 'rock the boat'. The landslide election further strengthened Baldwin and MacDonald who was also anxious for a large measure of Indian self-government.

The second Round Table Conference lasted for over three months. Its proceedings might have been quicker if Gandhi had again decided on a boycott. His presence led to endless disputation. The complications of creating a federal legislature seemed so great that Hoare considered postponement till after provincial self-government had been established. The news leaked, and created an uproar in Congress which was at once convinced it was a device for indefinite delay. MacDonald, however, reaffirmed that responsible government for an all-India federation as well as the provinces was a specific commitment. The second conference ended on 31 December. It was not self-evident that there had to be a third. A franchise committee under Lord Lothian had been sent to India. Legislation could have followed its report. Hoare hoped to escape yet another long repetition of Indian discords and grievances. Gandhi, however, during 1932 became involved in 'non-violent' disputation with the Viceroy Lord Willingdon, and it seemed wrong to ruin the credibility of the small Liberal Party – the only Hindu group prepared to talk – by refusing another conference. Opened on 17 November 1932, it ended on 24 December and was followed by a White Paper outlining the proposed legislation published on 17 March 1933. A joint select committee of sixteen from each House with some Indians as 'assessors' was set up to consider the question and take evidence before the Bill was introduced. It sat for some eighteen months; its proceedings were enlivened by Churchill in April 1934 accusing Hoare and Lord Derby of putting improper pressure on the Manchester Chamber of Commerce to change its evidence in a direction more favourable to the White Paper. He invoked the Committee of Privileges which on 8 June completely acquitted Hoare and Derby of the slightest impropriety. Churchill cut a poor figure in the subsequent debate. His intemperate language in the various India debates damaged his credibility on far more important matters where he was in the right.

No one could say that the India Bill, introduced by Hoare on the second reading in February 1935, lacked preparation. There had been the massive Simon Report, three meetings of the Round Table Conference, Lord Lothian's Franchise Committee, an India Committee of the Cabinet, a White Paper and the Joint Select Committee of both Houses which endorsed by a large majority the principal features of the

White Paper. At almost every stage there had been opportunities for parliamentary debate, and there were of course even more during the stages of the Bill: Churchill used every weapon, fair or unfair, to discredit the government's policy, but he never got more than seventy-nine diehards into the lobby with him. He fared better in the extra-parliamentary field and in February 1933 his motion in the Central Council of the National Union was lost by only 189 to 150 though there were a great many abstentions. At his final battle in that organization he scored his highest number of votes – 390 in December 1934 – but the government too had pulled out all the stops and mustered 712.

The India Act which finally became law on 2 August 1935 did not attract the attention in Britain that the packed columns in Hansard and the correspondence pages of the serious dailies would suggest. A section of the middle and upper class felt deeply about it. Most people were bored. The Act probably represented as much agreement among the contending factions as any measure could. A unitary British India dominated by the Congress Party would have been, as Hoare appreciated, anathema even to moderate Conservatives – and it was to appease them that the select committee had been set up. But responsible government at provincial level only, as Simon had suggested, was no longer acceptable even to moderate Indians. How well the Act would have worked no one can say. It never came into full effect. Provincial autonomy was indeed established in 1937, but responsible government at the centre depended, under the Act, on a measure of assent from the princes because of their treaty relations with the Crown – in fact the agreement of rulers representing more than half the population (some 80 million) of the princely states. This had not been obtained by 1939. When constitutional reform was revived after the war both India and Britain had moved into another world.

If India produced one set of acute constitutional problems, Ireland constituted another. In 1932 the government party, Cumann na nGaedheal, led by Cosgrave, which had been in office for the last ten years, lost the general election to de Valera's Fianna Fail. The electoral system was one of proportional representation and de Valera did not win outright, but the minor parties were on balance in his favour giving him a majority of seventy-nine to seventy-four in the Dáil. It looked slender but he was to be in office for the next sixteen years. The result was caused less by constitutional than economic discontent – general depression and cuts in public expenditure because of the slump. De Valera, however, resolved to attack on both fronts – to remove the Oath of Allegiance to the Crown from the constitution and to suspend the payment of land annuities to the British Treasury. These were repayments taken over by the Irish government in 1923 of loans advanced by the British government under the various pre-1922 Land Acts to enable Irish peasant tenants to buy their freeholds from the owners who were largely members of the old Anglo-Irish 'Ascendancy'. De Valera argued that the land had been stolen by the English and it was for them not the Irish to compensate the bought-out owners. The latter of course had had their money long ago, and the new proprietors went on paying the annuities whether or not Dublin passed them on to London. It was an inter-governmental battle. When de Valera cut off payment, Britain riposted by imposing twenty per cent duties on the principal Irish agricultural imports into Britain. Ireland naturally hit back with various counter-measures but it is as certain as it can be in an area where hard figures are notoriously difficult to obtain, that in the economic warfare which lasted till 1938 Ireland lost proportionately much more than Britain. Although under the agreement of that year the Irish got off with a lump sum payment of £10 million in settlement of claims amounting to ten times as much, the reasons for Britain's acquiescence were political expediency, not defeat in an economic battle which could have been protracted for many years.

On the constitutional side, de Valera was furnished with a weapon which had only recently been forged, the Statute of

Westminster. Under the Irish Free State Act of 1922 the twenty-six counties were to have the same constitutional status as the dominions, in particular Canada. Any country less like Canada than Ireland it would be hard to imagine. The dominions were relatively new countries which were separated by thousands of miles from the 'motherland', and had reached their current constitutional status by a process of peaceful evolution, except in the case of South Africa. Ireland in Professor Lyon's words 'was an ancient nation which was a motherland second only in the Anglo-Saxon world to England herself'. Conquered and 'colonized' by an alien English aristocracy, Ireland was entangled with England by geography and the history of a long love–hate relationship (mostly hate). She had achieved her constitutional status not by peaceful progress but by a bloody revolution followed by a no less bloody civil war. Nevertheless, dominion status on the Canadian model was written into the Act. When that status was defined, as it was in 1931, to enhance the independence of the dominions, Ireland was able to profit.

A long intricate and esoteric constitutional argument followed. Learned lawyers disputed energetically about it at the time and have done so though with diminishing fervour ever since. It is enough to say that de Valera abolished the oath, the appeal to the Judicial Committee of the Privy Council, and, for all practical purposes, the office of Governor-General. An obscure principle of 'external association' with Britain was enunciated. There is much to be said for obscurity, and the principle, whatever it meant, turned out to be a useful precedent for other separatist countries, like India, reluctant to be called dominions but anxious to preserve some sort of relationship with Britain. At the end of this haggle a new Irish constitution was produced in 1937 after the old Senate had been abolished and a puppet upper house substituted to carry out the change. The constitution was virtually republican but de Valera shied off calling it as such. Why? There is no clear answer. He could have done so without serious challenge. It would have meant at that time leaving the Commonwealth, but this could not have greatly mattered although there were some advantages in retaining the use of Britain's global diplomatic service. Perhaps the notion of a republic was too much associated with the dream of including all thirty-two counties of the Emerald Isle, and perhaps de Valera preferred to leave the name to the dreamers.

3

From the beginning of 1933 MacDonald gradually sank into physical and political decline. His eyesight deteriorated and he had operations for glaucoma, which involved long periods of minimal reading. Someone gregarious like Lloyd George could have absorbed information through talk, chatter and gossip. MacDonald, a natural solitary, depended on memoranda, minutes and white papers. His health declined in other ways – insomnia, headaches and loss of memory. He became rambling and incoherent in Cabinet. His public speeches often verged upon – and sometimes fell into – gibberish. He described Lloyd George as having 'a hawk-like desire for action without bridle or saddle across the Atlantic'. He was sadly conscious of his own condition. 'Machine run down: stupid in mind & can do no work & sick in body,' he wrote in his diary in March 1934. Churchill rightly describes him as 'dwindling into senility', although he was only sixty-nine when he resigned as Prime Minister in 1935.

Politically too he was a waning asset. By-elections went against the government from April 1932 onwards – among them a sensational disaster at East Fulham on 23 October 1933. Conservatives could not blame MacDonald, but they soon had their eyes on future prospects. Forgetting the asset he was to them in 1931 they thought of the liability he might be at the next election. Early in 1935 the government received heavy blows from left and right. On 17 January Lloyd George launched at Bangor a grand challenge to current orthodoxy – a campaign for loan-financed national development on the

THE DECLINE OF POWER

lines of Roosevelt's New Deal. This appealed to a great many of the younger Conservatives as well as to Liberals and floating voters. On 6 February Churchill's son, Randolph, standing as an independent Conservative at the Wavertree Division of Liverpool on a programme of higher arms expenditure and opposition to the government's India policy won 10,000 votes, ousting the official candidate and letting Labour in. It was one thing to cope with a diehard revolt in the House, quite another to deal with an outbreak in the constituencies. The Conservative Party was now seething with discontent.

MacDonald contemplated an invitation to Lloyd George but this was vetoed by Neville Chamberlain. In March he told Baldwin that he planned to resign that year. Baldwin, who had originally said that he would retire at the same time, asked to be released from the promise. Arrangements were set in motion to make the change. On 7 June Baldwin became Prime Minister and MacDonald took his place as Lord President. There had been two major liabilities in MacDonald's Cabinet: Sir John Simon, whose style as Foreign Secretary was increasingly under fire and who seemed to be better at putting to international conferences the case for almost any other nation than Britain; and Lord Londonderry, the Secretary for Air, who had made a series of tactless and misleading speeches. Sir Samuel Hoare became Foreign Secretary with Anthony Eden, also in the Cabinet, as Minister for League Affairs, and Simon went to the Home Office replacing Sir John Gilmour. Cunliffe-Lister became Air Minister in place of Londonderry who, bitterly complaining, accepted the leadership of the House of Lords. MacDonald should have resigned earlier, and a party leader less kindly than Baldwin would probably have got him out before 1935, though the difficulty of evicting even an ailing Prime Minister ought not to be underestimated. More tragic still was MacDonald's decision to stay on in the Cabinet and in Parliament after June 1935, increasingly confused and useless – 'chief mourner at his own protracted funeral', as Rosebery said of

Lord Randolph Churchill. In the 1935 election MacDonald lost his seat at Seaham Harbour to Emanuel Shinwell. Another, however, was found for him – the Combined Scottish Universities. He resigned office along with Baldwin in May 1937 and died on a sea voyage a few months later on 9 November. MacDonald has had a bad press. He was hated in his last years and posthumously by the Labour Party, while the Conservatives regarded him with indifference or contempt. He had many weaknesses but posterity has been too harsh on him. After all he did in a sense sacrifice his party for his country, as Peel did in 1846 over the repeal of the Corn Laws. There was, however, one great difference. Peel was right about free trade which he carried and which greatly benefited the Britain of those days. MacDonald was wrong about the gold standard which he failed to preserve and which was doing more harm than good anyway.

Chapter Ten

REARMAMENT AND ABDICATION

I

The most important and controversial issue of the 1930s was the question of defence and rearmament. It has to be seen against certain assumptions consistently if unwisely held from 1919 to March 1939. These derived from changes in the global balance of power dating from the turn of the century. By then it was already evident that the navy, pillar of British strategy from the days of the Armada, was no longer able to dominate the oceans. Britain's weak point was the Pacific. Hence the Anglo-Japanese Alliance of 1902. Twenty years later it came to an end, and the events of the decade after that caused a further decline in British strength. Sea power counted for less and Britain was less able to hold her share of it. The 1914–18 war was the first in which her naval superiority was seriously challenged. It was also the first in which she was obliged to make a major contribution on land. The long tradition of fighting by proxy reinforced by ships and money to the last German, Austrian, Frenchman or Dutchman came to an end.

How was Britain to maintain her security and her empire's after 1918? There seemed to be two choices. One was to rely on the League of Nations, but this was regarded as a dead letter from the start – anyway by the Conservative Cabinets which ruled for most of the inter-war years. They had no intention of fighting solo for the cause of 'collective security'. Labour often invoked it but scarcely less often voted against the armaments needed to support it. Labour ministers never had a working majority in this period. But if they had been confronted by the challenge to collective security posed by the Japanese dispute with Manchuria in 1931–2 and the Italian dispute with Abyssinia in 1935–6, it is doubtful whether they would have done anything different from the Conservatives – i.e. nothing whatever.

The second choice was to build up a system of alliances as in 1902–14. The problem was to find allies. America retreated into neutrality, Russia into enigmatic obscurity. Japan and Italy were, like Germany, potential enemies. This left only France. It was assumed that France would be Britain's ally, for she no more than Britain could afford to see the Low Countries overrun by Germany. Why, then, was no attempt made till the last moment to hold staff talks and coordinate military plans? There were three reasons. One was irritation at France's perpetual insistence on security, which was widely believed to have wrecked disarmament and provoked Hitler into repudiating Versailles – as if he would not have rearmed and thrown off his treaty obligations in any case whenever it suited him! The second and more important reason was the reluctance of public opinion and hence of governments to admit that war would again entail a continental commitment. But such an admission was inevitable if staff talks began.

A third reason was British determination not to be pulled into a war through the French system of east European alliances. This had been made categorically clear at Locarno when Britain firmly limited her guarantees to western Europe. It was a consistent feature of British policy till early in 1939 and it is the key to Chamberlain's behaviour in the Munich crisis. Britain would go to war for France if France was invaded, but not if France attacked Germany in support of the Czechs. This policy was reversed only after the occupation of Prague in March 1939, although the decision to hold staff talks was taken slightly earlier after rumours of an impending German invasion of Holland.

There was moreover an important element in 'the climate of opinion' which influenced successive governments for a large part of the 1930s – a mood of pacifism and revulsion against war, idealistic support of the League, hatred of arms and their manufacturers. In February 1933 the Oxford Union by 275 to 153 passed the most famous motion in its history – 'This House will under no circumstances fight for its King and Country' – an episode trivial to those who knew Oxford but portentous to outsiders. In October a by-election at East Fulham converted a Conservative majority of 14,521 to a Labour one of 4,840. This startling result was believed to be due to the Conservative candidate's advocacy of rearmament and his opponent's charge of 'warmongering'.

There was also the question of the national economy. What could the country afford? Cuts in civilian expenditure in 1931 had been as severe as in defence. Restoration of the former had a high electoral priority. It is true that the economy recovered more rapidly than was expected, but the Cabinet had to think in terms of financial feasibility and of a confused public opinion in which the spirits of Scrooge and of Good Will on Earth were curiously mingled. Although there were some who refused to recognize the threat of Hitler or even to see any great harm in him, the makers of British policy were not as blind as is sometimes made out. MacDonald, Baldwin, Chamberlain, Simon, Hoare, Halifax knew that the Nazi regime was detestable and that Germany constituted the greatest single menace to British security. But they did not know what to do about it within the limits imposed by public opinion, strategic realities and fiscal constraints.

As a result of the Japanese action in Manchuria, the government abandoned the Ten Year Rule on 22 March 1932, but nothing practical was done for another eighteen months. The reasons were the economic crisis and the futile proceedings of the Disarmament Conference which was still hoped to result in a reduction rather than an increase in arms. Hitler's withdrawal both from the conference and the League on 14 October 1933 jolted the Cabinet into action. A committee of officials called the Defence Requirement Sub-Committee (DRC) held its first meeting on 14 November. It consisted of the Chiefs of Staff and the three most powerful civil servants in the country, Sir Maurice Hankey, Secretary to the Cabinet, Sir Robert Vansittart, Head of the Foreign Office and Sir Warren Fisher, Head of the Treasury. Its first report, made in February 1934, recommended expenditure of some £75 million over the next five years. The principal objects were to replace the battle fleet and make good the deficiencies of naval bases in the Far East, in particular Singapore; to create an army expeditionary force capable in five years' time of mobilization in a month and geared to prevent Germany from establishing air-bases in the Low Countries; and to bring the RAF Home Defence squadrons up by ten to the fifty-two which had been promised under the unfulfilled 1923 programme.

The Cabinet did not move at all rapidly. It was not until 2 May that the report was referred to the Ministerial Committee on Disarmament. That committee's recommendations were approved on 18 July, and there was a full dress debate in Parliament on the RAF aspect of the programme on 30 July. The Ministerial Committee, largely at the instance of Neville Chamberlain, made some major changes in the original proposals of the DRC. It reduced the expenditure by a third to £50 million. The biggest cut was inflicted on the army which had its allocation reduced from £40 million to £20 million. The objective of creating an expeditionary force was not abandoned, merely postponed on the grounds that Germany would not be in a position to wage war in five years' time. Since a war started by Hitler broke out almost exactly five years later, this was not a particularly good prediction. Chamberlain also successfully attacked the navy's programme arguing that Germany was the principal threat, that a two-power standard fleet was impossible on fiscal grounds, and that the navy's demands for replacement of capital ships was based on the assumption of a war with Japan which Britain simply could not fight if she was also engaged in European hostilities at the same time. He agreed, however, to the fortification of Singapore to placate the dominions but reduced the naval deficiency programme from £21 million to £13 million.

On the other hand, he favoured more squadrons for the RAF than were recommended by the DRC – seventy-five instead of fifty-two – though partly at the expense of the generous provision made by the DRC for war reserves. The revised programme made no allowance at all for these and incurred the criticism of 'window-dressing'. Chamberlain did not mind. He and his supporters considered that the announcement of so large a programme would in itself act as a deterrent, and would also be a gesture to public opinion much agitated at the time about the threat from the *Luftwaffe*. This was the only part of the new policy revealed for public debate. Even the limited rearmament now agreed for the army and navy was not a popular cry.

The European scene did not improve during 1934. The brutality of Hitler's regime was confirmed by the murder in June of Ernest Roehm and most of the leaders of the SA. It was in part a bargain with the army which hated this rival force. Hitler received the *quid pro quo* when on Hindenburg's death a month later he became President as well as Chancellor and the army swore its oath of loyalty to him personally as head of state. In July the Nazi party in Austria attempted a coup against the Chancellor, Dolfuss. He was killed but Mussolini marched troops to the Brenner Pass, and Hitler, disclaiming all responsibility, took no action. In October the French Foreign Minister Louis Barthou, who was trying to build up an east European pact with France, was assassinated by a Croat fanatic in Marseilles along with King Alexander of Yugoslavia. He was the last French politician to pursue the old hard-line policy of Poincaré. His successor, Pierre Laval, was an appeaser and in the end a traitor. In December occurred the Wal-Wal incident, the germ of Italy's eventual conquest of Abyssinia.

Meanwhile, alarming information about the scale of German rearmament was reaching London. The Air Ministry in July had reckoned that by October 1935 Germany might have 500 first-line aircraft, and perhaps 1,000 by 1939. It now appeared that, although the 1935 figure was not far out

(576), Germany would have at least 1,300 as early as October 1936. The Cabinet set up a small committee to investigate the whole situation. It found that the German Army, limited to 100,000 men at Versailles, had reached 300,000. The navy, limited to six battleships of not more than 10,000 tons, six light cruisers and twelve destroyers, already consisted of seven capital ships, eight cruisers and sixteen destroyers, with two battleships, one cruiser and four destroyers under construction. The air figures were confirmed. The government decided to speed up its air programme and provide twenty-two squadrons for home defence in the next two years together with three squadrons for the Fleet Air Arm – these to be additional to four RAF squadrons already being formed that year. On 29 November 1934 Churchill uttered grave warnings in Parliament, declaring that by November 1935 Germany would be at least as strong in the air as Britain, that by the end of 1936 she would be fifty per cent stronger and by the end of 1937 twice as strong.

Baldwin replied to the debate. He stated that, whereas Britain had 880 first-line aircraft – 560 available for service in the UK – Germany had not got more than 600 in all, and since many of them lacked essential components, the effective strength was under 300. He reckoned that Britain would have a fifty per cent superiority by the end of 1935 and 1,200 first-line planes a year later. He said nothing about German strength in 1936 and observed that 1937 was too far away for predictions, but the general impression given was that no great danger impended. Although his picture of the current situation and the prospective one for 1935 was much closer to the truth than Churchill's, his speech was misleading if only by omission. On the Air Ministry's own figures Germany would have a lead of 100 to 200 first-line planes by the end of 1936, and the speed with which she was overtaking Britain was a bad sign for 1937.

The German rearmament sparked off a series of talks between Britain, France and Italy, culminating in the Stresa Conference in April 1935. The first of these at Rome between France and Italy resulted in an agreement to clear up certain colonial differences. It was an almost suspiciously bad bargain for Mussolini. Secretly, however, he had secured from Laval a free hand to deal with the Abyssinian dispute which was simmering in its early stages. No one in Britain smelt a rat. There followed Anglo-French discussions in London early in February 1935. The British government wanted to legalize past German rearmament, accept it as a fact, and try to limit it in future in the hope of bringing Germany back to Geneva and the League. The French were not prepared to abrogate Part V of the Versailles Treaty – the disarmament provisions – unless 'teeth' were put into Locarno. They wanted an 'air convention' under which the signatories of Locarno would guarantee aerial action to protect any of the relevant powers threatened with unprovoked aggression by another.

Nothing concrete came out of all this. On 4 March the White Paper on defence was published, clearly directed at German rearmament. Hitler caught a 'diplomatic cold' and put off a proposed visit by Simon to Berlin. On 15 March the French Prime Minister, M. Flandin, carried a measure to increase military service from one to two years. Next day Hitler announced conscription for a German army of thirty-six divisions. The postponed Berlin talks led nowhere. The representatives of Britain, France and Italy met at Stresa on 11 April 1935. Nothing was said about Abyssinia; it has been alleged that Mussolini pointedly added the words 'in Europe' after 'maintenance of peace' in the Stresa declaration and that MacDonald and Simon silently consented, thus condoning Italian plans for Africa. This is a myth. The words were in the draft from the very beginning. The upshot of Stresa was a more or less meaningless statement about support of Locarno, but at the very least it could be reasonably assumed that the three powers would act in concert and not let Germany engage in piecemeal negotiations with any one of them. This assumption was quickly belied by the least defensible of all British inter-war transactions, the Anglo-German Naval Agreement of 18 June, which allowed Germany to build a navy up to thirty-five per cent of the size of Britain's. In the narrow terms of the Admiralty's anxiety about Japan, it made sense of a sort to limit the naval construction of a European enemy. But the argument presupposed that Germany would not cheat over the crucial details or denounce the agreement as soon as it suited her – both of which she did. It also ignored the probable reaction of the French who were furious at a flagrant breach of the spirit, if not the letter, of Stresa. The change of government on 7 June, when Simon was replaced at the Foreign Office by Hoare exhausted after his long battle over the India Bill and unfamiliar with his new field, may partly explain the blunder.

Meanwhile, there had been important changes over air policy. When Simon and Eden went to Berlin at the end of March 1935 Hitler told them, quite untruly, that Germany had already achieved air parity with England. The effect of this lie was perhaps from Hitler's point of view counter-productive. The Cabinet at once pushed up the figures in their programme. The old fifty-two-squadron scheme of 1923 meant 598 first-line planes. The so-called Scheme A of July 1934 aimed at 836. The new target agreed on 22 May 1935 was 123 squadrons – 1,512 first-line planes – to be completed by 31 March 1937. Baldwin made a celebrated speech in which he admitted unnecessarily that he had been wrong about German air strength when he spoke the previous November. He had certainly committed errors but not that particular one. The figures he gave then were broadly correct and Hitler had not achieved parity four months later. Nevertheless it was true that the Air Ministry had greatly underestimated the rapidity with which Germany could, and would, expand its air force from now onwards.

From early summer it became increasingly clear that Mussolini intended, despite League attempts at mediation, to attack Abyssinia. In fact, as we now know, he had decided as early as 30 December 1934 to destroy the Emperor Haile

Selassie's forces and annex the country. He planned to begin operations on 1 October 1935. The British Cabinet, strongly supported by Vansittart and the Chiefs of Staff, was determined not to fight Italy on behalf of the League. It was not true, as sometimes claimed, that the Chiefs of Staff had any serious doubts about winning such a war even if France stayed neutral, though they certainly advised that it should not be deliberately undertaken without French cooperation. Sanctions, especially oil sanctions, were regarded with scarcely more enthusiasm than hostilities, since they might provoke Italy into military action. An inter-departmental committee chaired by Sir John Maffey advised on 18 June that no vital British interest was at stake if Italy conquered Abyssinia. The French of course had no intention whatever of fighting. Laval, who had done the secret deal with Mussolini in January, was now Prime Minister. Like Vansittart, and in common with much official opinion in England, Laval believed that war with Italy would give Germany and possibly Japan a chance to make trouble. It was bound to result in some material losses and neither country could afford any in the light of German rearmament and the dangerous situation in the Far East. The French were no doubt even less inclined to cooperate with Britain after the Anglo-German Naval Agreement.

The British government, however, had to deal with a public opinion very different from the French. This was the high water mark of pacifism and of a related but separate sentiment – 'Leagueomania'. At the end of June the results of a house-to-house questionnaire erroneously known as the 'Peace Ballot' and organized by the League of Nations Union were announced. The questions formulated in October 1934 invited the answer 'yes'. Were people in favour of Britain remaining in the League, and, by international agreement, reducing arms, abolishing war planes and prohibiting the private manufacture and sale of armaments? Obviously they were, though events since October had made disarmament an unreal issue. Out of 11.5 million answers, over 10 million were affirmative in each case. A fifth question was more topical. Should an aggressor be compelled to desist by (a) economic measures and (b) if necessary military measures? Over 10 million said yes to (a); 6.78 million said yes to (b); 2.35 million said no; and another 2 million abstained. No government, with an imminent general election at least on the cards even if the date was not yet settled, could disregard this vote for 'collective security'. On 11 September Hoare made a speech at the League of Nations Assembly in which he vigorously reaffirmed his government's commitment to the League Covenant. He affirmed without specific reference to Italy that collective action against an aggressor would be strongly supported by Britain. Although he made it clear that 'collective' meant what it said – action by all, and no obligation to act individually – the style of his address minimized the reservations. It was generally regarded as a declaration of intent to 'stop' Mussolini, and applauded as such by the League's supporters.

Meanwhile, the problem of armaments and collective security had produced a convulsion in the attenuated Labour Party led since 1931 by George Lansbury, now seventy-six, a rhetorical, old-fashioned left-wing Christian pacifist. The credibility of Labour's foreign and defence policies was raised at the Trades Union Congress meeting at Margate early in September. There was an overwhelming vote for League sanctions even if they led to war. A month later at the Labour Party Conference in Brighton held on 1 October on the very eve of Mussolini's invasion of Abyssinia, a similar motion was carried over the opposition of Lansbury who resigned a week later. It was famous for Ernest Bevin's reference to Lansbury 'taking [according to other versions 'trailing' or 'hawking'] his conscience from body to body to be told what you ought to do with it'. The Parliamentary Labour Party chose Lansbury's deputy to act as leader for the rest of the session. In this interim manner Clement Attlee whose position was confirmed after a party vote following the 1935 election entered on a leadership that lasted for over twenty years.

National sentiment for strong action through the League reached its apogee that autumn. Baldwin had been hesitating whether to dissolve then or in January 1936, as the party managers advised. Mussolini's invasion of Abyssinia on 2 October decided him to go to the country as soon as possible to seek a mandate for rearmament in the interests of Britain, world peace and collective security. He announced on 25 October that a general election would be held on 14 November. The result was a notable triumph for Baldwin. To repeat the results of 1931 would have been inconceivable. To lose as little as he did – less than 100 seats – was a remarkable success in the light of recent by-elections. It was the first election since 1880 to be fought mainly on foreign policy and there has been none since. The government still called 'national' won 432 seats along with its now indistinguishable Liberal national allies. Labour won 154 and the Samuelite Liberals 21.

Few governments have got into greater trouble sooner – and on the very issue which it had made as the principal plank of its platform. There was never any intention to risk war for the League but the question of economic sanctions, in particular an embargo on oil imports, raised the possibility of military reprisals by Italy. The Foreign Office, led by Vansittart who was violently anti-German, wanted to reach a settlement before the League imposed sanctions and drove Italy into the arms of Germany. Hoare, who was far from well, suffered from fainting fits and badly needed a holiday, decided to go to Switzerland. He passed through Paris accompanied by Vansittart on 7 December when he could have an urgently requested talk with Laval. His mandate from the Cabinet was to press on with peace talks, secure French cooperation and avoid war, the clear implication being recognition of Italian predominance in Abyssinia and at least some transfer of territory. The ensuing bargain which would have reduced the country to two-fifths of its size was leaked – no one to this day knows by whom – to the Paris press. It looked like a sell-out and there was a public uproar in London.

Hoare, who thought he had secured a diplomatic coup, went on to Switzerland where he broke his nose skating, and on return to London was too ill to defend himself to the craven Cabinet which demanded his resignation. He was replaced by Anthony Eden. Hoare's treatment was one of the least creditable episodes in Baldwin's career. The deal with Laval was repudiated, and sanctions of a sort were imposed, though there was no embargo on oil which was the only commodity that mattered. The Italians overran and annexed Abyssinia early in 1936. Haile Selassie would have done better under the Hoare–Laval pact. Mussolini got what he wanted but with the maximum of ill will all round. These transactions effectively killed the League.

Although Eden was more of a Leagueophile than Hoare he was no more successful in saving Abyssinia. But it could well be argued that the survival of that remote and backward country was not a British interest. Far more serious was Eden's first major diplomatic confrontation in Europe. On 27 February 1936 the French Chamber of Deputies ratified the Franco-Soviet Treaty of mutual assistance signed in the previous May. Hitler claimed to regard this as a breach of Locarno. On 7 March German troops marched into the Rhineland zone demilitarized under the Treaty of Versailles. The method might be deplored but it was a concession Britain had long been ready to make. The Germans in the famous words of Lord Lothian were 'only walking into their back garden', and no British government, if it could help it, was willing to go to war to stop them. This attitude was supported by both the Labour and Liberal parties. The French were divided. Their army was not prepared for action, although the French Commission of Inquiry after the war concluded that France could have forced Hitler out of the Rhineland. On the other hand, the French Chief of Staff, General Gamelin, was pessimistic about the upshot of a war; he could not be sure that military action would 'call Hitler's bluff' and result in German withdrawal. If France had acted instantly and invoked Locarno, the British Cabinet could not have refused its support. Flandin lost the chance when he agreed to parley in London. No doubt, he meant to lose it. The result was a triumph for Hitler and a major strategic setback for France. British public opinion was dead against war. *The Times* headlined its leader on the Rhineland crisis, 'A Chance to Reconstruct'. Hitler made no more major moves for the next two years. He had effectively wrecked the Versailles settlement as far as Germany was concerned. He could now rearm as much as he pleased. The period described by Churchill in his Memoirs as 'The Loaded Pause' had begun.

The Defence Requirement Sub-Committee (DRC) made its third report to the Cabinet on 21 November 1935, and a new defence programme was presented to the House by Baldwin on 9 March 1936. The report as amended by the Cabinet was in many ways a landmark in the history of British defence policy. It recognized for the first time the need to consider a two-power naval standard. It recommended a programme of substantial reinforcement by the Territorial Army for a continental expeditionary force, although the Cabinet modified the DRC's original proposals. It reiterated the July 1935 proposals for a front-line strength of 1,512 aircraft by April 1937 and gave the Air Ministry discretion to go further if necessary. It dealt with the question of industrial production and advised the creation of 'shadow factories'. Firms which did not normally manufacture arms were given modest orders on condition that they expanded their works and machinery far more than was necessary for peace production in order to be able to switch to munitions.

These steps were symptoms of widespread anxiety, and were helped by economic recovery. In 1934 a deficiency programme of £50 million over five years had been added to regular defence estimates of £120 million. In 1936 the regular estimates were only slightly higher but extra expenditure over the next five years was pitched at £400 million – eight times as much as in 1934. This meant a total of £200 million per year. There remained many obscurities and inadequacies. A two-power naval standard had not yet been agreed. The expeditionary force was still based on an ambivalent principle of limited liability. Industrial production was constrained by the attitude of 'business as usual'. There was no attempt to direct labour or lay down priorities in allocating commodities. The appointment on 13 March of Sir Thomas Inskip, the Attorney-General, as Minister for Coordination of Defence seemed to some people a sign of governmental feebleness and the quip attributed to Churchill who expected the job for himself that it was the oddest choice 'since the Emperor Caligula made his horse a Consul' caused merriment especially among those who did not recognize plagiarism from a remark of Gladstone fifty-six years earlier, or know that Caligula never did it anyway. In fact Inskip proved to be a much abler minister than his critics expected, and Churchill in the immediate aftermath of the great row about India would not have been an acceptable alternative. These criticisms of the defence programme of 1936 should not be allowed to blur a notable step forward. It is, however, right to remember that on the government's own reckoning Germany was already spending £500 million a year on its armed services.

2

Shortly before midnight on 20 January 1936 King George V died at Sandringham at the age of seventy. A gruff, naval martinet who was little known before succeeding to the throne in 1910, he had become in the course of his twenty-five years' reign a much loved father figure. His annual Christmas radio broadcasts were listened to in almost every home. His Silver Jubilee in the summer of 1935 was celebrated with enthusiasm and devotion. No twentieth-century monarch has had a larger number of constitutional problems to deal with. The King's good sense enabled him to make what posterity has endorsed as the right decision in every case. There was a real sense of national grief at his death.

His successor, Edward Prince of Wales, was very different.

He too was immensely popular, but in personality and character he was a charming lightweight – small, fair haired, good looking and remarkably youthful in appearance for a man of forty-two. Like his father and grandfather – though unlike the Prince Consort – he was not at all intellectual. 'Bookish he will never be.' Thus, in one of the understatements of the age, wrote Sir Herbert Warren, the royalty-loving President of Magdalen College Oxford, where the Prince spent two years before the outbreak of war in 1914. Like many of his Hanoverian forebears he was highly sexed. After a brief affair with Lord Leicester's daughter-in-law Lady Coke – he invariably went for married women – he fell, in the words of his biographer, Lady Donaldson,[1] 'abjectly' in love with Mrs Dudley Ward, wife of one of the Liberal Whips. By an extraordinary coincidence they first met early in 1918 at the house of a Mrs Kerr-Smiley, sister of Mr Simpson whose career was to be strangely entwined with that of the Prince many years later. The Prince's love for Mrs Dudley Ward was a case of total infatuation and total surrender. The affair which lasted for sixteen years was widely known in London society but it was conducted with great discretion and no breath of it ever got into the gossip columns. Indeed to this day very little has been said about it in print. It ruled out any sort of appropriate royal marriage, though not the occasional escapade on a royal tour or short affair with someone else, for example the American-born Lady Furness. One can surmise that the Prince's preference was not accidental. Probably he was already showing consciously or unconsciously his revulsion against the regal role. Perhaps too he was seeking the maternal affection which was denied him as a boy.

The Prince's entanglement naturally did not please his parents. King George V had never been an easy father, but his younger sons after making highly respectable marriages got on well enough with him. The Prince of Wales was in a different category. His relationship with Mrs Dudley Ward, added to his love of nightclubs and various other non-

Victorian manifestations of society, not to mention his chronic unpunctuality and the modernity of his clothes – turn-up trousers being a particular bone of contention – caused an ever widening gap between father and son.

Worse, however, was to follow. Early in 1934 the Prince fell passionately in love with Mrs Wallis Simpson, a twice married American from Baltimore. Mrs Dudley Ward, who had been for some weeks nursing a sick daughter, suddenly noticed the silence from York House, the Prince's residence. When she telephoned she was told that orders had been given for her calls to be refused. She never saw him again. The Prince was now with Mrs Simpson wherever he went. This new relationship soon became as widely known as the old one. There was, however, an important difference. Mrs Dudley Ward, no more than Mrs Fitzherbert or the Duchess of Kendall, aspired to be Queen of England. Mrs Simpson did. She failed to see the impossibility of a twice divorced woman ascending the throne. It is hard to believe that the new King did not encourage her in this delusion. With his desire to be dominated he was as 'abjectly' in love with her as he had been with Mrs Dudley Ward. He wished to please her every whim. On minor issues he had successfully defied the old order. Whether he deluded himself that he could do it on a matter of this magnitude will never be known. Nor can one say what Mrs Simpson would have done if she had recognized, in Lady Donaldson's words, 'that the choice was not between being Queen of England or the King's mistress, but between mistress of the King and exile'.[2] George V knew about this new infatuation which is said to have hastened his death, but neither he nor Queen Mary could bring themselves to say anything to the Prince.

The foreign press became even more full of stories about Mrs Simpson after the Prince's accession and such persons as the Prime Minister, the Archbishop of Canterbury and even Queen Mary were bombarded with letters, but the British papers preserved a discreet silence – all the more remarkable since the King was anything but discreet himself, e.g. putting Mrs Simpson's name in the Court circular. Meanwhile, he proceeded to conduct the monarchy in a style which distressed close observers. Three examples are enough. The clocks at Sandringham had during the late reign always been set half an hour fast. King George V's body was still warm when, at his son's order, they were all put back to Greenwich time. No one would have expected this idiosyncratic feature of the old order to be preserved for long, but to obliterate it at that of all moments seemed heartless and shocked King George's old servants who were soon to be even more shocked by the extreme stinginess of their new master. Then came the episode of the Privileged Bodies which by long usage separately present loyal addresses to a new monarch. These are some twenty, including the universities of Oxford and Cambridge, the Royal Academy, the Bank of England, etc. Instead of receiving and replying to each on its own, the King lumped them together and made one reply to the lot. A third instance was when a photographer caught the expression of sulky *ennui* on his face while women and girls were curtseying to him at a presentation party in the garden of Buckingham Palace.

Of course the King remained in general very popular. These episodes affected only a few people and perhaps were in themselves trivial. There were, however, more serious causes for anxiety. The Foreign Office believed that Mrs Simpson had contacts with highly placed Germans, which made it necessary to keep her under surveillance. No evidence has emerged to substantiate these suspicions, but keeping her under observation meant keeping the King too, and he was much more of a security risk than she. He refused to have any of his staff at Fort Belvedere. The red boxes which went there were left lying about sometimes for weeks with no precautions taken. In addition, the King made no secret of his strong pro-German views. If the accounts of his opinions which have appeared in some of the captured Nazi documents are based on any substratum of truth at all he was wildly indiscreet at the time of the remilitarization of the

Rhineland and on other occasions too. The Foreign Office decided to screen the papers sent to him and to hold back anything that would do real harm if it fell into the wrong hands – probably a unique episode in the history of the monarchy.

Scandalous stories about Mrs Simpson could not raise any constitutional problem while she remained married to Mr Simpson. No one can ask a King about his private life. The news in October that Mrs Simpson was instituting divorce proceedings against her husband transformed the situation. Under the English law as it then stood divorce was not only unobtainable by mutual consent, but unobtainable if both parties had committed adultery. A mysterious official called the King's Proctor had the duty to intervene if he received evidence that these rules had been broken. The custom was for the 'guilty party,' i.e. the husband in all these collusive cases, to occupy a hotel bedroom with some woman paid for the purpose. Servants could then give evidence which was accepted as proof of adultery, although of course it was extremely rare for any sexual act to occur in these dismal, prearranged conditions. The interval between a decree of divorce *nisi* (i.e. unless such objections could be brought) and becoming 'absolute' was six months. Knowledge that these proceedings impended made Baldwin, after strong pressure by the royal Private Secretary, Alexander Hardinge, seek an audience with the King on 20 October. He referred to the stories about Mrs Simpson and urged him to use his influence to put off the divorce. The King replied that it was a private matter in which he could not interfere. Nothing was said about marriage. On 27 October a decree *nisi* against Mr Simpson was pronounced at Ipswich. It prompted a famous headline in an American newspaper – 'King's Moll Reno'd in Wolsey's Home Town'. On 13 November Hardinge, to whom the King had said no word about Mrs Simpson, wrote him a letter warning that the silence of the British press would at any moment be broken and asking that Mrs Simpson should be urged to go abroad 'without further delay'. He received no reply. Henceforth the King dealt with the Cabinet through Sir Walter Monckton, an old Oxford friend, a distinguished barrister and legal adviser to the Duchy of Cornwall.

Three days later on 16 November the King summoned Baldwin to Buckingham Palace. He said that he understood the Cabinet to be worried about his relations with Mrs Simpson. Baldwin confirmed that this was so and that in his opinion the country would not approve of Mrs Simpson as Queen. Whether a reigning monarch needs the Cabinet's assent for his marriage is an arguable question. The King never pressed the point, declaring at once that if the government disapproved of the marriage he would abdicate and marry Mrs Simpson as soon as he could. Baldwin replied that this was 'grievous news' and he could not comment that day. On the same evening the King dined with his mother and told her his decision. Queen Mary was profoundly shocked and very angry. She implored him to reconsider it. He would not do so, and next day informed his three brothers.

Much has been written about events between then and the formal act of abdication on 10 December, but it is clear that the decision, if not yet irrevocable, was already very difficult to revoke. Moreover, it had been taken before the King's famous visit on 18 and 19 November to the depressed areas of south Wales when he said that 'something must be done' and before the Bishop of Bradford rebuked him for his mode of life in the somewhat cryptic sermon on 1 December, which sparked off the press, long smouldering under self-imposed silence, into a sudden blaze. The abdication was neither the result of a political plot to get rid of a 'radical' monarch who seemed to be criticizing the Cabinet's economic policy nor an episcopal plot to remove a King who refused to abide by the Church's rulings on divorce. Baldwin was well aware that the King's views were anything but 'left', and the Bishop who had never even heard of Mrs Simpson was referring to the irregularity of the King's attendances at church.

At this juncture a new proposal was floated. Esmond

Harmsworth, Lord Rothermere's son, suggested to Mrs Simpson the possibility of a 'morganatic' marriage, i.e. one in which the wife and the children do not inherit the title of the husband nor any of his entailed property. The King, encouraged by glowing reports especially in the Harmsworth-owned *Daily Mail* of his Welsh visit, began to think twice about abdication and saw Harmsworth's plan as a way out of the impasse. The snag was that the status of a morganatic wife is unknown to British law. The plan would require special legislation and not only by the British but by all the dominion Parliaments as well. Baldwin, though most reluctant to propose it, felt obliged to consult the dominion Prime Ministers and the leaders of the British opposition parties. The answers were, with varying degrees of emphasis, negative. On 2 December the Cabinet rejected morganatic marriage. Abdication was now inevitable. The question had in effect been settled before the vast majority of the British public even knew that there was a question to settle.

On 3 December the press broke its silence, and banner headlines everywhere proclaimed the news of the crisis. The reaction of the papers for the next week dismayed the King. Far from seeing him as the hero of the love affair of the century the newspapers, reflecting the views of so many people who had been and were to be ready to die for their country, wrote in terms of abandoning his post. On the evening of 3 December Mrs Simpson left for France. The King made one last attempt to promote the morganatic marriage. He proposed to broadcast his case direct to the nation. He would then go abroad and await the verdict of his people. Just how this would be secured was not clear, but in any case Baldwin vetoed the appeal as unconstitutional – which it certainly would have been.

An ineffective effort was made to raise a 'King's party'. The Beaverbrook–Rothermere press supported the King. Sir Oswald Mosley came out on his side. Churchill did his best to plead for delay. But Parliament was virtually unanimous and there has never been any real evidence that the public was seriously divided on the question. The King was not prepared to fight. His intention to abdicate was formally announced to Baldwin on Saturday, 5 December. On 7 December at question time in the House of Commons Churchill attempted to get an assurance that no irrevocable step had been taken. He was howled down. His political standing, already much damaged by the fight over India, reached its nadir. The Cabinet did, however, make one last attempt to persuade the King not to abdicate. It was unsuccessful. On Thursday, 10 December the formalities of abdication were completed. The following evening the ex-King announced, at his brother's instructions, as 'His Royal Highness Prince Edward', was able to make his final broadcast unrestrained by the government. It was a moving and dignified performance. He left the country that night. The new King's coronation took place on 12 May 1937, the day appointed for King Edward's. One of his first acts after it was to create the latter Duke of Windsor. On 3 June the Duke married Mrs Simpson in France, having received on the eve of the wedding the disagreeable news that, although King George VI had conferred the title of HRH on him, it was not to be used by his wife or any children. This exclusion which was of questionable legality rankled for the rest of his life. It was one, though not the only, reason why it could never be said of the Duke and the Duchess of Windsor that 'they lived happily ever after'.

The abdication did no harm to the Crown. It was the monarchy which enjoyed deep rooted public esteem not the monarch whose popularity could quickly evaporate if he put a foot wrong. King George VI and his wife, Queen Elizabeth, were soon as much loved and respected as his father and mother had been. He was conscientious, hard-working and punctilious. The slight aloofness occasioned by a defect in his speech was more than counter-balanced by the Queen's charm and friendliness. The social world which had surrounded King Edward and Mrs Simpson scurried for cover. It was difficult before long to find anyone who would admit to having known them – a situation encapsulated in the title of

Osbert Sitwell's unpublished poem, 'Rat Week'. However there were limits to this swing of opinion. When Cosmo Gordon Lang, Archbishop of Canterbury, gave a condemnatory broadcast about the ex-King on Sunday, 13 December there was an uproar. He said what a great many people felt, but they did not like him saying it. No archbishop in modern history has been more roundly abused. But the row soon died away, and before long the abdication faded from the nation's collective memory. News about the Duke and Duchess of Windsor often appeared in the press but they were no longer a part of English history.

Chapter Eleven

PRELUDE TO WAR

The abdication occurred against a darkening international scene. On 9 May 1936 Mussolini annexed Abyssinia. A month later Neville Chamberlain, deliberately omitting to consult Eden, described the continuation of sanctions as 'the very midsummer of madness'. Formal abandonment on 18 June caused Harold Macmillan and one other Conservative MP to vote with the opposition in a motion of censure and resign the Conservative Whip. On 16 July the international scene abruptly changed: civil war broke out in Spain. It followed an attempt by General Franco to overthrow the shallow-rooted Republic which had replaced the monarchy in 1931. The ideological cleavage reflected in heightened form all the major politico-religious conflicts of post-war Europe. Perhaps it is not too fanciful to believe that it also reflected the harsh contrasts of climate and landscape. In Spain the Church was more bigoted, the aristocracy more entrenched, the army more reactionary,[1] the socialists more divided, the anarchists more turbulent, the legislature more chaotic, the poor more resentful, and the anti-clericals more virulent than anywhere else in Europe.

The struggle between the Nationalists and the Republicans was cruel and brutal. After thirty-two months and 600,000 deaths Franco finally crushed the Republic in March 1939. Germany and Italy intervened with different degrees of vigour on his side, partly for ideological reasons (though his Catholicism inspired no sympathy), partly to try out their armaments, partly to establish a hostile government on France's western border, capable in the event of war of threatening the Anglo-French position in the Mediterrranean. This calculation proved erroneous. The help that Franco gave to Mussolini and Hitler after 1939 was minimal, nor had his coup been in any way concerted with them. The German –Italian intervention did, however, at a time when Mussolini's foreign policy was in the balance, tip it towards alliance with Hitler, and to that extent weaken Britain and France. Stalin after much vacillation gave ambiguous support to the Republic, but he was more concerned with protracting the war than winning it. The Popular Front Government in Paris headed by Leon Blum was at first inclined to supply arms to the Republic but, under strong pressure from London, in the end, adopted the British policy of 'non-intervention'. This seemed the best way to avert the danger that a general war would break out if foreign 'volunteers' fought against each other in Spain. It was the official attitude of Germany and Italy too but it did not stop the latter pouring in about 50,000 men and the former sending 10,000, including many air crew, along with planes in large numbers, not to mention guns and ammunition. The solemn meetings of the non-intervention committee in London were a futile and hypocritical exercise in diplomacy unrivalled in the inter-war years.

In the world of those European countries which still enjoyed freedom of expression Spain aroused intense feeling, and nowhere more than in England. The struggle seemed to be one between tyranny and liberty, fascism and democracy, capitalism and socialism. In reality this was an absurd oversimplification; the victory of the Republican 'Popular Front' heavily penetrated, indeed largely controlled, by the Communists would have been in no sense a victory for democracy. But opinions are affected by appearance, not reality. The writers and intellectuals were overwhelmingly on the side of the Republic. Here was a cause and a crusade. Its emotional impact was like that of the French Revolution, the Greek War of Independence or the events of 1848. A dissenting minority, it is true, saw the battle as one between Christian religion and Communist atheism. Evelyn Waugh,

Edmund Blunden and the South African poet, Roy Campbell, were pro-Franco. For the same reason the Labour Party which for historical reasons had a good deal of Roman Catholic support stemming from the Irish vote in England, was more divided than one would have expected, though the official policy was strongly pro-Republican.

Labour was divided for another reason. This was the heyday of the Left Book Club founded just before the outbreak of the war by Victor Gollancz with the aid of John Strachey and Harold Laski. All three took their line from the Communist Party. The books chosen were heavily slanted and had great influence on the left generally. One of the Communist objectives was the creation of a Popular Front on the model of France and Spain, an alliance of all the anti-fascist elements. The Communists hoped to establish over it the sort of control which they had secured in Spain. Communism as a creed became more respectable than at any time before or since. It flourished in the universities, particularly in Cambridge. Of course it was always a minority creed even in Trinity College, and it was only a minority within a minority who became spies and traitors like Burgess, Maclean, Philby and Blunt. The full horrors of Soviet Russia were little known at the time and Stalin's policy of judicially murdering first the entire Communist old guard and then most of his generals had only just begun. Nevertheless, the Labour leaders saw the danger soon enough. No Popular Front was ever established in England and those who proclaimed the cause were quickly ejected from the Labour Party.

The real threat to Britain in the thirties was not Franco or Mussolini or even Stalin. It was Hitler, and the Spanish war had a divisive effect on those who sought to create a sense of urgency and unity against him. The Conservatives had little sympathy with the Republic, and the right-wing Conservatives had even less than the rest. Drawn largely from the aristocratic element of the party they saw all too clearly what was happening to their opposite numbers in Spain. The sort of Spaniards they knew were counts, marquesses and dukes who got short shrift if they fell into the hands of the Popular Front. 'Non-intervention' may have prevented a general war from occurring earlier, and it may be true that Hitler and Mussolini got less out of Franco's success than they expected. The fact remains that the course of events strengthened the Axis, weakened the western Allies and discredited British diplomacy.

Shortly after the coronation of George VI, Baldwin resigned as Prime Minister on 28 May. There could be no question about his successor. Neville Chamberlain had been the inevitable heir since 1930. He made the minimum changes in the Cabinet. Simon became Chancellor of the Exchequer. Hoare moved from the Admiralty to the Home Office and Duff Cooper took his place. Hore-Belisha, a recent entry to the Cabinet as Minister of Transport whose name is remembered for his 'beacons', went to the War Office. Baldwin adorned with the Garter and an earldom departed in a blaze of glory. He was widely believed to have handled the abdication brilliantly. In fact it is hard to see that he did anything that anyone else would not have done. The obverse side of the undoubted fact that he did not plan to push the King out is that he did not plan anything at all. As so often he played by ear and instinct. His reputation evaporated soon enough. After the outbreak of war he was blamed for Britain's deficiency in arms, and most of the ills of the 1930s were attributed to his allegedly feeble leadership. This version of history contributed to the Conservative defeat in 1945. Later there was a reaction which went too far and Baldwin was invested with a prescience which he never possessed. He was not a great statesman. He was a shrewd politician, kindly, decent and honourable.

Neville Chamberlain was harder, clearer and more abrasive. He did not conceal his contempt for the Labour Party and it reciprocated with a real dislike unusual in politics. He built up no fund of the goodwill on which Baldwin could draw even from the opposition when things went wrong. It was the same with his own backbenchers. Efforts to bring him into the smoking room of the House of Commons and make him display the genial common touch over a drink were counter-productive. He said little and looked bored, as no doubt he was. No one could dispute his integrity, energy and efficiency. He was respected, even admired, but he was not loved.

From the beginning Chamberlain made it clear that foreign policy was one of his main interests. At first Eden welcomed this change from the days of Baldwin who had seemed indifferent, but it soon became clear that Chamberlain's views were not the same as Eden's and relations began to deteriorate. The divergence was one of style and timing rather than purpose. Eden was not a Churchillian. He had been emphatic on the impossibility of British action over the Rhineland. He had not objected to the abandonment of sanctions against Italy in June 1936, and he was certainly not prepared to enter into the sort of continental commitments implied in the 'collective security' which Churchill had been preaching for several years. Whereas Churchill emphasized the threat of Germany and spoke politely about Italian fascism, Eden seems to have regarded Mussolini with greater hostility than he did Hitler. It is true that Eden from time to time used League language, and to that extent seemed nearer to Churchill than he was to Chamberlain who frankly regarded the League as dead. In this way Eden's style was more acceptable to the left than Chamberlain's but there was no real difference of content.

Chamberlain was coolly realistic. Events during 1936 and 1937 had moved against Britain. In his eyes very little was being done about it, and he had no use for the Foreign Office. In summer 1936 the holding of the Olympic Games at Berlin gave Hitler a notable propaganda triumph. In November while the British Cabinet was absorbed in the 'King's business' two disagreeable developments occurred. Conversations between Hitler and Mussolini led to the agreement known as the Rome–Berlin Axis, and German negotiations with Japan resulted in the anti-Commintern Pact, which, though not directly aimed at Britain had serious implications for the Franco-Soviet alliance which had been Hitler's original excuse for reoccupying the Rhineland. A year later the pact was joined by Italy.

It was clear to Chamberlain at an early stage that Britain might find herself confronting these three major powers simultaneously, with France as her only ally, and an uncertain one at that. The danger became even greater with the outbreak of war in 1937 between Japan and China. He believed that it was simply not possible to rearm on a scale needed to fight against Italy, Germany and Japan at the same time. His view was not based merely on the difficulty of securing the necessary sacrifices from a parliamentary democracy still at peace. The point was that the British economy's ability to generate foreign exchange was in itself an important weapon of war. If rearmament was undertaken on so vast a scale the economy would be greatly weakened. It is important to remember that in those years there was a powerful and well founded Treasury view about the limits to the burden which the national economy could bear in peacetime without irreparably damaging its future strength in wartime. The likelihood of the American help which was to save the day in the end seemed remote in the extreme in 1937–9, and no prudent statesman could have banked on it.

The logic of this assessment, given the collapse of the League and collective security (though the collapse was of course denied by Labour, Liberals and Churchill), led to the necessity of doing a deal of some sort with one or both of the European dictators – the policy which came to be known as 'Appeasement'. It was supported by the Treasury, by the Chiefs of Staff and by the dominions, especially Australia and New Zealand alarmed at Japanese chauvinism and anxious for Britain to build up her forces in the Far East. Appeasement did not imply moral condonation of Hitler's Germany. Chamberlain was shocked like all decent Englishmen at the treatment of the Jews. On the other hand there were dictatorships just as bad – Soviet Russia being at the top of the list and sought as an ally by the left. Germany had legitimate complaints and a moral case in some matters. If she was to be freed from the shackles of Versailles she was bound to become the dominant power in eastern Europe, and self-determination for the German-speaking populations of Austria, Czechoslovakia and Poland commanded more sympathy in England from the left than the right. It would add to Hitler's territory and numbers but perhaps a Germany whose grievances were removed by peaceful negotiations under international law would be a better European neighbour. It might abandon further territorial demands and even adopt a less barbaric internal policy. Similar arguments could be used about Mussolini.

It has been argued that there was an alternative policy – a Franco–Russian–British military alliance. This was the sort of thing talked about at undergraduate clubs in Oxford and no doubt many other places where people knew very little about reality. Chamberlain regarded it with the deepest repugnance. Even if he had not, he could never have carried it in his party. Apart from the ideological issue, Stalin's slaughter, in a series of still puzzling 'purges', of most of his top generals made him an unconvincing military ally and Russia separated by a *cordon sanitaire* of hostile states was ill placed to put pressure on Germany.

Appeasement was not a disreputable policy. It always presupposed that there were some British interests on which there could be no concession – the integrity of France and the Low Countries for example, or the route to India. Eastern Europe and even the former German African colonies did not seem to be so important. Eden half went along with this policy but only half. He seemed to hanker after the League Covenant and he was most reluctant to follow Chamberlain's approaches to the dictators, though he never proposed a clear alternative. He disliked Halifax's visit to Goering in November 1937 when Halifax indicated that Britain would not object to a peaceful German settlement with Austria,

Czechoslovakia and Poland, but he was quite ready to get rid of Vansittart (or rather push him upstairs) soon afterwards, less perhaps on account of his anti-German tirades than because he behaved too much like a Secretary of State.

The crunch with Chamberlain came over two matters. In January 1938 President Roosevelt suggested an *omnium gatherum* diplomatic conference to discuss the problems of the world. Eden was away on holiday. Without consulting him, Chamberlain, who believed that his own direct approaches to the dictators might be compromised, politely requested postponement. Eden, apprised by the Foreign Office, flew back from the South of France and persuaded Chamberlain to send a follow-up telegram reversing the earlier one, but nothing came of it. The episode has been blown up into a great lost opportunity, largely by Churchill and Eden. American historians take the view that Roosevelt never intended more than a gesture, but naturally Eden was much upset. The last straw was Chamberlain's decision to start conversations with Mussolini in February on the basis of *de jure* recognition of the Italian conquest of Abyssinia in return for a promise to withdraw Italian volunteers from Spain. Chamberlain also wanted Mussolini to use a moderating influence on Hitler in the crisis which was clearly about to erupt over Austria, and he hoped generally to detach Italy from Germany. Eden dug in his toes. He did not openly object to *de jure* recognition, though one may guess that privately he saw it as a blow to the Leagueophiles whom he had come to represent, nor did he object in principle to conversations, but he insisted that they should not formally begin until Mussolini had actually shown some evidence that he was withdrawing volunteers from Spain. Meanwhile informal discussion could take place 'to prepare the ground and settle the details first'.[2] Chamberlain was adamant for his own proposed course and he was supported by the Cabinet. But Eden, after many efforts had been made to dissuade him, resigned on 20 February, along with his under-secretary, Lord Cranborne, grandson of the great Lord Salisbury. The actual issue may seem narrow as it usually does in such cases, but it was the culmination of a long series of differences; there had been charges by each side of press leaks, and the Prime Minister mistrusted Eden to the extent of by-passing him by communicating direct with Count Grandi, the Italian ambassador via a Conservative Party official and ex-member of MI5, Sir Joseph Ball. He also received much information from his widowed sister-in-law Lady Chamberlain[3] who lived in Rome and was in close touch with the top Italian ministers. Mussolini was well informed too. A spy in the Rome Embassy supplied him with all the most secret correspondence between the ambassador and the Foreign Office.

In the debate on Eden's resignation twenty-five MPs abstained. Eden's speech was conciliatory. Cranborne's was not, and Chamberlain never forgave him for it. In 1940 when he was Lord President and Cranborne came to be sworn in as a Privy Counsellor he refused to shake hands.[4] In Eden's place Chamberlain appointed Halifax who had for some time been a mediatory figure and was well informed on foreign affairs. He was the only person among the 'appeasers' whose reputation, thanks to his integrity and flexibility, was to remain uninjured. His under-secretary was R. A. Butler. Barely had they taken office than Hitler took Austria. This had been expected ever since the formation of the Axis, and neither Britain nor France intended to do anything about it. One did not need to be a prophet to predict that Czechoslovakia would be next on the list, or rather its German-inhabited area known as the Sudetenland. This was a more perilous problem. Austria was wholly German-speaking and would have joined Germany in 1919 but for a French veto. The annexation of the Sudetenland would, however, mean the dismemberment of one of the few show pieces of the post-war settlement – a parliamentary democracy of high repute with a considerable army and an industrial base most of which was unfortunately in the Sudetenland itself.

We now know that Hitler had decided early in November the previous year that Germany had nothing to gain from prolongation of peace. His armaments were now superior to anyone else's but would become obsolete in 1943-5 or even earlier. He informed his military leaders and the head of the German Foreign Office on 5 November 1937 that expansion *(lebensraum)* into Poland and the rich black land of the Ukraine was essential and could be achieved only by the threat or use of force. The first steps would be the annexation of Austria and the destruction of Czechoslovakia. He recognized that Germany had to reckon with 'two hateful antagonists, England and France', but he did not believe they would go to war. At the time of this conference, recorded in a document of great historical importance by his adjutant, Friedrich Hossbach, he did not regard the matter as urgent, but he soon changed his mind possibly because of the changes in the British Foreign Office – Vansittart's supersession and the departure of Eden and Cranborne. Whatever his motives Hitler suddenly speeded up his programme early in 1938. The annexation of Austria on 13 March was uncontested by Britain and France. Italy also acquiesced. He now moved without a pause to the destruction of Czechoslovakia – that 'French aircraft carrier in the middle of Europe', as he described it. His public argument was the alleged oppression of the Sudeten Germans but he carefully arranged that every concession by Prague was followed by further disruptive demands from the Sudeten leader, Konrad Henlein. Hitler planned to invade Czechoslovakia on 30 September.

Czech integrity was guaranteed by a treaty with Russia and France. The Russians, however, were obliged to act only if France did so first and then invoked the treaty. The French were determined not to move without British support, and the British government was equally determined not to give it. As Chamberlain was to put the matter in a broadcast on 27 September, it was 'fantastic and incredible' to be involved in a war 'because of a quarrel in a far-away country between people of whom we know nothing'. The Chiefs of Staff were strongly against war, as indeed were their German counterparts but Chamberlain was less influenced by military advice than by his belief that diplomacy could still avert European cataclysm through peaceful revision of Versailles.

From 19 to 21 May there was a war scare. It was widely believed that Hitler was about to attack Czechoslovakia. Britain and France displayed a degree of support for the Czechs which was never repeated. The ensuing German denial was genuine, though only in the sense that the attack was scheduled not for 19 May but 30 September. The widespread impression that Anglo-French solidarity had prevented a German attack infuriated Hitler. He was more determined than ever to destroy Czechoslovakia and he stepped up the Sudeten agitation. Convinced that there was now a major threat to European peace Chamberlain in August sent out Lord Runciman, a Liberal national who had been President of the Board of Trade from 1931 to 1937 to mediate between Czechs and Sudeten Germans. He returned empty-handed. Henlein's orders precluded any settlement short of outright cession of the German-speaking areas, and he was supported in a striking *Times* leader on 7 September.

Chamberlain was not yet ready to go to quite this length. On 15 September he took the then sensational decision to fly to meet Hitler at Berchtesgarten. He returned next day convinced that the only solution was to transfer the Sudetenland, and to persuade France to agree. This was pushing at an open door. The last thing the French wanted was war. Their army, geared to a purely defensive role, was incapable of an attack on Germany's western frontier – the only move that could have helped the Czechs. Let down by their most important ally the Prague government had no option but to agree. Chamberlain returned to Germany on 22 September to meet Hitler at Godesberg. The German dictator, determined on his scheduled attack, had never expected a capitulation of this sort. He raised his terms even higher – so high that Chamberlain refused to accept what amounted to the total dismemberment of the country. For the next week war seemed imminent. Gas masks were distributed to the public, for gas was widely, though erroneously, expected to be a major weapon of war. I can vividly remember in a rural area of Norfolk an elderly lady rushing into our house crying, 'The devils have got us, the devils have got us', but the gas was only the smoke from an autumnal bonfire on that hot September afternoon. Trenches were dug in the London parks, a few anti-aircraft guns were manoeuvred into position, arrangements were made to evacuate school-children from London, the Fleet was mobilized.

Hitler may have expected, though no one can know for certain, that his new terms would result in a refusal from the Czechs who would then be abandoned by Britain and France. After that he could launch his invasion. The French, however, jibbed at such a total surrender despite British pressure, and London reluctantly agreed to support Paris. At this juncture Hitler climbed down – not far, but enough to satisfy the western allies. Why he did so is not clear. The German military authorities were strongly opposed to a war against France, Britain and Czechoslovakia. There is some evidence that they contemplated a coup against Hitler, and that this information was passed on to Halifax. Although the British government can hardly be blamed for not taking it very seriously the rumour may have stiffened them slightly. Military reluctance moreover must have affected Hitler, even if he knew nothing of any coup. For these or other reasons he decided to take the cherry in two bites, not one, and he allowed Mussolini to mediate. Chamberlain was aware of that possibility when he made a sombre speech on 28 September to a specially recalled House of Commons. Towards the end of his dismal recital a telegram was passed to him from Lord Halifax in the Peers Gallery via his parliamentary private secretary, Lord Dunglass (later to be Prime Minister as Sir Alec Douglas-Home). Chamberlain read out the news that Mussolini had persuaded Hitler to consent to a four-power conference at Munich. Almost the entire House rose to their feet and applauded this carefully stage-managed scene.

Churchill, Amery, Harold Nicolson and Willie Gallacher (the only Communist MP) remained seated. Eden either did the same or walked out 'pale with shame and anger' – the evidence conflicts.

Chamberlain flew to Germany for the third time on 29 September. The Munich Conference from which the Czech government was excluded comprised Britain, France, Germany and Italy. The territorial settlement was rather worse for Czechoslovakia than Chamberlain's Godesberg terms, but like those it did at least contain a four-power guarantee of the frontiers of the truncated state. Chamberlain and Hitler next day signed a statement that their two countries were resolved 'never to go to war with one another again'. On his return to London Chamberlain appeared at the window of 10 Downing Street and told the applauding multitude: 'This is the second time that there has come back from Germany to Downing Street peace with honour. I believe it is peace for our time.'

The Congress of Berlin to which he was alluding had resulted in an honourable peace which lasted with a few minor interruptions for thirty-six years. The Munich settlement was anything but honourable and it postponed war by less than one year. In Britain there was bitter controversy. People are inclined nowadays to regard Winston Churchill's writing as exaggerated and flamboyant. It sometimes is, but no one who lived through those times will deny the truth of this famous passage:

> It is not easy in these latter days ... to portray for another generation the passions which raged in Britain about the Munich Agreement. Among the Conservatives, families and friends in intimate contact were divided to a degree the like of which I have never seen. Men and women long bound together by party ties, social amenities and family connections glared upon one another in scorn and anger ... The Cabinet was shaken to its foundations.[5]

Churchill himself had good cause to be aware of the angry passions to which he alludes. On 5 October he made one of his most famous and eloquent speeches – splendid reading even today – in condemnation of Munich. It is worthy of Demosthenes or Cicero, but when he came to the words 'we have sustained a total and unmitigated defeat' he was compelled to pause because of the storm which he encountered. Munich created something of a generation gap. There was an element of euphoric relief among the middle aged and elderly at the avoidance of war. The articulate young were on the other side. They felt ashamed and humiliated. I can remember an Oxford friend and contemporary who refused to drink to the Prime Minister's health after his father had summoned champagne for the occasion. He was told to leave the house forthwith. He promptly did so and they were only reconciled shortly before his own death in action in the war that followed.

These disputes were largely confined to what Lord Salisbury called 'the classes'. No one knows how 'the masses' reacted. If by-elections are anything to go by Munich did not have a great effect. The swing against the Conservatives was much the same as it had been earlier in the year and was on the scale to be expected at this stage in the life of any government. There was a move towards setting up 'popular front' candidates. A. D. Lindsay, Master of Balliol, contested the Oxford City by-election on this basis in October against Quintin Hogg (now Lord Hailsham). It was the first trial of strength since Munich, but the verdict was ambiguous. Hogg won with a reduced majority. This was the general pattern with one notable exception – Bridgwater where Vernon Bartlett, a famous political commentator, defeated the Conservative candidate, polling 6,000 more votes than Labour and Liberal combined had secured in 1935, but there may well have been special reasons for this result.

Only one minister resigned – Duff Cooper, First Lord of the Admiralty, but he had gone along with so much of the government's policy that his reasons seemed rather narrow. Moreover, he was a lightweight in terms of political influence despite his high office. The Cabinet, however, was certainly

217

shaken. Its formal near-unanimity concealed many doubts and misgivings. A second Munich was out of the question. Although no Conservative MPs voted against Chamberlain there was a formidable list of abstentions, including Churchill, Eden, Cranborne, Amery, Macmillan, Bracken and Sandys. The Conservative Central Office favoured a snap election to exploit the temporary sense of relief that there was no war. Chamberlain was dissuaded by Halifax, and he was perhaps influenced too by a notable speech from Sir Sidney Herbert, a respected backbencher of the old order who referred to those who favoured a dissolution as 'some tiny Tammany Hall ring'.

The supporters of Munich could not have known that war would break out less than a year later. Nevertheless it has always been a subject of conjecture whether the interlude weakened or strengthened the western powers in relation to Germany, for one of the arguments used later to justify Chamberlain was that he was buying time to rearm. It has been urged equally strongly by Churchill among others that the year following Munich adversely affected the western powers which had lost a valuable ally without a shot being fired. There are too many imponderables for a clear answer and it is not enough to add up the number of divisions, ships and aircraft on both sides at the relevant dates without considering what other countries might have done. Russian policy remains a complete puzzle. Would Stalin have wished to intervene on the side of the Czechs and, if so, how could he have helped them when Russia was separated from the Czech frontier by Poland, Romania and Hungary – countries which feared him even more than they feared Hitler? And what would Poland and Hungary have done in the event of a German–Czech war? They were at least as likely to have joined Germany in dismembering Czechoslovakia as to have joined the west in a war against Hitler.

The truth is that military considerations played little part in Chamberlain's plans. Even if the British forces had been stronger and there had been a degree of coordination with the

French which was totally lacking in 1938 he would still have refused to involve Britain in the affairs of eastern Europe. He was following the well established policy of his predecessors since Locarno. There was no question of 'buying time' and, as Hitler believed, delaying in order to choose a better occasion for an inevitable conflict. British armed strength undoubtedly became greater during 1938–9 but this was largely because of decisions taken before Munich. It is wrong to think in terms of a nicely balanced decision made on strategic grounds. Chamberlain had no intention of going to war unless Germany threatened to invade the vital areas of the Low Countries and the French Channel coast. Of course this might have happened if France had fulfilled her obligations to Czechoslovakia but not necessarily; and until it did happen he was not going to move an inch.

Six months later Chamberlain made a complete *volte face* – one of the most startling 'U-turns' in the history of British foreign policy. The explanation lies in two developments, the first gradual, the second sudden. The first was the realization that Munich had made nonsense of the whole basis of French strategy. The destruction of France's only eastern ally enormously increased the danger of Germany overrunning the Low Countries and the north coast of France. It prompted the French to demand with increasing vehemence a revival of the continental commitment which had brought the British Expeditionary Force across the Channel in 1914. This meant the abandonment of the dogma of 'limited liability' in Europe to which successive governments had adhered since 1918. The Chiefs of State by February 1939 had become convinced that British security could not be maintained if France capitulated, and therefore that the defence of Britain 'may have to include a share in the land defence of France'.[6] Their argument converted Chamberlain, hitherto the leading exponent of 'limited liability'. The Cabinet decided to create an army of thirty-two divisions, six regular and twenty-six territorial – which meant doubling the Territorial Army and spending huge sums to equip it. Moreover, as the result of an erroneous report that Germany was about to attack Holland they at last authorized staff conversations with the French.

It was natural now to think again in terms of eastern European allies. At this juncture an unexpected development occurred in that very area. On 15 March, five days after Sir Samuel Hoare had made a particularly fatuous speech about peace and prosperity, and on the very day when a famous *Punch* cartoon appeared showing the nightmare of war vanishing from John Bull's bedroom window, Hitler marched his troops into Prague. He declared a German protectorate over Bohemia and Moravia and created Slovakia as a separate and puppet state. The seizure of a non-German country destroyed appeasement. No one could now imagine that Hitler's objectives were confined to remedying the grievances of Versailles. The 'doves' who believed in international morality and the 'hawks' who believed in the national interest were united, even as they had been a quarter of a century before by the German invasion of Belgium. The continental commitment suddenly became acceptable.

March 15 1939 is one of those rare days which can be described as a turning point in history. It may not have made war inevitable but it certainly made a great many English people think it inevitable. Not all, of course. Chamberlain and some of his Cabinet still clung to the view that it might be averted. Most people hoped for peace but few believed it. A notable fillip was given to war preparations of every kind. Recruitment to the Territorial Army and other volunteer branches of the services greatly increased. There was, however, none of the enthusiasm and idealism of 1914. The war ahead would not be one to end all wars or make the world safe for democracy. It would not be for a 'cause', for collective security, for racial equality, for international order. No doubt these notions played some part in some people's motives, but the real issue was patriotism, the survival of a Britain which, despite its defects, inspired the love and devotion of ninety-nine per cent of its citizens. The British would fight for self-preservation, to crush a destructive, ruthless, nihilistic power before it crushed them. In March 1939 joyless but determined the new war generation with a sombre sense of destiny and obligation accepted its duty.

Chamberlain's first reaction to Prague was legalistically negative; if Czechoslovakia had ceased to exist there was no state for Britain to guarantee. His speech in the House on 15 March was ill-received. Two days later he changed his tune, whether belatedly annoyed at being double-crossed by Hitler, or prompted by Lord Halifax's conscience or pressed by the Whips. At Birmingham on 17 March while defending Munich he ended with a sharp and loudly applauded condemnation of Hitler's action. Events now moved rapidly. An erroneous rumour, the second to influence British policy in the early months of 1939, suggested that Hitler was about to attack Romania. The Cabinet on 18 March resolved on a policy of inviting Russia, Poland, Romania, Yugoslavia, Greece and Turkey to join Britain and France in resistance to aggression in eastern Europe. The creation of an eastern front was a logical corollary to the continental commitment. The British Chiefs of Staff regarded it as important not only to block any German drive south-east towards the oil and grain of Romania and the ores of Yugoslavia but also to build a bastion in the eastern Mediterranean which would prevent German penetration into Britain's rebellious Middle Eastern empire and act as a launching pad for counter-attacks. This was the motive behind the search for alliances with Yugoslavia and Greece, the disastrous Greek campaign of 1941, the support for resistance movements after both countries had been overrun, and the vain negotiations for a deal with Turkey abandoned only in 1943. The trouble was that most of the countries which the Cabinet wished to win over hated Russia as much as Germany, and each other even more.

In fact Romania was not Hitler's next objective. Having swallowed up Czechoslovakia he reverted to irridentism. On 19 March he demanded and four days later obtained the cession of the German city of Memmel from Lithuania. At the same time he hotted up his many-month-old campaign for the return of Danzig, and on 21 March loaded the Polish ambassador in Berlin with a series of demands. At this juncture yet a third false report reached the British Cabinet. It was rumoured that German troops were about to attack Poland. Although Poland was under pressure to concede Danzig in return for future compensation in the Ukraine and to join the anti-Commintern Pact, Hitler had as yet no plans for invasion. Poland, however, appealed for help. On 31 March Chamberlain announced that along with France the British government would, if Poland were attacked, 'feel bound at once to lend the Polish government all support in their power'. Such an alliance was without precedent in English history. It was a complete reversal of the policy adopted ever since Locarno.

Viewed in cold blood the offer which was promptly accepted by Colonel Beck, the Polish Foreign Minister, seems insane. Britain and France could give no direct help whatever to Poland. The keys of war and peace were put into the hands of one of the most reckless, irresponsible, vain and volatile governments in Europe, a military dictatorship which did not even possess the virtue of military efficiency. The most likely *casus belli* was the Danzig question which of all Hitler's demands seemed the least unreasonable and the one with which the Cabinet had most sympathy. But the occupation of Prague made the guarantee acceptable to public opinion, just as it had also made the continental commitment acceptable. The Polish guarantee was probably intended to be a deterrent which Chamberlain hoped he would not have to implement. If so it was a major miscalculation. On 3 April, the very day on which the alliance was debated in the House of Commons, Hitler gave orders to his generals to make a contingency plan for the destruction of the Polish Army. On 28 April he denounced both the Anglo-German Naval Agreement of 1935 and German-Polish Non-Aggression Pact of 1934. Mussolini contributed his share to the general atmosphere of insecurity by annexing Albania on 7 April and shortly afterwards launching a bombastic anti-French campaign for the return to Italy of Tunis and Savoy. In May a formal Italo-German military alliance was concluded – the so-called Pact of Steel.

Chamberlain continued to resist any attempt to bring Churchill or Eden into his government. He announced at the end of April the establishment of a Ministry of Supply, though no minister was appointed till July and the first incumbent was not Churchill but a dim Liberal National called Leslie Burgin. At the same time a very limited form of conscription was introduced. It applied to future age groups on reaching twenty and they would only serve for six months when called up. It aroused furious opposition to alleged 'militarism' from Labour and Liberals alike.

It was to be five months before matters came to a head. The crucial question throughout that time was the attitude of Russia. Critics in Britain were quick to point out that the Polish guarantee made no military sense without a Russian alliance. But the Poles dreaded with good reason the entry of the Red Army on to their soil even if the purpose was to encounter German aggression. In Britain the political aims of the USSR were distrusted by the Cabinet and its military effectiveness by the Chiefs of Staff who believed that Russia was in no position to do more than defend itself. Who can say that they were wrong? Public opinion, however, expressed with vigour by Lloyd George, Churchill and the leaders of the Labour Party, forced Chamberlain reluctantly to seek an alliance. The ineluctable facts of geography and strategy, along with the charge of ideological prejudice against the 'Socialist Sixth of the World', brought him to initiate negotiations on 15 April. They were to be half-hearted, protracted and in the end abortive.

Chamberlain and Halifax do not seem to have hoped for much more than a vague anti-German threat by Stalin, which might, like their own specific guarantee to Poland, deter Hitler, and push him towards moderation. They still did not despair of a deal over Danzig and reconciliation with a Germany confined to limited objectives. The one thing they never expected was a bargain between Hitler and Stalin. Russian intentions and calculations are as obscure during this period as at the time of Munich. In retrospect one can guess that the dismissal on 3 May of the Commissar for Foreign Affairs, Litvinov, who was a Jew and favoured negotiations with the west, marked a turning point. His successor, Molotov, had no objection to dealing with the Nazis. Although there was at the time, and has been since, much criticism of the dilatory way in which Britain negotiated, it is unlikely that a different approach would have had any more success. It is impossible to say whether Stalin suspected Hitler's long-term plans. In the short run he could gain advantages which no western power could give – the reoccupation of the lands which Poland had acquired in 1920, and a free hand in Finland, Latvia, Estonia and Bessarabia. These items were part of the secret protocols to the Nazi–Soviet Pact which was announced on 23 August to the consternation of the western world. Hitler himself was candid enough in private. As he told Burckhardt, the Danzig High Commissioner on 11 August: 'Everything I undertake is directed against Russia. If the West is too blind and stupid to comprehend that, I will be forced to come to an understanding with the Russians, to smash the West and then, after its defeat, to turn against the Soviet Union with my assembled forces.'

The pact made war inevitable unless Hitler was prepared to obtain Danzig by diplomacy – which he probably could have done from the now sobered-down Poles. He was not. He planned to attack at dawn on 26 August. At the last moment he delayed, possibly because the Anglo-Polish alliance was formally if belatedly ratified on the previous day. There are some signs that he would have liked to appease Britain. His terms for a settlement were regarded as 'not unreasonable' by Neville Henderson and Halifax who urged Beck to negotiate. Beck refused, and the German armies attacked at 4.45 A.M. on 1 September.

There has been speculation about why Hitler struck when he did. The most probable explanation is that he had failed to get his war in 1938 and he was determined not to miss it now. What was the point, otherwise, of all his military preparations? Ribbentrop may well have spoken with his master's voice when in mid-August he was asked by Count Ciano, the Italian Foreign Minister: 'What is it that you want? Danzig? The Corridor?' He replied: 'We want war.' No doubt Hitler did not positively wish for war with Britain and France as well and he probably expected that, even if they fulfilled their formal obligations, they would drop them after the now inevitable destruction of Poland. But he did not regard their intervention as mattering much in comparison with the prospect of launching his armies on their first great foray into Europe.

The Polish government at once invoked the British alliance. There was a chilly response and a pause. The reason was later said to be the need for coordination with France whose government still hoped for a compromise based on rumours that, as in 1938, Mussolini was about to propose a mediatory conference. But Chamberlain and Halifax were also clutching at every straw. Poland too was a far-off country of which few Britons knew anything. Parliament forced a reluctant government into war. Chamberlain on 2 September hinted at a conference. When Arthur Greenwood, acting for Attlee who was ill, got up to reply, Leo Amery cried out: 'Arthur, speak for England.' Greenwood referred to the danger of 'imperilling the very foundations of our national honour'. The House adjourned in a state of indignation, and Chamberlain was made fully aware of a potential Cabinet revolt. At 9 A.M. the next day the delayed British ultimatum was sent. It expired without reply at 11 A.M., and war was declared. The French glumly followed suit six hours later.

Chapter Twelve

WAR

I

Hitler's invasion of Poland launched a war that involved all the major powers in the world and did not end till his total defeat in 1945. The war was confined at first to France, Poland (quickly destroyed), the British Empire and Germany. It extended to Italy in 1940, to the Soviet Union, Japan and America during 1941. It engulfed the whole of Europe, apart from Switzerland, Sweden and the Iberian peninsula. It was fought in the Middle East, Africa, Burma, Malaysia and China and in the skies and oceans. Some 45 million people were killed, divided almost equally between combatants and civilians. Britain suffered far less than others, but these fearful figures have conditioned the world to which Britain belongs from that day to this.

The British declaration of war constitutionally brought in India, Burma and the colonies, but not the dominions. Australia, New Zealand and Canada followed Britain. In South Africa there was a minor constitutional crisis. Hertzog, the Prime Minister, introduced on 4 September a motion favouring neutrality. Smuts carried by eighty votes to sixty-seven an amendment in favour of entry into war. Hertzog then asked for a dissolution of Parliament but the Governor-General refused and when Hertzog resigned on 6 September appointed Smuts who declared war the same day. He retained office until 1948. Chamberlain made a modest reconstruction of his government. Labour and Liberals declined to join, but Churchill and Eden were included – as First Lord of the Admiralty and Dominions Secretary respectively.

The Cabinet was slimmed down from twenty-one to nine. The inner ring of the appeasers was included – Hoare, Simon and Halifax. Eden was not a member of the Cabinet. A number of new non-Cabinet ministries were created – Economic Warfare, Food, Shipping, Information. Chamberlain like Asquith was not by nature a wartime Prime Minister. He could not cope with a situation in which, as he said in his gloomy broadcast on 3 September: '... everything that I have worked for, everything that I have hoped, everything that I have believed in during my public life, has crashed in ruins.' There was little drive and less coordination. The service chiefs conducted war on a departmental basis.

Not that there was at first very much war to conduct. Neither Britain nor France could do anything about Poland, rapidly obliterated in the blazing heat of that terrible September. The Polish forces, brave, archaic, horse-drawn and cavalry-dominated, rapidly crumpled under a bold, mobile, mechanized attack. The Germans did not possess the formidable arms with which they were credited then and later. They had no heavy tanks, and only a few medium ones. Their six armoured divisions consisted mainly of light tanks with very thin armour and liable to frequent breakdown. The German Army was not ready for war. But it did possess overwhelming air superiority, and its formidable force of Stuka dive-bombers had a devastating effect. These black rook-like planes screaming suddenly down from a sky, empty a few seconds earlier, epitomized the *Blitzkrieg*, the lightning war. On 17 September, the Russians marched in to occupy the territory agreed to be theirs under the terms of the Nazi–Soviet Pact. At the end of the month Poland capitulated. Her casualties were immense, and her capital devastated.

All, however, was quiet on the western front and continued to be so for many months. The ponderous mobilization of the French Army was not completed till 17 September. By then the imminence of Polish defeat excused an inactivity which would have occurred anyway. The army was not trained for an offensive. Nor, given the neutrality of the Low Countries, was there an obvious route for launching one without defiance of international law. Thereafter attack was out of the question as the victorious German troops moved to the west. During September and October the four divisions of the British Expeditionary Force arrived to take up station south of Lille on the Belgian frontier. By March 1940 the number had risen to ten and the line was extended. The government resolved to build the army up to fifty-five divisions instead of thirty-two, but this would take many months to achieve.

The RAF was equally quiescent. The potential effects of German bombing were grossly exaggerated. Since the *Luftwaffe* showed no signs of attacking, it was regarded as dangerous to provoke reprisals. For similar reasons the French vetoed Churchill's plan to drop mines in the Rhine. The RAF confined itself to scattering propaganda leaflets, a singularly futile operation against an enemy flushed with victory. The navy was the only branch of the services which was superior to its German counterpart. It was also the only one to be involved in any serious fighting in the early months of the war, though with mixed success. U-boat and commerce raiders sank some 800,000 tons of merchant shipping before the 'real' war began. On 17 September a U-boat torpedoed the aircraft carrier *Courageous*. On 14 October Lieutenant Prien commanding the U47 managed with great skill and courage to penetrate the defences of Scapa Flow and sink the battleship *Royal Oak*, with the loss of nearly 800 men. On 23 November the armed merchantman *Rawalpindi*, patrolling between Iceland and the Faroes, went down in flames to the guns of the *Scharnhorst*, one of the two fast ultramodern battle cruisers which, along with the *Gneisenau*, threatened the convoys in the North Atlantic. The two battle cruisers turned back for fear of discovery and, despite a hunt involving most of the available ships in the British and French navies, arrived safely in the Baltic. Not surprisingly the navy's prestige was at a low ebb until confidence was restored by the action on 13 December off the river Plate where the pocket battleship *Graf Spee*, which had sunk nine cargo ships in the southern seas was found by Commodore Harwood's 'hunting group'. Although his three cruisers had inferior gun power he was able to drive the *Graf Spee* into Montevideo where on orders from Hitler she was scuttled four days later.

On 6 October Hitler urged Britain and France to accept a *fait accompli* and discuss with him the remaining problems of Europe. It is unlikely that he expected agreement and his invitation was turned down after a few days, but even before that he issued instructions for a major offensive against the western powers to begin as soon as possible and not later than mid-November. The German generals were horrified. They knew how much had gone wrong behind the scenes in Poland. They were short of ammunition and spare parts, they had fewer divisions than their opponents – 98 to 114 (including the BEF), or in terms of 'active' divisions 62 to 69 – they had fewer tanks, and they had not yet themselves fully appreciated the significance of their own air superiority. There was even talk of a military coup against Hitler but nothing came of it. The weather which suddenly worsened in early November and remained exceptionally bad all over western Europe for the whole winter caused numerous postponements. Eventually Hitler decided to allow Christmas leave and launch the offensive in the New Year.

Meanwhile the USSR was taking every precaution against her new ally. As soon as the Soviet troops had marched into Poland the frightened foreign ministers of the Baltic states were summoned to Moscow to sign 'non-aggression pacts' which gave Russia the right to install garrisons. Early in October pressure was put on Finland to make similar concessions. Surprisingly the Finns refused, and on 30 November the Russians attacked. Even more surprisingly they were repulsed. The invaders were to be held up for three months before sheer numbers forced Finland to come to terms. There was universal disgust in the west at this piece of Soviet aggression. Gallant little Finland in 1939 matched gallant little Belgium in 1914. By the end of the year Churchill was pressing a plan to send an expeditionary force via the northernmost Norwegian port of Narvik. The idea which was later taken up with enthusiasm by the French was not dictated solely by sympathy with a small nation wantonly invaded. A by-product of the use of Narvik would be to enable the Allies to cut off the supply of Swedish iron ore to Germany. It is true that both Norway and Sweden were neutral but, as Churchill said in his memorandum of 16 December 1939: 'Small nations must not tie our hands when we are fighting for their freedom . . . Humanity, rather than legality, must be our guide.' The Cabinet was however not prepared to be so cavalier at this stage. The year ended with no clear decision taken, but with agreement to make plans for landing a force at Narvik if necessary.

At home the declaration of war was almost unanimously supported in Parliament, and there was virtually no dissent in the country. The pro-Nazi groups active up to Munich had become silent after Prague. The Communist Party lost a third of its membership, small anyway, when it toadied to the Stalinist line a few weeks after the Nazi–Soviet Pact. Pacifists were treated more generously than in 1914 and there were too few of them to matter politically. The government took emergency powers which entitled it to do almost anything by regulation or decree but it was chary of exercising them. Petrol rationing was introduced but on a generous scale at first. Food rationing did not come in till the New Year and more from pressure of public demand than ministerial conviction. The railways and the major industries were brought nominally under government control but in practice they were run by committees of their own top management. Rich people could still send themselves or their money abroad and quite a number did both. Five thousand people left for America in the first two days of the war. Others took themselves to the north and the west of England or to Wales and Scotland, and, if they were over military age, spent a not uncomfortable war in an area far less affected than the south and east. Some 2 million are supposed to have moved, not of course all of them permanently.

This was a piece of private enterprise. Far more sensational was the effect of the government's plan to evacuate school-children from the danger areas where German bombing was expected and to billet them in safe places. Arrangements had been made to move 4 million mothers, children, babies, teachers and helpers. In the event about 1.5 million went. This shortfall was a help in some ways but in others not. The careful allocation of schools to particular trains for particular places went by the board. The evacuees filled up the first train to go, without regard to destination. At the other end, as Angus Calder points out in his vivid account,[1] those on whom the evacuees actually were billeted, although quasi-volunteers, had a legitimate grievance – 'Why me?' And the same indignation was expressed between neighbouring villages, some of which had every place taken, others none. The verminous condition of the children, most of whom came from the poorest inner city areas, was an acute shock to middle-class householders. Every sort of mismatching and confrontation occurred. It would require the pen of Dickens to do justice to the scenes that followed. The pen of Evelyn Waugh has indeed done justice to a limited aspect in *Put Out More Flags*, one of the funniest books ever written. In the end it was all rather like the Grand Old Duke of York. No bombs fell. Mothers and children moved back to the familiarity of the slums. By the New Year nearly a million had returned. The 'two nations' certainly knew more about each other but whether they liked what they knew is another matter.

The other notable impact on life was the ubiquity of the blackout. No single measure of the government transformed ordinary life more completely. It came into force at dusk on 1 September, before war had even been declared. Street lamps, neon signs, shop windows were extinguished. To use a torch or strike a match was to run the risk of prosecution. The historian might console himself with the reflection that he now knew from personal experience what urban life must have been like after dark in the middle ages, but even he cannot have enjoyed the contusions suffered by falling down a man-hole, bumping into a lamp post, tripping over a paving stone, or simply colliding with another citizen. Motorists had to use sidelights, and as a result deaths on the road doubled during September. Every householder was obliged to ensure by the use of black paper or heavy curtains that no chink of light could be seen outside. Air raid wardens who enforced all these regulations, often with irritating officiousness, came to be a much disliked class.

Common sense resulted in some modification in October. Torches with a double thickness of tissue paper were permitted. Cars were allowed to use masked headlights. At Christmas illuminated signs were allowed for cinemas and a very limited degree of lighting for shops and stalls. Street lamps too could be used, if modified so as to project a very thin beam downwards. The blackout embodied the most striking contrast between the years of peace and war. Many soldiers who went out by the Cape route to the Middle East in 1941–2 can still remember the shock of seeing the normal city lights at ports like Cape Town or Durban. After the blackout it was a revelation.

The country became without much urgency a military training camp. By the end of 1939 over 1.5 million men were in the armed services, nearly all in the army. Men between eighteen and forty-one were liable to call-up, but the process was leisurely; twenty-seven-year-olds were not required till May 1940. It was possible to volunteer earlier and over a million did so, including 43,000 in the Women's Auxiliary Services. There were no white feathers, none of the hysteria of 1914, and there was a whole category of reserved occupations where people were enjoined to remain in the national interest. Employers could ask for 'deferment' of call-up. Individuals could argue a case on 'personal hardship'.

2

In the early months of 1940 some crucial decisions were taken which shaped the course of the war and, perhaps, of world politics ever since. The principal decision – Hitler's change of plan for the attack on the west – is a striking example of the part that chance can play in history. The original German plan modelled on that of Count von Schlieffen in 1914 was an attack through Belgium, with Holland added in for good measure. The main armoured thrust would have come from the German right. The French Commander-in-Chief, General Gamelin, expected this and planned to riposte with an Anglo-French sweep into Belgium. It might have been more prudent to stay on the defensive lines built along the Belgian frontier. But even so, a campaign fought among the rivers, canals, marshes and big cities of the Low Countries would have been most unfavourable to German armour and would almost certainly have ended in a stalemate. This point was made to Hitler by some of his advisers. Nevertheless, on 10 January he decided to launch his attack a week later, without modification.

On that very day, in circumstances still obscure, a German officer flying from Munster to Bonn with a copy of the entire operational plan made a forced landing in Belgium. He tried unsuccessfully to burn his papers but they were impounded by the Belgian authorities and passed on to the French and British High Command. Hitler could not know for certain what had happened but he obviously had to change his plans. At the instance of General von Manstein he decided to put his main armoured thrust not on the right but on the left through the hilly, forested Ardennes. This was an area hitherto regarded by both sides as untraversable by tanks. Despite doubts expressed both by Churchill and Hore-Belisha, who was dismissed for his pains, the front from the northern end of the Maginot Line along the Meuse and through Sedan to the southern end of the area held by the BEF was thinly defended by second-class French troops and inadequate fortification. Manstein reckoned that it was physically possible for tanks to go through the Ardennes provided that there was no opposition. If they moved with sufficient speed and secrecy they would be over the Meuse before the defenders could do anything. Once they were across, they could fan out on the rolling plains of northern France, ideal territory for armoured divisions, and drive for the Channel ports thus cutting off the BEF and the flower of the French armies from their bases. The change which involved completely recasting the German plan involved a delay of four months but the time was used more profitably by the Germans than the Allies. Surprisingly, the French High Command made no attempt to recast their own plans in the light of their curious windfall. They convinced themselves that it was an elaborate piece of deception; yet it is hard to see what the German staff were supposed to gain by alerting the Belgians who on the strength of this discovery, might legitimately have invited the Anglo-French forces into their country, thus constituting the very threat to the Ruhr which Hitler dreaded – 'our Achilles' heel', he called it.

Meanwhile, enthusiasm mounted in the British and French governments for a Scandinavian expedition. Churchill had long been anxious to mine the 'Leads' – the narrow strip of Norwegian territorial waters which provided a passage for Swedish iron ore during the winter months. The signs were so obvious that the leader of a Norwegian Nazi-type party, Vikdun Quisling, who was to give his name to such movements all over Europe, visited Hitler in December 1939 and urged him to forestall Britain. Hitler preferred a neutral Scandinavia but was ready to act if there was a clear British intention to occupy Norway. On 27 January 1940 he gave orders to plan against this contingency. On 5 February the Supreme Allied War Council met in Paris and decided to send two British divisions along with a smaller French force to Narvik early in March, the 'cover' being aid to Finland, the real purpose the occupation of the Gällivare orefield. Eleven days later in Norwegian territorial waters the British Navy under the noses of two Norwegian gunboats seized the *Altmark*, a German vessel carrying the prisoners taken by the *Graf Spee*. This episode wrongly convinced Hitler that the Norwegian government was hand in glove with Britain. He gave orders on 1 March for the preparation of plans for invasion, although he still felt reluctant to take the final plunge. On 8 March the British Cabinet decided to occupy twelve days later the key Norwegian ports of Trondheim, Bergen and Stavanger as well as Narvik. On 13 March, however, Finland capitulated. There was now no pretext for invasion and the Allies hesitated.

At this juncture the French Prime Minister, Edouard Daladier, was replaced by Paul Reynaud who was expected to infuse more vigour into the prosecution of the war. The same sentiment prevailed in England, and at a meeting of the Supreme Allied War Council on 28 March Chamberlain pressed not only for action in Norway, both mining the 'Leads' and seizing the ports, but also for Churchill's favourite plan of launching or dropping a stream of fluvial mines in the Rhine and other German rivers. Reynaud was all for invading Norway but dubious about the Rhine. A fatal pause ensued. Chamberlain wanted the two operations to take place simultaneously. The mining of the 'Leads' had been fixed for 5 April, and the expeditionary force was to sail for Narvik on the 8th. The French War Council jibbed at mines in the Rhine. Chamberlain decided to postpone the Norwegian operation for three days and send Churchill to Paris on what turned out to be an unsuccessful mission to persuade the French. Meanwhile on 1 April Hitler had at last decided to strike. The Germans occupied Denmark and in the early hours of 9 April German troops conveyed in warships seized, to the astonishment of the Allies, Oslo and all the principal Norwegian ports. The British and French governments had of course no difficulty in denouncing the moral obliquity of an action which they had been on the very brink of taking themselves.

The ensuing campaign was a catalogue of disasters. The Germans with an inferior navy and far fewer troops defeated the Allies at every turn. There has seldom in British history been greater confusion of council, more contradictory orders and less planning. However, one should remember that the

Germans possessed overwhelming air power. It was this which made the Admiralty hesitate to cut off the supply route through the Skagerrak between Denmark and Norway, and which defeated all attempts to capture Trondheim. Narvik was briefly occupied on 27 May but relinquished on 7 June. By then much had happened.

The Norwegian campaign brought down Chamberlain and put in Churchill. This was in some ways an ironic turn of events. If any one minister could be held accountable for the débâcle it was the First Lord of the Admiralty. To his credit Churchill never disclaimed his responsibility and in the two-day debate which began on 7 May vigorously defended the government. Amery attacked Chamberlain, quoting Cromwell's words to the Rump Parliament: 'Depart, I say, and let us have done with you. In the name of God, go!' The Labour leaders had not intended to force a division but changed their minds overnight. Next day Lloyd George, who hated Chamberlain, referred acidly to the Prime Minister's appeal for 'sacrifice'. He urged him to set an example 'because there is nothing that can contribute more to victory in this war than that he should sacrifice the seals of office'. In the ensuing vote the government's usual majority of over two hundred fell to eighty-one; of its normal supporters forty-one, including thirty-three Conservatives, voted with the opposition, and over sixty abstained.

This palpable rebuff and manifestation of disunity resolved Chamberlain to try to create an all-party coalition. The dissident Conservatives made the attempt a condition of their own adherence. Chamberlain still hoped to remain as Prime Minister but he knew that Labour and Liberals might refuse to serve under him, and therefore that he might have to recommend to the King a name for the succession. To the general public Churchill was the obvious man but to those in the corridors of power the answer was not so certain. He had made a great many enemies, and he was reputed to be reckless. Halifax seemed a safer bet, and we now know that the King, Chamberlain and the principal figures in the

Labour and Liberal parties preferred him. Moreover, Churchill had frequently declared that he would serve under anyone acceptable in a crisis such as this. Chamberlain summoned the two men to meet him, along with Margesson, the Chief Whip, on the afternoon of 9 May. Brendan Bracken extracted a promise from Churchill to remain silent if asked whether he would serve under Halifax, and on no account to offer to do so. Churchill kept his promise and left it to Halifax to say that it would be difficult for a peer to be Prime Minister. In fact there would have been no difficulty, and no one else used the argument. An *ad hominem* bill could easily have been passed to allow him to speak and sit in the Commons.

At the end of the interview it was clear that Churchill would be Chamberlain's successor if he resigned, but it was not so clear that he would resign. In the early hours of the following morning Hitler's western offensive began. Chamberlain at first regarded it as his duty to remain, but Attlee whom he had consulted the night before sent a message from the party conference at Bournemouth. The National Executive authorized Labour to join a coalition – but under a new Prime Minister. Sir Kingsley Wood who was something of a Tory barometer urged Chamberlain to resign. He did so, telling the King that Halifax was 'not enthusiastic'. He advised him to send for Churchill who accordingly became on 10 May Prime Minister at the age of sixty-four. He was to remain in office for five years. By the end Germany and Italy had been totally defeated, Europe had been 'liberated' and Britain had survived. But America had become the foremost western power, the Indian and colonial empires were on the first downward step in a decline which within thirty years was to leave only a few small, shadowy dependencies, and Russia, a totalitarian power as hostile as Nazi Germany to western values, dominated eastern Europe and has done so ever since.

Churchill's concern was 'English' survival and the defeat of Hitler. The measure of his strategic contribution has been, and long will be argued. There can be no doubt about his contribution to morale. He had the power of language to a supreme degree. At this desperate moment – France surrendered at the end of June and the battle of Britain began on 10 July – rhetoric really mattered whether on radio or in print, and Churchill was one of the greatest orators in England's history. 'I have nothing to offer but blood, toil, tears and sweat,' he said when he first addressed the House of Commons as Prime Minister. On a later occasion he declared: 'We shall defend our island, whatever the cost may be. We shall fight in the beaches, we shall fight on the landing grounds. We shall fight in the fields and in the streets, we shall fight in the hills, we shall never surrender.'[2] After the defeat of France he said: 'I expect that the Battle of Britain is about to begin. Upon this battle depends the survival of Christian civilization. Let us so bear ourselves that, if the British Commonwealth and Empire lasts for a thousand years, men will still say, "This was their finest hour".' Much else could be quoted. Long after his death and the deaths of those who heard him, his words will echo down the centuries.

Churchill reduced the War Cabinet to five at first (though it later rose to eight): two Labour, Attlee and Greenwood, and three Conservatives, himself, Halifax and Neville Chamberlain who was a better loser than Asquith in 1916 and agreed to serve as Lord Privy Seal. Chamberlain also retained the leadership of the Conservative Party which would not at that time have been readily bestowed upon Churchill. Five months later ill health obliged him to resign – he died soon afterwards – and Churchill ignoring some well intended advice about being 'above party' had no difficulty in getting himself elected; he knew the perils of being a Prime Minister without a party machine. The non-Cabinet posts were largely monopolized by Conservatives (fifteen) and non-party figures of Conservative sympathy like Sir John Anderson, Sir John Reith and Lord Woolton. There was no proscription of the Men of Munich. Only Hoare was shunted off to the embassy in Madrid. Labour had four posts, and the Liberals one. Among key appointments were Lord Beaverbrook as Minister of Aircraft Production – a new creation – and Ernest Bevin as Minister of Labour. There was a party truce on by-elections though there was nothing to stop an individual contesting one without party endorsement if he wanted to. Churchill treated Parliament with impeccable correctitude. It met throughout the war and, as far as possible, he made all his major pronouncements to the House.

Churchill initiated two important administrative changes. The first was to call himself Minister of Defence. The War Cabinet agreed, but Parliament was not consulted and no statutory provision was passed for this new office. At the same time he wound up the Committee for Military Coordination replacing it by the Defence Committee of which he himself became chairman. It had two panels, 'Operations' and 'Supply'. The former was the one that mattered. The deputy Prime Minister, the three service Ministers, and later the Foreign Secretary were members, but more significantly than the actual membership was the convention that the three Chiefs of Staff were always in attendance. This gave them a direct and continuous contact with the Prime Minister, which had never existed before. They continued to have their own regular meetings but Churchill's voice was heard through General Sir Hastings Ismay who was his representative on the Chiefs of Staff Committee. The practical effect of these changes was that the service ministers became much less important, administrators rather than policy-makers. The direction of the war was effectively in the hands of Churchill together with the Chiefs of Staff. Formal responsibility lay with the War Cabinet, but in practice it almost always rubber-stamped the decisions of the Prime Minister and the chiefs. There was very little change in personnel during the war. Sir John Dill was CIGS till December 1941 when he became Churchill's personal military representative in Washington and was succeeded by Sir Alan Brooke. Sir Cyril Newall, Chief of Air Staff, retired in September 1940 and was followed by Sir Charles Portal. Brooke, Portal and Ismay remained in post till the end of hostilities. The First Sea Lord was Sir Dudley Pound who died in 1943. His successor, Sir Andrew Cunningham, saw out the war.

Churchill infused a sense of furious energy and fertile imagination into the war effort. Some of his proposals were eccentric and impracticable, and he caused the Chiefs of Staff and their subordinates to waste much valuable time in demonstrating that this was so. He did not always treat his commanders fairly. Sir Hugh Dowding who won the battle of Britain is a classic example. Others, like Generals Wavell and Auchinleck who successively commanded at Cairo, could complain of being pushed into campaigns which they had opposed and blamed for failures which they had predicted. These are blemishes but they count little in the balance against the courage, the leadership and the determination of the statesman who symbolized the British will to win and who led his country for more than five years of unprecedented stress and strain.

3

The crisis that faced Churchill was as grave as it could be. The revamped German plan for attack in the west succeeded brilliantly. The French had more divisions than Germany but far too many of them were in the Maginot Line. French tanks were better than the German armour and there were more of them but they were scattered in penny packets all over the place. As in Poland and Norway, Hitler had air superiority, and his generals – or some of them – knew that a sudden, unexpected armoured thrust could revolutionize war as hitherto conducted. The tank drive through the Ardennes led by General Guderian, one of the ablest German commanders, did just what Manstein hoped it would do, assisted by Guderian's readiness to disregard orders and go ahead. By the afternoon of 14 May the main weight of German armour was sweeping towards the Channel ports. The plan to cut the BEF and the élite of the French army was helped by Gamelin's unwise decision to advance at once into Belgium.

Early on 15 May Reynaud telephoned Churchill: 'We have lost the battle.' Guderian's armour reached Abbeville on 20 May and then headed north, isolating Boulogne and Calais.

It was clear that nothing could now save France, and on 11 June Italy declared war. Churchill made a last-minute appeal for an indissoluble union between France and Britain. It was rejected, and a new government under the venerable Marshal Pétain sought an armistice on 22 June. The whole of northern France, including Paris and the coastline to the Pyrenees, now came under German occupation. The remainder became a neutral and nominally independent state ruled from Vichy by Pétain whose authority was recognized by the vast majority of French generals, admirals and colonial governors. The French Navy now loomed large in British eyes. If acquired by Germany it could tilt the whole balance of sea power against Britain. Under the German agreement with Pétain it was to be disarmed, and the Germans promised not to use it against Britain. In fact the French commanders had secret orders to scuttle their ships rather than let them fall into German hands, but this was not known outside, and the German guarantee was not trusted. The French ships in British ports and in Alexandria were taken over, but the main force was at Oran. On 3 July, failing to obtain its surrender, Admiral Somerville opened fire and sank two battleships and a battle cruiser with heavy casualties. This action embittered Anglo-French relations for years, but in the circumstances was inevitable.

Two decisions, neither of them by Churchill, were responsible for Britain's survival. Lord Gort's BEF from 23 May onwards had only one port of escape, Dunkirk. It could easily have been cut off, but, for reasons still obscure, Hitler gave orders on 24 May to halt his armour. It did not move for three days. The result was 'the miracle of Dunkirk'. By a splendid effort of the navy 224,000 British and 95,000 French soldiers were conveyed to England between 26 May and 2 June. They lost all their arms (except rifles), their transport and other equipment, but they survived to fight again another day.

The other decision was that of Sir Hugh Dowding, the head of Fighter Command. The air staff estimated that fifty-two fighter squadrons were the minimum to prevent the *Luftwaffe* gaining the total air supremacy essential for the invasion of England. French pressure for fighter aid was intense, and Churchill was anxious to help. But by 13 May over 200 Hurricanes had been lost and Dowding was down to thirty-six squadrons in England. He took his case on appeal to the War Cabinet on 15 May – a drastic step for a commander. The French wanted at least ten squadrons. Dowding, to Churchill's displeasure, persuaded the Cabinet to send none. After his departure Churchill converted a rump Cabinet into sending four. But the effect of Dowding's *démarche* was felt when Churchill, having flown next day to Paris, pressed for another six. The War Cabinet seemingly agreed but insisted that they should do what they could from forward bases in southern England, not from France. In the battle of Britain three months later, thanks to Lord Beaverbrook's galvanic effect on aircraft production, Dowding had about fifty squadrons and he won by the narrowest of margins. If he had had six less he would have been defeated.

Hitler expected Britain to come to terms after the fall of France. He had made no dispositions for an invasion nor had his generals given any thought to the problems involved. On 22 June he ordered the demobilization of thirty-five divisions. A month later on 19 July he made a speech offering peace. It was taken for granted in England that this was impossible. Churchill on 3 August publicly defined Britain's conditions which were obviously unacceptable. Already, on 16 July, Hitler in a slightly half-hearted way had ordered the preparation of an invasion code-named 'Operation Sealion' to be ready by the middle of August. The German military and naval authorities were unenthusiastic, but since air supremacy was vital and Goering declared that the *Luftwaffe* could obtain it, they saw no harm in letting him try.

The ensuing struggle was not the David and Goliath affair depicted at the time and for many years afterwards. The rival air forces were more evenly matched than is usually believed. Goering had 875 high-level bombers poorly armed and needing fighter escort. He also had just over 300 dive-bombers which were so vulnerable as to be useless. He possessed 929 fighters, mostly short-range ME109s but including 227 ME110s, twin-engined and relatively long range. Dowding had by mid-July got back to his numbers before the attack on France began, some 650 Hurricanes and Spitfires. They were faster and more manoeuvrable than the Messerschmitts but their eight machine-guns were not as devastating as the 20 mm cannon of the German planes. The pilots on both sides were skilled and brave. The RAF was numerically weaker. Dowding had only 1,434 fighter pilots at the beginning of August and at the end of that nerve-racking month he was down to 840. During the same period only 260 were turned out by the training units. By September inexperience was causing an even heavier toll.

The RAF possessed three great assets. The first was far superior air intelligence, thanks to their chain of coastal radar stations and the increasing success of Ultra, the name given to the decryptography of German radio ciphers.[3] The second was an equally superior communication system – ground-to-air radio which enabled the group controllers to guide and coordinate the fighter squadrons. German radio was poor and there were no effective links with base. The third was Dowding himself, prickly, withdrawn, and awkward, but a commander of genius. He had planned the battle for years, whereas Goering was slapdash and ignorant. One would expect victory to go to an austere Wykehamist rather than a Neronic sybarite. And so it did.

But the margin was very narrow. The battle began from early July onwards with attacks on Channel convoys. The damage was severe but not disastrous. Dowding declined to commit his forces on a large scale. From 3 July to 11 August, German losses in bombers and fighters came to 364, while Dowding lost 203 fighters. On 13 August – *Adlertag* or Eagle Day – Goering launched the attack which was intended to destroy the RAF and prepare the way for invasion. He rightly decided to bomb the radar stations and the fighter airfields in the south-east. He believed that his bombers with fighter escort could win, given four days of good weather. They failed in the end, though the struggle continued for over a month. It is not easy to pinpoint moments of decision. On 15 August the RAF shot down seventy-five German planes losing thirty-six of its fighters. It is regarded by some as the crucial day. 'Never in the field of human conflict,' declared Churchill, 'was so much owed by so many to so few.' Dowding's knowledge through Ultra of the detailed German plans for that day was a vital element in his success, enabling him to hold back his fighters for the later raids and not waste them on the early ones. On 18 August the RAF made a similar relative score – seventy-one shot down at the loss of twenty-seven fighters. The worst moment was on 31 August when thirty-nine fighters were lost, and only forty-one German planes destroyed. England's air-bases had been badly damaged, and in the month of August the country had lost 338 fighters to Germany's 177, though a large number of bombers have to be added to the German casualties.

But on 3 September Goering made a major error. He decided to switch his bombers to London. The assault took place on 7 September both by day and night and did much damage, but the immediate relief for fighter command was crucial. A few more attacks on its airfields, and the defence of Britain might have been broken. On 13 September, 'Battle of Britain Day', renewed attacks on London resulted in sixty German aircraft being shot down (the estimate at the time was 185) at the cost of twenty-six RAF fighters. Two days later Hitler called off 'Sealion' until further notice. The threat of invasion lingered on for several months but German attention was now directed towards the east. From September onwards plans for an attack on Russia were being made. On 18 December Hitler gave orders to prepare for the operation known as 'Barbarossa' – invasion of Russia on a huge scale in May the following year. Meanwhile in the west the *Luftwaffe* had shifted its activities to the night bombing of London which had already begun on 7 September. From that date onwards for fifty-seven nights running London was attacked by an average force of 160 bombers. On 14 November a series of raids was launched on other cities. A new technique was the use of 'pathfinders' guided on a radio beam to drop incendiary bombs and light up the target for the rest of the force. The first victim was Coventry, which was devastated in brilliant moonlight. A myth grew up that Churchill knew from some secret source that the raid was coming but gave orders to do nothing lest the source was compromised. There is no truth in this. Ultra did indeed show that a major attack involving three targets impended, but there was no way of deducing what they were. Nor could much have been done even if Coventry had been specifically named, given the inadequacy of night-fighting equipment at that time.

The 'Blitz', as Goering's offensive was inappropriately called, lasted with varying degrees of severity through the autumn, winter and spring of 1940–41. The final efforts were two particularly severe raids – on London (10 May) and Birmingham (16 May). After that the bulk of the *Luftwaffe* was moved east in support of 'Barbarossa'. The blitz had little effect on war production or communications. The German bomber pilots had been trained to cooperate with the army. An independent night offensive had never been planned. The German raids, about 100 tons a night, bore no relation to the immense British bomber offensive in 1943–4, with a delivery sixteen times as great. Even this did not in itself defeat Germany. But the blitz killed 30,000 civilians and rendered millions homeless by the destruction of some 3.5 million houses. It wrecked the House of Commons, damaged Buckingham Palace – the King and Queen were, however, glad to share their subjects' experience – and it devastated great areas of London and other major cities. It disrupted and darkened life for most of the population of England.

Chapter Thirteen

REVERSES

I

At the end of 1940 Britain could claim to have survived – but little more. Nations like individuals, however, can be swept by euphoria. The plans of the Chiefs of Staff in September 1940 emanated from cloud cuckoo land. It was a strange article of faith, even when the war began, that Germany was on the verge of economic collapse. It was even stranger to believe this after Hitler had conquered much of Europe. In fact, till 1943 Germany ran on a 'peacetime war economy' with no serious consumer shortages of anything. Yet the staff view remained that economic disaster and the discontent of subject peoples would by 1942 enable a British and empire army of fifty-five divisions to invade, without great loss, a Nazi regime on the verge of collapse because of these non-existent dangers.

It was nonsense but there is such a thing as useful nonsense. It sustained morale, and morale was crucial. Moreover, just as an individual's optimism sometimes turns out to be justified because of events over which he has no control, so can a nation's. Few people could have been confident that Hitler would attack Russia, still less that if he did he would be defeated. It was not certain that Japan would enter the war, still less that, when it did, Hitler would declare war on America. The British hung on, buoyed up by fantasy. They could not have reckoned upon any of those events, but the events happened.

Britain did, however, possess one asset of supreme importance. It was the best kept secret of the war, although thousands of people in the UK and later in America knew about it. Ultra has already been mentioned. The veil on this vital source of information was not lifted till 1974 when Group Captain Winterbotham, Air Intelligence Officer in the Secret Service, was allowed to publish his memoirs, *The Ultra Secret*. In 1977 copies of some of the decrypted German intercepts were made available in the Public Record Office. In 1979 Ronald Lewin wrote *Ultra Goes to War* – the most authoritative account so far of the contribution of the cryptographers. It is no exaggeration to say that every study, biography and autobiography concerned with the conduct of the 1939-45 war needs revision if it was published before 1974.

Ultra was the name given sometimes to the decoded intercepts, sometimes to the process of decoding them, often to both. Thanks partly to pre-war aid from the Polish intelligence services it became possible to read from April 1940 onwards some of the most confidential German radio communications transmitted by the 'Enigma' machine believed by the Germans throughout the war to be 'unbreakable'. Expressions such as 'secret' or 'sure' sources, 'a spy in Rommel's headquarters', an 'agent in the German Foreign Office' and many others, recognizable by those who knew, were covers for this crucial 'leak'. The body responsible was an offshoot of the Secret Service, the Government Code and Cipher School (GC and CS) stationed at Bletchley Park in Buckinghamshire, which developed into a vast organization by the end of the war.

Not all German ciphers were cracked all the time. The *Luftwaffe*'s were the first and least difficult – which was just as well since Britain's first struggle after it stood alone was a battle for the skies. The army ciphers could be read in the battle of France, but too slowly to make any difference. In any case all the intelligence in the world can have little effect against a fast-moving army crushing the slow defeatist forces of its enemy. The German naval ciphers were not cracked till the capture of the U110's Enigma machine in May 1941 (see below page 265). But, although there were gaps, often big ones – it took for example two years to break the Abwehr (German Secret Service) ciphers – the advantages of being able to read the enemy's mind were enormous. Churchill saw it at once. The arrangements made to convey Ultra to him via his close friend Sir Desmond Morton, who selected pieces but always sent them in their original form, has been well described by Mr Lewin who also describes the unobtrusive Special Liaison Units (SLU) which accompanied top commanders in the field and passed Ultra on to them.

It would be wrong to claim too much for Ultra. It was one of many sources of intelligence – very important but always needing interpretation and imagination if it was to be properly used. It did not produce the 'miracle of Dunkirk' or the sinking of the *Bismarck*, although Bletchley believed otherwise. Its effect on the battle of Britain was significant but radar was even more important. It was of little use in the mobile hour-to-hour fighting in North Africa. It may even have done harm there by moving Churchill to bully his generals into premature attack because he read Rommel's dismal picture of the German situation, not realizing that it was often deliberately exaggerated in order to persuade Hitler to send more reinforcements. On the other hand, Ultra was the key to the battles of the Atlantic and the Mediterranean. If properly used it could have saved Crete in 1941 and the PQ17 convoy in 1942. Above all it was essential for the elaborate deception plan without which OVERLORD, the assault on Normandy in 1944, might never have come off. Finally, we should remember that much information about its use still remains suppressed.

2

There was one unexpected gleam of light at the end of 1940 and it came from an unexpected quarter. Italy's declaration of war had been anticipated much earlier; substantial naval forces had been stationed at Malta and a small military force under General Sir Archibald Wavell in Egypt. The object was to defend the Mediterranean route to India via Suez, and help to protect French communications with North Africa. The collapse of France transformed the situation. The Mediterranean route became almost unusable and communications between France and North Africa no longer mattered. On 16 June Sir Dudley Pound drew the logical conclusion. He would have moved part of the fleet to Gibraltar and part to Aden, closed the Suez Canal and abandoned Egypt. Given the solemn pledges to protect Australia and New Zealand against Japan, this made sense. Britain could not hold both Egypt and Singapore.

Churchill refused. He was to take the same line in spring 1941, overruling a recommendation made this time by all three Chiefs of Staff – one of the very rare occasions when he did so. Japan, however menacing, was still neutral. He reckoned that America would somehow come to the rescue in the Far East – an area of which he knew little. Egypt was a country in which he had fought and Britain's post-war Middle Eastern empire was partly his creation. The die was cast early in August 1940 when Wavell's request for reinforcements to deal with the double Italian threat from Libya and Ethiopia was accepted – a bold step just as the battle of Britain was beginning. It was a decisive commitment which shaped the whole course of British strategy, making the Mediterranean shores Britain's main theatre of operations for the next three years.

Italy's empire in Africa consisted of Libya in the north, Abyssinia, Eritrea and Italian Somaliland in the east. To Churchill's wrath the British forces in British Somaliland were forced to evacuate in August. Shortly after that, in September six divisions (about 80,000 men) of the Italian army in Libya moved ponderously across the frontier to Sidi Barrani and halted fifty miles west of the British positions at Mersa Matruh. Marshal Graziani disposed of forces amounting to 300,000 men. Wavell, after reinforcements had arrived in October, had only 56,000, but he had 275 tanks (including

fifty heavily armoured 'Matildas') to the Italians' 120. In East
Africa he now had 75,000 men in Kenya and 28,000 in the
Sudan, opposing Italian forces of some 200,000. A further
complication was added to the scene of Italian operations
when at the end of October Mussolini invaded Greece from
Albania, to Hitler's surprise. The Italians failed to make any
headway. The Greeks decided not to invoke their alliance
with Britain for fear of provoking German intervention.

On 8 December Wavell launched what was intended to be
little more than a 'spoiling offensive' against the Italian
positions at Sidi Barrani to forestall Italian attack and cover
the diversion of some of his forces to the Sudan. General
O'Connor who commanded a force of 30,000 men succeeded
beyond his or Wavell's wildest dreams. Graziani's army
collapsed like a pack of cards. O'Connor broke through Sidi
Barrani on 11 December and captured Bardia on 4 January,
Tobruk on 22 January, and destroyed the rest of the Italian
forces at Beda Fomm on the west coast of Cyrenaica on 5
February. By 9 February 1941 his advance guard was at El
Agheila, the key to Tripoli itself. Some 125,000 prisoners,
1,000 guns, and vast quantities of equipment were captured.
The road to Tripoli was now wide open but at this juncture
orders came to halt. The Cabinet had decided that aid to
Greece was the top priority.

Thanks to Ultra and other sources it was known that Hitler
intended to rescue the Italians and thus forestall any danger
to his rear from the Balkans when 'Barbarossa' (also known in
detail through Ultra) was launched. It was to be a two-fold
salvage operation – North Africa and Greece. On 6 February,
the same day as O'Connor's victory at Beda Fomm, Hitler
summoned Lt-General Rommel, one of the ablest and most
dashing of his younger tank commanders. On 12 February
Rommel arrived in Tripoli, followed two days later by his
advance guard, but no tanks were available for another month
and the main body, 15th Panzer Division, not till May. A
pause followed in the desert.

Hitler also decided that Greece must be knocked out, if

only for fear of a British landing at Salonika. He planned to begin this operation in March. On 19 February Eden and Dill arrived in Cairo. Three days later they flew with Wavell to Athens. Churchill now began to have misgivings. 'Do not consider yourselves obligated to a Greek enterprise,' he telegraphed on 20 February, 'if in your hearts you feel it will be only another Norwegian fiasco.' This was exactly what it was to be, but Eden was strong for action and the Greek government now welcomed military aid. On 7 March, though Churchill was still in doubt, the War Cabinet took the plunge, and the first detachments of an army of 50,000 men landed in Greece. Churchill's acquiescence was not solely dictated by loyalty to the Greek alliance. He hoped to build up a Balkan front – Yugoslavia, Greece, Turkey. It was not a very promising plan. Each hated the other, their armies were museum pieces, and Yugoslavia was in the Axis camp. On 27 March, however, a coup in Belgrade resulted in a pro-Allied government. Hitler, at this affront, lost his temper. He heavily reinforced the army intended for Greece in order to crush Yugoslavia too. On 6 April he launched his attack.

Disaster followed upon disaster for Britain and its allies. The two countries were rapidly overrun. Belgrade devastated by bombing was occupied on 13 April. Greece capitulated on 24 April. For the third time the navy had to bail out British forces from the countries they had entered to assist. Losses, in dead and prisoners were 12,000, and in equipment almost everything. Meanwhile, there had been a major reverse in the desert. Wavell was aware from Ultra of the reinforcements Rommel had received. These seemed quite inadequate on orthodox rules about supplies and distances. Rommel, however, decided not to wait for his main body of tanks. He was a brilliant, unorthodox improviser and he commanded excellent soldiers. On 30 March he began an offensive as damaging to the UK and dominion forces as O'Connor's had been to those of Marshal Graziani. By 13 April O'Connor and his relief, General Neame, were prisoners, and the British Army had been thrown back hundreds of miles to the

Egyptian frontier at Sollum, leaving an exiguous garrison at Tobruk. Rommel tried twice to assault it but failed; these were the first rebuffs, albeit minor, that any German commander had so far received. It was a very thin silver lining to a black cloud about to be made blacker by the German airborne seizure of Crete after ferocious fighting from 20 to 27 May. The defeat was not, as has been claimed, the result of surprise. It was the result of miscalculation. The commander at Crete, General Freyberg, was fully informed in advance through Ultra of the details and timing of the German attack but he failed to appreciate the importance of airfields. He could easily have prevented their capture. From this blunder all else stemmed. In Churchill's words 'we had to face once again the bitter and dismal task of evacuation'. Out of 30,000 troops some 16,500 were rescued. German casualties were, however, so heavy that Hitler never attempted a similar assault again.

The Greek campaign was an error of the first magnitude. If in February O'Connor in the western desert had been reinforced or simply allowed to go ahead with his existing force he could have driven the Italians out of North Africa before Rommel gained a foothold. The course of the war would then have been very different. An *ex post facto* justification – it was not a consideration at the time – is that the Greek campaign held up 'Barbarossa' by six weeks and so made all the difference to Hitler's attempt to reach Moscow before Christmas. There is not much in this argument. Hitler gave orders at the end of March to postpone 'Barbarossa' from 15 May, and in the end fixed it for 22 June. But it was the coup in Belgrade which prompted him because he had to use far larger forces than intended. He had already allowed for the British intervention in Greece. Apart from other considerations the weather was so bad in eastern Europe during May and early June that he could not have invaded Russia earlier, whatever happened in the Balkans.

The kaleidoscopic months of early 1941 were not all packed with disaster. Although little noticed at the time a campaign beginning on 14 January with General Platt's attack from the northern Sudan and ending with the capture of the Keren heights on 27 March resulted in British seizure of Eritrea. An offensive from Kenya launched by General Cunningham in February led to the capture of Mogadishu on 23 February and Addis Ababa on 6 April. The Duke of Aosta, Viceroy of Ethiopia, surrendered on 19 May. This was the end of Mussolini's short-lived East African empire. Large reinforcements were now available for the forces in the Middle East.

These were not the only 'side-shows' to distract Whitehall and Cairo. At the end of March a pro-Axis coup forced the Regent of Iraq into exile and put Rashid Ali (known to the troops as 'Wretched Ally') into the premiership. He was a friend of the Grand Mufti who had made so much trouble in Palestine. Britain had a treaty with Iraq which gave valuable military facilities including an air-base at Habbaniya and the right of transit for troops in an emergency. The oilfields of Iraq and Iran were obviously important and the possibility of a German air-borne attack was in the minds of British strategists, though Hitler had no such plans. Churchill insisted on action. Wavell was reluctant, prophesied disaster but obeyed orders. Hostilities began on 30 April and Iraq surrendered a month later on 31 May. By the autumn officers in pink coats were hunting jackal near Habbaniya just as they had in peacetime. Churchill had long been doubtful about Wavell's judgement. The Iraq affair confirmed his doubts. A similar incident occurred over Syria, governed by Vichy France. It was believed that the Germans intended to use air-bases there. Again Churchill pressed for intervention, with the aid of de Gaulle's Free French forces which at this time he wished to encourage. Again Wavell had doubts, and again accepted orders. On 8 June British and Free French troops entered Syria and Lebanon. The fighting was tough and the Vichy French did not surrender till 11 July. Before then Wavell had gone.

As early as 19 May Churchill decided to swap him with Sir

Claude Auchinleck, Commander-in-Chief India, but took no immediate action. Reading the exchanges between the two men one can sympathize with both; they were by temperament wholly incompatible – exuberance, optimism and perpetual nagging on the one side, caution, professionalism and growing weariness on the other. On 5 May, Churchill, overruling naval advice, told Wavell that he was sending some 300 tanks by a fast convoy known as 'Tiger' through the Mediterranean. It arrived on 12 May. The Prime Minister now put the strongest pressure on Wavell to launch an immediate offensive. The tanks – 'Tiger cubs' as Churchill called them – were in poor condition and much had to be done in the workshops. The soldiers who were to man them were inexperienced, and Wavell did not possess the air superiority with which he was credited in London. The attack known as 'Battleaxe' launched on 14 June was a complete failure. The tanks on both sides were about equal in numbers but the German armour was better handled and mechanically more reliable. It was also the first occasion when Rommel used his 88mm anti-aircraft guns against tanks. They were devastating when dug into defensive positions. It is astonishing that the British at no stage in the desert war employed their own very similar 3.7inch AA guns in the same role. Wavell lost ninety-one tanks to Rommel's twelve and the British forces were back to their base by 17 June. Five days later Wavell was offered the Indian command and replaced by Auchinleck. On the same day Hitler attacked Russia.

'Barbarossa' is not a part of English history. Thanks to Ultra, it had been possible to tell Stalin what was impending, though the source could not be revealed. He behaved as if he had been taken completely by surprise. Hitler now concentrated almost exclusively on Russia. The Mediterranean became for him a 'side-show', and the majority of his forces were engaged henceforth on the eastern front till the end of the war. There was a deeper significance for Britain. One of the lessons of both world wars is that if opponents were at all evenly matched the casualties on both sides were bound to be immense. Yet in 1939–45 Britain lost only 400,000 killed, of whom 60,000 were civilians and 35,000 were in the merchant navy. In the First World War casualties were nearly twice as high, and French losses twice as much again. It was on the desolate plains of eastern Europe that the Sommes and Passchendaeles of the Second World War were to be fought.

The course of these terrible campaigns belongs to German and Russian history. Hitler's forces nearly broke through to Moscow in 1941, but just failed. They nearly broke through to the Caucasian oilfields in 1942. Again they failed and the surrender of their encircled army in Stalingrad on 31 January 1943 marks the turning point in German fortunes. The next two years saw a gradual but irreversible ebb. By the end of 1944 the German Army had been cleared out of Russia. In April 1945 Russian troops entered Berlin.

Churchill at once broadcast Britain's unreserved support for the USSR. 'If Hitler invaded Hell I would at least make a favourable reference to the Devil in the House of Commons,' he said to one of his private secretaries. There was not much he could do to help. Stalin at once began a series of importunate demands which continued till the end of the war; a second front now – which was out of the question; supplies of every kind, which were desperately short. Nor was the one branch of the services which might have done something – Bomber Command – particularly effective. Under the influence of Lord Trenchard, the RAF had become committed to the doctrine that the war could be won by an independent strategic air offensive. This was a piece of inter-service politics designed to preserve the independence of the RAF rather than a blueprint for practical action. No adequate force of long-range bombers existed in 1939, and no one had analysed just how strategic bombing could actually win a war.

Throughout 1940 and 1941 the inaccuracy of night bombers was lamentable. In August 1941 a report found that only one-tenth got within five miles of their targets. Even in 1942 after Air Chief Marshal Sir Arthur Harris, the new Commander-in-Chief, had infused fresh energy into an attack helped by the latest radar aids to navigation, German war production rose by fifty per cent. There was a natural, though in the end regrettable, move away from military targets to 'area bombing' in order to 'undermine the morale of the German people' – in plain language 'terrorization'. This was never publicly admitted but it was what happened, culminating in the destruction of Dresden in 1944.

3

In August 1941 Churchill had the first of nine meetings with Roosevelt. He regarded American economic aid as crucial and he saw a military alliance with America as Britain's hope of survival. He and the President had been exchanging messages (largely deciphered by the Germans but luckily assumed by them to be a double-cross) from the beginning of the war. Roosevelt regarded Britain, especially in her empire role, without enthusiasm, and America was pledged to neutrality. But he was convinced that a British defeat would be disastrous to American interests. For Britain, American supplies were vital. Dollars to buy them were rapidly diminishing. Within and sometimes beyond the constitutional limits of the presidency Roosevelt gave all the help he could. The swapping of fifty destroyers for bases in the West Indies in September 1940 was a gesture. 'Lend-lease', an arrangement under which American goods would be provided without immediate cash payment from February 1941 onwards, was a major element in Britain's survival. The meeting in August at Placentia Bay, Newfoundland, produced nothing beyond the Atlantic Charter, a long forgotten document of virtuous goodwill about the future. The Americans declined to be drawn closely into military plans, though they revealed their scepticism about strategic bombing and their doubts about the chances of holding the Middle East.

Before Placentia a crucial Anglo-American decision had been taken. It shaped the whole future of the war and turned it from a European into a global struggle. The Japanese, bogged down in a war with China, which they could scarcely lose but found hard to win, were impatient to bring matters to a conclusion. The collapse of France and Holland, and the pressure on Britain made the Far Eastern colonies of those powers a tempting target. In July Japan took over French Indo-China. Roosevelt, who had long regarded Japanese expansion as a threat, promptly declared a trade embargo. Britain and the Dutch government in London followed suit. In effect this was a declaration of war. Japan imported eighty-eight per cent of her peacetime oil needs, and most of her requirements of tin and rubber. She would have to abandon the war in China or else strike southwards and seize the oilfields of the Dutch East Indies and the rubber plantations and tin-mines of Malaysia.

For four months the question of war or peace was debated in Tokyo. The battle if it took place would be largely naval, but of a new kind. The Japanese were on paper about evenly matched with the combined Allied fleets in the south-west Pacific but there was one important exception. The Japanese had ten aircraft carriers to America's three. Britain had none. Aircraft carriers were to be of paramount importance for this strange and novel form of sea warfare in which opposing fleets bombarded each other at vast distances without ever setting eyes on an enemy ship. Both in quantity and quality the Japanese planes were superior to those of the Allies. Their land forces were numerically slightly inferior, but well trained in the techniques of jungle warfare, night attacks and amphibious landings. Japanese soldiers were tougher and more hardy, and could live on less. They were sustained by a fanatical zeal which regarded surrender as eternal dishonour, and they treated their prisoners with corresponding contempt.

A campaign to establish a 'Greater East Asia Co-Prosperity Sphere', as it was called, protected by a concentric defensive ring from the Aleutian Islands to Burma was not such a gamble as it seemed. The one real threat was the US Fleet at Pearl Harbor in Hawaii. Admiral Yamamoto solved the problem by using his carriers in a surprise attack which during the early hours of 7 December sank four of the eight battleships anchored there and knocked out the rest for several months to come.

These events transformed the situation. America was now Britain's ally with all the momentous consequences which followed. Churchill declared war at once. He quoted words spoken to him by Sir Edward Grey thirty years earlier. America was like 'a gigantic boiler. Once the fire is lighted under it, there is no limit to the power it can generate'. Pearl Harbor lifted one British fear. Japan could have attacked Malaya, Java and Sumatra, and left the Americans alone – in which case they might have stayed neutral. But, if victory was now assured in the long run, there was a contingency which could have made the run even longer. Pearl Harbor did not automatically bring in the European Axis powers. They could have remained neutral towards Japan. If they had, would the USA have declared war on Germany? It is by no means certain. Luckily for Britain Hitler, whose reasons are to this day obscure, declared war against America on 11 December though he was under no treaty obligation to do so. It was a disastrous move. There had been since early 1941 an agreement between the American and British Chiefs of Staff that *if* – and it was a big 'if' at the time – the two countries were jointly involved in war against the three Axis powers, the main effort should be made in Europe. Hitler's action made it certain that the full weight of America's immense power would be directed first at Germany, only later at Japan.

4

The war now became a part of world rather than British history. Britain would be on the victorious side. It had made and would make a notable contribution to victory. It would become for good or ill more committed to 'total' war than all other belligerents except the USSR and with a greater efficiency than any of them. But the hard facts of wealth, resources and manpower meant that Britain became a secondary nation, a junior partner in a war which encircled the globe, extinguished the Third Reich and left America and Russia as the only 'great powers' in the world, glowering at each other across Western Europe and the Atlantic, as they have done ever since.

Whatever fillip the events of December 1941 gave to Allied prospects, the short-term effects were disastrous. Japanese bombers sank the battleship *Prince of Wales* and the battle cruiser *Repulse* on 10 December off Kuantan on the east coast of Malay. There were now no Allied capital ships left in the south-west Pacific. Hong Kong fell on Christmas Day. Malaya was conquered by 31 January 1942 largely because, in Sir Basil Liddell Hart's acid words, 'the ground forces were widely dispersed to guard airfields that contained no airforces ... built to cover a naval base that contained no fleet'. With scarcely a pause the Japanese forces attacked Singapore whose defences were geared for attack from sea not land. General Perceval, the commander, surrendered on 15 February and some 60,000 men went into a cruel captivity. Their numbers were unhappily increased by the arrival in mid-January of the 18th British Division thrown into battle almost as soon as they landed after three months at sea. It was the worst humiliation for British arms since Kut, and on a much bigger scale. Neither the fall of Singapore nor that of Tobruk in June, a disaster almost as bad, was the subject of a formal inquiry then or later. There are dark aspects of both which have never been explored and now never will be. The loss of Singapore was a landmark in imperial history. British prestige in India and the east had always depended to some extent on bluff. That crushing blow by an Asiatic power was never forgotten. Britain's departure from India, Burma and Ceylon seven years later was foreshadowed in this defeat.

The Japanese now carried all before them. In the course of four months, Hong Kong, Malaya, South Burma, the Dutch East Indies, Borneo and the Celebes had been overrun. North Burma was evacuated early in May. The Americans defending the Philippines lasted rather longer, but on 9 June their resistance came to an end. The Japanese conquest was a remarkable feat accomplished by only eleven out of their fifty-one divisions for the loss of 15,000 men, four destroyers and less than 400 planes.

There were no counter-balancing successes nearer home. Auchinleck, Wavell's successor in the western desert, was as unwilling as Wavell to be hurried into a premature offensive. Being newly appointed he could insist. 'Operation Crusader', as it was codenamed, did not begin till 18 November 1941. In terms of aircraft and armour, Auchinleck's forces outweighed Rommel's. He had 710 gun-armed tanks against 174 German equivalents supported by 146 obsolete Italian tanks of little value. He had nearly 700 planes against 120 German and 200 Italian aircraft. But in this curious war where fair-skinned north Europeans fought each other in the western desert, hundreds of miles from home in blazing heat by day and bitter cold by night, varied with rain and sand storms which could suddenly change the whole scene, the Germans were more adaptable, better organized and more adventurous. It was the last 'gentleman's war'. There was something oddly exhilarating about it, the dry air, the hard brilliance of the moon and stars. Prisoners were honourably treated. Civilians were not starved, tortured or massacred – because there were none. It was also one of the few really mobile wars in history. Over these vast, dry, brown, sun-struck, mirage-filled plains which were deceptively flat – for there were many subtle undulations – it was possible to manoeuvre to an extent unparalleled anywhere else. The key problems were water and petrol at the end of a very long, thin supply line. The Prime Minister grumbled about the army's 'tail', but how could it be otherwise? Nevertheless, the evidence suggests that Rommel coped with the problems of logistics and tactics better than any opposing general. The quality of his tanks in terms of guns and armour was at no stage much better than the British weapons, and often not so good, although mechanically they were superior till the arrival of the

American-built Sherman late in 1942. The quantity was always less. But Rommel outmanoeuvred the British almost every time, and only succumbed in the end to the overwhelming strength and numbers supplied to General Montgomery for the second battle of El Alamein.

'Crusader' had a limited success. It began well. Rommel's intention to launch a major attack on Tobruk on 20 November was known, and 'Crusader', after a careful deception plan, was launched two days earlier catching him completely by surprise. The ensuing battle was one of bewildering complexity and vicissitudes. Tobruk was relieved and Rommel, abandoning his frontier garrisons at Bardia, retreated in the New Year to El Agheila where he had begun nine months earlier when he first attacked O'Connor. Auchinleck planned a final push to Tripoli in mid-February, but Rommel staged a remarkable come-back on 21 January. In the course of a fortnight he recovered Benghazi and drove the 8th Army, as the British forces were now called, back to the Gazala fortifications fifty miles west of Tobruk, running from the sea to Bir Hacheim where the Free French held the left of the line.

A pause followed while both sides prepared for the next round. This time Rommel got his blow in first. On the brilliant moonlit night of 26 May his two panzer divisions supported by some 10,000 vehicles swept round Bir Hacheim and then turned north towards the sea, to cut off the divisions on the Gazala Line. The British armour at this time, contrary to later mythology, was, tank for tank, as good as the German, and there was much more of it; the new American-made Grant tanks had a more powerful gun and a thicker hull than any German tank, although the gun was mounted on the side, instead of in the turret. It thus had a limited traverse and could not easily exploit the 'hull down' position. The British had 850 tanks of which 170 were Grants. Rommel commanded a total of 560, but half were either light or obsolete Italian tanks. His effective force was 280, which gave the British in theory a 3 to 1 advantage. In terms of air power the two sides

261

were roughly equal, but in artillery the British had a numerical advantage of 3 to 2. The German 88mm gun, however, remained the most formidable anti-tank weapon on either side. Rommel had only forty-eight of them, but he exploited these devastating weapons brilliantly.

No satisfactory account has ever been written of this extraordinary battle. Rommel's initial thrust to the sea failed; at one stage it looked as if his forces would be trapped in a pocket against the minefields of the Gazala Line. On 30 May, having lost a third of his armour, he took up a defensive position. Yet a fortnight later on 14 June General Ritchie, who commanded the 8th Army, gave orders contrary to Auchinleck's instructions – to abandon the Gazala Line and retreat to the Egyptian frontier. At Churchill's insistence he left the 2nd South African Division, the Guards Brigade and the 32nd Army Tank Brigade to garrison Tobruk whose fortifications had been neglected since November. Rommel seized the opportunity on 20 June to launch a surprise attack on the eastern perimeter. General Klopper, the South African commander, surrendered next day, and 35,000 men together with a vast amount of stores fell into German hands. On 22 June the 8th Army abandoned Sollum near the frontier and fled across the desert with Rommel in hot pursuit, though he now had only sixty tanks left.

What had happened during the critical fortnight between 30 May and 14 June? The Duke of Wellington said that writing the history of a battle is like writing the history of a ball. Certainly the neat maps with arrows and diagrams beloved of military historians can tell us only a fragment of the reality. At one stage in the Gazala battle a sand storm stopped almost all action for forty-eight hours. A metaphorical sand storm is still swirling round the dim outline of events. The two most popular theories are incorrect. In addition to the myth of German tank superiority there is the myth that a single disastrous day, 13 June, saw huge British tank losses which turned the scales. The truth, rather, seems to be that Ritchie who was quite unsuited to this sort of command never concentrated his armour but threw it against Rommel in a series of piecemeal attacks during each of which Rommel had just enough of a margin to win. By the evening of 13 June Ritchie had only 100 tanks left, and Rommel now possessed overall superiority.

Auchinleck who took over personal command from Ritchie decided to retreat to El Alamein, the only defensible line before Alexandria, flanked on the right by the sea, and on the left by the impassable Quattara Depression. Rommel, now only sixty miles from his goal, arrived there on 30 June. Panic raged in Cairo. July 1 was known as 'Ash Wednesday' because of the burning of the files at GHQ. In retrospect it can be seen as a turning point. This was Rommel's best chance of a breakthrough with incalculable consequences. Auchinleck, just, but only just, prevented the now exhausted Afrika Korps from sweeping on to Alexandria. He had to call off his counter-attack three weeks later, but the real threat was over. This did not save Auchinleck whom Churchill replaced on 8 August by General Alexander. At the same time General Montgomery was given command of the 8th Army – a second choice in place of General Gott shot down by a German plane on 7 August.

The fall of Tobruk was a heavy blow to British prestige and a personal humiliation for Churchill who was in Washington when it happened. Roosevelt behaved with remarkable generosity. He agreed to send 300 new Sherman tanks and 100 self-propelled 105mm guns to Egypt. The Sherman proved to be the best tank of the war on the Allied side, and Montgomery's victory at El Alamein in the autumn was largely due to them. At this meeting in Washington the whole question of Allied strategy was in the balance. Should there be, as Stalin demanded, and the American Chiefs of Staff appeared to favour, a 'second front' i.e. an invasion of northern France in 1942? Churchill effectively vetoed this proposal on 8 July when he was back in London.

His own plan, adumbrated as long ago as Christmas 1941, was to launch an Anglo-American invasion of French North-

West Africa in conjunction with an offensive from the east and thus to clear the Axis powers out of Africa altogether. General Marshall saw that the momentum, shipping and logistics of such an operation, whatever promises were made, would in practice preclude a second front in 1943 as well as 1942. He now favoured building up a force for the invasion of northern France in 1943 and avoiding any major offensive in 1942 – a rational, soldier's decision. Roosevelt, a politician to the finger tips, was determined that something should be done in the west in 1942. American public opinion might otherwise insist on major diversion to the Pacific. Churchill was even more anxious to go ahead in view of the setback in the western desert. The upshot of these deliberations was the decision on 5 September, after much haggling, to launch the operation known as 'Torch' early in November.

On 30 August Rommel made a last attempt to break through at El Alamein. Montgomery repulsed it after a few days. His much vaunted ability to 'read the enemy's mind' was in fact the ability of Bletchley to read Rommel's signals. The battle of Alam Halfa might have been even more successful if he had followed it up. Montgomery, however, would not move until he had overwhelming force. The second battle of El Alamein began on 23 October. He had three times as many troops as Rommel, six times as many effective tanks and overpowering air superiority. The British Navy dominated the Mediterranean, and Rommel's supply line was long and vulnerable. Even so, it was a hotly contested affair with very heavy casualties, but by 4 November Rommel began a retreat which was to take him the whole way back to Tunis. It was the first clear British victory since the war began.

5

To Churchill it was especially welcome. He had been Prime Minister for two and a half years during which almost every possible disaster had occurred except the ultimate one. The first ten months of 1942 were particularly bad – the Japanese conquests, the reverses in the desert and the losses of the RAF. Moreover the struggle for the Atlantic routes took a marked turn for the worse. The previous year had been better. The destruction of the *Bismarck*, the most powerful battleship in the world, on 27 May 1941, after she had sunk the *Hood* off Iceland with the loss of all her crew but three, had given a boost to morale. The damage she could have inflicted on the convoys, one of which was taking the 50th Division to the Middle East at that very time, was incalculable. As so often in war there was a good deal of luck involved. If a Catalina flying boat had not spotted her and a Swordfish torpedo plane had not put her steering gear out of action, the *Bismarck* might have escaped.

A few days earlier a coup had been achieved, which affected the whole history of the war. On 8 May 1941 the commander of the U110 abandoned his ship off Greenland, leaving an intact Enigma machine and all his codes. The demolition charges failed to explode. Horrified at this calamity the German commander committed suicide. With great skill and in nerve-wracking circumstances – the charges could have gone off at any moment – Sub-Lieutenant David Balme brought a boarding party to the U-boat and recovered the machine; it was quickly conveyed under extreme secrecy to Bletchley. The German naval code 'Hydra', hitherto unreadable, could now be cracked. As Ronald Lewin puts it: 'History is written in terms of Trafalgars and Jutlands, but by any standard the seizure of the U110 should rate as a major victory at sea.' The war had many turning points. This was certainly one of them.

The immediate effect was a notable fall in shipping losses and the destruction of Admiral Doenitz's surface supply system for raiders and submarines. By the end of the year the former ceased to count and the latter could be supplied only by 'milch-cow U-boats'. But the vicissitudes of this strange cryptographical combat were not finished. In February 1942

265

a new system was adopted for U-boats, called 'Triton'. For ten months it was unbroken, and British shipping losses reached a peak in that terrible year of 6 million tons. When it was cracked in December – and but for the capture of the Enigma machine it probably never would have been – an instant relief followed. The figures for January 1943 (203,000 tons) and February (360,000 tons) were much lower, but in March the cipher was changed again and they shot up to 627,000 tons. Bletchley, however, managed to break into the new 'Triton' with astonishing speed. A number of technical changes, better radar, more long-range aircraft and well equipped escort vessels helped to produce yet another reversal. On 24 May Doenitz gave up. His losses were too heavy to sustain. Two-thirds of all the U-boat crews were killed before the war ended.

This relief lay in the future. During 1942 there were two other naval reverses. Although again thanks to Ultra, the move was known well in advance, the pocket battleships, *Scharnhorst* and *Gneisenau* managed on 17 and 18 February to escape from Brest and sail through the English Channel to Kiel. 'Nothing more mortifying to the pride of sea-power has happened in home waters since the 17th century,' thundered *The Times*.

In July a much bigger disaster occurred. Under great pressure from Roosevelt, Churchill, despite his own misgivings and contrary to all the best naval opinion, agreed to send to Archangel thirty-four cargo ships which had been banked off Iceland for many weeks loaded with American supplies for Russia. This was the ill-fated Arctic convoy, PQ17 which sailed on 27 June. On 4 July it became known through Ultra that the battleship *Tirpitz* plus two pocket battleships and a heavy cruiser had moved from Trondheim to Altenfjord, the most northerly anchorage in Norway. Would they put to sea and attack? The question was crucial. If the *Tirpitz* attacked, the only hope of saving any ships was for the convoy to scatter (each ship had its own orders what to do in that event) and for its escort to withdraw. To keep together was certain doom. If on the other hand no surface attack was intended, scattering was the worst possible course. U-boats and planes would pick the ships off one by one. Admiral Denning in charge of Admiralty intelligence assured the First Sea Lord at about 7 P.M. that the *Tirpitz* had not left Altenfjord, and that he would be sure to know if and when she did. Sir Dudley Pound tragically refused to accept this advice. He had convinced himself that the great battleship must have already sailed. At 9.30 P.M. he gave the order to scatter. The *Tirpitz* remained in harbour. Twenty-three out of thirty-four ships of the PQ17 were sunk by U-boats and the *Luftwaffe*. It was not till after the war that even Churchill knew who was responsible. By then Sir Dudley Pound had died of a tumour of the brain, on Trafalgar Day, 21 October 1943.

During 1942 Churchill came under increasing criticism. Sensing this he demanded and received a vote of confidence in the House on 29 January by 464 to 1, but he felt obliged to reconstruct his government and he made Beaverbrook Minister of War Production on 4 February. Beaverbrook could not work with Bevin, Minister of Labour. Frustration produced asthma. Three weeks later he resigned. Sir Stafford Cripps sent as ambassador to Moscow – 'Left speaking to Left' – became suddenly an important figure. He returned from Russia ludicrously credited with having brought Stalin into the war; Hitler was the only man who did that. Churchill made him Leader of the House and a member of the War Cabinet, and then shuffled him off to India to placate Gandhi – with no success. Discontent reached its height when a vote of no confidence was moved on 2 July, after the fall of Tobruk, by a prominent Conservative backbencher, Sir John Wardlaw-Milne, supported by Hore-Belisha and Admiral Sir Roger Keyes, hero of Zebrugge in the First World War. It was the only serious parliamentary attack on the Prime Minister during the war, but its seriousness was diminished by the mover's suggestion that the Duke of Gloucester, an amiable but not very clever royal figurehead,

should be made Commander-in-Chief. It was defeated by
475 votes to 25, with about 40 abstentions. Events soon
turned the other way and Churchill's position was never
threatened again.

Chapter Fourteen

THE TURN OF THE TIDE

I

'Torch' was launched under the command of General Eisenhower on 8 November with landings at Casablanca, Oran and Algiers; the first two landings were exclusively American, the third was a joint Anglo-American affair. The plan was a compromise after much haggling between General Marshall's preference for confining it to Casablanca because of the perils of the Straits of Gibraltar and the British desire to go as far east as possible – to Philippeville, Bone or even closer to Tunisia, the country which really mattered. The British were right. A major landing at Bone could have reaped great dividends.

A serious question was the attitude of the French. The Commander of all Vichy forces and successor designate to Marshal Pétain was Admiral Darlan whose great-grandfather had been killed at Trafalgar. He hated the British and he never forgave the attack on the French fleet at Mers-el-Kebir in 1940. In the opinion of Roosevelt, who believed himself to have a *rapport* with Vichy through his ambassador, Admiral Leahy, the less the British were involved, the better the chances of French non-resistance. This was a doubtful theory and it had the result of giving to American forces an excessive share in the long drawn-out campaign that ensued. Much cloak-and-dagger work preceded the invasion. Who was to be chosen and persuaded to rally the French troops to the Allied side? These were substantial – at least 120,000 men. De Gaulle, regarded as a traitor by Vichy and most of the officer corps, was out of the question. Roosevelt insisted that he should not even be told of the operation in advance. General Juin who commanded in French North Africa sat on the fence. Roosevelt plumped for General Giraud, hero of two remarkable escapes, but vain and stupid. He expected, incredibly, to command 'Torch' and was only conciliated by an offer to be High Commissioner and Commander-in-Chief of French forces in North Africa. It soon became clear that he cut no more ice than de Gaulle with the elements whose cooperation was essential.

Fortunately – and purely by chance – Darlan was in Algiers visiting a sick son on the very day of the landings. Stiff fighting occurred at all points. The French authorities arrested, released and re-arrested each other. Darlan to whom Pétain had conferred secret plenipotentiary powers and who was thus alone in a position to give orders to the French troops was persuaded to order a cease-fire on 9 November. This was a boon and a stroke of luck. The allies promptly reneged on Giraud. He was now made Commander-in-Chief *under* Darlan who was to be High Commissioner. Darlan had been built up in the western press as a sinister pro-Nazi. An uproar followed in both Britain and America among those who believed that the war was a crusade for democracy.

Hitler promptly landed troops by air in Tunis on the afternoon of 9 November, and marched six divisions into unoccupied France at midnight on 11 November. The Fleet in Toulon at once became a serious risk for the Allies. Darlan ordered it to move to North Africa. The commander, Admiral de Laborde, was even more anti-English than Darlan. He waited until the Germans were about to seize it on 27 November and then at last obeyed the long-standing order to scuttle.

The German occupation of Tunisia was effected with great speed. General Anderson, who commanded the 1st Army, as the Anglo-American forces were now called, did not begin his drive for Bizerta till 25 November; his earlier probings had been defeated by brilliant German bluff, based on a force which, though boldly called '90th Corps', did not amount to a division even by the end of the month. Anderson's effort failed partly from bad weather, partly from the inexperience of his troops. Before the end of the year the German commander, General von Arnim, had a force of 50,000 men and twenty-two tanks. In December the rains came down. On Christmas Eve the attack was called off. 'The race for Tunis' had been lost. There was no chance now of trapping Rommel, still in Tripolitania, between a thrust to the east from Tunis and an attack by Montgomery to the west.

Having blown up the harbour of Tripoli Rommel retreated eighty miles inside the Tunisian frontier to the Mareth Line built originally by the French to forestall an Italian invasion. Rommel and von Arnim disliked each other, and neither was in sole command of the Axis forces. But they agreed that their position in men and materials in the early months of 1943 was as favourable as it ever would be and that the advantages of 'interior lines' gave a chance of victory. The plan was for Rommel behind the shelter of the Mareth Line to make a left hook to the north-west and seize the US base and airfield at Tebessa. This would render the whole Allied position in Tunisia untenable. He would then switch east and catch Montgomery's advance divisions thin on the ground at Medenine just east of Mareth.

It nearly worked. Rommel captured the Kasserine Pass and inflicted severe losses on the inexperienced Americans, some of whom abandoned their equipment with deplorable rapidity. But on 22 February after eight days' fighting he broke off the attack. He now turned east. Montgomery, fully warned by Ultra both of the place and day of attack, 6 March, brought up heavy reinforcements just in time. The battle of Medenine was a heavy defeat for Rommel who retired with the loss of forty tanks after only twenty-four hours' fighting.

This was the end for the Axis in North Africa. Rommel, now a sick man, decided that the battle could be continued only if the German–Italian forces were withdrawn to a perimeter round Tunis and Bizerta and could be guaranteed 140,000 tons of supplies per month. On 9 March he flew out to tell Mussolini and Hitler, but the two dictators had lost all contact with reality. Hitler chided Rommel as a 'pessimist'. He would, he said, keep him in Germany to get fit in order to launch an attack on Casablanca! The command was given to von Arnim, but when he pressed for the instant withdrawal of the Afrika Korps towards Tunis and Bizerta, Hitler insisted on holding the Mareth Line. Montgomery attacked on 20 March, launching a head-on assault on a narrow front against its strongest sector in the north. This was a predictably expensive failure. One can only wonder why, despite the knowledge at his disposal from Ultra and other sources, Montgomery did it at all. But he quickly changed his plans and forced the Afrika Korps to withdraw by a brilliantly executed outflanking movement many miles inland.

From now onwards Allied victory was inevitable. Many changes contributed to it. There was an improved system of command. In January 1943 General Alexander was made deputy Commander-in-Chief to Eisenhower and Commander of '18th Army Group' comprising Anderson's 1st Army and Montgomery's 8th Army. The Americans, after cruel rebuffs, rapidly learned the art of war. Great quantities of ammunition and arms poured in. But the key factor was the cutting of German supplies, again largely due to Ultra, which enabled the Allied naval and air forces to know every detail about almost every convoy. The effect on von Arnim's forces was catastrophic and far more significant than Allied skill in fighting. Rommel had asked for 140,000 tons a month, probably an excessive figure, but the supply in March was only 29,000, in April 23,000, and in the first twelve days of May, 2,000. There was hard, bitter fighting which demonstrated the continued capacity of defensive power. The collapse when it came was sudden and complete. By 13 May when the surrender took place, the Germans had run out of ammunition entirely. By 1 June there would have been no more food. Von Arnim and some 150,000 men fell into Allied hands.

Hitler made a major error in thus reinforcing a cause

which was doubtful from the start and hopeless after 6 March. He deprived himself of the tried though youthful veterans of the Mediterranean war, who might have made the subsequent invasion of Sicily impossible. In that sense, as Sir Basil Liddell Hart observes, the Allied failure to seize Tunis after 'Torch' was 'one of the biggest blessings in disguise that could have happened'. It is ironical to reflect that, if Hitler a year before the Tunisian surrender had given his North African forces even a small proportion of the men and supplies that he tried to pour into Tunis from 9 November onwards, Rommel might well have broken through to the Delta with incalculable consequences for the future of the war.

2

In January 1943 a meeting of great importance was held at Casablanca, attended by Roosevelt, Churchill and their Chiefs of Staff – on the British side General Sir Alan Brooke and Air Chief Marshal Sir Charles (Peter) Portal, on the American side General George C. Marshall and Admiral Ernest J. King. The whole future strategy of the war came under consideration. There were three views. Admiral King was for devoting everything to the defeat of Japan. His policy was not a serious runner. Roosevelt was firmly against it, though the Admiral was able in the end to divert much more *matériel* to the Pacific theatre than the President intended. General Marshall was in favour of the earliest possible invasion of Europe in 1943 from the north which gave the quickest route into Germany. Brooke was convinced that this was impossible and that the right thing to do after the capture of Tunis was to invade Italy via Sicily. Portal took the same view and so did Lord Louis Mountbatten, Chief of Combined Operations, though he preferred Sardinia to Sicily.

Churchill had not at first agreed with his military advisers. Although he was strongly against a second front in 1942, he still believed in the possibility of a cross-Channel invasion during the summer of 1943. When informing Stalin in Moscow in August 1942 that a second front was not 'on' that year he had given a virtual promise that it would be established during the next year. Paradoxically it was the American combined Chiefs of Staff who regarded 'Torch' as precluding 'Round-up', the code name for a cross-Channel attack in 1943. General Marshall came to take a different view later, but in November 1942 he gave orders, subsequently countermanded, to slow down the build-up of forces in England. By early January 1943, however, the lines of difference were clearly drawn. The Americans favoured 'Round-up' in 1943 and remaining in Africa after Tunis had been cleared. The British wished to follow up 'Torch' with landings in Sicily. They did not preclude an invasion of northern France that year if conditions made it feasible but it was not their top priority.

The Casablanca Conference, 14 to 24 January, was called to resolve these differences. The British view prevailed all along the line. Although 'Round-up' was still kept on the agenda for 1943, it was agreed that Sicily should be the next target after the capture of Tunis. Nothing was said about invasion of Italy. By consenting to this programme Marshall was in effect agreeing to postpone the invasion of France till 1944. The only possible way at this stage of launching 'Round-up' in 1943 would have been to wind up the North African campaign at once, adopt a defensive posture in Tunis, leaving the German forces to rot away through lack of supplies, and transfer troops, equipment and landing craft to England as soon as possible. Marshall did not suggest this; it would have been psychologically unacceptable to all concerned. The capture of Tunisia which took four more months was regarded as essential by both the American and British planners.

The contrary view has been expressed with clarity and vigour in Mr John Grigg's *1943, The Victory That Never Was* published in 1980. He argues that if it had been possible to invade northern France successfully in 1943 the war could have ended a year earlier with a great saving of life. On this most people would agree. But was it possible? The answer must be no, unless 'Torch' had never been launched in the first instance. It was not just a matter of treating Tunisia from the end of 1942 as a backwater (though it was one that could have produced some disagreeable waves). The numerous experts who examined the problem were unanimous that, in view of the Allied shortage of shipping – not, as so often claimed, landing craft – it was logistically impossible, once the Anglo-American forces had been committed to North Africa in 1942, to redeploy them for a cross-Channel landing before 1944. No one has ever refuted this argument, and there are many other reasons for doubting a success in 1943 – not least the amount of German armour that could have been switched at that time from the eastern front.

As so often in war the controversy became fogged by side-arguments, rationalizations and *ex post facto* judgements. Churchill, a reluctant convert to Brooke's view, became as had happened before – one could compare the Dardanelles – more papal than the Pope. His vehemence for the Mediterranean made the Americans suspect, unjustly, that the memory of British casualties on the western front in 1914–18 had determined him against 'Round-up' even in 1944. They felt that at Casablanca they had been 'bounced' and the feeling coloured relations for the rest of the war. Despite the urbane exchanges between Roosevelt and 'Former Naval Person' there was a barrier between them. At heart the President was suspicious of Britain and her empire. He was politically, if not on the left, certainly not conservative. To him Churchill was something of a fossil mentally, despite all his restless energy. His rhetoric and his grandiloquent monologues irked the President, and Churchill on his side was aware of an elusiveness and reticence which he could not penetrate, perhaps even a slipperiness which he could never grip.

There were two other important decisions at Casablanca. One was Roosevelt's declaration that the Allied objective was 'unconditional surrender' by the Axis powers. Much has been written about its origin and its wisdom. The objective was certainly agreed between Roosevelt and Churchill though it was not in the written communiqué issued to the press on 24 January. Nor had Churchill expected Roosevelt to mention it orally as he did. Churchill would have omitted Italy but the War Cabinet insisted otherwise – perhaps because of Eden's phobia against Mussolini. Not that its insistence made any difference. Roosevelt put in Italy without consulting Churchill who had no option but to agree.

As for the wisdom of the declaration, there will never be agreement. Some maintain that it had little or no effect, others that it prolonged resistance by depriving moderate elements in the Axis of any motive to press for a compromise peace. What is certain is that the decision was taken in a very slapdash manner. It may have led to unnecessary slowness in easing Italy out of the war, though there were delays in military planning which were equally significant. On balance the verdict must be 'non-proven'.

The other important decision was the go-ahead for the Anglo-American strategic air offensive, or rather two separate offensives, for the commanders of the two forces had to agree to differ. The Americans believed in daylight bombing of precise targets. The RAF doctrine was 'area' bombing by night which really meant intimidation of the civilian population. Harris maintained that Casablanca gave him authority to do this, and no one challenged him.

Both offensives had only limited success in 1943. The slow lumbering American 'Flying Fortresses', out of range of fighter escort, proved to be highly vulnerable. Losses were immense, culminating with the raid of 14 October on the ball-bearing plant at Schweinfurt. The attack cut production by nearly forty per cent and a repeat performance might have reduced it to nothing, but the US Air Force lost 60 out of 291 planes and had another 138 damaged. No bomber force could go on losing at this rate. The Americans now turned to what the RAF experts had always claimed to be impossible, the development of a really long-range escort fighter. This, the P51B Mustang, one of the finest weapons of the war, came into mass production at the end of the year and soon transformed the balance of power in the air.

Harris's night bombing of area targets had more effect than the daylight campaign in the sense that it killed an immense number of men, women and children, and destroyed a great quantity of houses. In Hamburg alone 50,000 people were killed and a quarter of a million houses rendered uninhabitable. Yet, even if one sets aside the ethics of this policy, as almost everyone did except George Bell, Bishop of Chichester, who thus forfeited his chances of Canterbury, one cannot regard it as a success. It had relatively little effect on war production. Precision bombing which was, after all, not impossible even by night would have produced better results. The losses in bombers rose steadily. The German night fighting techniques became more and more effective, and a raid on Nuremburg in March 1944 saw the loss of 94 out of 795 bombers and damage to another 71. At this juncture, fortunately for his repute, Harris was ordered much against his will to switch to the French railways in preparation for the cross-Channel invasion.

Churchill next met Roosevelt at Washington in May 1943. The target date for 'Round-up' now renamed 'Overlord' was fixed for 1 May 1944, and it was agreed, though not in any detail, that operations should be continued in the Mediterranean after the fall of Sicily. This vagueness had unfortunate results.

The attack on Sicily began on 10 July 1943, remarkably late in all the circumstances. It was mounted by 150,000 men later built up to half a million, and 2,000 ships. The German forces were about 60,000. The invasion was preceded by a brilliant deception plan. The cardinal feature was floating a corpse in officer's uniform ashore in Spain ('The Man Who Never Was') with documents which were sure to be photographed by the Abwehr and which suggested that Sardinia and Greece were the Allied objectives. Ultra enabled the

British Intelligence Services to monitor the effect and know that the Germans were completely taken in. Although Alexander's two army commanders – those equally bumptious figures Montgomery and the American General Patton – were on about as good terms as Rommel and Arnim in Tunis, Sicily was conquered by 17 August. But it was not a Dunkirk. No less than 40,000 Germans crossed to the mainland with fifty tanks, thousands of vehicles, nearly a hundred guns and 1,700 tons of supplies. It could have been much more than a Dunkirk if the Allies had landed even a small force in Calabria, the 'toe' of Italy, and cut off the German retreat.

Meanwhile, on 25 July Mussolini was overthrown by a coup worthy of Renaissance Florence, engineered by Marshal Badoglio who had been, along with others, in secret touch with the Allies for many months. Badoglio's government dared not at once break with Hitler. Negotiations of tortuous complexity followed. On 3 September 1943 an armistice treaty was secretly signed with the Allies. That same day the 8th Army crossed the Straits of Messina into Italy. Five days later General Mark Clark, American commander of the 5th (Anglo-American) Army, landed his advance forces at Salerno near Naples. At the same time the armistice was made public. The Germans, however, had been far quicker off the mark. As soon as Mussolini fell, Hitler ordered Rommel to take charge of a reserve army on the north Italian frontier. By the beginning of September he had eight divisions in readiness to reinforce Field-Marshal Kesselring's six in the south and two near Rome. Mussolini, interned in the Abruzzi, was rescued by German parachutists to the north and enabled to set up a puppet rival government to Badoglio's.

The 5th Army at Salerno barely held off an attack which nearly drove it back into the sea, but it survived, was joined by the 8th Army and captured Naples on 1 October. Little further progress was made. The features of the campaign were overinsurance and excessive caution. A virtually static front across the country some seventy miles north of Salerno was established late in December. 'The stagnation of the whole campaign on the Italian front is becoming scandalous,' wrote Churchill on 19 December. The reason was not just lack of enterprise. The truth was that the Americans were not interested in Italy or any Mediterranean campaign which might distract from 'Overlord'. Their suspicions about Churchill's commitment to the cross-Channel invasion were enhanced by his pressure for a breakthrough in Italy and even more by his disastrous decision in September to land troops on the Italian-garrisoned Aegean Islands, Leros, Kos and Samos. This was a part of his misguided belief – perhaps stemming from Gallipoli – of the importance of winning over the Turks to the Allied side. He had made an abortive visit to Ankara immediately after Casablanca for this hopeless cause, dreaming as in 1915 of convoys to Russia through the Black Sea. It is unlikely that Turkey would have joined in, even if the Aegean islands had been held, but they were not. Eisenhower refused all help. The Germans seized them with little difficulty. With the capture of Leros on 16 November the futile enterprise ended.

There was one aspect of the Italian capitulation on which history has been curiously silent till very recently.[1] Under a concordat between Hitler and Mussolini, Allied prisoners taken in North Africa were interned in Italian prisoner-of-war camps. There were some 70,000. Montgomery, characteristically assuming that he would clear Italy at once, had sent through the usual slow clandestine sources instructions to all senior British officers in prison camps to forbid the inmates to leave when the Italians capitulated; it would be tidier if they could be duly collected in an efficient organized manner instead of being scattered all over the place, drinking like fishes and sleeping with Italian girls. Too late in the day at Churchill's instigation these instructions were countermanded. In most camps the new orders were never received, the prisoners remained *in situ*, and were soon in German custody. About a seventh with much difficulty managed in the end to get away. The rest were transferred to Germany.

The year 1943 ended on a discouraging note for Britain. The balance of power among the western Allies had shifted to an America which had little but dislike for Britain's imperial role. On the shorter view, British forces had been held up in Italy and frustrated in the Aegean. The air offensives by both Britain and America had been expensive and relatively unproductive. It was true that the battle of the Atlantic had been won, also true that the great naval battle of Midway in June 1942 – a success largely due to the American equivalent of Ultra – had given the Japanese the first major defeat which led to their gradual decline during the next eighteen months. Moreover, on the eastern front the Axis had received blow after blow. The war would be won, but when?

3

By the end of 1943 Britain had become a 'socialist state' administered by a coalition government in which Conservatives were the major partner. No other country, apart from Russia of whose real system little is known, had moved so far towards complete *étatisme*. Every aspect of industrial and agricultural life, whether it involved ownership, management or labour, was controlled. Food, clothing and petrol were rigidly rationed. There was conscription of labour, and it even included women – a step which the German government resisted almost to the end. The contrast with Germany was remarkable in other respects. If one takes 100 as the base line for consumer goods in 1939 for both countries, the German figure in 1943 was 91, and in 1944 it was 85. No wonder the Allied troops were astonished at the prosperity of the German working class when they entered the country in 1945. In Britain the figure was 54 in both years. The British economy, in Mr A. J. P. Taylor's words, was 'socialism by consent, that is to say socialism with the difficulties left out'. The same author describes the war as 'a people's war'. He is right on both counts. It was only a unity of purpose among all classes of society that made the socialism

of the siege economy acceptable. That unity was to end with
the end of war.

But during the war there was a real sense of solidarity, not
only between the 'classes' but within the 'masses'. In the
previous war a profound gulf existed between the services and
the civilians whatever their social status – hence perhaps the
haunting verse and prose which it produced. In the Second
World War they were all much more mixed up together – this
especially applied to the RAF – they shared the same dangers
and except for the armies in the Mediterranean they were
based till 1944 on the same island. This solidarity did not
necessarily include the ever rising numbers of non-British
servicemen. By the spring of 1944 there were nearly 1·5
million, the vast majority being Americans who were the least
popular – 'overpaid, overfed, oversexed and over here', as the
saying was. It is common but fallacious for people to assume
that alien minorities, temporary or permanent, have inordinate
sexual vigour. Particular odium was attached to liaisons
between the GIs and the wives or girlfriends of British service
men overseas. The moralist may deplore but the realist cannot
wonder at these fleeting attachments between young men far
from home and girls whose husbands also far from home were
by no means always 'faithful', though their opportunities in the
jungles of Burma or the plains of the western desert were more
limited than those of their counterparts in England.

The acceptance of total war by the 'masses' was helped by a
policy which increased wages compared with dividends, rents,
and salaries. Subsidies kept down prices. The rich were
heavily taxed, and, although fortunes were made during the
war in agriculture and industry they were not on the blatant
scale of 1914–18. There was a black market and a grey market,
as in all controlled economies. No one will ever know quite
how big they were, but there is nothing to suggest that they
operated on a very large scale. By and large the public was
patriotic and committed to the war, and the army of 'snoopers'
maintained by various ministries had at least some deterrent
effect.

The health of the country is a moot question. It is generally said that rationing and allocation of milk, etc., led to an improvement for children. Teenagers probably fared worse, for rationing gave 'equal' not 'fair' shares and different people have different needs. The war saw a great increase in tuberculosis, owing to long, cold hours of work, and of course in syphilis and gonorrhoea – regular concomitants of war since the sixteenth century.

One lasting revolution in the treatment of wounds and diseases was achieved when Sir Howard (later Lord) Florey, an Australian medical scientist of genius, made possible the production of penicillin on a major scale. The drug had been discovered before the war by Alexander Fleming whose name is always associated with it, but its practical success was Florey's. No single person – if one can personify at all – has saved more lives. It was, however, a sign of Britain's relative decline that the country lacked the resources to exploit Florey's achievement, and so the patents all went to America.

The mood of the country became markedly more left-wing. 'Socialism' seemed to be working in war. Why not in peace? There was a great faith in Russia which was bearing the main brunt of the war. The time-serving duplicity of Stalin from 1939 to 1941 was forgotten, though not by everyone; and those who knew about the cruelty, barbarism and brutality of his regime which was as bad as Hitler's kept silent. Russia was still vaguely regarded, if not as a socialist Utopia, at least as a country which was moving in the proper direction. All this fuelled the flame of agitation for a 'second front' in 1942. Some who supported it – Lord Beaverbrook and Sir Stafford Cripps – were anything but fellow-travellers, others were ideologically more sympathetic, and the Communist Party, always influential among the trade unions, agitated, vigorously instructed from above. In autumn 1942 the King ordered the making of a special sword to be presented to the people of Stalingrad. The 'Sword of Stalingrad' was sent on a tour of England and Scotland, to be gazed at by reverent queues of sightseers. A high point of Russomania was the celebration of 'Red Army Day' on 23 February 1943. Official demonstrations addressed by ministers took place in a dozen great cities. Louis MacNeice wrote a verse play 'Salute to the Red Army'. Sir Alexander Cadogan who vetted it on behalf of the Foreign Office wrote: 'This is sorry stuff but I am glad to see that there are *some* references to Britain's part in the war.' If governmental encouragement of these pro-Russian manifestations seems almost incredible today and indeed seemed very strange quite soon after the war, one has to remember the widespread fear that Stalin might sign a separate peace with Hitler. It appeared important, even to politicians who deeply detested communism, to show solidarity with Russia. After all, the Red Army was doing most of the fighting. We can now see that the brutalities committed by the Germans in occupied Russia made any sort of deal out of the question but this was not clear at the time.

Pro-Russianism among the intelligentsia and a large section of both the middle and working classes was one symptom among many of a decisive swing to the left. The 'Postscripts' of J. B. Priestley on the radio, the answers on 'The Brains Trust', the lectures by the Army Education Corps and by the Army Bureau of Current Affairs (ABCA), the documentary film movement, the Penguin Specials, the Left Book Club, the *Daily Mirror*, *Picture Post* – one could compile an endless list – all had their effect. But, contrary to the beliefs of most Tories, they were symptoms as well as causes of the new mood. By-elections, which owing to the party truce were fought only by independents, told a similar tale. People were voting against the Conservatives. They were almost certain to vote for Labour when they had the chance. It is significant that by 1942, if the findings of Mass Observation were correct, most people who answered the question at all believed that Labour would win the next general election. The cry of 'Guilty Men' who brought Britain unprepared into war, the popular denunciations of unemployment and poverty in the 1930s, the memory of what had happened after 1918 all produced a climate of opinion that was anti-Conservative, egalitarian and hopeful of major changes in post-war society.

Nowhere was the new mood more clearly shown than in the reception of the Beveridge Report which was published on 1 December 1942. The Committee on Social Insurance and Allied Services was set up by Arthur Greenwood, Minister of Reconstruction in June 1941, under the chairmanship of Sir William Beveridge, Master of University College, Oxford, since 1937. He was a notable – perhaps the last – 'all-round' social reformer. The government did not expect any major policy recommendations to emerge and Bevin unrealistically wanted it to stick to technical details. Anyone who expected this to happen reckoned without the chairman. Beveridge, who was vain and egotistical as well as very clever, was determined to propose a revolution in social policy and he had the powerful support of Keynes in the Treasury. He dominated the committee and he lobbied ceaselessly among the media, ensuring mammoth publicity, to the fury of Whitehall, even before the report came out. In a moment of folly he told a *Daily Telegraph* journalist that his proposals would take the country 'half way to Moscow'. He was never again to play any part in official policy-making whether under Labour or Conservative administrations.

The report was not as revolutionary as is sometimes said but it undoubtedly appealed to the public. No less than 650,000 copies were sold, which must be a record for a Stationery Office publication. It came out at a good moment – after the turn of the tide at Alamein, and the 'Torch' landings in North Africa. What he proposed was the unification of the existing separate pre-war schemes of social insurance and the inclusion of everyone in a single scheme to cover health, unemployment and old age. He boldly assumed as requirements full employment – or at any rate much fuller than before the war – and a National Health Service. Although Beveridge was not a member of the Labour Party his proposals had more appeal there than among the Conservatives. Churchill did not conceal his boredom with the whole business. There was a backbench Labour rebellion on 18 February 1943 when in the debate on the proposals James Griffiths put down an amendment in favour of prompt action, which got 118 votes.

The principal social reform measures which were accepted before the end of the war nearly all stemmed from Beveridge, for example the White Papers of 1943 on a National Health Service and that of 1944 on Full Employment. The exception was the Education Act of 1944 brought in by R. A. Butler, which created the tripartite system of grammar, secondary modern and technical schools, defused the explosive question of religious education, raised the school leaving age to fifteen (sixteen as soon as possible – which turned out to be 1973) and proposed, on the recommendation of the Fleming Committee, that the public (i.e. private) schools should take a quarter of their number from within the state system. Nothing came of this last proposal, but it kept the critics at bay for the time being. The Bill as a by-product caused a backbench revolt. By a majority of one the House carried equal pay for women teachers, but Churchill forced the rescission of the vote.

The Conservatives did not ignore social reform or the factors leading to its demand, but they did not seem as clear-headed and enthusiastic as Labour. There were a hundred indications by the end of 1943 and early 1944 that Labour would win the next election. One will suffice. In June 1943 voting intentions, according to the British Institute of Public Opinion were: Conservative 31, Labour 38, and Liberal 9. By December the figures were respectively: 27, 40 and 10. In April 1945 they were to be not very different: 23, 40 and 12. It seems in retrospect unlikely that the Conservatives, despite all Churchill's prestige, could have won an election any time after 1940.

Chapter Fifteen

VICTORY

At the end of 1943 a series of high-level Allied conferences took place first in Cairo on 22 to 26 November, attended by Roosevelt, Churchill and their Combined Chiefs of Staff; then in Teheran from 28 November to 1 December, attended by the same Anglo-American team with Stalin and his principal military advisers; finally in Cairo again from 3 to 7 December, confined to the Anglo-Americans. The meeting with the Russians was the most important, for it settled the shape of the war for the next six months. It also marked the first signs of Churchill's isolation and of Roosevelt's desire not to 'gang up' on Stalin – soon difficult to distinguish from a positive inclination to 'gang up' on Churchill. He fully exploited Stalin's unwavering support for a second front in 1944 in order to check any British backsliding. The meeting was also the origin of 'Anvil' – the auxiliary invasion of the south of France.

The Americans misunderstood the British attitude. Churchill was genuinely committed to 'Overlord'; there was no question of going back on the agreement confirmed at Quebec in August 1943. Neither then nor later did he wish to substitute an invasion of the Balkans; General Smuts in September urged him to press for full-scale invasion of southern Europe, and postponement of 'Overlord', while stepping up the strategic bombing of Germany. The idea was not foolish, in itself. South-eastern Europe contained valuable supplies of ore, grain and oil. The number of German divisions retained in the Balkans showed Hitler's anxiety. But the Americans would never have consented to a reshuffle of this sort. 'I hope you realize,' Churchill replied, 'that British loyalty to "Overlord" is the keystone of the arch of Anglo-American cooperation.'

The British plan never went beyond diversionary activities in the Mediterranean to support 'Overlord'. The success of a cross-Channel invasion turned, not on the number of German divisions in western Europe but on the number actually ready to cope with the landings during the first few days. Anything which could be done to confuse the German High Command or distract forces towards the south would be highly profitable. Time was the key to the operation. The American fear was that these diversionary attempts would, by an insidious series of gradations, become objectives in themselves and draw away the necessary resources for the principal purpose of the whole strategy, namely the invasion of northern France.

At the end of the second Cairo conference there was broad agreement. 'Overlord' and 'Anvil' would be launched in May 1944. Because of 'Anvil', the assault shipping to exploit openings in Italy and the Aegean would not be removed from the Mediterranean as had at one time been the plan. To make 'Anvil' possible 'Buccaneer' – an amphibious operation which Mountbatten had planned to launch in March 1944 against the Andaman Islands twenty-two miles south west of Rangoon – was cancelled by Roosevelt (the Americans were in sole control of Far Eastern strategy).

There remained the problem of the command of 'Overlord'. Churchill agreed that the post should go to an American and that Marshall should be the man. A series of intrigues followed in Washington. Could Marshall combine the command of 'Overlord' with being Chief of Staff? The other American Chiefs said no. Could he become commander not only of 'Overlord' but of the entire western Allied forces in Europe? Churchill and the British Chiefs said no. Roosevelt in the end kept Marshall where he was and appointed Eisenhower to command 'Overlord' – probably the best result.

It was agreed that Montgomery, under Eisenhower, would be in charge of the initial Anglo-American assault on northern France. Thereafter Eisenhower would take over, and under him General Omar Bradley would command the American group of armies and Montgomery the British. Air Chief Marshal Tedder was to be Eisenhower's deputy. The Mediterranean was left to the British; Maitland Wilson, a diplomatic general, was the supremo but the key figure was Alexander who commanded in Italy.

In terms of war strategy Teheran and Cairo were successful. The pattern of operations for 1944 was settled. The decision of all three Allies to use their full power against Japan after the defeat of Germany was confirmed. Politically the upshot was less clear. Stalin's determination to keep the gains of the Ribbentrop–Molotov pact received the secret acquiescence of Roosevelt who met him privately behind Churchill's back and agreed to a shift of Poland's western frontier to the Oder as a 'compensation' for the loss of the territory east of the 'Curzon Line' of 1920. Roosevelt also agreed to the Russian annexation of the Baltic republics. Stalin had a free hand henceforth in this part of north-east Europe and he was to exploit it ruthlessly to the dismay of Churchill who could not forget that, formally at least, Britain unlike the USA had gone to war to preserve Poland. On the future of Germany nothing very clear emerged other than vague ideas about its dismemberment. Churchill was dubious about this and very indignant at Stalin's suggestion, half-endorsed by Roosevelt, that 50,000 German officers should be shot at the end of the war. This has been long regarded as a joke by Stalin – albeit in bad taste. The Katyn massacre suggests that it was nothing of the sort.

The decision to invade southern France ('Anvil') in May left resources of shipping and landing craft in the Mediterranean temporarily unused. It made sense to employ them in January for an amphibious flank-turning operation in Italy where the main Allied forces had become frozen outside Cassino ninety miles south of Rome. The plan was to land a force at Anzio thirty miles south of Rome and compel the Germans to retreat from their mountain line, thus opening the road to Rome. The idea was good, the execution by the slow, cautious General Mark Clark was not. 'Anzio' began on 22 January. The Germans nearly drove Clark's forces into the sea. The landings did little to help the hard slog up the 'spine' of Italy. Clark's troops became a beleaguered garrison. Their entry into Rome, on 4 June nearly five months later, flattered the vanity of their commander who owed more to the hard sloggers than to his own troops. Meanwhile, all hopes of a renewed attack on the Dodecanese vanished and the invasion of southern France appeared to be a more and more doubtful proposition in view of the shipping and reinforcements needed for Anzio. Maitland Wilson was for cancelling it – rightly. But it lingered on – an American dream – implemented in the end, but many weeks after it had any relevance to 'Overlord'.

Plans for the invasion of northern France had been gestating since March 1943 when General Morgan was appointed as Chief of Staff to the Supreme Allied Commander (Designate), 'Cossac' for short. He saw two possible places for landings, either the Pas de Calais between Gravelines and the Somme, or the Caen–Cotentin area. He decided on the latter. It was further from Allied air-bases and involved a longer sea-passage. But it was less obvious and it embraced two major ports, Cherbourg and Le Havre. Cossac envisaged a three division sea-borne landing in the Caen sector of the Normandy coast, supported by two air-borne divisions. Success required three conditions; first, facilities to maintain a force of eighteen divisions across the beaches while the captured ports were restored; secondly, the elimination of German fighter planes in north-west Europe; thirdly, that on D-Day the Germans should not have more than twelve mobile divisions in France and Belgium and should not be in a position to move more than fifteen from other parts of Europe during the first two months of the campaign. These last figures were averages to cover a number of contingencies. The plan stipulated an elaborate deception scheme to achieve the maximum of surprise.

Early in January 1944 Eisenhower and Montgomery examined these proposals. They decided that the front of attack was too narrow and the number of divisions too few. Their final figure was six sea-borne divisions in the first assault and two American air-borne divisions. The attack would not be confined to the twenty miles of coast north of Caen but would include a landing at La Madeleine on the eastern base of the Cotentin peninsula north-west of the Vire estuary and another at Vierville some fifteen miles east of the estuary. The landings north of Caen between Carentan and the river Orne were to be accomplished by General Dempsey's British 2nd Army (two British divisions and one Canadian); the landings further west by General Bradley's US 1st Army. These forces and the heavy reinforcements which it was planned to pour in after the beach heads had been captured were known as 21st Army Group and were commanded by Montgomery. By D-Day+15 there should be some twenty Allied divisions in France.

It was agreed by the planners that the German Air Force must be driven from the skies and that the greatest possible delay must be imposed on German troop movements. There was the further threat, known to be imminent, of new German weapons which came to be called the V1 and V2 – the 'flying bomb' and the rocket. German experts had been deeply involved in developing these throughout the war. By June 1943 their feasibility had been demonstrated. Hitler told his military entourage that by the end of the year London would be obliterated and Britain forced to capitulate. In July the order was given for mass production of the weapons and the construction of launching sites. Allied intelligence was aware from April 1943 that something was afoot, although details were hard to come by. Photo-reconnaissance of a very high order revealed the location of some of the launching sites and key factories. Here was yet another task for the USAAF and the RAF.

The question from January 1944 onwards was how best to employ the Allied air forces. Obviously the factories and launching sites of the new weapons must be destroyed if this could be accurately done. The delay in their use – the first V1 did not appear over London till 13 June, a week after D-Day – was largely due to Allied bombing. A bigger problem was the choice of targets to assist 'Overlord'. Since June 1943 the top priority in strategic bombing had been the destruction of the German fighter aircraft industry; operation 'Pointblank' was the codename. It had been ineffective. The strength of the German fighter forces rose steadily. However, Harris for the RAF and General Spaatz for the US Air Force believed that the American long-range escort fighters would change the scene. If German oil installations were added to their targets, strategic bombing over the next three months would achieve the twin objectives of neutralizing the *Luftwaffe* and disrupting communications by destroying oil supplies. After that in May the air arm could be switched to the tactical needs of 'Overlord', a short and heavy bombardment of communications. Then it could be switched back again to the old objective of destroying the German economy and morale.

The 'Overlord' authorities disagreed. Although in favour of the destruction of fighter production, they believed that the Germans had plenty of oil in France and that the bombing of oil installations in Germany would not produce the sort of disruption of communications which could result from a prolonged direct attack on railways, roads and bridges in France and Belgium. They favoured as a rival to 'Pointblank' what came to be known as the 'Transportation Plan'. The ensuing dispute was acrimonious, especially as it affected a crucial question of command. Under 'Pointblank' the air forces would be autonomous. Under the 'Transportation Plan' they would be subordinated to Eisenhower or in practice to Tedder. Proposals and counter-proposals whizzed to and fro. Spaatz suggested a compromise which Tedder rejected. There was the problem of French civilian casualties – a matter which particularly disturbed Churchill. In the end the 'Transportation Plan' prevailed. From 25 March the strategic air objectives would be divided between the German aircraft industry and the communications system – above all railways – in France and Belgium. There can be little doubt that the decision was correct. The *Luftwaffe* was effectively driven from the skies by D-Day, the disruption of the railways, though never complete, was enough to have a crippling effect on the arrival of new German divisions, and French casualties were far fewer than were feared.

Deception was one of the keys of success. Nothing could conceal the Allied intention to invade northern Europe from Britain in 1944. It was thus essential to keep Hitler guessing where the blow would fall. An elaborate system of double-agents, bogus wireless traffic and constant monitoring by Ultra of the German reaction achieved astonishing success. Fictitious armies were created, one threatening the Balkans, another Norway. The Germans kept twenty-four divisions in the Balkans and did not move troops from Norway till D-Day+10. These were mere ancillary diversions. The crucial area was northern France. Once again a non-existent force was created. It was supposed to be under General Patton's command, and to be assembled in south-east England for an assault on the Pas de Calais. It was named FUSAG or First US Army Group. With great skill the impression was given that the main assault would be there, and that an earlier attack in Normandy would be a diversionary feint. The Germans were deceived, and, thanks to Ultra, the Allies knew that they had been deceived.

Hitler had fifty-eight divisions in France, half of them static and some of poor quality, but the figure included no less than ten panzer divisions. The Allies had thirty-five divisions and three air-borne divisions but they had effectively given the impression to Hitler, von Rundstedt, the Commander-in-Chief in the west, and Rommel who commanded the forces on the Channel coast, of having eighty-five to ninety divisions and seven air-borne divisions. When the assault began Rommel's 7th Army was in Normandy and his 15th Army comprising eighteen divisions was in the Pas de Calais. He kept the 15th Army where it was. If he had moved it at once to Normandy 'Overlord' might well have ended in disaster.

On Eisenhower, and on him alone, fell the choice of D-Day. Moon and tide were the determining factors. He resolved to attack at half-flood to avoid underwater devices. His ships needed darkness for the voyage of approach but moonlight to identify their objectives when they arrived. These conditions meant a day when the moon rose between 1 A.M. and 2 A.M. and the tide was at half-flood forty minutes after dawn – requirements which could be met only a few days in any month. The first was 5 June and Eisenhower chose it. Another necessity was that the weather should be reasonably calm and fine. By the end of May all was ready, and the last few days of the month were clear and sunny, but on 1 June a sinister change occurred – heavy low cloud and a rising wind. The next day or two were even worse. The 'great armada', as Churchill called it was already in formation but at 4.15 A.M. on 4 June as a result of a dismal weather forecast Eisenhower postponed the attack for twenty-four hours. If he did not go ahead by 7 June at latest, nothing could be done for at least a fortnight. At 9.15 P.M. on 4 June he again consulted his chief meteorologist who now predicted a lull on 6 June followed by an indefinite spell of bad weather. Eisenhower resolved to go ahead. The German meteorologists also predicted the bad weather, but not the lull, thus giving the invasion a further, if adventitious element of surprise.

The Allied meteorologists were right. There was a lull on 6 June. After a tremendous sea and air bombardment which, among other achievements, knocked out nearly all the German coastal radar stations, landings were effected on all the beaches. On 6 and 7 June 185,000 men and 19,000 vehicles were landed by, or under the protection of 4,000 landing craft, 1,300 merchant ships and 1,200 warships; 19,000 men were conveyed by air, and the assault was supported by 10,000 planes. Two large artificial harbours known as 'Mulberrys' were put in position to handle 12,000 tons of stores and 2,500 vehicles daily. It was a remarkable performance. By mid-June there were nine American and seven British divisions ashore, the beach heads had been linked up and the forward troops were well inland. Caen which Montgomery intended to capture on the first day, and could have done but for over-cautious command on the spot, was still in German hands, and the American advance up the Cotentin peninsula was slower than expected, but in view of the enormous hazards and the powerful fortifications of the 'Atlantic Wall', the Allies had managed well.

At this juncture they had a stroke of bad luck. On 19 June the worst gale in that month for forty years struck the Channel. Convoys were scattered. One of the two artificial harbours was wrecked, the other badly damaged. A week of stormy weather followed and the rate of supplies fell disastrously. As a result Caen did not fall to the British 2nd Army which did most of the fighting until 18 July. On 31 July the Americans broke through on the west at Avranches. A large part of Rommel's forces was trapped in the 'Falaise pocket' between the British and American forces. The victory owed much to Ultra – Hitler's reckless decision to order a counter-attack towards the sea was known in advance, and preparations were made. Some eight German divisions had been annihilated by 20 August, but a considerable force managed to escape towards the Seine. Overwhelming air superiority and supplies of armour, guns and ammunition, along with the ability to read the German ciphers contributed to victory over an enemy who could still fight with great tenacity, despite convulsive events at home. Indeed, the latest historian – Max Hastings in his *Overlord* – considers that man for man the German Army was superior to those of the Allies throughout the Normandy campaign.[1] When numbers were near to equality the Germans usually won. They displayed greater initiative, greater resourcefulness, and were prepared to fight to the end. They were very tough enemies. In weapon strength, their machine-guns, hand grenades, mortars and, above all, their tanks were far superior to those of their opponents. The Sherman could be supplied in almost unlimited numbers but compared with the German Panther and Tiger it was under-armoured and under-gunned. Good though the Allied artillery was, neither America nor Britain ever produced anything to rival the German 88mm anti-tank gun. What the Allies did possess was total air superiority and this was one of the keys of success even though there has been much criticism of the way it was used.

On 20 July an attempt was made to blow up Hitler at his eastern HQ. It failed, and the vengeance which he took on all, however remotely connected with the aristocratic military plotters, was characteristically ferocious. Some 5,000 people are said to have been executed – many by methods of the utmost barbarity. Von Klüge who had replaced Von Rundstedt killed himself, as did many others. Rommel, badly wounded on 17 July, was also implicated. Nursed back to health in October he was given the option of trial before a 'people's court', or suicide which he preferred to slow strangulation on a thin wire suspended from a meat hook – the fate of the principal conspirators.

The Allied armies moved rapidly through northern France and Belgium. On 15 August 'Anvil', renamed 'Dragoon', was launched in the south. It met little opposition, but did no particular good. The next three weeks saw the entry of de Gaulle into Paris, the capture of Brussels, Antwerp, Namur and Verdun, and a great sweep by Patton's 3rd Army through Orleans and Troyes towards Alsace. At the same time a major offensive had been launched by the Russians with notable success. There was a general sense of euphoria. In Italy Alexander, despite the removal of seven divisions to the south of France believed that he could reach the north Italian plain and swing north through the so-called 'Ljubljana Gap' to Vienna before winter. He was far too optimistic. However, by mid-September his forces had broken through the 'Gothic Line' (which ran from north of

Pesaro to a few miles south of Spezia), and the prospects seemed good.

Yet within a few weeks of the capture of Antwerp all this euphoria evaporated. By the end of October the Allies had been checked everywhere in northern Europe, the Russians had been halted outside Budapest and Warsaw[2] and on the frontier of East Prussia, while Alexander's offensive had petered out. It was plain to all that the war would not end in 1944. This was a European tragedy of the greatest magnitude. Millions more men and women were killed and wounded, millions more Jews were marched into the gas chambers. Vast additional damage was done to homes and factories. Could it have been averted? The answer is yes.

The missed opportunity was in the west. It was not in Italy which was a 'side-show' in terms of general strategy. Nor was it on the eastern front where the German Army was at its most formidable. But in the west the Germans were in a state of total disarray for a brief period. They could only oppose 100 serviceable tanks to the Allies' 2,000 and 570 aircraft to over 14,000. The Allies were, however, hampered by shortage of supplies. Le Havre did not fall till 12 September, Boulogne till 22 September, Calais till 30 September. The capture of Antwerp on 4 September was useless until the Germans on both sides of the Schelde had been eliminated. This would have been possible if there had been quick action. In the event they hung on till November.

From 1 August the Allied forces had been split into two army groups, British 21st under Montgomery (1st Canadian and 2nd British armies), US 12th under Bradley (1st and 3rd American armies), but Montgomery still retained overall operational command. Eisenhower favoured a 'broad front' approach after the Normandy breakthrough. This was a cautious and reasonable strategy, but it was devised before D-Day on the assumption that the Germans would still be in fair strength and good order. Both Montgomery and Bradley, however, believed that the Germans were on the run and wanted a single rapid concentrated thrust on a narrower sector, Montgomery in the north through the Low Countries aiming at the Rhine on each side of the Ruhr, Bradley in the centre crossing the Rhine between Mainz and Karlsruhe. Montgomery was ready if necessary to let Bradley lead the northern offensive which had the advantage of clearing the Pas de Calais and the Channel ports. Both were agreed that, whichever sector was chosen, all available resources should be concentrated on it and that there should be only one commander. The debate has gone on ever since, but the balance of opinion favours the two army group commanders.

Eisenhower, however, had to consider the political aspect which was also part of the military. Montgomery, though a hero to the British public, was very unpopular with the top American command because of his conceit and egotism. He had moreover done himself great harm not only with the American but with the British High Command by maintaining throughout the Normandy campaign that his thrust for Caen was going, or had gone, according to plan when it was obviously doing nothing of the sort. Bradley was a relatively neutral figure but his key subordinate, Patton, was the hero of the American public, and like Montgomery neither modest nor tactful; the British military hierarchy detested him. To stop either Patton or Montgomery in their tracks and concentrate everything on either the north or the centre was to court a major political rumpus and to upset the Allied command structure which Eisenhower had been at immense pains to build up into a harmonious team. Accordingly on 1 September, as had been agreed all along, he took over operational command himself. He saw the advantage of some concentration on the north and 'lent' Montgomery the American 1st Army till the occupation of Antwerp, cutting down on the US 3rd Army's supplies, to the fury of Patton. But he was determined after that to revert to the broad front.

Montgomery made a renewed *démarche* after the fall of Antwerp, but to no avail. Although Eisenhower fully authorized the air-borne attempt on 17 September to secure a bridgehead across the Rhine at Arnhem, it was never intended to do more than consolidate a position. It was not the *point d'appui* of a major thrust. The defeat at Arnhem, largely caused by the accidental arrival of a panzer division near the point of landing and refusal to heed the intelligence reports which showed its presence, did not, as is often believed, stop a breakthrough into northern Germany, for none was planned. Much went wrong with the 21st Army Group's northward move. There were plans for an air-borne attack near Tournai which wasted six days of air supplies and was cancelled because ground troops arrived before it was needed. The Allies had extravagant notions about supply and failed to see that when the enemy was in flight petrol mattered more than ammunition. No less than 1,400 newly arrived trucks were found to have faulty pistons. Montgomery was slow after Antwerp either to make a quick move north-east or to clear the Schelde. Nevertheless, his basic strategy was right. Given enough support he could have won the war in 1944.

Arnhem, where a part of the flower of the British Army was lost despite immense courage, has gone down to posterity as one of those gallant defeats which will always figure in the annals of Britain's military history. It may not have been a strategical defeat, but it was certainly a blow to morale – a clear signal that the Germans had not been beaten. Their power of recuperation was astonishing. They exploited the pause after Arnhem by a series of resourceful improvisations. Clearly they could not now win the war even with the V weapons but Hitler, sick and half-mad, still retained his charismatic power. All centres of opposition to him had been destroyed. He convinced himself that the USSR and the eastern Allies must quarrel irrevocably before long. If not, it was better for the peoples of the Third Reich to perish in flames along with the leader of whom they were unworthy, than to surrender to these hateful enemies.

On 12 to 16 September when the Arnhem campaign was about to be launched Churchill met Roosevelt at a second Quebec Conference. He was a worried man. He was not convinced, despite the optimism of the military, that the war would end in 1944. He knew that Britain's relative contribution to the Allied war effort must decline and would be accompanied by a similar diminution in his power to influence the post-war settlement. Nor was all well at home. The civilian population had had enough. The flying bombs killed only 6,000 but their effect was morally very damaging – the clanking noise, the sudden silent cut-off and the ensuing explosion. One and a half million people left London between 13 June and the end of July. On 8 September just when the V1 had been conquered by fighters and AA gunnery, the first rockets (V2) – portents of a new military technology – fell on London. They killed another 2,750. This was a trivial figure, but unlike the 'flying bomb' the rocket could not be destroyed *en route*. London would have been rendered uninhabitable if the launching pads had not been overrun so soon. Had the device come into production only a few months earlier the course of the war could have been very different. Fortunately the Germans showed no sign of being anywhere near to the secret of the second major invention about to revolutionize war – the atomic bomb.

Britain's relative decline was emphasized at Quebec by the reluctance of the American Chiefs of Staff to countenance a British naval force in the Pacific. Churchill pressed it for political reasons and Roosevelt, to placate him, overruled the chiefs. But American ascendancy in terms of naval and air power was now so vast that the British contribution appeared militarily trivial and politically inconvenient. This was the last Anglo-American meeting to be mainly concerned with grand strategy. It was discussed, despite Churchill's doubts, largely on the assumption that Germany would be defeated in a few weeks. The conference was also the occasion for thought about the post-war world. Churchill was worried about the future of 'Lend-lease' and much concerned that it should be continued until the defeat of Japan not expected before 1946 or even later. The question became tangled with the future of Germany. At Teheran in December 1943 Stalin had floated the idea of dismembering and 'de-industrializing' Germany. This was taken up with enthusiasm by Henry Morgenthau, the US Secretary of the Treasury, and by Lord Cherwell (Professor Lindemann), Churchill's old friend and by no means unerring scientific adviser, who loathed Germans. The 'Morgenthau plan' would have turned Germany into a depopulated rural slum.

Churchill, by nature generous, repudiated it at first but later accepted it – possibly as a *quid pro quo*, unlikely in practice to be exacted, for 6.5 billion dollars of 'Lend-lease'. Eden strongly protested, and the American officials were no less hostile. In the end Roosevelt and Churchill silently abandoned a proposal which survives only in the history books – a memorial to the vindictive and impracticable folly which could seduce even the leaders of liberal democracy. It soon leaked in Washington, as most things did and do – a splendid bonus for Goebbels's propaganda machine and far more effective than 'unconditional surrender' in prolonging German resistance.

Although the Russian offensive had been halted in the north, the Soviet armies gained great successes in the south. By the end of August they had seized Bucharest and the Romanian oilfields. Bulgaria also surrendered, and the German forces in Greece were ordered to retreat on 7 October. The future of south-east Europe was now a major question. Churchill went indefatigably to Moscow from 9 to 17 October. He submitted to Stalin a curious percentage plan of predominance – Romania to be ninety per cent Russian; Greece ninety per cent British; Yugoslavia and Hungary fifty per cent each; Bulgaria, for some reason, seventy-five per cent Russian. Stalin ticked the paper with his large blue pencil. Churchill observed after a pause: 'Might it not be thought rather cynical if it seemed we had disposed of these issues, so fateful to millions of people, in such an off-hand manner? Let us burn the paper.' 'No, you keep it,' replied Stalin. The transaction meant little except for Greece. Everywhere else Stalin soon took 100 per cent, but in Greece he kept his word. In the winter of 1944 – 5 British troops suppressed the pro-communist forces (ELAS) to the fury of Labour, Liberals and *The Times* at home, while America looked on in frosty neutrality. Stalin never lifted a finger in aid of ELAS.

The war of movement died away in October both in northern Europe and in Italy where Alexander's forces made little progress after penetrating the Gothic Line. Then there occurred something which none of the Allies expected. In great secrecy, with complete radio silence Hitler personally prepared a counter-attack in the Ardennes, the very area in which his armies had swept through to victory in 1940. Aided by fog, rain and low cloud it began on 16 December and took the Americans, who held that sector thinly with detachments of their 1st Army, completely by surprise. The plan was to cross the Meuse between Huy and Liège, drive for Antwerp, cut off the 21st Army Group from its base and achieve another Dunkirk. Although the attack achieved alarming initial success, and inflicted some heavy defeats on the US 1st Army, Hitler lacked the resources in fuel and ammunition to follow it through. When his armies came to a halt ten days later they had advanced in places up to fifty miles, but they never looked like crossing the Meuse. The campaign was a curious repetition of March 1918, and had the same damaging longer-term consequences to the German forces. Counter-attacks were launched by Montgomery from the north and Patton from the south. By mid-January the Germans with a loss of 120,000 men and 600 tanks were everywhere half way or more back to their starting line.

The second and last meeting of the Big Three took place at Yalta in the Crimea from 4 to 10 February 1945. It was preceded by Anglo-American discussions in Malta from 30 January onwards, briefly joined by the President *en route* for the Crimea on 2 February. He displayed little desire to discuss details before the tripartite meeting with Stalin. This reluctance has been attributed to his health, but contemporary accounts do not suggest that it was as bad as it appeared with hindsight – for example to Lord Moran, Churchill's doctor. It is just as likely that Roosevelt did not want to get involved in talks which might cut across his plans for cooperation with Stalin. American policy was to change sharply after the President's death, though not at once, but this should not blur its original assumptions. The Far East was the main question. The British were committed to war with Japan. The Russians had said that they would join. But would they when it came to the point? The atomic bomb was not at this stage certain to work. The British Empire in the Far East could be a barrier to the sort of anti-colonial peace settlement envisaged by Roosevelt.

The President got what mattered most to him, a promise signed, sealed and delivered that Russia would enter the war against Japan not more than three months after Germany had been defeated. The bargain, concluded behind Churchill's back, involved some disagreeable features for Britain, though the Prime Minister felt obliged to sign. The President also secured Stalin's agreement to his system of voting in the United Nations – a matter to which he attached great importance. The Polish question was settled by *force majeure*. Russian will was stamped upon a people which detested them then and has ever since. Churchill reluctantly agreed to recognize the communist puppet government with some face-saving provisos. His decision sparked off a minor Tory revolt. A junior minister, Harry Strauss (later Lord Conesford), resigned, and twenty-five Conservative backbenchers voted against a motion to approve Yalta, including two of subsequent eminence – Lord Home (then Lord Dunglass MP) and Peter (Lord) Thorneycroft. The carve-up of occupied Germany into British, US and Russian zones was confirmed, with the addition of a French zone to be sliced out of the British and American.

At the time of Yalta it was far from clear when the war would end. The Ardennes offensive made the Allied commanders as cautious as they had been optimistic; they talked in terms of late June or early July. In fact the German forces after an astonishing display of tenacity had almost reached the end of their power to resist. The strategic air offensive resumed by both the USAAF and the RAF in the autumn of 1944 at last began, under long-range fighter escort, to do what its supporters had wrongly claimed that it had been doing ever since 1942. The Americans still favoured precision bombing on oil targets and communications. Portal agreed and so did Tedder. Harris was adamant for 'area' bombing. He was by now a popular hero like Montgomery. He won his way but lost his peerage. The destruction of Dresden on 14 February at the cost of 60,000 civilian deaths was authorized by Churchill and the War Cabinet, but it was a superfluous piece of terrorism and those who were cajoled into its support were uneasy. Churchill ignored Bomber Command in his victory broadcast. It is fair to say that Churchill advised Attlee who was by then Prime Minister to recommend Harris for a peerage. For whatever reasons Attlee would not do so. After Churchill returned to office he offered Harris a peerage in April 1952, but the latter had made his home in South Africa, where the House of Lords meant nothing. He preferred a baronetcy which was duly conferred on him. He died in April 1984, aged ninety-one.

The German armies collapsed in March and early April. There has been much talk about the territorial advances which Eisenhower might have gained to the detriment of Russia. In fact the zones had been settled at Yalta or earlier. Anglo-American occupation of the area allocated to Russia would have made no difference unless there was to be diplomatic rupture inconceivable at that time. On 12 April Roosevelt died. He was succeeded by Harry S. Truman, the Vice-President who rose to the occasion for which he was singularly ill-prepared. Hitler, by now almost insane, drew a curious analogy with the survival of Frederick the Great in 1782 thanks to the death of Tsarina Elizabeth. But the Russian armies were on the outskirts of Berlin. On 30 April Hitler and his mistress Eva Braun whom he had married the previous day committed suicide in the Berlin 'bunker' along with Goebbels and his family. Two days earlier Mussolini

303

and his mistress had been shot by the Italian 'partisans'. Thus perished two of the most odious tyrants in European history. On 7 May Hitler's designated successor, Admiral Doenitz, surrendered unconditionally on all fronts. The war in Europe, after five years and eight months of misery, destruction and slaughter had at last ended.

Chapter Sixteen

THE TRIUMPH OF LABOUR

I

VE (Victory in Europe) Day was decreed as a national holiday on 8 May, prudently followed by another day of rest on 9 May. It was dull and slightly raining in the morning but the sun came out in the afternoon. Churchill's broadcast to the nation relayed to a vast crowd in Parliament Square took place at three o'clock, after a thanksgiving service at St Margaret's, Westminster, attended by ministers and members of both Houses. During the evening the King and Queen stood on the balcony of Buckingham Palace. Everything that could be floodlit was. Fireworks blazed away in the skies. There was a mild sense of saturnalia in the streets. People were fairly drunk though not offensively. As night fell the unrailed parks were given over to love-making and it was hard to walk through them without tripping over writhing couples thus occupied well into the small hours of the morning.

Politically, the most urgent question was the continuation of the coalition. The parties had run out of domestic policies on which they could agree. The last straw perhaps was, as Michael Foot maintained in his life of Aneurin Bevan, the land question. Labour had long adhered to nationalization, its old panacea. In September 1943 the party modified its position to the extent of substituting nationalization of 'development rights' as recommended by a committee under the chairmanship of Mr Justice Uthwatt. But this was scarcely less odious to Conservative views on private property. Nationalization or variations of it came to be the sticking point

305

between the two major parties. In October 1944 Labour's National Executive Committee declared that the party would fight the next election independently. Their feelings were soon enhanced by Churchill's Greek policy which showed that foreign affairs could also be a bone of contention. Although people like Attlee, Dalton and Bevin had few delusions about communism, a growing number of youngish, idealistic, and rather naïve Labour supporters saw Europe in terms of a struggle between the 'bad', aristocratic, capitalist royalist classes and the 'good' popular forces struggling in guerrilla and underground movements to break the thraldom of the old order as well as that of Hitler and Mussolini. 'The upper classes in every country,' observed Major Denis Healey at the Labour Party Conference in May 1945, 'are selfish, depraved, dissolute and decadent.'

The Labour rank and file wanted an early end to the coalition – which meant an early election – whereas their leaders, on the analogy of Lloyd George's success in 1918, feared that an early election would give Churchill a similar victory. They wished it to be postponed till October and were prepared to continue the coalition until then. Churchill would have none of this. On 18 May he gave Attlee the choice of either continuation of the coalition until the defeat of Japan, then not expected for another eighteen months, or an immediate election. He was concerned not only with national unity against Japan but against the Russians with whom relations had been fast deteriorating since the closing months of the European war. Attlee and Bevin would have agreed but the National Executive Committee on the eve of the Labour Conference refused, and certainly reflected the views of the conference itself. On 23 May Churchill resigned as Prime Minister of the coalition and the King reappointed him within an hour or so as head of a Conservative, National Liberal (the real Liberals withdrew) and non-party 'caretaker' government, pending the general election. This was fixed for 5 July, but, because of the delay involved in getting in the service voting papers, the ballot boxes were not to be opened until 25 July. Meanwhile Churchill invited Attlee to attend the Potsdam Conference in the middle of the month to discuss with Stalin and Truman the future of Europe.

Anyone who remembers those weeks will confirm that Churchill was expected to win easily. Even if some people had doubts about him as a peacetime Prime Minister, peace still seemed a long way off. In retrospect, however, one can see many signals that Labour would win. The public opinion surveys have already been mentioned, and they showed a consistently wide Labour lead over the Conservatives. By-elections too boded no good for them. An example was the celebrated contest in Derbyshire West early in 1944 when the Cavendish (Duke of Devonshire) family supremacy, uninterrupted in that area for three centuries except in 1918–23, was broken by a son of the man who had done the same thing twenty-five years earlier. The young Lord Hartington who inherited a majority of 5,500 was easily beaten. The Independent Labour candidate, Charlie White, won by 4,500 votes. Some Labour leaders correctly read the signs of the times. Both Herbert Morrison and Ernest Bevin expected to win. Attlee, however, was very surprised; opinion polls were non-proven in those days, and by-elections have often been misleading.

There was plenty of mud-slinging in the campaign. Oddly enough, it was inaugurated by Attlee who summarily dismissed Churchill's suggestion of a referendum to decide whether the coalition might continue without a general election till Japan had been defeated. A referendum, he said, had 'all too often been the instrument of Nazidom and Fascism'. But Churchill gave as good as he got and more, when he suggested in a broadcast that socialism could only be enforced by 'some form of Gestapo', a phrase to which Lord Beaverbrook gave maximum publicity in the *Daily Express*. It was based on F. A. Hayek's famous book, *The Road to Serfdom* published in 1944. The campaign was complicated by Professor Harold Laski, a notable guru of the left, who happened to be Labour

Party Chairman that year. He declared that Attlee could not bind the party to any agreement achieved at Potsdam. The extent of the power of the NEC at once became an issue, and it is one which has never been settled from that day to this. Churchill and Attlee exchanged much acid public correspondence about the affair. One can doubt whether these verbal exchanges made any great difference. Labour would probably have won, whatever Churchill, Attlee, Laski or anyone else had said.

The 'verdict' of the electorate announced on 26 July confounded most prophets. Labour won 393 seats, the Conservatives 213 and the Liberals a mere 12. All British elections greatly distort the 'popular vote' in terms of parliamentary representation. The Labour voters numbered 11,995,152 (47.8 per cent of the total vote), Conservatives 9,988,306 (39.8 per cent), the Liberals 2,248,226 (9 per cent), the rest 854,294 (2.8 per cent). Nevertheless, the result on any interpretation was a decisive repudiation of the Conservatives. It was their worst defeat since the 'landslide' of 1906. The increasingly acerbic Potsdam Conference had been adjourned for three days for the election. To the astonishment of Stalin a new British delegation appeared on 28 July. It would be interesting to see, if they exist at all, the papers in the Russian archives on an episode which must have puzzled the Kremlin. Churchill resigned at 7 P.M. on the day of the announcement of the results. In the small hours of the morning he had had a hunch that he might lose. Although the reality was a shock, he was characteristically magnanimous. Next day Lord Moran, finding him 'in a brown study', referred to the ingratitude of the people. '"Oh no," he answered at once, "I wouldn't call it that. They have had a very hard time."'[1]

All sorts of reasons were ascribed at the time to explain this *bouleversement*. The Conservative organization was said to be run down because its agents were serving in the forces whereas Labour's equivalents were trade unionist stay-at-homes who escaped conscription. There seems no truth in this. Certainly the Conservative organization was a feeble affair compared with pre-war days, but Labour's was even feebler. Anyway electoral swings of this magnitude do not depend on organization. Churchill's 'Gestapo' speech and alleged dependence on Lord Beaverbrook's advice were other causes that were invoked – not very plausibly. Absence of Churchillian enthusiasm for the Beveridge Report was perhaps a more serious factor, and the very marked Labour preponderance in the service vote, said to have been fostered by ABCA and the Army Education Corps, was another, though in fact only half those eligible voted. These were symptoms, not causes. The labour victory had a deeper cause – the conversion of the opinion-formers to collectivism and Keynsianism which dominated British politics for a quarter of a century after the end of the war and has only recently started to break down.

Attlee's government was one of elder statesmen: Ernest Bevin at the Foreign Office, Hugh Dalton at the Exchequer, Herbert Morrison, Lord President and Leader of the House, Viscount Addison at the Commonwealth Relations Office, Arthur Greenwood, Lord Privy Seal, Stafford Cripps, Minister of Economic Affairs, and Attlee himself had all been active in politics before 1914. When Addison replaced Greenwood as Lord Privy Seal in October 1947 a man of seventy-eight succeeded one of sixty-eight. The only younger figure of significance was Aneurin Bevan, a brilliant Welsh orator who went straight from the backbenches into the Cabinet as Minister of Health, one of the hottest seats of all. In Attlee's original list, Dalton was Foreign Secretary, Bevin Chancellor of the Exchequer. George VI suggested that the places should be reversed, and Attlee agreed, though whether because of the King's suggestion or because he had changed his mind on other grounds is not clear.

2

During the weeks of the caretaker government two major questions dominated the counsels of the Allies: the intransigence of Russia, and the war in Japan. The Russians soon made it clear that they would stick to Yalta only in so far as it was convenient. In the countries which their forces had 'liberated' they would pursue their own way regardless. The situation was exacerbated by one of Truman's least happy executive actions, an ill-considered notice to terminate 'Lend-lease' arrangements with Russia on 11 May. He withdrew the order later but the harm had been done. Russian suspicion and resentment remained, and the Potsdam Conference produced no real agreement on the questions at issue, though a façade of solidarity was preserved. Relations between the western Allies and Russia deteriorated steadily from then onwards; the widening gap has dominated international relations ever since.

The Japanese war was tied up with the problem of the atomic bomb. This belongs to American rather than English history, but there was an English involvement which cannot be disregarded. German-born scientists working in Britain, notably Professor Rudolf Peierls and Dr Otto Frisch, explained in a memorandum of spring 1940 how it might be possible to produce an explosion of colossal violence by bombarding uranium atoms with neutrons, and that 'the critical mass', i.e. the minimum quantity of material needed to produce a 'chain reaction', could be contained in a bomb, though a very large one. Churchill, despite some expert misgivings, decided in 1941 to go ahead with the manufacture of this terrifying weapon, although the cost and resources involved were immense. American scientists were also proceeding on the same lines from 1939 onwards, and in August 1941 the head of their National Defense Research Committee, Dr Bush, suggested that the two countries should cooperate and make the bomb as a joint project. The

British attitude, largely conditioned by Lord Cherwell on grounds of security, was negative, but the American entry into the war in December changed the situation, and British experts visiting America early in 1942 discovered that their US colleagues were very much further ahead than had been realized in Britain and of course had far greater resources behind them. Unless the British cooperated quickly while they still had something to contribute, they would find themselves elbowed out of an operation which, it was now clear, could be effectively conducted only in America. Churchill in June 1942 discussed the matter with Roosevelt in Washington. He urged that the process of manufacturing the bomb, codenamed 'Tube Alloys', should take place in America and that there should be full disclosure and cooperation on both sides. He believed that the President had agreed, and in August Sir John Anderson, the Cabinet Minister responsible, sent a formal proposal to this effect to Dr Bush. But the boot was now on the other foot. No exchanges took place and in October his defence scientists advised Roosevelt against disclosing their secrets to the British. It was not till July 1943 that Roosevelt decided to stick to his original bargain, and he confirmed it at the first Quebec Conference in August. There was to be a full exchange and the permission of both countries would be needed for the use of the bomb.

By the end of March 1945 the experts were fairly confident that the bomb could be made to work by the late summer. It was reckoned at this stage that, despite the enormous damage being done by 'conventional' bombing on the Japanese mainland, and despite the destruction of nearly all their shipping and most of their planes, the Japanese would capitulate only after an invasion of their mainland. This was expected to be very costly, and it could not even be attempted before November. In these circumstances it was hardly conceivable that the bomb would not be used. It was argued later that the Japanese would have surrendered before the end of the year under other pressures, but this, even if true, could not be known with any certainty.

British assent in principle to the dropping of the bomb was given on 1 July by Churchill and conveyed to the Combined Policy Committee in Washington on 4 July. Neither the British War Cabinet nor the Chiefs of Staff were consulted, nor did Churchill, Anderson or any British authority even see the arguments for and against the use of 'The Weapon' which were circulated at the top secret level in Washington. Churchill agreed before the Americans themselves had decided to drop the bomb. On 16 July an atomic device was successfully exploded at Alamagordo. On 24 July at Potsdam Truman casually informed Stalin that America had a new bomb of great power. Stalin seemed pleased but showed no particular surprise. At the time it was assumed that he did not understand. In retrospect one can guess that, thanks to the treachery of Klaus Fuchs and other spies, he knew about it already. On 26 July an ultimatum was sent to Japan from Washington. On 6 August the first atomic bomb was dropped on Hiroshima killing 80,000 people. The world was never to be the same again.

On 9 August Russia declared war on Japan. That same morning a second atomic bomb was dropped, this time on Nagasaki. It exhausted the existing supply, but the Americans were geared to produce these weapons at the rate of three a month. The following day the Emperor insisted that the war must end. The message of surrender was received in Washington on 14 August; 2 September was celebrated as VJ Day. Lord Mountbatten received the formal capitulation of the Japanese forces in Malaya at Singapore on 12 September.

3

The ending of the Japanese war had a catastrophic effect on the British economy. It had been taken for granted that 'Lend-lease' would continue for at least a year if only because there seemed no likelihood of Japanese surrender any earlier. On 17 August Truman withdrew American aid and on 2 September he terminated 'Lend-lease'. Since 1939 Britain had sold over £1,100 million of overseas investments and run up sterling debts to the tune of nearly another £3,100 million in order to finance the war. 'Invisible' exports (transport, tourism, finance) were far below pre-war levels, partly because the country had lost thirty per cent of its merchant shipping. It was reckoned that Britain would have to raise its exports to about 175 per cent of the pre-war value to meet the deficit. The Treasury thought that this could be achieved in three or four years – an estimate that was not far out, for the target was reached by 1950. But it was reached largely because Britain's chief pre-war rivals, Japan and Germany, were temporarily ruined; as a result British exporters fell into the habit of thinking that they could get away with anything – an attitude which was to be very damaging later when the rival economies recovered. Meanwhile, the only way of meeting the import bill was an American loan. This was duly negotiated – £1,100 million on very easy terms, though not, as the British negotiators hoped, interest free. One of the conditions was that there should be no further expansion of the Ottawa Imperial Preferences – which provoked a minor explosion by Lord Beaverbrook in the House of Lords. The pound was fixed at $4·03, its 1939 rate – a level which was too high but had that best of reasons; no one could plausibly argue for any other. There was a second awkward condition of the loan; non-British owners of sterling must be allowed to convert their balances into dollars not later than fifteen months after the loan came into effect i.e. 15 July 1947. The result was that the loan ran out more quickly than expected. The assumption in America that Britain would recover her economic position as quickly as she had after 1918 proved over-optimistic. In 1947 five weeks of convertibility were disastrous and exchange controls had to be reinstated on 20 August.

The need to maximize exports and minimize imports had already made Britain an even more dismal, though less perilous, country to live in than in the latter years of the war. Almost everything – clothes, food, petrol – continued to be rationed. Restrictions remained unabated and were sometimes enhanced. Bread was rationed for the first time in July 1946 and continued to be for the next two years. In restaurants where meals, as in wartime, were limited to three courses bread now counted as a course, though not if it was part of a dish e.g. welsh rarebit. Customers who had taken bread with their soup were refused a pudding. Whale steaks became an unloved substitute for meat, and in May 1948 a peculiarly repulsive tinned South African fish called snoek came on to the market. Dr Edith Summerskill, parliamentary under-secretary to the Minister of Food, held a special snoek-tasting party at the Ministry, but to no avail: the public would not eat it, despite rations which by then were lower than at any time in the war. An adult's weekly allowance was now only thirteen ounces of meat, one and a half of cheese, six of butter or margarine, one of cooking fat, eight of sugar, two pints of milk and one egg. The drink situation was equally gloomy. Whisky was severely rationed by the suppliers, most of it going to America. Beer, already much weakened in wartime, was 'devalued' by another ten per cent in 1946. There was plenty of gin – of a faintly disagreeable flavour but nothing to drink it with, except synthetic fruit juices. As for wine, it was scarcely obtainable. The *Daily Mirror* headline, 'Wine from Weeds', did not encourage many people to make the experiment. One had to queue for almost every commodity, even potatoes and fruit. It was calculated by someone in 1947 that the average woman in England was spending at least an hour a day in a queue.

Matters were made no better by the descent early in January 1947 of the worst winter of the century. By the end of the month the whole of Britain was blanketed by snow, including the Scilly and Channel Islands. Transport was paralysed, industry came grinding to a halt through shortage of electricity, and at the end of the first week of February 2 million men were out of work. It was reckoned that over 20,000 acres of winter wheat were destroyed by frost, and another 70,000 by the floods which followed in March. Thousands of sheep died in the hills. The Minister of Food

314

was John Strachey and of Power and Fuel Emmanuel Shinwell. 'Starve with Strachey and Shiver with Shinwell' became the Tory slogan. Ironically this grim winter was succeeded by a rainless summer of blazing heat which produced water shortages in several parts of the country, and much discomfort in those days of few refrigerators.

This joyless background against which the Labour Cabinet tried to carry out its electoral programme was to have an intangible, unquantifiable but important effect on the elections of 1950 and 1951 when the party lost ground so heavily. However unfair – and it was not entirely unfair – the impression was gained that Ministers took a certain relish in 'austerity'; the bleak puritanism of Sir Stafford Cripps seemed to epitomize their attitude. The Labour Ministers were probably neither more nor less fond of pleasure than any others, but the very process of having to defend one cut after another led some of them to move by insensible gradations from the argument of disagreeable necessity to the argument of moral virtue. The spirit of national unity which had made these hardships acceptable vanished very quickly, especially as they became worse when war ended. 'Don't you know there's a war on?' – a favourite answer of curmudgeonly waitresses or shop-assistants to every complaint – was less convincing when the war had ceased to be 'on'.

Labour could hardly have won the 1945 election so conclusively without a substantial accession of 'middle-class' voters, but they soon were disenchanted. It was for that section of society a particularly painful period. The incomes of the professional classes had not risen in proportion to those of the wage-earners. Servants had vanished, and washing-machines had not yet appeared. There was a black market as there had been in the war though more blatant. But the middle and upper classes for the most part still had patriotic doubts about exploiting it. Their patriotism did not, however, extend to a willing acceptance of the new world of high wages, full employment and ubiquitous red tape. They felt beleaguered, bewildered, uneasy, resentful. Taxation re-

315

mained very heavy. Dividends were restricted. Petrol was severely rationed. The foreign exchange allowance for a holiday abroad was only £50. Those who did manage a visit to Europe found that in France and Italy life had almost been restored to pre-war normality. There was no rationing, and wine flowed like water. The contrast with the home life of their own dear country was striking. Something of the bitterness of the middle classes emerges from the novels of Angela Thirkell, *Peace Breaks Out* (1946), *Love among the Ruins* (1948) and others. As novels they are not very good but as pictures of the scene from a certain social angle they deserve to be remembered by the historian of the times.

The Labour Party's election manifesto pledged them to a sweeping programme of nationalization, and the government carried most of their promised measures in 1945–8. The Bank of England, civil aviation, the coal-mines, gas, electricity, the railways and a large sector of road transport, were all taken into public ownership, without any very great controversy. The Bank of England had always been subject to the control of any Chancellor of the Exchequer who knew his own mind, for example Neville Chamberlain. Gas, then a declining industry, and electricity were already to a large extent under public control. Road, rail and air transport had in effect been nationalized in war, and the same people continued to run them. Both coal-mining and the railways were unprofitable and needed a heavy injection of capital which private enterprise at that time was ill-placed to provide. The Conservatives accepted the situation without enthusiasm but without resentment. The nationalization of iron and steel which Labour had also promised was a different matter. Alone of the party's targets it was a manufacturing industry which had been profitable in the past and might well become so again. The steel-workers, unlike the coal-miners, were lukewarm about nationalization, and the Cabinet itself was rumoured to have doubts about the exact method if not the principle. The Conservatives resolved to fight it as hard as they could and to use the House of Lords in the process.

The Government did not get round to planning what was bound to be a very complicated measure till the summer of 1947. The Minister of Supply, George Strauss, was asked to produce a bill for the autumn session. He replied that it was impossible before October 1948. This meant that the Lords would be able to delay the measure till after the latest date for the next general election. Labour, therefore, brought in a measure to reduce their delaying power from two years to one.

In addition to nationalization Labour was strongly committed to the 'welfare state', as it came to be known. Here lay the importance of the Beveridge Report, and, although the legislation of 1945–50 by no means followed Sir William Beveridge's recommendations to the letter, it was very largely inspired by them. Between 1946 and 1948 a series of major measures had been enacted in this field – the National Insurance Act, the Industrial Injuries Act, the National Assistance Act, and a Local Government Act which tilted exchequer aid towards the poorer authorities. Aneurin Bevan who was responsible for the last two had also brought in what was perhaps the most important of all pieces of legislation in this area – the National Health Service Act. It was bitterly opposed by the spokesmen of the medical profession, but Bevan displayed a skill, patience, tact and charm which amazed those who thought of him as a wild fanatical revolutionary. The dispute had an almost uncanny resemblance to Lloyd George's struggle with the doctors over the National Health Insurance Act of 1913. In both cases the doctors feared loss of independence and professional status, and threatened to boycott the schemes. In both cases they joined despite the threats, and in both cases found that their fears were not warranted. In spite of some defects, the Health Service has proved to be one of the most successful and lasting measures of the Attlee administration. In his life of Aneurin Bevan Michael Foot quotes the verdict of Professor Almont Lindsay of the University of Virginia who conducted a detailed survey published in 1963:

In the light of past accomplishment and future goals the Health Service cannot very well be excluded from any list of notable achievements of the twentieth century. So much has it become part of the British way of life, it is difficult for the average Englishman to imagine what it would be like without those services which have contributed so much to his physical and mental well-being.[2]

One other piece of legislation should be mentioned. The trades unions were still the financial backbone of the Labour party. Labour had long declared its intention of repealing the Trades Disputes Act of 1927 which made general strikes illegal, forbade civil servants to belong to a union and insisted that those who wished to pay the political levy must 'contract in'. This was repealed in 1946 amidst great jubilation among Labour MPs. On the third reading of the Bill which replaced it Sir Hartley (later Lord) Shawcross, the Attorney-General, made a remark often misquoted as 'We are the masters now'. What he actually said was: 'We are the masters at the moment – and not only for the moment but for a very long time to come.' The sentiment is much the same but the garbled version sounded worse when Conservative speakers quoted it as typical of Labour arrogance.

Politicians are constantly having to speak. It is not surprising that every now and then they use phrases which turn out to have an unexpected and unwelcome celebrity. Two others are worth mentioning. Early in 1948 Shinwell declared on a public platform that the working class were the only people who mattered. For his part, he said, he did not care 'a tinker's cuss' for any of the others. The Conservatives naturally gave this remark the maximum publicity. Then, on the very eve of the day (5 July 1948) when the Health Service Act was to come into operation, Bevan made an even more notorious observation. Speaking at a rally in Belle Vue Manchester on Sunday, 4 July he referred to the harshness of the Means Test in his youth: 'That is why no amount of cajolery can eradicate from my heart a deep burning hatred for the Tory

Party that inflicted those experiences on me. So far as I am concerned they are lower than vermin.' The uproar was tremendous. Even the Prime Minister felt obliged to send a confidential rebuke. Nor was it any good to claim that Bevan was only referring to the Tories of his youth, for he went out of his way in the same speech to say: '. . . they have not changed – if they have they are slightly worse than they were.' Some Conservatives formed 'Vermin Clubs'. Some even wore 'Vermin' badges. Bevan's meetings were liable to be punctuated by hecklers with cries of 'vermin, vermin'. The word echoed for months to come, but one must take with many grains of salt Harold Laski's guess that it gave 2 million votes to the Conservatives in the 1950 election. It probably did little more than symbolize the profound class conflict of the time.

The middle classes had been knocked out of balance by the 1945 election. For the first year or two they treated the policy of the new government with a half-stunned resignation; the continued restrictions could be accepted as a carry-over from war, likewise the heavy taxation. The nationalization measures had no very direct effect. The appalling winter of 1947 produced, like war itself, a brief sense of national unity in the face of external danger. The opposition of the doctors was the first post-war case of a powerful and deeply conservative pressure group hitting back at a government which seemed to be gunning for the whole of its class in society. Bevan beat them, but not by much and only after a long cliff-hanging struggle which may have taken its toll of his nerves as well as theirs. Hence perhaps the remark about 'vermin', and the bitterness with which it was greeted. 'VERMIN VILLA HOME OF A LOUD MOUTHED RAT' were the words scrawled in gigantic letters across his house at 23 Clivedon Place.

In retrospect Labour Ministers put the date when their fortunes began to decline rather earlier. The summer of 1947 is often seen as the crucial moment from which the party did not recover for seventeen years. The crisis caused by the enforced convertibility of sterling on 15 July has already been mentioned. It is surprising that the government, though warned by Keynes at the time of the loan negotiations that convertibility was quite impracticable at such an early date, did not invoke the emergency clause in the agreement and insist on postponement. Now, after the run on sterling had virtually wiped out the loan, it seemed possible to save the situation only by more drastic restrictions than ever. The meat ration was heavily cut, the bacon ration was halved, the basic petrol ration (for those who simply wanted to drive for pleasure) was abolished and so was the meagre £50 allowance for foreign travel. The last two measures were bound to infuriate the middle class more than any other section of the community. The wage-earners did not yet own cars or take holidays on the Costa Brava. However, no one welcomed cuts in meat, and a Gallup poll gave the Conservatives an eleven point lead which was confirmed by their subsequent crushing victory at the local elections held in those days in the autumn.

An important by-product of the policy of austerity imposed by the Treasury was a cut in the housing programme. Britain's total supply of houses in 1939 was 12·5 million, of which over a third had been damaged and some 700,000 had been totally destroyed or rendered uninhabitable. Housing had been a major issue in the 1945 election campaign, and Bevan under whose department it came was determined to meet the demand. In fact it turned out to be far greater than expected, and the figure of 750,000 new houses regarded by the Ministry officials in 1945 as the proper target turned out to be wholly inadequate, largely because of an unexpected boom in marriages and births. Under Bevan who operated largely through the local authorities some 55,000 houses were built in 1946 and 140,000 in 1947. In 1948 the figure shot up to 285,000, and there is every reason to believe that the magical figure of 300,000, which was to be pressed on the Conservative Shadow Cabinet at the Party Conference in 1950 and triumphantly achieved by Harold Macmillan, would have been reached in 1949, if the Treasury had not insisted on the cut as part of its package to meet the dollar crisis. This decision which Bevan strongly opposed could not affect 1948, but it reduced the average for the three years after that to 210,000. The contrast with Macmillan's performance was not the result of narrow-mindedness, myopia or incompetence on the part of Bevan or his officials.[3] It was the responsibility of the Cabinet. The policy may have been right on general economic grounds but it was to be highly damaging to the government on this most sensitive of electoral issues.

The 1947 crisis led to a move to oust the Prime Minister. Dalton, Cripps and Morrison were the principal figures in the plot, and they made approaches to Ernest Bevin whom they regarded as the most plausible successor. He was not prepared to play along with them. He already had all the power he needed, for Attlee invariably backed him; he did not care about the pomp and circumstance; and he had a strong sense of loyalty. At this juncture the principal plotter, Dalton, made a disastrous gaffe. There was to be a special November budget, and in a moment of folly he gave a hint of its contents to an importunate journalist just before he introduced it. No one could have made a penny out of the indiscretion. It was merely an example of the congenital defect of politicians – talking too much; but Dalton had to resign. He was succeeded by Cripps who as Minister of Economic Affairs had already been deeply involved in the crisis. Britain was spared the worst austerity by the Marshall Plan (see below page 326) from which she was to receive all told some £700 million with no obligation to repay. This, however, was announced in broad outline only at the end of June 1947 and it did not operate till the following year. No one could tell in advance what sum Congress would actually vote, and severe restrictions on consumption continued.

In 1949 there was a renewed dollar crisis, though for opposite reasons from those that caused the earlier one. In 1947 an American boom had put up the price of dollar imports and caused the loan to run out even faster than it would have anyway. In 1949 a sharp recession occurred in

America and suddenly hit the American demand for British exports. In the first quarter of 1949 the dollar gap was lower than it had been for years, £82 million, but in the second quarter it almost doubled to £157 million. This led to a run on the pound, which made devaluation inevitable. The decision was delayed, owing to Cripps's conscience, for longer than it should have been, and the reduction might have been less if the signals had been read more promptly. On 18 September the pound was devalued by thirty per cent – from $4·03 to $2·80, where it was to remain till 1967. At the time it seemed a great symbol of national decline. In fact, almost all European currencies had to be devalued in terms of the dollar during the aftermath of war. Most countries did it quietly and discreetly. Only Britain, with her hangover of great power status made it a matter of masochistic breast-beating. Naturally the opposition exploited this 'humiliation' to the full; it was probably another element in the decline of Labour's fortunes in the election of 1950.

4

The year 1947 was not only portentous in terms of Britain's declining economy. It was also – and the two changes were closely connected – an outward and visible turning point in the country's long period as a 'great power'. If ever one can choose a twelve-month period for the Decline of Power, this is the year. The greatest imperial revolution of all was the abandonment of the British Raj. India had been for a century the very symbol of imperial grandeur. There was something strangely romantic about British rule in that alien sub-continent. A few thousand Britons, compared by Curzon, one of India's most eminent Viceroys, to the white foam on a dark and unfathomable ocean, had ruled India without serious challenge for nearly a century since the Mutiny. It is sometimes said that their authority was a gigantic piece of bluff. This is only partially true. There were formidable sanctions which a determined government could have brought to bear at any time before 1939. The war changed the scene to some extent economically and militarily. Even so Britain did not need to withdraw in 1947, and there were elements in the British middle class which felt deeply affronted – those who had made their careers as administrators and had come to regard the British Raj as a part of their being. Unlike their eighteenth- and nineteenth-century predecessors they were not corrupt. They believed in a vague way that they had moral responsibility for the 'progress' i.e. westernization of the congeries of religions and races entrusted to their rule. They would in theory have subscribed to Macaulay's dictum that the day when free European institutions were granted to India 'will be the proudest day in English history'. But there can be vested interests in 'moral responsibility' as in more tangible matters such as the style of life which sustained that moral responsibility.

Britain had no clear policy about India when the war broke out. The federal plan embodied in Hoare's India Act of 1935 which Churchill had so bitterly opposed was a dead letter because of the opposition of the Princes. But the Japanese successes which demonstrated for the second time (the first being the Russo-Japanese war of 1904–5) that Asiatics could defeat Europeans shook British hegemony to the core.

On 29 March 1942 the British government made a declaration about Indian policy, usually called the 'Cripps Offer' because Sir Stafford Cripps had been charged with the task of 'selling' it to the Viceroy, the Commander-in-Chief and the principal Indian leaders. It gave India the right to determine her own constitution after the end of the war, either as a dominion or an independent state. Princes and provinces could then secede if they chose. Meanwhile there would be an Indianized quasi-cabinet. The Viceroy would become a constitutional monarch though he would retain some special responsibilities and a right of veto. The British government through the Commander-in-Chief would remain in charge of defence till the war ended. Partition was thus for the first time officially admitted as an option. On the other hand, an Indianized quasi-cabinet might have accustomed the Muslim and Hindu leaders to work together. However, Churchill and the Viceroy, Lord Linlithgow, were always dubious about the scheme and they knew that they were backed by the Conservative Party. The Congress leaders were equally sceptical and disliked the reserve powers of the Viceroy and Commander-in-Chief. The Cripps mission collapsed. 'Indianization' was postponed, though the declaration was never repudiated as a basis for a post-war settlement. The Congress leaders turned down the Cripps offer, withdrew from all the provincial governments and embarked on a mass non-cooperation movement. For three years the party of Gandhi and Nehru was out of effective action, and Jinnah, leader of the Muslim League, was well placed to consolidate its position and extend its influence in the provinces where the Muslims had a majority. Partition had become unavoidable. Linlithgow left in 1943, and was replaced by Wavell who obstinately pursued the now hopeless chimera of unity. In 1946 there was another Cripps mission and another failure. Nehru demanded too much and Jinnah dug in his heels. On 20 February 1947 the Prime Minister announced that Indian independence would be granted not later than June 1948, and that Lord Mountbatten would become Viceroy instead of Wavell. The latter was given the minimum of notice in a curt letter from Attlee. He had been a narrow and unperceptive Viceroy but he did not deserve this discourtesy.

The idea of unity was still cherished in England. Mountbatten himself expected to achieve it when he first went out. He soon saw its impossibility. The plan for partition was evolved by an able Indian, V. P. Menon, who advised the Viceroy on all the major questions and knew through his civil service experience the limits of consensus and compromise. Having secured agreement, reluctant or otherwise, from Jinnah and Nehru, Mountbatten pushed hard for an even earlier date of independence, 15 August 1947. Partition of India into two states led to mass migration both ways. Neither Hindus nor Muslims felt safe where they were outnumbered.

The situation was made worse by the Sikhs who claimed a national identity of their own that was never conceded. The ensuing slaughter was appalling. There is no agreed figure of the dead but the lowest estimate is 200,000. It may have been three times that figure. Personal blame is hard to assess. The 'old India hands' never forgave Mountbatten, and Lady Mountbatten's alleged relations with Nehru exacerbated their fury. Perhaps the Viceroy could be accused of being a middle-aged man in a hurry, but the savagery of the communal mayhem after Independence Day caught all the governing classes – English, Hindu, Muslim – by surprise. The tragedy only confirms how ignorant governors can be about those they govern.

The loss of India was not the only symbol during 1947 of Britain's decline as a major power. The second episode arose from the 'Cold War'. In March 1946 Churchill had made one of his most famous speeches. The place was Fulton, Missouri.

> From Stettin in the Baltic . . . to Trieste in the Adriatic an iron curtain has descended across the Continent. Behind that line lie all the capitals of the ancient States of Central and Eastern Europe . . . The Communist parties which were very small . . . have been raised to pre-eminence and power far beyond their numbers and are seeking everywhere to obtain totalitarian control.

This speech, fully justified by later events, went down badly in London where belief in cooperation with Russia still lingered in some circles. Bevin wanted Attlee to make a formal repudiation, but the Prime Minister refused. Even Anthony Eden remained conspicuously silent. But the Foreign Secretary soon had to follow the Churchill line. The exact date when the Cold War began will always be disputed. The myth of Russia as an ally and a symbol of the socialist Utopia lingered long after the realities destroyed it. Perhaps the moment was 24 March 1945 when the mortally sick President

Roosevelt receiving a telegram from Averell Harriman, his ambassador in Moscow, declared: 'Averell is right, we can't do business with Stalin. He has broken every one of the promises he made at Yalta.' But euphoric goodwill lingered longer, and, in retrospect, it seems odd that the USSR did not exploit it more successfully. There were many potential dupes.

However that may be, the year 1947 was crucial in this matter as in many others. The British government decided that it must abandon the military and economic aid it was giving to Greece and Turkey in order to defeat communist subversion. Britain had been closely involved in the affairs of Greece since December 1944, to the deep disapproval at that time of both the American administration and the British left. The Communists had been crushed at the time but their revival was possible. Turkey was another potential victim of Russian expansionism. Both countries were believed to be of vital importance in the control of the Mediterranean. But Britain's economy could no longer sustain foreign aid. The Cabinet's decision to withdraw was communicated to the American Secretary of State, General Marshall, on 21 February. On 12 March President Truman made a speech which has affected world history ever since. He asked Congress for $400 million in aid of Greece and Turkey: 'I believe that it must be the policy of the United States to support free peoples who are resisting attempted subjugation by armed minorities or by outside pressures.' He was in effect declaring that American dollars and influence would henceforth be used against Stalinist expansion and that America was prepared to take Britain's place in areas which had for many generations been regarded as British spheres of influence.

The Truman Doctrine, as it came to be called, was followed by the Marshall Plan announced in June to provide dollar aid to reconstruct war-shattered Europe. The offer was seized with alacrity by Bevin. The idea that he and the Foreign Office were torpid is a myth. The offer included the communist bloc, but was firmly refused by the Kremlin. This was one of the most imaginative acts of enlightened self-interest ever performed by a great nation. It saved western Europe from Russian domination. At the start of the year there were powerful Communist parties represented in the coalition governments of both France and Italy. By the end of 1947 both had been ousted. 'Revisionist' historians date the Cold War from the Truman Doctrine alleged to be worded so as to make participation by the communist bloc impossible. This is nonsense. The Cold War had begun already. One could argue that Stalin did not control Greek communist guerrillas, and that it was just possible to condone his refusal to allow free elections in Poland, Romania and Bulgaria by reference to that curious 'percentage' deal with Churchill in October 1944 (see pp. 300–301). But his dealings with Hungary were indefensible. There the 'percentage' was 50:50, and in 1946 genuine free elections were held. The Communists obtained only sixteen per cent of the popular vote. In January 1947, two months before the promulgation of the Truman Doctrine, Stalin, conjuring up an imaginary right-wing plot, ordered the Russian military in Budapest to arrest Bela Kovacs, General Secretary, along with seven leading members of the Smallholders Party which had won fifty-seven per cent of the 1946 vote. By the end of the year the Communists were in total control. There has never been a free election in Hungary from that day to this.

The Cold War soon hardened. In February 1948 the only surviving democracy in eastern Europe was extinguished by a communist coup in Prague. This was followed by a Russian blockade of the land routes to Berlin. Britain, America and France formed along with Russia the quadripartite administration of the conquered capital. The western powers considered an armed convoy by road but chose instead an airlift. The supplies required were 4,500 tons a day, which seemed impossible. Thanks to the organizing genius of the American General Lucius D. Clay the figure was easily achieved, and by the spring of 1949 8,000 tons a day were being flown in. In

May the Soviet blockade was lifted after ten months – a notable victory for the west.

Meanwhile there had been important diplomatic developments in the west. On 17 March 1948 a defence pact was signed in Brussels between Britain, France, Belgium, the Netherlands and Luxemburg. Just over a year later it was converted on 4 April 1949 into the North Atlantic Treaty Organization (NATO) with the accession of America, Canada, Italy, Portugal, Denmark, Norway and Iceland. In 1948 Britain took two further steps. The period of conscription was raised from twelve to eighteen months and a decision was taken with the minimum of Cabinet consultation to manufacture the atomic bomb. In May 1949 the Federal Republic of Germany comprising the French, British and American zones of occupation came into being. It was only a matter of time before it joined NATO as a rearmed military ally. Russia riposted by creating a puppet communist state in her own zone, the so-called German Democratic Republic.

5

An important event which had no connection with the Cold War was the abandonment of the British Mandate for Palestine – another episode in that fateful year, 1947. In the long story of decolonization this was one of the earliest and least creditable transactions. It stands in marked contrast with the transfer of power in India. Partition of the sub-continent was, it is true, followed by fearful inter-communal massacres, but these could scarcely be blamed on the British who departed with goodwill from Hindus and Muslims alike. In Palestine the British exit was attended with the maximum of ill-will all round and it left a legacy of bitterness, violence and strife which still dominates the Middle East and shows no sign of going away.

It is fair to say that the Balfour Declaration which was the pledge under which Britain took on the Palestine Mandate comprised two fundamentally inconsistent objectives – 'the establishment of a National Home for the Jewish People' without 'prejudice to the civil and religious rights of existing non-Jewish communities in Palestine'. This was impossible. What the half million Arabs living in Palestine in 1917 saw as their civil and religious rights could never be squared with the unlimited immigration which the Jews regarded as implied by the creation of a National Home. The realities were masked until the rise of Hitler because the supply of Jewish immigrants was very limited. The Soviet government put a stopper on the principal pre-war source, the Jews of Russia. The Jews of western Europe and America felt no inclination to migrate to a barbarous and backward country full of enemies. Till the early 1930s the annual rate of immigration was only about 10,000. After that it shot up, reaching 60,000 in 1936. Communal violence escalated and for three years a large part of the British Army was engaged in the ungrateful task of preserving peace and order. In 1939 amidst strong Zionist protests a British White Paper announced that the figure was not to exceed 75,000 over the next five years. In practice, however, the European war prevented even this low figure being achieved.

The outbreak of peace worsened the situation. The Holocaust gave a notable impetus to the Zionist cause and there was worldwide sympathy for the 600,000 survivors many of whom were living in squalid refugee camps in Germany. A combination of genuine compassion and acute awareness of the Jewish vote in New York State caused Truman to support the Jewish Agency's plea for the immediate entry of 100,000 Jews into Palestine. The advent of a Labour government in Britain might have been expected to advance this cause. True, Churchill, always a strong Zionist sympathizer, was out, but most Conservatives tended to be pro-Arab, whereas Labour had long been committed to Zionism. In fact the arguments of defence and foreign policy soon prevailed. Egyptian nationalism already threatened Britain's Suez Canal base. Palestine with its central strategic position was a possible alternative but would be useless if Britain engaged in a confrontation with the Arab world. Middle East oil was vital to British armed forces and industry. Bevin was strongly opposed to, and much irritated by, Zionist demands. He was not, as is often alleged, anti-semitic, although he did on occasions make observations of remarkable insensitivity and he never understood the strength of Jewish nationalism. What motivated him was British strategic interests, and his view was fully endorsed by the Cabinet committee which in September 1945 recommended a quota of 1,500 a month.

This proposal did not begin to satisfy Zionist American-backed demands. Acts of terrorism had already occurred in wartime Palestine including the murder in 1944 of Lord Moyne, the British Minister Resident. These were now stepped up. Bevin, anxious to invoke American aid for a settlement, agreed in November 1945 to the appointment of an Anglo-American Committee of Inquiry. Its report was published on 1 May 1946, advance copies having gone to both governments a week or two before. The report recommended the immediate admission of 100,000 immigrants, the creation of a unitary state, the abolition of discriminatory restrictions on land purchase, and cooperation by the Jewish Agency in suppressing terrorism and illegal immigration, though the latter was not made a condition for the deal. This unanimous report was attacked by Zionists and Arabs alike. Nevertheless Lord Bullock, Bevin's biographer, believes that it was the best chance of a settlement. The moderate Jews faced with the choice of 100,000 immigrants and no Jewish state or no immigrants and the shadowy prospect of statehood might well have chosen the former. The Americans would, moreover, be bound to participate in implementing the scheme. Attlee and Bevin decided to make no official pronouncement until a joint body of experts had looked into details and they asked the American State Department to do the same. Unfortunately, Truman, influenced by Zionist pressures, publicly called for the immediate admission of the 100,000 and postponement of the other issues as soon as the report was published. Attlee and Bevin were extremely angry and now declared that they would not countenance immigration unless the illegal Jewish organizations in Palestine were dissolved and disarmed – a new condition which made Anglo-American cooperation even less easy to obtain.

Negotiations continued nevertheless, and an alternative scheme was propounded for division into two autonomous provinces, Jewish and Arab under a central trustee government. The 100,000 would be admitted and the scheme left open the options of federation or partition according to the way matters developed. The Zionists made it clear that this was no good, they would settle for nothing short of partition now. At this juncture a series of violent actions culminated on 22 July with the blowing up of the King David Hotel in Jerusalem by an organization called *Irgun* led by Menachim Begin, later to be Prime Minister of Israel. Nearly a hundred people were killed. The anger felt in Britain was only rivalled by the anger which Zionist propaganda managed to stir up in America over the strong reaction of the British authorities. Truman refused to back the plans for autonomous provinces. Neither Jews nor Arabs would attend a conference called in London in September to discuss the scheme. On 4 October Truman, on the eve of mid-term elections, made a speech advocating immediate and unconditional admission of 100,000 immigrants. This was the last straw for Attlee and Bevin, and the Prime Minister despatched a terse and cutting reproof to the President. Anglo-American relations were now as frosty as at any time before the Suez crisis of 1956–7. There were powerful arguments for partition and for admitting the hundred thousand, but both were bitterly opposed by the Arabs, and this was a fact which Britain, unlike the Americans and the Zionists, could not ignore, given historical obligations and strategic needs.

The truth was that there was no way of squaring this circle. Early in 1947 the British government abandoned the attempt and decided to hand back the Mandate to the United Nations. By now relations with the Jews had been steadily deteriorating. The turning back of illegal refugee ships,

331

murders, reprisals, bomb outrages – it was a sombre cycle of violence and terror. In the worldwide war of propaganda Britain was losing all along the line, and had an unfortunate gift of playing straight into its opponents' hands. The best example was in July 1947. The ship *Exodus*, carrying 4,500 illegal refugees, was boarded by the Royal Navy off Palestine and after some roughish treatment turned back. It disembarked at Marseilles. The immigrants were free to stay in France but all, bar a handful, insisted on Palestine or nothing. The *Irgun* had just hanged two young captured British sergeants as a reprisal for the execution of three terrorists. To land the *Exodus* refugees in Britain invited anti-semitic demonstrations. It was decided to send them to Hamburg, part of the British zone in Germany. The decision resulted from expediency and insensitivity rather than brutality but it gave an obvious lever to Zionist propoganda. The Zionists had another asset. However much they might publicly denounce the British as Nazis, they knew privately that no British government would ever try to crush terrorism by the ruthless methods of Hitler in occupied Europe.

The rest of the sad story can be quickly told. The United Nations produced a plan of partition backed by Truman which was geographically absurd and totally unacceptable to the Arabs. The British government declined responsibility for any plan unacceptable to one or other of the parties concerned and thus requiring force for its implementation. It was only slowly that the UN authorities realized that Attlee and his Cabinet actually meant what they said. Britain was fed up with Jews, Arabs, Zionists, Americans and the United Nations. In December the government declared that it would relinquish the Mandate on 15 May 1948; it would do nothing to obstruct but also nothing to enforce the UN plan. To this line Bevin adhered rigidly despite the belated alarm of Washington which put all possible pressure on Britain to stay in a trusteeship role. If Britain would not enforce the UN plan who would? Certainly not the Americans. On 14 March the State of Israel was proclaimed. Truman without consulting anyone gave official recognition just sixteen minutes later. Civil war had already begun. It now spread all over Palestine. The Israelis were victorious on every front. Early in 1949 Britain reluctantly recognized Israel and in the course of the next few months armistices were established between Israel and the five Arab states which had hoped to 'drive the Jews into the sea'.

Chapter Seventeen

THE CONSERVATIVE
RECOVERY

I

The Labour government had been in power for over four
years at the time of the traumatic devaluation on 18 September 1949. The next general election could not be held later
than July the following year. There was much argument about
the date. Should it be autumn 1949, February 1950 or June
1950? Attlee was against the autumn, and Cripps believed
that his spring budget would have to be so stringent that
electoral defeat would be inevitable. In December 1949 the
Prime Minister and six senior colleagues together with the
Chief Whip decided for 23 February, despite the risk of
power cuts and general gloom. They expected, however, to
win. At a dinner given by Cripps after the dissolution had
been announced fourteen ministers were present with their
wives, and betted a shilling (5p) on the result. Eleven
plumped for a victory of seventy seats or more. Gaitskell, the
least optimistic, put it at thirty. He scooped the pool. Labour
did win – but only by six seats.

The campaign turned on Labour's defence of its achievements since 1945, recollections of unemployment under the
Tories in the 1930s, the Conservative denunciation of the
bleakness, austerity and allegedly doctrinaire Labour policy
which had caused them. The proportion of the electorate
which voted was 84 per cent compared with 72.7 per cent in
1945. The figures were: Conservatives 12,502,567; Labour
13,266,592; Liberals 2,621,548; others 381,964. Labour won
315 seats, Conservatives 298, Liberals 9, others 3. These
statistics are not easy to interpret. If the Conservatives scored

about 2·5 million more votes than in 1945, Labour could claim a big rise too – 1·7 million. Perhaps one should look at the constituencies. Their boundaries had been redrawn to create greater equality, and the peculiar position of Labour with huge 'wasted' majorities in seats like Ebbw Vale or Durham, hitherto compensated by monopolist fiefs in diminishing inner city slum constituencies, was adversely affected. Labour's loss was to some degree counter-balanced by the abolition of university seats under the Representation of the People Act of 1948 which also removed both plural voting and the business franchise. But the net result was that for the decade 1950–60, which included four general elections, Labour had to gain two per cent more of the popular vote to equal the Conservatives in parliamentary seats. Geographically and socially the election of 1950 was also significant. The working-class constituencies usually remained Labour, but the county and suburban middle-class seats south of the Trent swung the other way; they did not swing back till 1966, and then only to a limited extent.

The 1950 election is often claimed as a success for the Conservatives even though they lost it. But, in view of the difficulties of the post-war years, the inevitable unpopularity of any government then in office and the general gloom of the times, one could argue that the Conservatives ought to have done much better. A great deal of work was put into improving their machine and their image, notably by Lord Woolton, a party manager of genius who reformed the party's organization on a popular basis, and by R. A. Butler who presided over its newly furbished ideology. The first was more important than the second. Tory democracy had long been the object of lip-service. Lord Woolton actually made Toryism democratic for the first time, in the sense of creating real popular participation. He brought to an end the system by which wealthy men bought their seats, and he created an organization under which a great many people produced small subscriptions instead of a few giving very big ones. The change obliged party agents to canvass on a large scale for money, and the process helped to spread the gospel.

The party had also made a serious effort to bring its policies up to date. Oliver Stanley, Harold Macmillan, Oliver Lyttelton, R. A. Butler and David Maxwell-Fyfe were the principal members of the shadow Cabinet involved in this enterprise. They were from the first up against a difficulty; Churchill did not believe in it. 'When an Opposition spells out its policy,' he told Butler, 'the Government becomes the Opposition and attacks the Opposition which becomes the Government. So having failed to win the sweets of office, it fails equally to enjoy the benefits of being out of office.' Writing many years later Butler conceded: 'There is rather more truth and tactic in this than I was prepared to admit at the time.'[1] However, even Churchill felt obliged to concede a little to the overwhelming demand of the 1946 Conservative conference for some reformulation of policy, and the Conservative Research Department was given the go-ahead. Some of the ablest of the younger Tories worked there; among those who later made a mark were Reginald Maudling, Enoch Powell and Iain Macleod. The department produced the *Industrial Charter* in 1947, followed by the *Agricultural Charter* and *Imperial Policy*. These were consolidated in *The Right Road for Britain* promulgated in 1949, the basis of the 1950 manifesto. It is questionable whether these statements of policy were particularly relevant when the Conservatives returned to office. The problems which they had to deal with were as usual by then quite different. Nor is it at all clear that the party's near miss in 1950 and narrow victory the following year had anything much to do with the charters. But they did at least show that the party was not 'the stupid party' and that it had some sort of constructive policy. Moreover they gave employment to a number of clever young men who otherwise might have drifted away from politics altogether.

On the morrow of the election it was assumed that a government with a majority of only six – if the Liberals voted with the Conservatives – could not last. The feat of legerdemain performed by Harold Wilson in 1964–6 and by first him and then James Callaghan between 1974 and 1979 lay far in the future. The Labour Cabinet was elderly and weary. Its principal members had served for ten years of great strain and continuous emergency. One has to go back to the days of Pitt, Perceval, Liverpool and Castlereagh for a precedent. The Conservatives used every ploy compatible with the parliamentary rules to harry and exhaust a party whose MPs were on average older than the opposition which had received much new blood in the 1950 election. The high point was the campaign in March 1951 to put down Prayers against Ministerial Orders. These could only be discussed after ordinary business, and the debates lasted all night until the Labour Whips found a procedural counter-move. The government had few new ideas beyond the mutualization of insurance companies and a rather half-hearted extension of state ownership to sugar and cement. It did manage to put through, despite furious Conservative hostility, one piece of unfinished business from the 1945–50 parliament – the nationalization of iron and steel. It survived for eighteen months – far longer than the pundits predicted, and the end when it came was caused by foreign rather than home affairs.

In June 1950 North Korean forces armed with Russian weapons invaded South Korea. At a time when Communist China seemed part of a monolithic Soviet sphere of influence, this act of aggression produced an even more hostile confrontation between east and west. The immediate effect in Britain was that the stockpiling of commodities caused a sharp rise in the cost of imports. There was also strong pressure for rearmament which hit the standard of living just at the moment when it seemed to be improving. The proportion of the national income annually spent on defence was seven per cent even before Korea – a high figure by the standards of the inter-war years. In August the Cabinet agreed to raise it to ten per cent – a three-year programme which would involve a total expenditure of £3,600 million – and in February 1951 to fourteen per cent i.e. £4,700 million over the same period. At the same time National Service was

337

extended to two years – which put a further strain on the supply of labour for industry. These developments resulted from the fluctuations of the fortunes of war. Thanks to a boycott by the USSR of the Security Council, it was conducted under UN auspices, no Soviet representative being present to apply the usual veto. The North Korean troops carried all before them in the summer of 1950 but the UN forces, predominantly American, though with a small British and an even smaller Australian contingent in support, hit back in October and swept towards the Chinese frontier. The Chinese then intervened in force in November and pushed back the UN Army south of the 38th parallel.

General MacArthur, the militant American proconsul who governed Japan and commanded the UN Army, proposed to riposte by bombing mainland China. Early in December Attlee flew to Washington to argue against this widening of the war. Whether or not his visit had any effect – and Truman maintains in his memoirs that his decision had already been taken – the war was not widened. The President firmly laid down that fighting must be limited to the defence of South Korea. The situation became stabilized early in 1951, and in April Truman dismissed MacArthur who still openly advocated hostilities against China. It was not until July 1953 that an armistice and exchange of prisoners was achieved. The division of the two Koreas at the 38th parallel has lasted ever since.

Korea was not the only foreign problem for the 1950–51 Labour government. In December 1950 the Iranian government refused to confirm an arrangement made with the Anglo-Iranian Oil Company about royalties. The Iranian Prime Minister, General Rasmara, was murdered in March 1951 and succeeded by Dr Mossadeq, a fanatical enemy of the company, who passed a bill to nationalize it. The British Labour government could not very well object to nationalization in principle but it insisted on arbitration about compensation figures, and strongly objected to the suspension of oil operations while these discussions were going on. Britain procured an injunction from the Hague Court in July, but, after further negotiations and an attempt at American mediation, the company's remaining technicians were withdrawn early in October to avoid incidents or violence. The episode was to play a big part in the ensuing British general election.

Two important changes occurred in the Cabinet during 1950–51. In October 1950 Stafford Cripps, who had long been ailing, finally resigned, and was succeeded as Chancellor of the Exchequer by Hugh Gaitskell. This caused a strong protest to Attlee from Bevan whose biographer, however, states that he did not so much want it for himself as disapprove of the promotion of a middle-class Wykehamist intellectual who had little standing with Labour's rank and file.[2] Cripps who was deeply hurt at the King's failure to say a word of thanks when he gave up the seals of office died eighteen months later. In March 1951 ill health removed an even more important figure. Ernest Bevin had been the linchpin of the government since 1945, but by now he was palpably failing. He resigned the Foreign Office, became briefly Lord Privy Seal, and died on 14 April. His successor was Herbert Morrison. Bevin will always have a high place in the pantheon of Foreign Secretaries. He is to be numbered with Castlereagh, Canning, Palmerston, Salisbury, Grey and Eden. Morrison was ill-suited to the office and his brief tenure was unhappy.

Gaitskell's first and only budget produced a major crisis. To find some of the finance needed for the rearmament programme he decided to breach the principle of a free health service by imposing charges for false teeth and spectacles. This roused the wrath of Bevan who, though moved to the Ministry of Labour in January, still regarded the service as his own brainchild. On 3 April he publicly told a heckler at Bermondsey that he could not remain a member of a government that imposed charges on the patient. When Gaitskell saw the King about the budget and said that it looked as if either he or Bevan would have to resign, the King according to Gaitskell said: "He [Bevan] must be mad to resign over a thing like that. I really don't see why people should have free false teeth any more than they have free shoes," waving his foot at me as he said it. He is of course a fairly reactionary person.'[3] Attlee in hospital backed Gaitskell who introduced his budget on 10 April 1951. Bevan did not at once resign but he made his dissent widely known. On 20 April the Prime Minister gave him an ultimatum. He resigned next day along with Harold Wilson and John Freeman, the parliamentary under-secretary at the Ministry of Supply. It was widely believed that this was the writing on the wall for Attlee's Cabinet.

On the question of free dentures and spectacles most people probably felt like George VI. It was an inflated issue, and Bevan got little sympathy or support even in his own party. The wider question of the necessity and feasibility of the rearmament programme was another matter. It is highly complicated and has been the subject of controversy ever since, thrashed out most recently by the sharply differing biographers of Bevan and Gaitskell.[4] The case against the feasibility of the £4,700 million programme was principally made by Harold Wilson but it is wrong to think that Bevan only tagged on at the end. It was apparently vindicated by events, for Churchill, soon after entering office in November 1951, calmly announced that the government could not spend £4,700 million in three years; part of it would have to roll forward to a fourth. But the other argument used against it, namely that the danger from Russia was grossly exaggerated and that a programme of rearmament on this scale was wholly unnecessary, cannot be substantiated. We will never know whether western rearmament deterred Stalin from a move into Europe, which there is at least some reason to suppose that he contemplated, if the much later evidence of a Czech defector is correct.[5] The American Chiefs of Staff believed that there was a real danger, and the British War Office warned the Cabinet early in January 1951: 'War possible in 1951, probable in 1952.' It was hard to ignore intelligence of this sort. The Russians had 175 divisions, NATO only fourteen. British rearmament on a very substantial scale – the Americans had pressed for £6,000 million – was essential if Truman was to persuade a Republican Congress wedded to 'Fortress America' and 'Asia First' that Europe was also vital. Unless Europe showed some ability to help itself there was little chance of getting help from America. France and Italy were weak and divided. In both countries there were powerful Communist opposition parties. Although the Americans at a NATO meeting in September 1950 had insisted on West German rearmament, the process had scarcely begun in 1951. Britain was the only European power of military significance and her example would be crucial. There was a strong case for promising to spend the £4,700 million even if one doubted whether the promise could be fulfilled.

One sensational episode occurred during Morrison's brief tenure of the Foreign Office. In the last week of May 1951 Donald Maclean, a member of the Diplomatic Service, fled the country along with Guy Burgess, a homosexual alcoholic who had just been sacked from the Foreign Office for outrageous conduct. Both were communist spies recruited in Cambridge in the 1930s. Maclean was married but had latent homosexual tendencies, which manifested themselves under the influence of alcohol, for he too was a heavy drinker, though was rather more discreet in his cups than Burgess. He was also much more dangerous, passing on information of the highest importance to Russia about atomic bombs while he was in the Washington embassy from 1945 to 1948. His activities had been discovered and he was about to be interrogated. Nothing further was heard of the couple till 1955, though it was generally assumed – and correctly – that they had been wafted away to Moscow. Rumours were rife of a 'third man' who had tipped them off. These were true and the person was Harold ('Kim') Philby who held high office in MI6; he was another communist addict of the bottle though heterosexual. There was no legal proof at the time. After repeated interrogation he was simply asked to retire. The public knew nothing of these details at the time but had the

341

general impression of a cover-up. His guilt was not revealed till 1963 when he too fled to Russia where he still lives – a KGB general.

2

The autumn of 1951 saw another serious balance of payments crisis. It was partly produced by American bidding up of the price of commodities in order to rearm. The NATO countries were thus in absurd competition with each other. An additional trouble was the situation in Iran, then the only important oil-producing country in the sterling area. In retrospect the episode can be seen as the first attempt by the countries of the Middle East to get even with the west whose industries depended more and more on oil. The effect on Britain was to increase her need for dollar oil imports. Armed intervention was seriously considered by the Cabinet, though rejected in the end. The American opposition to force seemed in Britain to be dictated as much by the interests of their own oil companies as love of peace. The Conservatives made the most of Labour's alleged pusillanimity, but the argument became a double-edged weapon in the election campaign.

As early as May Attlee had been thinking in terms of an autumn dissolution. The political situation was precarious. It was not in the national interest to have a series of cliff-hanging votes, and he was influenced to some extent by the King's proposed visit for five or six months in the New Year to Australasia. It would have been very awkward to have a political crisis while he was away but there were many other reasons for having an autumn election. In the event the King's grave illness, cancer of one lung, precluded the visit. The general election was held on 25 October. The Iranian situation was a prominent issue, but Churchill's charge of cowardice was countered by that of 'war-mongering', culminating with the *Daily Mirror*'s reiterated theme: 'Whose finger do you want on the trigger?' which led to a libel action by Churchill settled out of court in his favour many months later. The upshot of the election was a narrow Conservative majority in terms of parliamentary seats based on a minority of votes cast – a result which, though unusual, is possible under the British electoral system. It had occurred in 1929 and was to occur again in February 1974. The Conservatives with 13,717,538 votes (48 per cent of those cast) won 321 seats; Labour with 13,948,605 (48.8 per cent) won 295; and the Liberals who put up only 109 candidates compared with 475 in 1950 won 6 seats on a total vote of 730,556 (2.5 per cent). The turnout at 82.5 per cent was slightly down on the 1950 figure of 84 per cent, probably because of Liberal abstentions in seats where they had no candidate. The result was something of a disappointment to the Conservatives and a relief to Labour. Opinion polls had suggested a much bigger win for the former. As is usually the case in closely contested elections, it is impossible to explain the result with any confidence. Few people would have predicted that it would be followed by thirteen years of Conservative ascendancy.

Churchill in no way deterred by his age, seventy-six, promptly formed his government. The principal figures were Eden at the Foreign Office (also Leader of the House), Butler at the Exchequer, Maxwell-Fyfe at the Home Office and Oliver Lyttelton at the Colonial Office. An attempt to create one or two 'super-ministers' or 'overlords', members of the Upper House in charge of coordinating various departments, was soon dropped. Churchill, as in war, assumed the Ministry of Defence but quickly found that he had to pass it on – to Earl Alexander in March 1952. Similarly, Eden could not be expected to combine his two offices, and in May Harry Crookshank became Leader of the House. Harold Macmillan became Minister of Housing, not a post high in the Cabinet hierarchy but important because of the pledge to build 300,000 houses in the government's first year, given to placate a revolt during the party conference in October 1950. 'Every humble home will bless you if you succeed,' he was told by Churchill. He did succeed, and, whether or not he was blessed by humble home dwellers, his prestige was much enhanced.

This was not the only matter which helped the Conservatives on the domestic front. The diminution of hostilities in Korea caused the terms of trade to turn in favour of the western powers. The Conservatives were the beneficiaries of a change which might have been equally helpful to Labour if Attlee had not dissolved when he did. There had been biennial sterling crises in 1947, 1949 and 1951, but the pattern was broken in 1953, and there was not another till 1955. The economy, however, went through a bad patch in the first few months of the new administration. The drain on sterling continued, and Butler's Chancellorship began with a vigorous dispute hidden from the public about the merits of a plan curiously codenamed 'Robot'. The gist of it was to block eighty to ninety per cent of existing sterling balances, while allowing the residue and subsequent additions to be freely convertible at a rate left to find its own level and thus relieve the strain on the reserves. The scheme which was supported by the Chancellor and his Treasury team, and by the Governor of the Bank of England, C. F. (later Lord) Cobbold, appealed to the Prime Minister whose instinct was to 'free the pound'. It would have had the merit, as Lord Butler puts it, of creating 'an external regulator to the balance of payments corresponding to the internal regulator provided principally by Bank rate'. It might have prevented the hiccups of 'stop–go' economics which punctuated the rest of the Conservative period in office. It might also have forestalled the abrupt and demoralizing devaluation from $2·80 to $2·40 which was forced on the Labour government in 1967.

Butler's effort to float the pound failed. He was able with the full support of Cobbold to inject some realism into the bank rate. The two per cent level had become a Labour sacred cow and he scandalized the opposition by announcing a four per cent rate along with his budget of 1952. The budget, however, was orthodox, and 'Robot' did not go through. It would have involved an abrupt reversal of the

344

policies announced to a Commonwealth Finance Ministers' Conference as recently as November 1951, and its opponents believed that relief of the strain on the reserves could mean a burden on the economy in the form of higher interest rates, higher prices and higher unemployment; low unemployment was another Labour sacred cow, worshipped in those days by many Conservatives too. 'Robot' was strongly opposed by Lord Cherwell and Lord Salter, but despite claims in various biographies, their opposition does not seem to have been decisive. The evidence is not conclusive, but opposition from Lord Swinton, an elder statesman of weight, and above all from Eden who made one of his rare incursions into domestic politics appears to have delivered the *coup de grâce*.[6] There was general coolness too among all the senior ministers except Oliver Lyttelton.[7]

The economic climate in 1952 changed in Britain's favour, though the causes were as much outside Britain's control as those of the dismal weather earlier. A sense of prosperity and well being quite suddenly succeeded drab despondency. Industrial production which had been growing at nearly four per cent a year between 1945 and the Korean war, in fact increased rather less rapidly during the four years of Churchill's government, but the contrast with the earlier period seemed favourable because so much of the increase in the post-war years had been diverted into defence and social services and away from consumer products. Butler talked of doubling the standard of living in twenty-five years – a target which in the event was very nearly achieved. Rationing still tight during 1951 was soon relaxed and by the end of 1953 it had almost vanished.

The boom of the early 1950s, which with slight hiccups in 1955, 1957 and 1961 continued for the rest of our period, concealed certain economic weaknesses. The textile industry, once Britain's greatest pride, was palpably on the decline, as Japan and India began to compete. The revival of the German, Japanese and later the French economies cut into the export markets where Britain's post-war monopoly had led to a 'take it or leave it' attitude which caused resentment and readiness to switch to other countries. In 1952 the gross national products of the western powers in billions of dollars were USA 350, Britain 44, West Germany 32, France 29, Japan 16. Ten years later West Germany had passed Britain, and France was very close behind. The figures were USA 560, Britain 81, West Germany 89, France 74, Japan 59. By 1972 Britain was bottom of the league. Its position relative to the USA had not greatly changed since 1952 but the other three had caught up and easily surpassed it. These trends were not predictable in 1952, and much of Britain's imperial, foreign and defence policy at that time and later can be explained in terms of a country still regarding itself as the third industrial power in the world, admittedly a long way behind the USA and the USSR but well ahead of the others.

The 1950s saw the arrival of new consumer goods on a larger scale than ever before. The age of austerity soon became a matter of wry half-mocking memory. Black-and-white television sets – colour came later – motor cars, washing-machines, refrigerators, cheap synthetic fibres and plastic products of every sort proliferated. This 'Americanization' of British life was deplored by the left and also by the more old-fashioned figures on the right. Television probably changed people's style of life more than anything else. It largely destroyed the cinemas, and the newspapers have never really recovered from its impact. A notable battle was fought on the question of commercial television. The government, thanks to skilful and continuous persuasion by a powerful pressure group under the leadership of some of the bitterest opponents of the BBC, decided in favour of it. Labour was strongly opposed and so were a number of peers drawn from the more traditional elements of the Conservative Party. The Cabinet had some difficulty in getting the bill through the House of Lords but it passed in the end – a victory for the 'adventurers' against the 'establishment'. There was no question of Labour repealing it in 1964, any more than there had been of the Conservatives abolishing the welfare state in 1951. Both were far too popular.

In the early hours of 6 February 1952 King George VI, after a happy day's shooting, died in his sleep at Sandringham. He was only fifty-six. His health had never been robust and his unexpected succession was a great strain for a man who suffered from an acute stammer. In 1948 he was diagnosed as suffering from the early stages of arteriosclerosis in his right leg. A lumbar sympathectomy operation was performed and he seemed to recover, although he had to take life more easily. This led to the first postponement of his Australasian tour. Originally fixed for 1949 it was now to be in 1952. But in September 1951 cancer of his left lung was diagnosed and it had to be removed. The operation was successful and the King was never told that he had suffered from cancer. His doctors were well aware of the risk of a coronary thrombosis during or soon after the operation, and this was the cause of his death.

He was succeeded by his elder daughter whose marriage with traditional pageantry in November 1947 to Lieutenant Philip Mountbatten, as he was when they became engaged, had done something to cheer the public depressed by the austerities of that bleak year. She was in Kenya at the time of her father's death and flew back to England to be duly proclaimed as 'Queen Elizabeth the Second, by the Grace of God, Queen of this Realm and of all Her other Realms and Territories, Head of the Commonwealth, Defender of the Faith'. The title reflected the change in the status of what was once the 'British Dominions beyond the seas'. The title, 'Head of the Commonwealth' enabled the new Commonwealth republics, of which India was the first, to retain their association with the Crown, without swearing allegiance to it.

George VI had been an unknown figure when he succeeded. By the end of his reign he was popular and respected, and his death was sincerely mourned. He did not have to cope with the many constitutional problems involving the discretionary powers of the Crown which faced his father; the

347

House of Lords crisis in 1911, the Ulster question in 1912–14, the succession to Asquith in 1916, the appointment of Baldwin in 1923; the formation of the national government in 1931. But London was in the front line from 1940 to 1945 and Buckingham Palace was bombed while the King and Queen were there. It was hit nine times in the course of the war. Moreover, he sustained a personal blow which was spared to his father when his youngest brother, the Duke of Kent, to whom he was devoted, was killed in an air crash in 1942. The war years were exhausting for a King whose conscientiousness made him go far beyond the call of duty. They may well have contributed to his death.

3

In foreign affairs the years from 1951 to 1955 were the heyday of Anthony Eden. He had a series of diplomatic successes. He enjoyed immense prestige within the government – what Maxwell-Fyfe (later Lord Kilmuir) called 'a silencing authority' where foreign policy was concerned. No one dared challenge him in the Cabinet room, and, although he had some serious battles with Churchill which he did not always win, these were settled for the most part in private. There were four areas which were diplomatically important during this period – Korea, Iran, Egypt and Indo-China – and there was one major problem, how to reconcile France to German rearmament if NATO was to survive. In all these matters Britain had to take second place to America, and in nearly every case the American view differed at least in some degree and often considerably from the British. Since America possessed far superior military force and a GNP eight times that of Britain, the American attitude, when clear and definite, prevailed but if there was hesitation or uncertainty, the British had a chance.

Eden's memoirs personalize these issues too much. The differences are presented as a running battle between himself and John Foster Dulles, Eisenhower's Secretary of State.

But, as Eden's most recent biographer points out, it is easy to forget that Dean Acheson headed the State Department for the first fifteen months of Eden's tenure and the differences were just as sharp then.[8] Moreover, even if Dulles was a strong Secretary of State, Eisenhower was not a weak President. His decisions were even more important especially in the final show-down over Suez, though Eden naturally did not dwell on this in his book, *Full Circle* published in 1960. Dulles was dead by then but Eisenhower was still in office. In fact the problem was not personal, though personalities may have exacerbated it. The difference was one of political judgement and divergent national attitudes.

Eden regarded London as a balancing influence between the American continent, Europe and the Commonwealth. The Americans regarded their continent as their monopoly, the Commonwealth as obsolescent and Britain as just another European country. They saw the general situation since 1947 in terms of a worldwide challenge by international communism against the liberal values of the west. Eden was a late convert to belief in the threat of communism, and thought in terms of 'spheres of influence' and traditional British interest. He preferred to leave the Far East to America. He was anxious to avoid a war with China which would mean the loss of Hong Kong and might cause Russia, then to all appearances China's ally, to retaliate in Europe. The Middle East on the other hand was 'British'. To withdraw from Egypt would threaten the Suez Canal route. If Mossadeq succeeded in nationalizing the Anglo-Iranian Oil Company without compensation, British investments would be at peril all over the world. Better for Iran to be engulfed by communism than risk such a disaster.

The Americans believed that communism was on the march in the Far East, and had to be checked lest other powers fell in turn to its militant advance – the domino theory derived from Hitler's successes in 1936–9. To them the cautious British approach towards first a Korean settlement and then the ending of the colonial war between the French

349

and Vietminh in Indo-China echoed Munich. In the Middle East, on the other hand, the Americans regarded communism as merely an incipient threat. It might exploit nationalist movements if they were frustrated but, if they succeeded, it might never get a foothold at all. Britain, by clinging on to a quasi-colonial position whether directly as in Egypt or indirectly through the AIOC, was driving the nationalists into the communists' arms. If too much pressure was put on Mossadeq he would move into the communist camp or else he would fall and be replaced by the Tudeh (Communist) Party. Of course there was room for differing judgements. It was possible that Mossadeq would fall to a more moderate regime, in which case all would be well. Acheson was pessimistic and wished to bolster Mossadeq with funds – an attitude which infuriated Eden.

The Eisenhower administration, however, took a different view and acquiesced in a British plan, in conjunction with the CIA which was headed by Foster Dulles's brother, Allen, to overthrow the Iranian Prime Minister. This was successfully achieved by Kermit Roosevelt, a CIA officer, in August 1953. The Shah took over and the Iranian problem was temporarily settled. Some details of the coup have been revealed; [9] the British part is obscure, and likely to remain so till the relevant archives are opened if they ever are. It is fair to remember, as the author of the best up-to-date book on Iran points out, that the coup was pushing at an open door.[10] The Mossadeq regime was in desperate straits, thanks to an international boycott of Iranian oil, and the Shah had a reserve of popularity which was not dissipated till much later.

Egypt involved a similar dispute with America at first, though there was subsequent agreement which in the event did not last. In October 1951 King Farouk's government abrogated the Anglo-Egyptian Treaty of 1936. Eden made this rebuff a part of the Conservative electoral campaign – an attack on Labour weakness. Early in 1952 there was major disorder in Cairo and Ismailia involving British punitive action and several deaths. Acheson wanted Britain to recognize the King's claim to be king of the Sudan as well as Egypt. Eden refused, and in July a military coup exiled the King, along with his remarkable collection of pornographic clocks, to Europe. General Neguib who led the coup was soon deposed and succeeded by Colonel Nasser. There was strong American pressure for a deal and, whether or not for that reason, Eden agreed in 1954 to the evacuation of the Suez base, Cyprus being the inadequate substitute. Churchill was privately indignant. Publicly a number of Conservative MPs led by Captain Charles Waterhouse bitterly opposed the withdrawal. 'The Suez Group', as they came to be called, was a thorn in Eden's flesh for the rest of his political life.

In the Far East in 1954 Eden scored his most striking success against the anti-communist containment strategy of the USA. He had already in the previous year helped to negotiate an armistice in Korea but the gravest problem was in French Indo-China. The French colonial war against the Vietminh raised the American 'China Lobby' to boiling point, and the increasing likelihood of French defeat prompted America to threaten armed intervention. The US administration was, however, unwilling to 'go it alone', and Congress seemed unlikely to support action which might be regarded as supporting 'colonialism' unless it had international backing. This gave Eden his leverage. He regarded the possibility, however remote, of a third world war as something to which Britain would be far more vulnerable than the USA. It was better to accept a slight diminution of anti-communist strength than run that risk. A partition arrangement in which Dulles reluctantly acquiesced was eventually achieved. It seemed a relief at the time but the promise of united elections in 1956 was never realized, nor could Eden have believed otherwise. The settlement was only a lull in a thirty-year war.

Eden's greatest triumph concerned German rearmament. In 1954 the French Assembly voted down the proposal for EDC (European Defence Community) supported by the Prime Minister, Pierre Mendès-France. This had been expected, for it seemed to involve a closer integration at a lower level between the various forces than was likely to be acceptable. Eden's suggestion for an alternative form of alliance, above all his offer at just the right psychological moment to maintain four British divisions in Europe persuaded the French, convinced the Germans and rescued NATO from ruin. The settlement has lasted ever since.

Eden could notch up two further achievements to his credit. The question of Trieste had been a wearisome frontier problem between Yugoslavia and Italy from the end of the war. Largely thanks to Eden's patient efforts an agreement was reached in October 1954 which has stood the test of time. Eden was also much involved in the Austrian settlement. This hung fire for many years owing to Soviet intransigence. Just after Eden had become Prime Minister and in the middle of his election campaign Molotov, surprisingly, agreed to a treaty in April 1955. It is the only case of Russia voluntarily quitting an occupied territory.

Churchill regarded himself as above these details. He wanted a summit conference with the USA and USSR. The accession of Eisenhower to the Presidency late in 1952 and the death of Stalin early in 1953 encouraged his hopes. Eden, with whom his relations had long been uneasy, thought that there was little to be gained, and so did Eisenhower. But in spring 1953 Eden had a bile duct operation which was not a success and had to be repaired later in Boston. He was out of action from April to October. Churchill took over the Foreign Office and seized the opportunity to press Eisenhower once again for a meeting between the western powers and the USSR. Eisenhower agreed reluctantly to a preliminary meeting in Bermuda in July to discuss the idea but insisted, to Churchill's chagrin, that the French should be there too. The President wished to bury the 'special relationship'. At this juncture Churchill in his turn was put out of action late in July 1953 – by a stroke from which he made a remarkable but never complete recovery. The seriousness of his illness was concealed from all except a few intimates, and the summer season made public appearances unnecessary. The Bermuda meeting was postponed till December, and turned out to be of no great consequence anyway. In 1954 Churchill by-passing the Cabinet persuaded both Eisenhower and Eden to agree to his seeing Malenkov on his own. The Russians rebuffed the offer. This was lucky for Churchill. There could well have been some major Cabinet resignations if the offer had been accepted.

Churchill ought to have resigned after his stroke. He justified his continuance in office by Eden's illness; had he resigned, his successor would have been Butler who was acting Prime Minister, and this would have deprived Eden, the Conservative crown prince, of his rightful inheritance. The argument was thin. Churchill may have preferred Eden to Butler but it is not clear that he thought very highly of either and when Eden recovered Churchill did not resign. He continued for another eighteen months, and might not have gone even then but for a veiled ultimatum from Macmillan who had no axe to grind since his own prospects for the premiership at that time seemed negligible; Eden was youn-ger and Butler, next in line, younger still.

Churchill treated Eden badly. The alleged 'father and son' relationship does not stand up to scrutiny, except in the sense that fathers and sons do not always get on well together. They would have been rivals for the succession if the anti-appeasers had overthrown Chamberlain. Churchill received a decisive boost, oddly enough from Chamberlain, by being made a member of the War Cabinet and First Lord of the Admiralty in 1939 whereas Eden was kept out of it in the minor post of Dominions Secretary. When Churchill became Prime Minister he let seven months pass before he made Eden Foreign Secretary and a member of the inner circle. Their differences were frequent and sometimes sharp. It is true that Churchill, after a request from the King in 1942 to nominate his successor in case he was killed, named Eden. In 1945 sitting in the Cabinet Room after the last meeting of the caretaker government he said to Eden: 'Thirty years of my life have been passed in this room. I shall never sit in it again.

You will but I shall not.' Eden must have expected Churchill to bow out after Labour's landslide victory, if not at once, at a decent interval. That Churchill should return to office in 1951 and still be Prime Minister in 1955 would have seemed incredible. How far Eden's own conduct of the premiership was affected by this frustrating delay can only be a matter of conjecture.

Chapter Eighteen

THE SUEZ CRISIS

I

Churchill formally resigned on 6 April 1955. A press strike spoilt the publicity for a great occasion. Eden succeeded inevitably and smoothly. He made minimal cabinet changes. Lord Swinton was retired with an earldom. The Foreign Office went to Macmillan. Eden would have preferred Lord Salisbury but for his peerage and said so in his memoirs which appeared in 1960. Macmillan, by then Prime Minister, may have derived some pleasure in making Lord Home Foreign Secretary later that year. No problem arose, nor did it in 1979 when Margaret Thatcher appointed Lord Carrington.

Eden had to decide on the date of the next election. He was not obliged to dissolve before October 1956, but there was a good case for a new Prime Minister obtaining a new mandate, and the Conservative prospects seemed favourable. The economy was booming. Since 1951 the number of cars in the country had gone up by a third, and television sets fourfold. Unemployment was negligible, and living standards were rising. In the last four years an Englishman had conquered Everest, another had run a four-minute mile and England had regained and held the Ashes. Queen Elizabeth II had been crowned. The foreign scene, thanks largely to Eden, seemed less stormy than for many years past.

There was another matter to consider. The Labour Party was in disarray. Bevan's dissidence had contributed to the Conservative victory of 1951. Since then, his opposition to Attlee had caused bitter dispute. The battle was partly about

355

defence and foreign policy but it was also a personal struggle between Bevan and Gaitskell for the Labour leadership generally expected to become vacant very soon after the 1951 election. Attlee, however, like many party leaders before him, showed no sign of going. Yet he became curiously indecisive about the dispute. An attempt was made in March 1955 to expel Bevan from the PLP. It failed, but Attlee could easily have prevented it being made at all, or ensured its success. The Labour Party was ill-placed to cope with an early general election.

On 15 April Eden announced a dissolution and fixed the date of the election for 26 May. It was a bold decision and failure would have given him the disagreeable record of the shortest holder of his office since Earl Waldegrave (four days) in 1757. The Conservatives won easily, helped by a tax-reducing budget and a well run campaign in which television played a major part for the first time. Eden appealing to the concept of 'a property-owning democracy' was very effective. He disregarded 'received wisdom', addressing his audience face to face, solo and unscripted. If his words were somewhat platitudinous their sincerity was obvious and the contrast with Churchill's high rhetoric may have been an asset. Significantly, Churchill was not asked to broadcast. The Conservatives won 344 seats, Labour 277, Liberals 6, the rest 3. The voting figures, on a turnout of 76.7 per cent of the electorate, were: Conservatives 13,286,569; Labour 12,404,970; Liberals (with only 110 candidates) 722,405. The Conservatives seemed well set for several years in office and indeed they were to enjoy a longer continuous tenure than any political party since 1830, but there were to be many dramas, convulsions and vicissitudes in the nine years before October 1964 when they at last fell from power.

The government soon ran into trouble. The newspaper strike had been followed by a strike of London busmen and dock-workers. This may have helped the Conservatives in the election, but when the train drivers (ASLEF) went on strike too on 29 May the government felt obliged to declare a state of emergency. Walter Monckton, a popular and conciliatory Minister of Labour, managed to settle the strike – but at a price which gave a further push to inflation. This soon appeared in the trade figures which had been deteriorating even in the last months of Churchill's regime. Butler's give-away budget now appeared in an unfavourable light – playing fast and loose with the economy for electioneering purposes. Matters were made no better by his decision in the spring to make sterling convertible at the current rate of exchange. It might have been better to 'float' the pound as the Bank of England preferred. A deflationary autumn budget had to be introduced on 26 October. It involved higher purchase tax on a number of goods, including kitchen utensils and the opposition dubbed it a 'pots and pans' budget. Butler was tired and exhausted. His first wife had died of cancer at the end of the previous year, and the loss had greatly affected him. Already in September Eden had decided to secure a more pliable Foreign Secretary. The only position to which Macmillan could be moved without loss of face was the Treasury but he pressed so strongly to remain that Eden postponed the reshuffle till 20 December. Macmillan then became Chancellor, Selwyn Lloyd Foreign Secretary and Butler Leader of the House. Eden had to agree to Macmillan's insistence that the change did not make Butler 'Deputy Prime Minister' – whatever that title meant. In fact, as Macmillan pointed out in a somewhat barbed letter to Eden the post was non-existent and outside the constitution, having been invented by Churchill only for wartime reasons.

A few days earlier an important change occurred in the Labour Party. Enigmatic and inscrutable to the end, Attlee who had led it for over twenty years resigned on 7 December abruptly and without warning except to the Chief Whip and Gaitskell. The succession lay between Morrison, Gaitskell and Bevan. Morrison, born in 1888 and by far the oldest competitor, might well have been the choice had Attlee resigned after the 1951 election, but this was one of the reasons why Attlee did not resign. Just as Macmillan in 1963 was determined not to be succeeded by Butler, so Attlee was determined not to be succeeded by Morrison. They had never been on friendly terms and Morrison had tried to block Attlee's accession as Prime Minister in 1945. Every year that passed diminished his chances, and Bevan by a series of explosive rows injured his own prospects too. A last minute effort by Shinwell to persuade both Bevan and Gaitskell to stand down in favour of Morrison failed. Bevan agreed, but Gaitskell and his supporters saw victory in their grasp. The voting in the Parliamentary Labour Party was announced on 14 December; Gaitskell 157, Bevan 70, Morrison 40. At forty-nine Gaitskell was the youngest party leader since 1900. 'If we *have* to have a Labour party,' wrote the famous hostess, Mrs Ian Fleming, 'it is as well that you should lead it.' Oddly enough, Morrison was to outlive both his younger rivals and was himself to be outlived by Attlee.

The election of a new leader cleared the air to some extent in the Labour Party. It also seemed to give the party a boost in its public rating. In a by-election at Torquay a week later, there was a nine per cent drop in the Conservatives' share of the poll and, though they had no difficulty in holding the seat, a swing of such size seemed far more portentous in those days than it would twenty years later. This setback among other things led to mounting personal criticism of the Prime Minister. Foremost in the attack was Winston Churchill's son, Randolph, who wrote a regular and malevolent column in the *Evening Standard*. Some people believed that personal animosity played a part. There was no love lost between him and his first cousin, Clarissa Churchill, who had become Eden's second wife in 1952. But he was far from being a solitary critic. The *Daily Mail* and the *Daily Telegraph*, both strongly Conservative organs, were also on the warpath. Rumours of resignation began to circulate and a signed article on 3 January 1956 by the deputy editor of the latter, Donald McLachlan, so annoyed the Prime Minister that he took the unprecedented step of publicly denying that he had any intention of retiring. In a speech in Bradford on 14

January he advised his audience not to believe what appeared in 'cantankerous' London newspapers. The commotion died away, but an impression of jitteriness remained.

Eden's premiership was dominated by foreign affairs. He was plunged at once into preparations for a conference of heads of the governments of the USA, Russia, France and the UK – represented respectively by Eisenhower and Dulles, Khrushchev and Bulganin, Faure and Pinay, Eden and Macmillan. It met in Geneva from 18 to 23 July 1955. The re-emergence of France weakened the status of Britain, hitherto the third of a Big Three with all its wartime associations but now a member of the junior pair of a Big Four. Eisenhower made no concessions to the old order and excused himself from visiting London on his way to Geneva. The conference came to nothing. Reunification of Germany, one of its objectives, was and remains unattainable. The Russians would only consent to a communist takeover. The west insisted on free elections which, as everyone knew on both sides of the Iron Curtain, would at once sweep away the East German regime. Disarmament, the other objective, was too closely connected with Germany to be separately soluble. The 'Eisenhower plan' and the 'Eden plan' are part of the debris of history. However, no positive ill will was created – and that was something. Bulganin and Khrushchev accepted Eden's invitation to visit Britain in the spring of 1956.

During discussions between Eden and Dulles a tangential question came up – the Baghdad Pact. There was a sharp disagreement which affected future events. The notion of Britain and the USA adhering to a defensive alliance between Turkey, Iran and Pakistan, the three Islamic states bordering on Russia's southern frontier, had been mooted while Eden was still in the Foreign Office. Dulles, though somewhat dilatory, seemed to favour it. But in March 1955 Eden without warning Dulles signed a British alliance with Turkey and Iraq (hence 'Baghdad Pact'). This was a very different affair, even though Iran and Pakistan adhered, later in the year. Iraq was not a part of the 'northern tier', and belonged moreover to the Arab League. The move had serious implications for American–Israeli relations. Iraq was widely regarded like Jordan as a British fief, and her adherence to the Baghdad Pact was bitterly resented by at least two other members of the league, Egypt and Saudi Arabia. Eden, ironically in view of later events, was regarded then as hostile to Israel. Dulles withdrew his support for the pact. Eden thought he had reneged on an agreement. 'There is something in Mr Dulles which particularly irritates the Prime Minister,' wrote Sir Ivone Kirkpatrick, head of the Foreign Office to Harold Macmillan on 20 August.[1]

In October Eden and Macmillan were involved in an awkward revival of the Burgess and Maclean affair of 1951, which did nothing to help relations with the Americans long suspicious of British feebleness towards communism. The two Soviet agents were now revealed as living in Moscow. The role of the 'third man' who had enabled them to escape was raised in Parliament by a Labour MP, Colonel Marcus Lipton, who named Philby. Philby was indeed strongly suspected by the authorities but there was still no legal proof. Macmillan who knew the evidence felt obliged to bend over backwards to endorse Philby's integrity. This was unwise and unnecessary. He could have observed the conventions with a terse and cautious reply. He must have wished he had when the matter came up again in the last year of his premiership and Philby's own escape to Russia conclusively proved his guilt.

Eden's embarrassment over issues of security had not come to an end. The promised nine-day visit of the Soviet leaders to Britain took place in April 1956. It went off smoothly enough apart from a public dispute during a dinner given to them by the Labour Party, at which George Brown was highly critical. But after the Russians returned they protested about espionage against the naval vessels that escorted them to Portsmouth. The Admiralty had already announced that a frogman, Commander Lionel Crabb, had failed to return from a test dive in connection with certain underwater apparatus. This was a cover story. Crabb had been spotted by Russian sailors, and his mission, of which the government knew nothing, was to inspect the Soviet hulls. Whether he was killed or died accidentally is unknown; the body was only recovered fourteen months later. But Eden was furious at this piece of private enterprise by MI6. The director would have been dismissed, had he not been on the verge of retiring. Eden appointed the head of MI5, Sir Dick White, who was a civilian, to succeed him. The two organizations were bitter enemies. No greater snub could have been given to MI6. When asked about the Crabb affair in the House, Eden took the unusual but justifiable course of stating that 'what was done was done without the authority or knowledge of Her Majesty's Ministers. Appropriate disciplinary steps are being taken'.

In January 1956 Eden and Lloyd left for Washington to discuss the Middle East. On 28 September 1955 it had become publicly known that Czechoslovakia was supplying the arms to Egypt refused by America. There was also the question of finance for the Aswan High Dam believed to be the answer to Egyptian poverty. It was discussed in Washington on the basis of ninety per cent to be loaned by the US and ten per cent by Britain but no clear decision was taken, and negotiations continued for many months.

On his return to Britain the Prime Minister was confronted by a serious domestic crisis. The Chancellor was determined to cut expenditure. High on Macmillan's list for the axe were subsidies for bread and milk. Eden had given a pledge at the election not to abolish these. He was now faced with a threat of resignation, and he settled on a compromise which gave Macmillan what he called in his memoirs 'four-fifths of my demands'. These measures, along with a rise in the bank rate from four and a half to five per cent and an increase in hire-purchase deposits were announced on 17 February. Two months later Macmillan presented his budget. It was neutral but produced one innovation which, though offending the non-conformist conscience, has lasted ever since – premium bonds.

Meanwhile, a disagreeable blow had been dealt to British prestige in the Middle East. On 1 March General John Glubb, commander of the Arab Legion, was summarily dismissed by the young King Hussein of Jordan. Eden's instinct was to break off all relations, for Glubb had been the very symbol of British prestige. Second thoughts prevailed. Eden decided that the real trouble-maker was Nasser whose pan-Arabist propaganda and subversive activities seemed likely to undermine the whole British position in the Middle East. It was not only a matter of prestige, but of economics – oil supplies and their route through the Suez Canal. He decided to play down the Jordan affair but his speech in the House of Commons on 7 March was a disaster. It deeply disturbed the Tory right. He could not afford again to look like an appeaser.

Two days later he was able to reverse that impression by brusquely deporting Archbishop Makarios to the Seychelles. The Archbishop was the leader of the Greek Cypriots clamouring for Enosis, i.e. union with Greece. No Greek government could afford to repudiate him. Cyprus had been a British colony since its acquisition by Disraeli from Turkey in 1878 and was regarded as strategically vital. Its population was seventy-five per cent Greek, the rest Turkish; but the Turks, with their atavistic and fully reciprocated hatred of the Greeks, were adamant against Enosis. The London Conference of 29 August 1955 between the various parties got nowhere. Protracted internal negotiations for limited self-government were equally abortive. Enosis was supported by a terrorist organization, EOKA. The Archbishop was suspiciously close to it. Violence mounted and on 9 March Eden took his decision. It greatly enhanced his prestige in the Conservative ranks, but whether it helped over Cyprus is at least doubtful.

A lull in both home and foreign affairs ensued. No startling events occurred in the spring and early summer of 1956.

2

Behind the scenes, diplomacy was at work and intrigue hummed. The British and American governments became more and more uneasy about the Aswan Dam. Pan-Arab propaganda from Cairo never ceased. It threatened the pro-British regimes in Iraq and Jordan and was bitterly hostile to Israel, an American protégé. To grant a vast loan to Nasser looked like rewarding an enemy at the expense of friends. Dulles wanted to build up oil-rich Saudi Arabia as a more effective anti-Egyptian bulwark than Iraq or Jordan, but, owing to a long-standing British dispute about the Buraimi oasis, Eden would have none of it. In May 1956 at a NATO meeting in Paris Dulles and Lloyd at least agreed on one thing; the Aswan loan should be allowed to 'wither on the vine'. Nasser already knew as early as March from an Iraqi source that the loan was unlikely to go through. Then or soon after he decided to use its probable cancellation as an excuse for nationalizing the Suez Canal Company – a coup which, he later told Dulles, he had been planning for two years.

Meanwhile he held his hand. The last British troops were due to leave the canal base on 13 June. Eden and Lloyd considered delay, but decided that there was not sufficient excuse to avoid alienating moderate Arab opinion. Nasser was now ready to act. He lulled suspicion by lowering the level of anti-British propaganda and concluding his protracted financial discussions with the Canal Company on a conciliatory basis. On 20 June the President of the International Bank made a final effort to settle the Aswan loan. Nasser riposted with a series of palpably unacceptable counter-proposals. Negotiations ceased, but were suddenly started up again a month later by the Egyptian ambassador in Washington. There is a conflict of evidence about what followed. The crucial day was 19 July. According to Egyptian sources the ambassador dropped all Nasser's previous conditions. According to Eisenhower and Robert Murphy, a high official in the State Department, the ambassador demanded many millions of dollars guaranteed over the next ten years – a proposal that would never have been accepted by Congress – and he added that if America would not agree he was sure Russia would fill the gap. It is claimed that Dulles replied: 'Well, as you have the money, you don't need any from us! My offer is withdrawn!'² He certainly cancelled the loan at very short notice, informing the British ambassador only an hour before and not consulting Eden or Lloyd. But the Egyptian demand had now made it impossible to let the offer 'wither on the vine'. The idea that Dulles 'provoked' the seizure of the Suez Canal Company has no substance. The withdrawal was a convenient propaganda excuse for Nasser to do what he had long planned to do and for which he would have found another excuse, or none at all, when it suited him.

A week later on 26 July, Nasser in an emotional and flamboyant speech to a mass audience in Alexandria announced the nationalization of the Canal Company, proclaimed martial law in the Canal Zone, and enjoined the company's employees to stay at their posts on pain of imprisonment. Egyptian troops occupied the company's offices. There would be compensation at current values for the shareholders, but Nasser's declaration that the canal revenues would be used to finance the Aswan Dam cast doubts on Egypt's ability to pay. Eden was entertaining King Feisal of Iraq and his Prime Minister Nuri-es-Said to dinner in Downing Street when the news came through. Selwyn Lloyd and Lords Salisbury and Home were also there. Nuri advised taking a strong line. When the guests had departed, an informal ministerial meeting was held in the Cabinet room. It included the Lord Chancellor Kilmuir, the First Sea Lord, Lord Mountbatten, the CIGS, Sir Gerald Templer, the Chief of Air Staff, Sir Dermot Boyle. The French ambassador and the US chargé d'affaires were also asked to attend. It was decided to concert common action between the three countries, and the Chiefs of Staff were invited to assess the prospects of military action. In the House of Commons at 11 A.M. next morning (a Friday)

the Suez coup was briefly debated. Gaitskell was as emphatic as Eden in denouncing 'this high handed and totally unjustifiable step', as he called it. The full Cabinet then met, and was informed by the Chairman of the Combined Chiefs of Staff, Sir William Dickson, that any military action would have to be amphibious and mounted from Malta. It would take six weeks to prepare. He ruled out an immediate descent by parachute troops. It was official military doctrine, based on Arnhem, that a parachute landing must be reinforced from the ground within twenty-four hours. The Egyptian forces in 1956 were a very different proposition from the Germans in 1944, however closely some people tried to compare Nasser with Hitler, but it would have been difficult for the Prime Minister to go against such clear professional advice. According to a book by the French Foreign Minister, Christian Pineau, Eden would have liked to take instant action.[3] Selwyn Lloyd in a book with a confusingly similar title asserted that the Cabinet regarded force as a last resort to be used only if diplomatic and economic pressure failed.[4] In America the impression was certainly gained that Eden meant to reoccupy the Canal Zone at once. If Eden had intended a quick military response, the advice of the Chiefs of Staff forced him to make a virtue of necessity and agree to negotiate for the time being, but the longer the negotiations continued the less easy it became to justify military action.

The precise legal position was far from clear. The Suez Canal Company was registered in Egypt and it could be argued that the Egyptian government, as long as it paid fair compensation, had the right to nationalize the company. There were powerful arguments the other way, and some of the foremost legal experts in Britain and elsewhere maintained that Nasser had broken international law. Even if he had, it was not certain that force could legitimately be used as a remedy. Here again opinions differed. Some maintained that it could only be used with the consent of the United Nations, others that the Suez Canal was so vital to Britain that she was entitled to take action under Article 51 of the

UN Charter which entitles a country to use force in self-defence, and is indeed the article under which the operation to regain the Falklands was taken in 1982.

It was, moreover, necessary to distinguish between the company and the canal itself. Most people, with vague memories of Disraeli and 'Madam you have it', were under the impression that Britain had somehow purchased the canal in 1875. In fact what Disraeli had done was to buy the Khedive's shares in the company. This gave the British the largest single holding though it was less than half the total. The canal itself was regulated by the Maritime Convention of 1888 under which Egypt guaranteed that it would be kept open to the ships of all nations in peace and war. It was true that in two world wars the British themselves had overridden this proviso. It was also true that for several years past Egypt had stopped Israeli ships from using it, and no one had taken action beyond a protest to the Security Council. However, if Nasser either through inability or malice failed to keep the canal open to shipping in general, then he would certainly be in breach of international law. In fact, he took good care not to do this until the actual Anglo-French invasion at the end of October, and the idea that the expertise of the company was essential for the smooth running of the canal proved to be a myth.

It was nevertheless undeniable that the forcible seizure of the company and its assets looked like a step towards using the leverage afforded by control of the canal in order to blackmail the west. In 1955, 14,666 ships passed through the canal; three-quarters of them belonged to NATO countries and one-third of them was British. Annually, 70 million tons of oil came through from the Gulf, of which 60 million went to western Europe, constituting two-thirds of the area's total oil imports. It would require twice the tonnage of tankers to bring it round the Cape. In these circumstances western alarm was understandable. Both Britain and France had further reasons for perturbation. Nasser's coup would give pan-Arabism a boost everywhere. In Algiers where France was fighting a bitter colonial war fuelled by Egyptian supplies and propaganda, the destruction of Nasser came more and more to be seen as a precondition of victory. Nasser's success also threatened the Baghdad Pact and the remaining pro-British regimes in the Middle East, especially Iraq. The French and British positions were, however, different in one important respect. France had cut her links with the Arab world and was on the very closest terms with Israel.

The American position was not the same. The threat to the canal did not greatly affect American interests. Certainly the administration disliked Nasser and his links with Russia; Dulles was especially annoyed by Egyptian recognition of the Chinese People's Republic, which at that time seemed to be an ally of Moscow. But both he and Eisenhower were reluctant to be associated with anything that savoured of 'colonialism', and they did not think Nasser's action sufficiently outrageous to produce the degree of sympathy in the non-communist countries, which, they believed, Britain and France would need for a military operation. Moreover, Eisenhower would be campaigning for re-election that autumn and an important plank in his programme was his role as a 'man of peace'. Various memoirs of British statesmen claim that the Americans did not rule out force as 'a last resort', but the documents so far published imply clearly enough that armed intervention would be supported by Washington – or even condoned – only if Nasser did something else, e.g. contravene the Maritime Convention. Neither Eisenhower nor Dulles ruled out military action if circumstances changed but both of them ruled it out if they remained the same. The French appreciated this point more clearly than the British. They were in no doubt about American disapproval but equally in no doubt that action should be taken whatever America said.

A great deal has been written about the Suez crisis but much remains obscure. Of the principal participants at the British end only Selwyn Lloyd has written memoirs of any value. These appeared in 1978. Eden's account given in *Full*

Circle (1960) omits all the matters of real controversy. The same can be said of Macmillan's in *Riding the Storm* (1971). Anthony Nutting's *No End of a Lesson* (1967) is certainly candid but he was not a member of the Cabinet. The best reconstruction of the episode is still Hugh Thomas's *The Suez Affair* (1967); it needs to be supplemented by *Anthony Eden* (1981) whose author David Carlton was able to use important American material available for the first time. The French have been much more open about their actions and motives, for example the memoirs of General Beaufre, General Challe and Christian Pineau. Under the thirty-year rule the British official papers will become available in 1987. There have been repeated rumours that much of the material has been destroyed, or, if not actually destroyed, will be suppressed far beyond 1987. These stories cannot be substantiated, but one can safely guess that material involving the intelligence departments is unlikely to be made available as early as 1987. And it is worth remembering that Cabinet minutes are written to record decisions, not to satisfy the curiosity of historians. The researchers who home in on the Record Office that year are likely to be disappointed.

3

The Cabinet meeting on 27 July determined the broad lines of British policy till mid-October. In concert with the French and, it was hoped, the Americans all possible economic, political and diplomatic pressure would be applied to Egypt. The object would be, not to reinstate the company – which was the obvious course – but to put the canal under some sort of international control. This cavalier treatment of the company was defended on the ground that the restoration of its position might alienate the newer states and raise the question of their right to nationalize; the company's concession to operate the canal would run out in 1968 anyway. If peaceful measures failed, then force would be used – but only in the last resort. The Chiefs of Staff were instructed to make preparations in cooperation with the French. An Egypt Committee of the Cabinet was set up to supervise the day-to-day conduct of the crisis. It consisted of Eden, Lloyd, Macmillan, Salisbury, Home and Walter Monckton (Minister of Defence). Selwyn Lloyd says that in practice membership was 'very fluid'. Contrary to some statements that have been made Butler was a frequent attender and so were several other ministers.

Eisenhower, to whom some fire-eating talk by Macmillan had been reported via Murphy, became alarmed lest military action was imminent. Macmillan could not have threatened this, for he was well aware that an Anglo-French force would not be ready at the latest till the end of the first week in September, but the evidence does suggest that he was one of the foremost 'hawks'. Eisenhower sent Dulles to London to pull Britain back from a brink which she had no immediate intention of overstepping nor even the ability to do so. The upshot was a diplomatic attempt – the calling of a conference in London of the twenty-four powers (two refused) most dependent upon the canal, including the signatories of the 1888 Convention. This was to meet at Lancaster House on 16 August to try to agree on proposals to Nasser. On 2 August there was a debate in the House of Commons at which Gaitskell used strong words about Nasser's coup; he said almost as an afterthought that force needed the consent of the United Nations, but this sounded like small print. *The Times*, the previous day, had produced a powerful leader: 'Quibbling over whether or not Nasser was "legally entitled" to make the grab will delight the finicky and comfort the faint-hearted, but entirely misses the real issues.' The writer compared Nasser's conduct with Hitler's over the Rhineland and Stalin's over Czechoslovakia. The article was entitled 'A Hinge of History'. Public opinion in general seemed firmly behind a strong line.

The conference which lasted for a week voted by eighteen to four in favour of Dulles's plan to put the canal under the control of an international board. A five-man mission led by

369

Robert Menzies, the Australian Prime Minister, was deputed to present these proposals in Cairo early in September. On 9 September Nasser rejected them, possibly influenced by a remark of Eisenhower reported on 5 September categorically repudiating the use of force. The British government now wanted to refer the matter to the Security Council. Parliament had been recalled for 12 September, and Eden hoped to make the announcement during the two-day debate. No doubt the Russians would veto any practical steps but the moral position of Britain and France would be strengthened. Dulles was against a reference to the Security Council, and had already on 4 September produced his own somewhat opaque plan for a Suez Canal Users' Association (SCUA). The users of the canal would manage it, employ their own pilots and collect the dues from the ships of the countries which adhered. Exactly how this was to work in practice was obscure. It certainly needed a degree of Egyptian cooperation which was unlikely to be forthcoming. Eden accepted it with reluctance on 10 September and Selwyn Lloyd was even more sceptical. The French government regarded it as an excuse for procrastination but being the junior partner in the alliance felt obliged to acquiesce. The French were right. SCUA made no sense unless it was backed by force and Dulles pulled the rug from under the Anglo-French feet on the evening of the second day of the debate in the House when he said at a press conference in Washington: 'We do not intend to shoot our way through. It may be that we have the right to do it, but we don't intend to do it as far as the United States is concerned.' However, the die was now cast and a second London conference was summoned for 19 September. It comprised the eighteen powers which had voted in favour of the Dulles proposals on 23 August. The conference agreed to have the inaugural meeting of SCUA in London on 1 October. Meanwhile, Eden ordered military plans to be prepared in case diplomacy failed. There were all along two objectives: to establish international control over the Canal and to 'topple' Nasser. If Nasser gave way to diplomacy he would probably, so it was argued, fall because of the damage to his prestige. If military action was needed, it would almost certainly bring him down as well as recover the canal. The toppling of Nasser was not a publicly avowed purpose, though Eden did not conceal it in his private messages to Eisenhower. The original Anglo-French plan was to land at Alexandria and advance on the canal via the region north of Cairo. This had the advantage of a shorter sea route and a greater likelihood of bringing down the Egyptian dictator. Eden at first vetoed it in favour of a direct attack on Port Said, but, if the account given by the French task force commander, General André Beaufre, is correct, he changed his mind on 14 August and agreed to an assault on Alexandria codenamed 'Musketeer'. According to the British commander, General Stockwell, the earliest date for this was fixed for 15 September later advanced to 8 September, but it remained a contingency plan and no decision had yet been taken to implement it. Early in September it was changed again, and on the 11th a new plan was adopted, 'Musketeer Revise', which reverted to the idea of a direct attack on the canal. The reason for the change was primarily political. It would seem like police action at the place of the offence whereas an attack on Alexandria might appear as aggression against Egypt. In the event it made the later excuse of intervention 'to separate the combatants', i.e. the Egyptians and Israelis, marginally less implausible, but this consideration was almost certainly not in Eden's mind in early September.

On 12 and 13 September Suez was again debated in Parliament. Dulles's remark about not shooting came through on the second day. Gaitskell and Labour with a few Conservative voices in support, pressed the Prime Minister to promise not to use force without reference to the UNO. In the Cabinet Butler was in favour of doing so but Macmillan was against. Eden compromised. He refused to accept Gaitskell's doctrine, and declined to give any absolute pledge, but he said that he would not use force without reference to the Security Council except in an emergency. This came near to saying that force would not be used simply to 'internationalize' the canal, but only if Nasser took some sort of further action or if a new crisis arose. Gaitskell nevertheless pressed the matter to a division and thus ineptly masked the extent of Eden's climb down.

On 22 September Eden decided, despite Selwyn Lloyd's misgivings and Dulles's disapproval, to refer the Suez question to the Security Council which agreed to consider it on 5 October. Meanwhile, the inaugural meeting of SCUA had taken place four days earlier. It soon became bogged down in futilities. On 2 October Dulles made an even more damaging remark than he had on 13 September about 'shooting through'. He referred to talk about the teeth having been drawn from SCUA: 'I know of no teeth; there were no teeth in it so far as I am aware.' In the same press conference he said that America could not identify itself 100 per cent with either 'the colonial powers' or the powers uniquely concerned with obtaining independence. There would, he hoped, always be close treaty relations between the US, the UK and France in the North Atlantic but in areas concerned with 'the problem of so-called colonialism', the US would be found 'playing a somewhat independent role'.

It may well be that these remarks were the last straw for Eden. Negotiation was clearly getting nowhere, and on 14 October Russia vetoed even the rather anodyne resolution which Selwyn Lloyd had extracted from the Security Council. The 'hawks' in the Conservative party led by Macmillan had become increasingly vociferous and the party conference on 13 and 14 October supported a strong line. Moreover, the forces and equipment mobilized could not be kept on ice for ever, and it was believed that the weather would prohibit an assault any later than the end of October. On the other hand, recourse to war was by now certain to meet strong opposition from the Labour Party and create misgivings among the Cabinet 'doves'; Monckton and Macleod, with Butler hovering somewhat ambiguously above

them. It would also be opposed by most of the Commonwealth, and, if words meant anything, by the American
administration too.

At some moment in the first half of October, Eden became
converted to a fourth option besides those of surrender,
negotiation or overt war. This was the French proposal to
play the Israeli card; the Israelis were increasingly alarmed at
the Soviet-aided build-up of arms in Syria and Egypt and
enraged by the Egyptian raids across the Sinai frontier. The
French plan was to use the pretext of a long contemplated
pre-emptive strike by Israel against Egypt in order to intervene along the Suez Canal. The excuse would be 'to separate
the combatants', and thus preserve the Suez Canal from the
interruption created by an Egyptian–Israeli war. Whether or
not Eden had received earlier intimations of the plan, the first
day when we know that it was put to him was 14 October. At
Chequers he and Anthony Nutting met General Challe and
Albert Gazier (representing the French Foreign Minister)
who brought with them a clear-cut proposal. Nutting, conscious of the Foreign Office's policy of good relations with
the Arabs, was deeply alarmed but Eden was enthusiastic; he
summoned Lloyd back from America and flew off with him to
Paris two days later for discussions so secret that even the top
officials and ambassadors were excluded.

The French proposal had two advantages. It provided the
new situation needed to justify military intervention after the
long period of inaction since the end of July. It also had the
appearance of preserving peace – 'separating the combatants', 'preventing the spread of a forest fire', and so on. The
occupation of the canal could be presented as a necessary
by-product of this process, whereas what an unnamed minister called 'the straight bash',[5] i.e. an operation designed
simply to take control of the canal, would at this stage look
like an act of aggression – provoked aggression no doubt but
aggression all the same. But the plan also had a major snag. It
involved close collaboration between the Israelis and the
French government which was in effect egging Israel on to

attack Egypt. This collaboration now had at least the connivance of the British Cabinet. It is one thing to separate the
combatants, quite another to do so when you have made no
attempt to stop the anticipated battle from beginning and
have actually encouraged the outbreak of hostilities.
However, it might have been possible for the British Cabinet
to pretend plausibly that Israeli intervention when it occurred
had come as a surprise to them, but for a crucial matter of
military logistics.

The Anglo-French intervention made no sense unless
there was some sort of threat to the canal, but the Israelis had
no reason, as far as their own interests were concerned, to go
anywhere near it. Their main objective was to eliminate
guerrilla or terrorist bases in Sinai. If they were to advance
towards the canal it was essential to knock out the Egyptian
Air Force. The Israelis were desperately short of planes.
There was not only the risk to their troops of advancing
across the desert without air cover but the possibility of Egypt
bombing their cities. Neither France nor Israel had the
means of 'taking out' the Egyptian Air Force. Britain alone of
the three powers could do so. But of course the plausibility of
being taken by surprise would be much diminished if the
affair began with a drastic British attack on Egypt's airfields.

On 18 October the Cabinet was informed – or at any rate
partly informed – about the plan agreed in Paris two days
before. But on 21 October Ben Gurion, the Israeli Prime
Minister, sent a message via Paris in which he made British
collaboration a *sine qua non* and insisted on direct talks. Eden
could have said no at this stage. Instead he sent Lloyd to
negotiate. It was a crucial turning point. On 22 October
Lloyd, in conditions of extreme secrecy, met Pineau first on
his own, then with Ben Gurion, Dayan and Peres, at a villa in
Sèvres. He reported next day to the Cabinet. Pineau flew to
London soon after, no doubt to steam up Lloyd who did not
seem too keen on the plan. Eden, however, persuaded him,
and it was agreed to have further talks at Sèvres. Lloyd was
tied by parliamentary business and Britain was represented by

Sir Patrick Dean, deputy under-secretary at the Foreign Office. A contingency plan was discussed and a 'record' was made of the discussion. It has never been published, but enough is known from Ben Gurion's diary and other sources to give an idea of its gist. The Israelis promised to take no action against Jordan. There seems no doubt that 29 October was named as the date of the Israeli attack, and that, on British insistence, it was agreed that the assault should seem to threaten the canal. A British air strike against Egypt was the *quid pro quo*, and only twelve hours were to be given for the ultimatum to both sides to withdraw from the Canal Zone while Anglo-French troops occupied it – peacefully if the ultimatum was accepted, forcibly if not. The date of 29 October was almost certainly chosen because it was believed – wrongly in the event – that the run-up to the presidential election on 6 November would preclude Eisenhower, on account of the Jewish vote, from taking strong action. The 'record' is alleged to have become an 'agreement' on 25 October when Eden after what seems to have been the decisive meeting of the Cabinet sent a letter to Mollet confirming that Britain would take the action proposed, and Mollet passed a copy on to Ben Gurion. On 27 October Israeli mobilization began, and on the evening of 29 October Israeli forces crossed the Sinai frontier. Next day at 4.30 P.M. Eden and Mollet sent the planned ultimatum. The Israelis predictably refused. Meanwhile, the Anglo-French expedition had already set out on its slow course towards Port Said.

4

The British system of government is ill-suited to 'conspir-acies' – and this was a conspiracy, even if inspired by sincere belief in the national interest. Apart from the Cabinet, the Chiefs of Staff and some of their planners, along with a very few top members of the Civil and Diplomatic Services, the government 'machine' was taken wholly by surprise. British ambassadors including those in Paris, Cairo and Moscow knew nothing officially in advance. As for Washington, whether by accident or design, there was no ambassador present. The normal parliamentary convention of taking the leaders of the opposition into the Prime Minister's confidence was ignored. Eden informed Gaitskell of the ultimatum only a quarter of an hour before its delivery, and never hinted that the Israeli attack was anything but a surprise.

The sea-borne landings were not due to take place until 6 November. The armada from Malta 1,000 miles away could steam only at the speed of its slowest vessels – landing craft incapable of exceeding five knots. This involved an eight-day voyage, and it meant that the air-borne descent on Port Said could not begin before 5 November. Meanwhile, on French insistence Eden ordered the bombers to attack from the night of 31 October/1 November onwards and the operation was completely successful.

A diplomatic and political row of the first magnitude now blew up. At Westminster the Labour Party was furious. Gaitskell, inheritor of the Gladstonian tradition of moralistic internationalism, denounced the government and appealed to dissident Conservatives to overthrow it, but Butler and Monckton, the only figures of the stature to lead such a revolt, swallowed their doubts. There were scenes in the House of Commons unparalleled since the Home Rule controversy of 1912–14. Yet the government survived and paradoxically the more obviously its policy had failed the more popular it became. By 14 November when the whole venture was in palpable disarray, a Gallup poll showed that Labour had lost its previous six-point lead over the Conservatives.

The American reaction was much more hostile than Eden or his colleagues seem to have expected. In the United Nations America's influence was thrown heavily against Britain and France, and the two countries twice had to use their power to veto resolutions. The general reaction of the Commonwealth countries was scarcely less hostile, though Australia and New Zealand supported Britain. A complicating factor was the Russian invasion of Hungary where an anti-communist revolution had been gathering strength for several weeks. The Russians intervened in force on 24 October. It is therefore not true that the Suez crisis provided them with 'cover', for it did not blow up till a week later. Nevertheless, Suez did to some extent distract the world from the far worse example of naked aggression in Hungary.

The Anglo-French air-borne forces duly landed near Port Said on Monday, 5 November followed by a sea-borne attack twenty-four hours later. Egyptian resistance was negligible, and there was no military obstacle to the occupation of the whole length of the canal. Nevertheless, as a result of great American pressure, the exact nature of which has not been revealed, Eden agreed to a cease-fire at midnight on 6 November and forced Mollet to agree also. The pressure partly took the form of massive sales of sterling in New York but there were steps which Britain could have been taking to minimize the consequences, and it may be that other sanctions were threatened. Whatever the truth Macmillan, who had been a 'hawk' hitherto, decided as Chancellor of the Exchequer that Britain could not afford to go on. There was also the difficulty that Britain's ostensible objective – to separate the combatants – had now been met and the fighting had stopped, though the canal itself was obstructed from end to end by ships sunk on Nasser's orders.

Eisenhower insisted on complete Anglo-French withdrawal, refused to allow Britain or France to unblock the canal and forbade them to take any part in the United Nations peace-keeping force which was being set up to police the Egypt–Israel frontier. His anger is understandable. Although in the event he won his election, the Suez affair had occurred at the most inconvenient moment possible and might have been very damaging. Moreover, he must soon have realized the astonishing duplicity practised by the British government, for there can be no doubt that Eden and Lloyd lied on a massive scale. The French being more cynical scarcely bothered to conceal the extent of their collusion with Israel and the real objectives of the expedition. The British combined humbug with deceit to a degree calculated to infuriate any ally. It is remarkable that Eisenhower made no public use of the knowledge which he soon acquired about Britain's relations with France and Israel.

The parliamentary scene became ever more chaotic. Labour was in a high state of moral outrage and rightly suspected the government of lying. Some Conservatives did also, and two junior ministers, Anthony Nutting and Edward Boyle resigned. But the majority sentiment of the party was not one of moral disapprobation, rather of bewilderment and, as time went on, indignation at Eden's failure to defy the Americans and occupy the whole of the canal. Exactly why he failed to do so remains to this day one of the many unanswered questions in the Suez imbroglio. Eden had been a sick man throughout the crisis, and on 21 November announced that his doctors had ordered him abroad for his health; he departed two days later to Jamaica to stay with Ian and Anne Fleming, causing consternation to his supporters. Butler acted as Prime Minister in his absence but he was not destined to be Eden's successor. On 9 January 1957 Eden announced his resignation to his colleagues on grounds of health.

The Conservative Party at that time had no machinery for electing its leader when the party was in power. It was not till 1965 that a system was devised by Sir Alec Douglas-Home. The choice of a successor to Eden lay with the Queen but it was understood that she would take the advice of the Party. Lords Salisbury and Kilmuir who being peers could not be contenders of the premiership[6] acted as assessors and interviewed each Cabinet Minister separately in the Privy Council offices. Their advice was heavily in favour of Macmillan rather than Butler whose equivocation over Suez and reputation for indecision had lowered his stock. They also saw the Chief Whip, Edward Heath, and the Chairman of the Conservative Party Organization and the 1922 Committee who confirmed this opinion though Parliament was not sitting. Lord Salisbury conveyed their collective advice to the Queen. Churchill too decided that it was his duty to advise the Queen, and favoured Macmillan. Contrary to many accounts including Macmillan's, she also consulted Eden. His advice is not known and could not have settled the matter, but it is a safe guess that he did not recommend Butler. In effect Macmillan was elected by the Cabinet – the first and probably last Prime Minister to be chosen in this way. (When George IV suggested the same method in 1827, Sir Robert Peel said it was unconstitutional.) After a quiet morning in perusal of *Pride and Prejudice* he was summoned to Buckingham Palace at two o'clock. The media, as usual out of touch with Conservative opinion, were taken entirely by surprise, but there was nothing surprising about it to those who moved in politics.

Chapter Nineteen

THE ASCENDANCY OF MACMILLAN

I

The situation which Macmillan inherited could hardly have looked blacker. When he first became Prime Minister he told the Queen that he could not be sure of surviving six weeks. She reminded him of this at an audience six years later. It was widely believed that the Conservatives would be out for the next twenty years. Most politicians and commentators thought that Macmillan had no chance of winning the next general election, let alone doing so by a much increased majority. They reckoned without the strange vicissitudes of politics, and perhaps did not understand the personality of the new Prime Minister. Macmillan, a curious and compli-cated character, had the strength of steel behind the façade of an Edwardian clubman. In many ways he resembled his hero Disraeli, though Disraeli unlike Macmillan was never 'clubb-able'. Both were brilliant actors with a flair for showmanship. Both were thinkers. Both led their party from left of centre but both had the knack of speaking in a right-wing tone of voice at the correct psychological moment. Like Disraeli, Macmillan, though in reality nervous and highly strung, had the gift of appearing cool and 'unflappable' in a crisis. 'Quiet, calm, deliberation disentangles every knot' was the notice he had hung on the door between the Cabinet room and the office of the private secretaries. Again like Disraeli, though unlike Eden, he believed in delegation and non-interference. The febrile atmosphere of the previous government quickly evaporated.

His first task was to form the Cabinet. He made few

changes. Butler would have liked the Foreign Office but he had to accept the Home Office instead. Macmillan had no intention of apologizing for Suez by moving Selwyn Lloyd. Peter Thorneycroft became Chancellor of the Exchequer, Duncan Sandys, Minister of Defence. Macmillan's second task was to establish his dominance both in the Cabinet and the House. This would not in itself guarantee electoral victory but if he failed in those two bodies defeat was certain. He had no problem with the Cabinet. When Lord Salisbury sent a letter of resignation at the end of March because of the decision to release Makarios from the Seychelles, Macmillan promptly accepted. He shrugged the matter off just as he was to do nine months later when the whole Treasury team resigned.

The House was less easy to deal with but Macmillan was well aware that if he controlled it, confidence would spread first to the party faithful and, if all went well, to the nation as a whole. He appreciated the importance of parliamentary oratory, and took immense trouble with his speeches. He had one important asset. Suez, on which the opposition harped too much for their own good, was a British setback which the mass of the public wanted to forget; it was a débâcle but there was a general feeling that, if Eden had erred, he had erred in the right direction. The harm done was not as great as opponents alleged. Petrol rationing imposed by the temporary closure of the canal soon ended. Britain would have to accept Nasser's terms for passage. This was a humiliation but most people blamed Washington. At this time Anglo-American relations were worse than at any moment in the post-war years. Macmillan, who knew Eisenhower well, was in a good position to repair the breach. He had the advantage over Eden of not being personally involved in deceiving him or Dulles. At Eisenhower's own request a conference was held at Bermuda late in March. No significant decisions were made but conversations were conducted in a relaxed atmosphere of friendly candour. The Americans too may well have wished to bury Suez. Their behaviour towards an old ally

381

confronted by an act of international brigandage had been far from blameless, whatever the faults on the other side.

Three important parliamentary debates took place in April and May. In the first on 1 April Macmillan, who was generally expected to be fighting for his life, turned the tables on Gaitskell. He brushed Suez aside and concentrated on the continuation of nuclear tests – an issue which deeply divided the Labour Party. The second on 17 April concerned the new Defence Paper, and once again the Prime Minister dominated the debate. On 16 May came what Macmillan called 'the canal turn'. He had to announce surrender to Nasser and face a motion skilfully worded to attract left-wing opponents as well as the Suez Group. After an indifferent opening speech he wound up the debate with a triumph which exposed Labour dissension and killed the Suez Group. The government won easily and the group faded into history. Gaitskell henceforth dropped the subject. It played no part in the 1959 election. By his triumph in the last of these debates Macmillan had ensured the survival of his government. He had also gone some way to establish his personal ascendancy both in the House and the Conservative Party.

The debate on 17 April led to one of the biggest revolutions ever achieved in defence policy during peacetime. Macmillan had given Sandys a very free hand. The cost of 'conventional' defence was widely regarded as excessive. Aided by Eisenhower's decision to deploy a number of intermediate range nuclear missiles in Britain, Sandys was able to set in train a process which greatly lowered expenditure and made possible the abolition of conscription in 1960. It involved reducing the British forces on the Rhine from 77,000 to 64,000 and the total manpower of the armed services from 690,000 to about 375,000. On 15 May the first British hydrogen bomb was exploded. Britain henceforth depended heavily on nuclear weapons – a decision which has shaped defence policy ever since.

The economic situation improved during the first half of the year despite pressure on sterling at the beginning, and a series of disputes in the motor, railway, shipping and engineering industries. Thorneycroft was able to bring in a budget with some modest tax concessions. Industrial troubles persuaded the government to set up in the summer an independent Council on Prices, Productivity and Incomes. Its trio of members was called 'The Three Wise Men'. Their powers were persuasive only – the first of many unsuccessful attempts to encourage voluntary wage restraint. Macmillan continued to be worried about inflation. On 20 July he made a speech at Bedford on this theme, but he used a phrase which was later jerked out of context to discredit him as a complacent materialist. 'Let's be frank about it; most of our people have never had it so good.' He was merely giving a fact about the standard of living and a warning about the difficulty of maintaining it.

The balance of payments deteriorated during the next few weeks. There was increasing pressure on the pound. The TUC repudiated wage restraint on the motion of Frank Cousins, head of the TGWU (Transport and General Workers' Union). He was one of the first post-war leaders of a major trades union to abandon compromise for confrontation. He soon replaced Bevan as the leading figure in Conservative demonology. The Treasury pressed for a drastic rise in the bank rate to stem the run on the reserves. The Prime Minister reluctantly acquiesced in an increase on 19 September from five to seven per cent which in the circumstances of the time was sensational. The medicine seemed to work but Macmillan did not like it. He was by instinct against deflation. He was haunted by memories of unemployment in the north country where he had been MP for Stockton in the 1920s, the place from which he was to take his belated title as an Earl on his ninetieth birthday. It may be that he was oversensitive on this matter in the very different climate of the 1950s. He was an admirer of Keynes whose books his firm had published and much influenced by Sir Roy Harrod, the eminent economist and Keynes's biographer. He was not going to yield readily again. There was one curious by-product of the change in the bank rate. Harold Wilson fastened on a rumour that Oliver Poole, the Party Chairman, had obtained advance knowledge from Thorneycroft of the rise and might have made improper use of it. After much debate during the autumn a judicial inquiry was held under the Tribunals Act. It reported on 21 January 1958. Poole was fully vindicated and so was the Chancellor of the Exchequer. The alleged bank rate 'leak' was shown up as a *canard*.

Long before this Poole had ceased to be chairman. Macmillan was alarmed at the fall of the Conservative barometer in the opinion polls. Poole was an administrator rather than an orator. Macmillan replaced him by Lord Hailsham, a born showman if ever there was one. The media were fascinated at the party conference in Brighton in October 1957 to meet a chairman who bathed every morning before breakfast with the maximum of publicity and opened proceedings by ringing a large bell. The delegates enjoyed this unexpected atmosphere of 'ballyhoo', and, whether or not it was cause and effect, the Conservative rating which had slumped heavily after the decision to raise the bank rate recovered some four points.

Early in the new year the battle between the Treasury and the Prime Minister came to a head. Thorneycroft spurred on by his two junior ministers, Enoch Powell and Nigel Birch, insisted that in line with the restrictions on public investment and bank advances, the following year's estimates should not be higher in cash terms than the current year's. This meant lower estimates in real terms and some painful cuts in social expenditure – in particular the abolition of the second child allowance. Macmillan was strongly against what he regarded as an unduly rigid approach and reckoned that Treasury estimates were usually wrong anyway. The Cabinet backed him. On 6 January after an acid and lengthy exchange of letters the entire Treasury team resigned and Derick Heathcoat Amory, the Minister of Agriculture, took Thorneycroft's place. Macmillan on the verge of an empire tour contrasted 'the wider vision of the Commonwealth' with 'these little local difficulties'.

His insouciance could not conceal the adverse effect on the party. Its popularity plummeted as badly as it had after the rise in the bank rate. Labour, moreover, had moved into calmer waters since Bevan, realizing that he could neither succeed nor topple Gaitskell, had decided to bury the hatchet. He repudiated nuclear disarmament, declaring that a British Prime Minister could not 'go naked into the conference chamber', and he worked hard for a compromise on nationalization. The Labour conference in October 1957 displayed an abnormal harmony. Before the end of the year Bevan and Gaitskell had each actually invited the other to lunch – 'really decisive events', wrote Crossman, 'in the life of these two men who have never had a drink with each other much less a meal in their whole lives'.[1] A price was paid for consensus. The resultant declarations of policy were so carefully drafted in order to spare sensitivities that they tended to be very dull. In the words of a journalist quoted by Philip Williams they made as much public impact as 'a jellyfish dropped from a fifth-floor window'.[2] However, it was something to have a degree of political unity which Labour had not enjoyed for many years.

The early part of 1958 saw further Conservative setbacks. At a by-election at Rochdale in February which Labour held they came in a bad third well behind the Liberals. At Kelvingrove in Glasgow, Walter Elliot's widow lost the seat vacated by her husband's death. At the end of March, just after Macmillan had returned from his Commonwealth tour, the Liberals won Torrington, their first by-election gain in thirty years. The new Chancellor's first budget was a cautious holding operation. The Treasury view that the economy was 'overheated and needed cooling' still prevailed, with its corollary that wages should be prevented from increases beyond those justified by increased productivity, but the report of 'The Three Wise Men' on these matters was stigmatized by Gaitskell as being 'not a scientific report but a

political tract'. There was no consensus on the wages problem then, nor has there been one since. A new bout of strikes
ensued – London busmen, railway workers and dockers.
These were all settled by compromises of one sort or another
before the end of June, the busmen's strike being the most
protracted. The government announced that it would use
troops if vital services were endangered, and outfaced Frank
Cousins's threat of calling out petrol drivers and electricity
workers. At the same time the bank rate was lowered, and the
economic prospect suddenly seemed brighter. In August for
the first time since the autumn of 1955 the Gallup poll gave
the Conservatives a small lead (four per cent). There was
speculation about an early election. Macmillan quashed it on
12 September saying that he would 'put the Opposition out of
their agony'. There is little else to recall on the domestic
front. Although the Conservatives slipped behind Labour in
the winter of 1958–9 the economy continued to boom and
Amory was able to make some striking tax reductions in the
1959 budget including 9d (4p) off the standard rate of income
tax. From then till the election was held in October the
Conservatives enjoyed a steadily increasing lead over Labour.

One constitutional measure of some importance came into
law on 30 April 1958. This was the Life Peerages Act. An
attempt by Palmerston to confer a barony for life had been
overruled by the Committee of Privileges on the ground that
the Royal Prerogative had no power to create anything but
hereditary peerages. The Judicature Act of 1871 conceded
the principle of life peerages but they were confined to a
limited number of judges of high legal eminence. The new
Act put no limitation on numbers or qualification and for the
first time made it possible to create women peers. There can
be no doubt that it gave a boost to what was becoming a
moribund institution, but the problem left in abeyance by the
Preamble to the Parliament Act of 1911, of creating a
rationally based second chamber, remains unsolved, and is
perhaps insoluble.

2

The rulers of England, Conservative and Labour alike, still thought of it as an important international power, a poor third no doubt to the USA and USSR, but, thanks partly to the Commonwealth connection, a cut above all the rest. When Macmillan came to write the memoirs of his premiership he devoted far more space to external than internal affairs. The historian of England should not follow his example but he cannot ignore international events if only because of their effects on home affairs. During 1957 the most important feature was the restoration of good relations with America. It culminated in July 1958 with the repeal of the McMahon Act of 1946 which had vetoed the transmission of atomic secrets to any foreign power and was the reason for Britain constructing her own nuclear bombs. This spirit of goodwill was displayed over Middle Eastern affairs. Early in 1958 Egypt and Syria formed a union which they called the 'United Arab Republic', joined soon after by the Yemen. In reply Jordan and Iraq formed the 'Arab Federation', in theory also a union of the two states. A wave of unrest swept over much of the area. There was trouble in Aden. More seriously, chaos developed in Lebanon. At the request of the Lebanese government American forces were landed at Beirut on 15 July. The day before, a major setback to British interests occurred in Baghdad. King Faisal and Prime Minister Nuri were murdered in barbaric circumstances by a disaffected section of the army. Thus ended the Hashemite monarchy, and Iraq was set upon a course of nationalist authoritarianism which shows no sign of changing. The prospects of the Jordanian monarchy now seemed far from bright, and King Hussein appealed for aid. On 17 July the British government despatched two battalions by air to Amman. Lebanon remained stable and so did Jordan. American troops withdrew from Lebanon on 25 October and the British forces retired from Jordan on 2 November. Several years of relative calm ensued in both countries. Iraq soon opted out of the Baghdad Pact but America joined it, and for the time being the Middle East seemed reasonably tranquil.

Two important changes of leadership among the major powers occurred in 1958. De Gaulle on an ambiguous programme of national rehabilitation was elected President of France under a new constitution which gave him great power. Khrushchev, that 'mixture of Peter the Great and Lord Beaverbrook', as Macmillan described him, became, with Bulganin's retirement, the unchallenged ruler of Russia. Encouraged perhaps by Russia's achievement of putting the first sputnik in orbit on 4 October 1957 the Russian leader adopted a noisy and aggressive posture which changed only after the Cuba episode in the autumn of 1962. Khrushchev's first move was to present an ultimatum on 10 November 1958 demanding the withdrawal of Allied forces within six months from West Berlin which would become a demilitarized free city. This naturally alarmed the German Chancellor, Dr Adenauer; the threat prompted Macmillan's celebrated visit in February 1959 to Moscow wearing a Finnish white fur hat twelve inches high. Much good vodka, bad food (caviare excepted) and worse wine were consumed. There was some plain speaking, and at one stage Khrushchev was so cross that he had an attack of diplomatic toothache. There was discussion of a 'summit' and the foreign ministers had a preparatory meeting on 11 May which came to nothing. In September Khrushchev visited Eisenhower and withdrew the Berlin ultimatum. The summit was fixed for 16 May 1960 in Paris.

One event little noticed in Britain occurred in 1957. On 25 March the six powers which had met at Messina in 1955 signed the Treaty of Rome which would on 1 January 1958 bring into being the European Economic Community (EEC). It was the culmination of negotiations dating from 1950. Britain had missed her chance to be a founding member with all the influence that this might have given her. She would have been welcome at the time but Labour was unsympathetic, Churchill lukewarm and Eden privately hostile. Macmillan could not have done much while Eden was Prime Minister but he could have been less obviously cool towards the project during 1955 while he was Foreign Secretary. When he became Chancellor of the Exchequer he was more concerned with what was called 'Plan G' than adherence to the EEC. This was the idea of a European Free Trade Area (EFTA) for everything except food stuffs which were the stumbling block to British entry into the EEC because of Commonwealth interests. In addition to the Six – France, Germany, Italy, Holland, Belgium and Luxemburg – EFTA would include Britain and another six countries of the OEEC, a total of thirteen. In August 1957 Macmillan appointed Reginald Maudling, one of the more promising young ministers, as a travelling salesman for the plan. Negotiations were prolonged. The agreement of France was essential but on 14 November de Gaulle politely but predictably vetoed the accession of the EEC to EFTA. It was the foretaste of a far greater setback later. There was a short-lived attempt to unite the EFTA countries into a feeble rival to the EEC but it soon expired.

During 1957–9 several steps were taken towards decolonization. The Gold Coast, renamed Ghana, became independent in March 1957. The Malay Federation achieved the same status in August. On 3 January 1958 the short-lived West Indian Federation was inaugurated, and on 3 June 1959 Singapore was given self-government. More important than any of these was the long delayed settlement in Cyprus. British bases were retained and an elaborate power-sharing constitution after seemingly endless haggling was approved by both Turkey and Greece. The agreement was signed on 19 February 1959. Full independence was granted, and the formal transfer of power was made on 15 August 1960. Makarios became the first president and opted to remain within the Commonwealth.

There were two 'colonial' episodes during those years, which caused much trouble to the government, each of them involving the possible resignation of the Minister, Alan

Lennox-Boyd. The first was the so-called 'Hola massacre'. There had been a prolonged rebellion in Kenya by a secret society of the dominant Kikuyu tribe, which was eventually suppressed in 1956. No less than 88,000 men had been detained in custody at one time or another. By 1959 there was a hard core of detainees in special camps. Eleven of these in a camp named Hola died of 'multiple bruising' at the hands of undisciplined prison guards. After the debate on 16 June Lennox-Boyd offered his resignation. It was a scandalous episode but Macmillan took the view that the Colonial Secretary could not be held responsible and talked him out of it.

No sooner had Hola occurred than another African rumpus broke out. In Nyasaland (now Malawi) African nationalists started a campaign of sabotage which obliged Sir Robert Armitage, the governor, to declare a state of emergency on 3 March. In the course of the disorders fifty-two Africans were killed by the security forces. An inquiry headed by Lord Devlin, a distinguished judge, was critical of the Nyasaland government and stigmatized the colony as 'a police state'. It was published on 24 July and debated four days later. Once again the Colonial Secretary offered to resign. This time Macmillan left it to the Cabinet, asking each member in turn. The verdict against resignation was unanimous. In his diary he says that he told them afterwards that he would himself have resigned, had it been different: 'But I had thought it unfair, *before* the decision to offer such a temptation to such a brilliant and properly ambitious set of men as composed the Cabinet.'

Macmillan had to decide early in 1959 on the timing of the general election. He could have held it as late as June 1960 but it is usually regarded as risky to let Parliament run to the limit, and the practical choice was narrowed to June or October 1959. The firm of Colman Prentis and Varley, advertising agents, had been in charge of Conservative publicity since June 1957. Its policy was to emphasize Conservative-claimed achievements, and ignore the Labour

Party. It also ignored the Prime Minister until late in the day when his personal popularity, having at one stage been lower than any Prime Minister's since Neville Chamberlain, suddenly rose. Lord Hailsham, after elaborate consultations, considered that a June election would give the Conservatives a majority of thirteen at best, and advised against it. Macmillan therefore plumped for October. The omens were propitious, and chance helped. Eisenhower had decided, before facing the visit from Khrushchev, to sound the ground in France, Germany and Britain. He appeared on television in August with Macmillan in a relaxed chat which could not have failed to improve the Prime Minister's image as a world statesman. On 7 September Macmillan asked the Queen for a dissolution, election day being 8 October. During the campaign Gaitskell may have made an error in promising extra expenditure on social services and alleging that it could be done without increasing income tax – a blow to his credibility. Macmillan never put a foot wrong and made a brilliant pre-recorded television performance on the eve of the poll. The Conservatives won easily. Their final score was 365 seats to Labour's 258 and the Liberals' 6. Their share of the popular vote was 13,749,830 (49.4 per cent) to Labour's 12,215,538 (43.8 per cent). It was the first time since 1865 that a party had won a majority in three successive elections by a larger margin on each occasion. A gigantic boom on the Stock Exchange ensued and there was a general atmosphere of euphoria among the possessing classes. Foolish commentators talked, as in 1945, of a one-party system for the foreseeable future – though a different party. Macmillan was too old a hand to be carried away, simply confiding to his diary 'it has all gone off rather well' and stating at a press conference his belief in 'the fundamental unity of our people'.

3

Macmillan made few immediate changes in the Cabinet. The most important vacancy was at the Colonial Office. Lennox-Boyd had indicated long before the election that he wished to retire from politics and would not stand again for Parliament. In his place Macmillan appointed the Minister of Labour, Iain Macleod, and Edward Heath succeeded Macleod. The appointment of Macleod was significant. Here was someone well to the left of centre in the Conservative spectrum occupying the position which was bound to come under the heaviest fire from the right. Macleod's objective which had Macmillan's full support was to apply to Africa the same policy of decolonization which had been followed in Asia. This was bound to be a painful process for the traditional party of empire.

The investment boom which followed the general election showed signs of 'overheating the economy', as the jargon of the day had it. In January the bank rate was again raised, though again with much reluctance on the part of the Prime Minister. It rose from four to five per cent. In April 1960 Amory introduced his last budget, a neutral compromise between the disinflationary wishes of the Chancellor and the Bank of England, and the optimism of the Prime Minister. 'A gentle squeeze may be right,' Macmillan wrote to the Chancellor of the Exchequer, 'but it cannot be sensible to cheer the economy on vigorously one moment and push it back violently the next.' In June the squeeze was slightly tightened by a further rise in the bank rate to six per cent. The Chancellor had been persuaded to stay till after the election only by strong pressure from Macmillan. Amory was determined to retire in the summer of 1960. This meant a major reconstruction of the Cabinet which was announced on 27 July. Selwyn Lloyd became Chancellor of the Exchequer. Lord Home, despite Labour protests at a peer occupying the position, became Foreign Secretary, Butler having refused.

Duncan Sandys succeeded Home at the Commonwealth Office. Macmillan brought back both Thorneycroft and Powell, the former as Minister of Aviation, the latter as Minister of Health.

For the next year the economy seemed reasonably buoyant. The Conservatives continued to be well ahead of Labour in the opinion polls until August 1961. No doubt they were helped by the widely publicized rifts in the Labour Party. Bevan died in July 1960 and his death exacerbated the situation. There were two major subjects of dispute – nationalization and unilateral nuclear disarmament. Gaitskell would have been happy to ditch nationalization enshrined in Clause 3(a) (usually called Clause 4) of the party constitution but he recognized that he would lose and so he compromised. On nuclear disarmament he was determined to fight. He was defeated at the 1960 Labour Conference in Scarborough. He proclaimed that he would 'fight and fight and fight again' to reverse it. Luckily for him two major unions changed their previous attitude in the same arbitrary and incalculable way in which they had originally adopted it. At Blackpool in October 1961 Gaitskell won handsomely. Already Conservative popularity was on the slide. As so often before and after, the balance of payments was in deficit. In April 1961 Selwyn Lloyd introduced a counter-inflationary budget. Although he raised the starting rate of surtax from its now obviously absurd level of £2,000 p.a. to £5,000, he imposed a 'payroll tax' and levied a surcharge on purchase tax. In July he announced cuts in public expenditure and put up the bank rate from five to seven per cent. Pointing out that wages had increased by eight per cent and productivity by only three per cent in the past year, he declared that 'there must be a pause until productivity has caught up'. His measures fended off the incipient sterling crisis but were very unpopular. The government could not directly affect wages in the private sector without special legislation but it engaged in a series of confrontations with the public sector unions – school-teachers, post office employees, railwaymen in the London underground. In August, Labour for the first time since the election took the lead over the Conservatives in the opinion polls and remained clearly ahead, though by varying margins, for the next three years. In March 1962 the Conservatives suffered a major setback at a by-election in Orpington though not at the hands of Labour. The Liberals won this hitherto safe seat with a rise of thirty-one per cent in votes. The 'pay pause' was the first attempt of many at an 'incomes policy'. None has succeeded. The institutions established in order to gain cooperation from both sides of industry achieved little. The National Economic Development Council (NEDC) set up in the spring of 1962, though described by Macmillan as an important and valuable part of our national machinery, has been little more than a talking shop. The Economic Committee of the TUC agreed to join on condition that it was not expected to preach wage-restraint to its affiliated unions, thus avoiding the only question that mattered. The National Incomes Commission adumbrated by the Prime Minister on 26 July of the same year was boycotted by the TUC. Efforts to placate that body were futile. A capital gains tax which, owing to inflation, soon turned into a capital levy was introduced in the 1962 budget as a gesture. As Macmillan himself says: 'The capitalist class was annoyed; the unions were not impressed.'

By the early summer the Prime Minister found himself more and more out of harmony with the Chancellor of the Exchequer who was giving, in his opinion, no real lead in the matter of an incomes policy. The 'pay pause' now coming to an end had only applied in practice to public employees – and not to all of them. How could it be extended to the private sector? But if it was not, how could the four objectives – full employment, stable prices, a favourable balance of payments and economic expansion – ever be obtained? They never have been, and the problem is with us still. But Macmillan saw a personal barrier in the form of a tired and not very cooperative Chancellor of the Exchequer. He decided to dismiss Lloyd. But he also decided – and, as he admitted in his memoirs, it was a major error – to combine the dismissal of the Chancellor with a major reconstruction of the Cabinet. It may have been desirable but it should have been left till later. The purge occurred on 14 July and involved the removal of a third of the Cabinet in circumstances so abrupt and peremptory as to leave lasting grievances. It looked like panic and perhaps it was. In addition to Selwyn Lloyd he dismissed Lord Kilmuir (the Lord Chancellor), Lord Mills (Paymaster General), Harold Watkinson (Minister of Defence), David Eccles (Minister of Education), Charles Hill (Minister of Housing) and J. S. Maclay (Scottish Office). Maudling who had succeeded Macleod at the Colonial Office (see below) now became Chancellor of the Exchequer, Thorneycroft went to Defence, Keith Joseph to Housing, Edward Boyle to Education, and the Colonial and Commonwealth Offices were united under Duncan Sandys. The 'July massacre' gave great offence within the Conservative Party, though a Labour vote of censure was easily defeated. The replacement of a much respected Lord Chancellor by the not very distinguished Attorney General, Sir Reginald Manningham Buller, caused particular disapproval.

In external affairs the government had also run into much trouble. Hopes for a successful summit meeting between Eisenhower, Khrushchev, de Gaulle, Adenauer and Macmillan in Paris in May 1960 had foundered with the shooting down over Russia of an American reconnaissance plane on 1 May. Eisenhower with naïve folly admitted that the flight was made with his knowledge and permission. The Russians broke up the conference. This seemed a setback at the time but summit conferences are just as likely to make things worse as better. So perhaps it did not matter. Meanwhile, Russian behaviour over Berlin, the Congo and many other trouble spots became more and more aggressive.

Throughout Macmillan's premiership there was the recurring theme of nuclear weapons. He was most anxious to negotiate a ban on atmospheric test explosions and eventually this was achieved in 1963. Even more difficult was the question of Britain's own nuclear weapons. Here the government had to face two problems, one public, one confidential. The public problem was the rising popular distaste for Britain possessing these horrific weapons at all. The early 1960s saw the heyday of the Campaign for Nuclear Disarmament (CND) which then went strangely into quiescence, only to be revived some twenty years later as inexplicably as it had faded out. This dispute was politically far more damaging to Labour who were divided than to the Conservatives.

But the question was, what sort of deterrent? Was it to be 'Blue Steel', an air-to-ground guided missile which could be propelled a long distance in advance (at least 200 miles) by RAF bombers? It was clear in the late 1950s that eventually something with an even longer range from a less vulnerable platform would be needed, and the government spent some £60 million developing a ground-to-ground missile called 'Blue Streak'. The trouble was that it fired from a fixed land site and there was increasing public agitation against this. Moreover, there was now a good prospect of eventually using submarines for this purpose, though 'Polaris' had not yet been fully developed. To make 'Blue Streak' effective another £500 million would have to be spent on rockets. On 24 February 1960 the Defence Committee of the Cabinet decided to cut its losses, abandon 'Blue Streak' and try to acquire 'Polaris' from America in due course. Meanwhile, the use of RAF bombers could be continued for many years by acquiring 'Skybolt'. This was a new air-to-ground missile being developed in America. It was superior to 'Blue Steel' in that it fired a rocket high into the atmosphere like a ground missile. Eisenhower agreed legally and formally to supply 'Skybolt'. In return the British Cabinet undertook to make a base available in Scotland for 'Polaris'. Informally Eisenhower also agreed that, if anything went wrong with 'Skybolt', Britain should have 'Polaris' and there the matter rested for the moment.

4

During the early 1960s the principal steps in 'decolonization' took place in Africa, the last remaining stronghold of British rule. These occurred at a speed which took most people by surprise and provoked bitter resentment in a section of the Conservative Party led by Lord Salisbury. The theory behind British colonialism had, it is true, always been that British rule was a preparation for indigenous self-government, but this acceleration, positively encouraged by Macmillan and Macleod, was, as Sir Nigel Fisher puts it in his life of the former, 'so radical that it amounted in practice to a change of policy', although Macmillan with characteristic appreciation of style as well as content never announced it as such.[3] Indeed, he accompanied it with enough right-wing noises to placate the backbenchers, rather like Disraeli during the debates on the Reform Act of 1867.

What was the reason for this revolution which was in no sense a part of his 'mandate' in 1959? Macmillan was greatly impressed by a conversation which he records in his memoirs with an experienced colonial governor.[4] Were the African leaders ready for freedom? he asked. To which the governor replied: 'Oh no, of course they are not ready for it.' 'When will they be ready?' 'Oh in perhaps fifteen or twenty years . . .' 'What then would you advise?' 'I should give it to them at once – as soon as possible.' And the governor explained that if the leaders of African opinion were willing to spend fifteen years learning the job, then he would be all for delay. But in practice they would not be. They would agitate and rebel. 'I will have to put them in prison. There they will learn nothing about administration, only about hatred and revenge . . . so I say, give them independence now.'

A conversation however interesting does not by itself explain the matter. The truth was that nationalism, the most powerful political force in the world during the last two centuries, having first transformed the map of Europe, then

397

of South America and then of Asia, had now reached Africa. Macmillan made a tour of some of the British dependencies on the continent and of the Dominion of South Africa early in 1960. At a state banquet in Accra he referred to 'the wind of change blowing through Africa'. It was a phrase first used by Lord Home and it attracted no special attention in Ghana. In Salisbury he issued an even plainer warning when he said: 'In all parts of this continent the tide of nationalism is flowing fast.' Then in Cape Town he addressed both Houses of Parliament and repeated the phrase about 'the wind of change'. This time it caused a sensation and made headlines in the world press. Right-wing Tories at once saw its implications. They founded the Monday Club in protest – to commemorate 'Black Monday', 3 February, the day on which the speech was made.

Macmillan had become convinced that the leisurely programme envisaged by the Colonial Office would no longer do – a view fully shared by Labour and Liberals. Hola and the Nyasaland troubles had demonstrated even before the election the disagreeable repercussions of African discontent on British politics. It was not that the government had lost its nerve or felt incapable of sustaining British rule. On the contrary, ministers were well aware that it could be preserved for many more years – at a price. Portugal, far weaker than Britain, managed to hang on to Angola and Mozambique till 1974. But why pay the price? Anyone of sense could see that the newly liberated territories would be worse governed than they were under the colonial regime, but this was their affair. Britain had no strategic or economic reasons for continuing to spend money and men on ruling mutinous peoples who only wanted to see the last of them. Decolonization was not the product of cowardice or altruism, rather of enlightened self-interest.

The transfer of power was comparatively easy in western Africa. No indigenous European society had established itself in the insalubrious areas long believed to be 'the white man's grave'. The climate in Tanganyika and Uganda was not so unhealthy but the same situation prevailed and there were few settlers. Ghana had already secured independence in 1957, Nigeria achieved the same status in 1960, Tanganyika (rechristened Tanzania) in 1961 and Uganda in 1962. But in the relatively cool and healthy highlands of Kenya, Nyasaland and the two Rhodesias it was a different story, and different in each place. In Kenya there was a substantial English ascendancy class engaged in farming and business, but juridically the country was a crown colony governed by a real Governor and took orders from the Colonial Office in Whitehall. The Kenyan whites would have had to stage a far more drastic rebellion than Ian Smith if they sought UDI, and they made no such attempt. After prolonged negotiations Kenya became independent under a black government in 1963.

Northern Rhodesia and Nyasaland were also crown colonies but their situation was complicated by their membership, along with Southern Rhodesia, of the Central African Federation created in 1953 with a constitution almost as elaborate as that of medieval Venice or seventeenth-century Holland. Southern Rhodesia's status was unique and quite unlike that of any other part of the Commonwealth. It had acquired in 1923 'responsible government'. In practice this meant that the white settlers, who were thicker on the ground than anywhere else in the Continent except South Africa, and amounted by 1960 to one in twelve of the population, had virtual autonomy based on a franchise which excluded all but a handful of Africans. But it was not complete autonomy. The UK government had a veto on some things particularly with regard to the franchise. There was a further complication. The Southern Rhodesian government dealt with the Commonwealth Office, as did the Federal government, whereas the governments of Northern Rhodesia and Nyasaland were controlled by the Colonial Office. Since the two departments had been at loggerheads for years and their political heads, Macleod and Sandys, were anything but friendly, the decolonization of Central Africa was bound to be difficult. Sir Roy Welensky, the pugilistic Prime Minister of the Federation, was unlikely to make it any easier. He had close links with the Tory right, and he was prepared to fight.

It was a losing battle. The African nationalist leaders in the two northern territories (Kenneth Kaunda in Northern Rhodesia, Hastings Banda in Nyasaland) were bitterly opposed to the Federation which they regarded as a manifestation of white sub-imperialism based on Salisbury. After some hesitation the Africans of Southern Rhodesia followed suit. Even before he left for his African tour, Macmillan had set up a Royal Commission to investigate the problem, headed by Walter Monckton. At Welensky's insistence its terms of reference excluded the possibility of secession by any of the territories. For this reason Gaitskell vetoed Labour participation. The commission reported in October 1960. Meanwhile there had been much rioting and violence throughout the three territories. To Welensky's justified fury the commission, among many far more complicated recommendations – about the franchise, the colour bar, the distribution of functions – suggested that in certain circumstances secession might be allowed. There is no doubt that a promise had been broken. But Welensky's claim that it sounded the death knell of the Federation is an exaggeration. It was dead already – from the moment in July 1960 when Nyasaland was given a constitution which ensured an African majority on its Legislative Council. This meant that one territory would certainly secede and Northern Rhodesia could hardly be denied the same right. The only alternative was to preserve the Federation by armed force.

There is no need to dwell on the complex negotiations about the Northern and Southern Rhodesian franchises, or – still more ephemeral – that of the Federation itself. The background of increasing chaos in the abruptly decolonized Belgian Congo (Zaire) should not be forgotten when one judges the white reaction to proposals for majority rule. Nor should the personality of Macleod be ignored. He was perhaps too keen on decolonization for his own good. He

inspired deep distrust in the white community which commanded a formidable lobby in London. Added to this was the
curious alliance between Lord Salisbury, head of one of the
grandest families in England, and Sir Roy Welensky of mixed
Polish, Jewish and Afrikaaner descent, who had fought his way
from nothing to the top. The issue was further complicated by
the attempted secession of Tshombe's Katanga from the
Congo supported by Welensky and by the Union Miniere, the
giant Belgian company in which a British firm, Tanganyika
Concessions (known in the City as 'Tanks'), had a substantial
interest. These forces saved neither Katanga nor the Federation, but they wrecked Macleod. Salisbury in February 1961
described him as 'too clever by half' in a speech in the House of
Lords where personal attacks on members of 'another place'
are contrary to convention. At this time the Tory right could
not have hoped to secure one of their own number as a
successor to the leadership, but they had an effective veto.
Macleod lost his chance but as he said later: 'You must just
take the consequences of the actions you believe to be right.'

Macmillan became weary of the in-fighting between
Sandys and Macleod and found the latter to be the more
tiresome of the two. In October 1961 he promoted him to the
leadership of the House and of the Party Organization.
Reginald Maudling became Colonial Secretary. Early in 1962
the Prime Minister belatedly removed Central Africa from
both departments, persuading Butler to take charge in March
1962 of a newly created Central African department. Any
chance of preserving the Federation had by now vanished
with the victory in December 1962 of the Rhodesian Front in
the Southern Rhodesian general election. The governments
of all three territories were now committed to secession.
Butler exercising much diplomatic skill dissolved the Federation at the Victoria Falls Conference which began on 28 June
1963. Nyasaland and Northern Rhodesia (rechristened
Malawi and Zambia) had by now secured independence or a
binding promise of it. Southern Rhodesia, despite subsequent recriminations, had not, and no such undertaking was

ever made by Butler or anyone else. Although the question was seriously considered, the decision was to leave the colony's status unchanged. The consequences, one of which was UDI, lie outside the scope of this book. The Federation was formally dissolved at midnight on 31 December 1963, and British rule in Africa, apart from a ghostly suzerainty over Southern Rhodesia which was to cause much tribulation over the next sixteen years, came to an end.

5

On 27 July 1961 the Cabinet applied to accede to the Treaty of Rome as a prelude to negotiation in detail. The European Movement began in 1947, a response to Churchill's Zurich speech the year before. The Marshall Plan led to the Organization for European Economic Community (OEEC) in 1948. In 1949 the North Atlantic Treaty Organization (NATO) was created, and the first meeting of the Council of Europe took place in Strasburg. West Germany joined it the following year. In 1951 the Schuman Plan for coal and steel was ratified by the six powers which later constituted the EEC. In 1954, after the failure of the European Defence Community (EDC) the Western European Union which included a rearmed West Germany came into being. In 1955 the 'six' met at Messina, and the Treaty of Rome became operative on 1 January 1958. De Gaulle's refusal to admit Britain and the other countries (the 'seven') outside the Common Market into a wider grouping has already been mentioned.

The decision to negotiate was not an easy one. The Conservative Party had a long tradition of supporting preferential trade arrangements with the Commonwealth. The Ottawa agreements were regarded by many people as the belated triumph of Joseph Chamberlain's policy of Tariff Reform. How would they fare now? The question of 'temperate food stuffs' arose – particularly applicable to Australia and New Zealand whose interests could be badly damaged by the

EEC's Common Agricultural Policy. Then there were questions of sovereignty. Would 'The Queen in Parliament' remain supreme? If the negotiation was a prelude to entering a European Federation, then, so Gaitskell declared in a famous television interview on 21 September 1962, 'it means the end of Britain as an independent nation; we become no more than "Texas" or "California" in the United States of Europe. It means the end of a thousand years of history'. On the other side was the view that European unity was of paramount political importance and that Britain and the Commonwealth economically would lose more if Britain stayed out than went in. The arguments have been rehearsed ever since; they are a part of current political debate. Their merits are not yet a matter for the historian.

It was clear at an early stage that de Gaulle was personally against British entry, and that if he carried France with him the other five powers could not override him. The negotiations with Europe and with the Commonwealth which occupied so much of the time and energy of ministers and officials, especially Edward Heath who first made a name for himself in this connection, might, therefore, be seen as obviously doomed to failure. But when the negotiations began it was not at all certain that de Gaulle would carry the day in France. He faced plenty of opposition, and his status, both constitutional and political, looked precarious. It was not till the referendum on the presidency at the end of October 1962, followed a month later by the sweeping victory of his party in the general election that de Gaulle was firmly in the saddle. Thereafter he could do what he wanted. On 14 January 1963 he gave a majestic press conference which palpably foreshadowed a formal veto. This was delivered to the negotiating powers in Brussels on 29 January. Macmillan had staked a great deal on success. It was not only a matter of electoral prospects. It was also a question of morale. Europe had become the government's 'theme'. 'All our policies at home and abroad are in ruins,' he wrote in his diary on 28 January. The Conservatives no longer had a theme.

De Gaulle's veto had been attributed to his deep-seated Americano-phobia dating from the war and his belief that Britain was too much tied up with America to be genuinely 'European'. This may be broadly true, but the particular examples usually cited are not very convincing. Macmillan certainly had cordial relations with Eisenhower's successor, Jack Kennedy, who took office early in 1961. There were family connections, and Kennedy enjoyed talking and listening to an older man whose long experience, urbane wit and deep sense of history made him a wise and delightful companion. During the Cuba crisis of October/November 1962, the President kept in constant touch with the Prime Minister. He had no such relationship with his other allies. Yet it would be hard to point to any decision which was taken on Macmillan's advice, certainly none that affected France. It is doubtful whether de Gaulle was much influenced by this case of Anglo-American friendship.

Another explanation is that he felt he had been tricked or slighted by the nuclear agreement between Britain and America announced on 21 December 1962 at Nassau. This was the settlement of one of the sharpest disputes between the two countries since Suez. It concerned 'Skybolt' upon which the British nuclear force depended after the cancellation of 'Blue Streak'. On 7 November Mr Macnamara, the US Secretary of Defense, recommended 'Skybolt's' cancellation on technical grounds. For causes that are still obscure there was no communication on the subject between the two governments until 12 December, when Macmillan heard the news from Thorneycroft who had just been told by Macnamara in Paris. The Prime Minister was horrified.

The conference at Bermuda had already been arranged but 'Skybolt' was not even on the agenda. It now took first place. There was deep British suspicion that the cancellation was a covert way of depriving Britain of nuclear independence. Macmillan was determined to insist on getting 'Polaris', the more so since he knew that de Gaulle meant to have an independent deterrent at whatever cost. Macmillan had already arranged to meet de Gaulle in Paris on the 13th, and he informed him about his plan to acquire 'Polaris'. It was afterwards alleged that the General vetoed the application to join the EEC because Macmillan had concealed his intention. This was not so, and the French President's objections had nothing to do with Britain's independent nuclear deterrent. At Bermuda after some very hard bargaining Kennedy reluctantly agreed that Britain should be supplied with 'Polaris' submarines for which she would make her own warheads. In return the submarines would be assigned to NATO, except in a case where Britain decided that her supreme national interests were at stake, in which case she reserved the right to use them independently. This was a victory for Macmillan.

De Gaulle's decision probably stemmed less from anti-Americanism than from the feeling that Britain would be an inconvenient rival to French supremacy, however many more nations were admitted to the EEC. De Gaulle stood in a long anti-English tradition – Joan of Arc, Louis XIV, Napoleon. These sentiments, atavistic or patriotic, have always been a part of the French heritage. France's national identity, like that of the Irish, originated in a revolt against English conquest. Alliance with England in two world wars modified but did not obliterate this sentiment. Neither Macmillan nor Heath could have done anything about it at that time.

One important and tragic event occurred shortly before de Gaulle's veto. Hugh Gaitskell was taken ill by a rare immuno-logical disease and died on 18 January. He was only fifty-six. An election for this unexpected vacancy took place in the Parliamentary Labour Party. On the second ballot, after James Callaghan had dropped out, Harold Wilson was elected by 144 votes to George Brown's 103.

Chapter Twenty

THE CONSERVATIVE DECLINE

I

The early 1960s saw one of those mysterious changes in 'the climate of opinion' which are as difficult to explain as they are easy to recognize. The extrovert confidence of the 1950s gave way to a mood of self-doubt and self-criticism. The first sign of change is sometimes dated back to John Osborne's play, *Look Back in Anger*, produced early in 1956. 'Don't clap too hard, we're all in a very old building,' one of the characters is made to say. That England was a tottering decrepit country seemed to be the burden of the message together with a nostalgia for a more noble past: 'people of our generation aren't able to die for good causes any more. We had all that done for us in the thirties and the forties when we were still kids. There aren't any good brave causes left.' This sense of resentment against the 'establishment' – a newly coined expression invented by the journalist Henry Fairlie – surfaced the following year when John Grigg (Lord Altrincham) in an otherwise mild article referred to the Queen as sounding like 'a priggish schoolgirl'. He was followed by the nineteen-year-old Marquis of Londonderry who attacked the royal family's 'toothpaste smiles' and 'appalling taste in clothes', and Malcolm Muggeridge who described the Queen as 'frumpish and banal'. Uproar ensued. Mr Grigg's face was slapped in the street. The Marquis was reproved by his seventy-seven-year-old grandmother and made a public apology. Malcolm Muggeridge was temporarily suspended by the BBC.

It did not pay to attack royalty. The Crown is the oldest,

toughest and most successful of all British institutions, but it seemed profitable to attack almost anything else. In 1961 the staging of *Beyond the Fringe* marked the revival of the art of political satire, and Harold Macmillan was one of the principal victims, shown as a decrepit old man travelling round the world 'on your behalf and at your expense'. In the same year *Private Eye* made its first appearance, as did David Frost's *That Was the Week That Was* on television. All three enterprises succeeded far beyond the expectations of their promoters and evidently corresponded to a hitherto unarticulated mood of ill-defined discontent. This may explain the widespread readership of a whole series of books about the 'condition of England'. Michael Shanks's paperback, *The Stagnant Society*, sold over 60,000 copies. Encouraged by these figures the publishers, Penguin Books, produced one series entitled *What's Wrong with . . .?* and another headed *Britain in the Sixties*. The Bishop of Woolwich, John Robinson, capped all these efforts. It might be perilous to criticize the monarchy, but at least one could look beyond mere English institutions and have a go at God. His celebrated book, *Honest to God* sold more than 250,000 copies in its first year. To many people it seemed to shake the very foundations of the Christianity in which they had hitherto believed. And it was written by a Bishop, even if he was a mere suffragan.

This spate of anti-establishment productions in print and the media was not specifically 'political' in the party sense of the word. It is probably true that, in the 1960s and ever since, most makers of programmes and most journalists have been on the 'radical' side of politics. As has been said, young Conservatives make money, young Radicals make programmes. But the mood of the period was more broadly based than that. It was a general dissatisfaction with the status quo. By 1963 the Conservatives had been in continuous office for over eleven years; *they* were the status quo. A generation had reached voting age, which scarcely remembered the last Labour government. This new sense of introversion, of inner doubt, of anxiety about Britain's role, of fear of the success of the EEC on the one hand and of America on the other, must have contributed towards the decline of the Conservatives' electoral fortunes. The party was losing the intellectual battle which it had won in the late 1940s and was to win again thirty years later. There was also a generation gap. The exponents of criticism and satire were too young – mostly under forty – to have been in the armed forces in the war. Perhaps they rebelled against those who had, or at least were bored by them. There was for a time a cult of youth. President Kennedy was contrasted with the ageing British leadership. In fact Kennedy was not so young as to have missed war service and he got on admirably with Harold Macmillan, but that did not affect the general image. No one could have been less like Kennedy than Harold Wilson but he managed, though not for long, to convey something of the same impression. The youth cult did not last. Perhaps it died with Kennedy.

Britain's decline in the economic league table was another important talking point. There were various attempted explanations. Was the state educational system with its tripartite divisions responsible? The abolition of the distinction between grammar, secondary modern and technical schools became a major left-wing objective which has since been achieved. Was the low number of graduates compared with America, Russia and the EEC countries a factor? The great university expansion based on the Robbins Report might have been expected to help in this respect. Yet it would be hard to argue that either comprehensive schooling or multiplication of universities has made much difference to Britain's industrial production or export competitiveness. Whatever the solution may be, it does not now seem likely to be found in either of those fields. But this is to write with the hindsight of two decades. In the early 1960s it was not unreasonable for idealists who believed in 'social engineering' to think that institutional changes of this sort would transform British society into one that could compete with rival industrial countries. It did not happen, but other benefits may have accrued which cannot be measured statistically.

Against this general background, the Conservatives were ill-placed to compete with a Labour Party which appeared more united than it had been for a long time past. They would need a run of luck in 1963 to win yet another election, but they were to stumble into a quite abnormal series of unhappy accidents.

2

Nineteen sixty-three can fairly be described as the year of scandal. By the summer, as Macmillan observes in his memoirs, an atmosphere prevailed that had no parallel since the days of Titus Oates. Every sort of evil rumour was rife about ministers and others in high places. There had been nothing like it before in the twentieth century – the Marconi affair was small beer in comparison – and there has been nothing like it since. The origin lay in a series of episodes connected with the security services. Early in 1961 there occurred the 'Portland' case in which a number of Soviet agents received long sentences for spying on the Underwater Weapons Establishment. A committee was appointed under Sir Charles Romer, a judge, to make recommendations about security procedures. It reported on 13 June. Meanwhile in April an even graver discovery occurred. George Blake, an employee of the security services, was tried and found guilty of treachery on a scale rivalled only by Philby. The details have never been disclosed but their seriousness can be gauged by the Lord Chief Justice's sentence of forty-two years' imprisonment – and also by the reaction of the KGB which contrived Blake's escape and removal to Russia some years later.

There was strong pressure for a further inquiry even though Romer had not yet reported. The Prime Minister set up another committee under the chairmanship of Lord Radcliffe with a wider remit which included the Romer findings. Lord Radcliffe's recommendations were in the hands of the government early in 1962 and were published in

April. The report revealed an alarming number of Communists among the civil service trade-union officials. Among other recommendations however it suggested that committed Communists were not the only threat; careful inquiry should be made into the antecedents of those who, for one reason or another, might be susceptible to Soviet influence or blackmail. A clear case of this danger came up in the same year. One J. W. C. Vassall was sentenced for espionage on 22 October for eighteen years. He was a homosexual whose proclivities had been discovered in 1956 by the KGB while he was attached to the British Embassy in Moscow, but not – unfortunately – by the British ambassador. Photographed in his bedroom, not alone and in a compromising posture he surrendered to blackmail. Homosexual acts were in those days criminal offences. He supplied the Russians with information for several years. By the time of his arrest he was an executive officer in the Admiralty. It was rumoured in the press that he had a homosexual link with Thomas (Tom) Galbraith, at one time Civil Lord of the Admiralty, subsequently an Under-Secretary of State for Scotland. British journalism reached its nadir at this time in terms of smear and innuendo. Lord Carrington, First Lord of the Admiralty, was freely accused of sheltering traitors. The Prime Minister felt obliged to convene a Tribunal under the 1921 Act to investigate the affair, and, once again, Lord Radcliffe was called in to preside. He completely exonerated Carrington and also Galbraith whose resignation Macmillan had temporarily accepted, and he insisted on two particularly scurrilous journalists giving their sources of information. What these were will remain unknown for the two men appealed to an alleged duty not to disclose them and were sent to prison in March 1963 for six months for contempt of court. The whole journalistic world was now up in arms, and furiously hostile to Macmillan and his colleagues, although the decision was a judicial one, in no way governmentally inspired. Galbraith was duly reinstated and the Prime Minister now felt very unhappy about having ever accepted his resignation in the first place.

Matters were made no better by the disclosure on 29 March that Philby really was the 'third man'. On the verge of being exposed as such, he had fled to Moscow from Beirut, where he was correspondent for the *Observer*. These prosecutions and exposures might reasonably have been regarded as successes for the security services, but in the feverish atmosphere of the time they seemed to point to an iceberg tip of cover-up, folly, incompetence and corruption on the part of the 'establishment'.

The atmosphere was therefore highly charged when the celebrated Profumo affair broke upon the public. Early in February the Prime Minister's private office received from a newspaper the story that John Profumo, the War Secretary, had had a liaison with a girl of dubious reputation called Christine Keeler. They had been introduced by one Stephen Ward at a party at Clivedon, seat of the third Viscount Astor. It was said that she was about to sell her memoirs to the press. The question of security arose – or rather was alleged to arise, for the claim had no foundation – because Profumo had shared her favours with the Russian Naval Attaché. The Prime Minister was abroad but his private secretary, Tim Bligh, and the Chief Whip Martin Redmayne, decided to interview Profumo at once. He denied all the charges. He admitted to having met Miss Keeler on half a dozen occasions in 1961 but said he had not seen her since; if these charges were made public he would take legal action. Macmillan accepted his denials but there was more trouble ahead. On 14 March Miss Keeler's name was mentioned in the courts. A West Indian man was charged with attempting to murder her. She was naturally enough the chief prosecution witness but she failed to turn up at the trial. Rumour soon had it that persons of high influence had arranged for her non-appearance.

At this juncture George (later Lord) Wigg, a Labour MP, took up the matter in Parliament. On the night of 21 March during a debate on the imprisoned journalists involved in the Vassall affair he made a definite charge against the War

Secretary. It was decided that Profumo should be interrogated again and, if he stuck to his story, he must give a personal denial next day in the House. After interrogation during the small hours by Macleod, Redmayne and the Law Officers he reiterated his innocence, and on 22 March made a personal statement in the Commons. He followed this up with successful libel actions against *Paris Match* and *Il Tempo* which had printed some of the allegations against him. This seemed conclusive. It is true that later Stephen Ward, whose career as a pimp and procurer was being investigated by the police, saw one of Macmillan's aides and told him that Profumo had lied, but this could easily be dismissed as an attempt to bring pressure on the government to call off the police inquiry. Macmillan had been blamed for credulity and for failing to interview Profumo himself, but a man who could deceive his hard-headed interrogators was well capable of deceiving the Prime Minister too, and Macmillan, unhappy at having accepted the resignation of the innocent Galbraith, can be forgiven for accepting these highly convincing denials.

On 4 June Profumo confessed to Bligh and Redmayne that Christine Keeler had been his mistress and that his statement to the contrary was untrue. He promptly resigned his office, his Privy Councillorship and his seat. The ensuing uproar was immense. Sensation followed sensation. Another West Indian was on trial for attacking Miss Keeler. On 8 June Stephen Ward was charged with living on immoral earnings. During the court proceedings a number of salacious sexual details emerged. He was certain to be convicted and he committed suicide on the eve of the last day of the trial. To cap it all Miss Keeler was charged with perjury. The press, glad to get their own back for the Vassall case, had a field day. The Conservative Party was gravely shaken and Macmillan was much criticized for blindness and complacency. In a debate on 17 June Nigel Birch made a short but deadly speech quoting Browning's poem, 'The Lost Leader', 'never glad confident morning again'. The government seemed about to fall; twenty-seven Tory MPs abstained on the ensuing vote of confidence. London was now agog with lurid gossip about the world of high politics. Stories of arcane perversions, orgies, blackmail, corruption, even treachery were rife. Macmillan decided that the air could only be cleared by giving *carte blanche* to a single individual of impeccable integrity to inquire into these rumours in total confidence and with no holds barred. He chose Lord Denning whose report was published on 26 September. His conclusion was clear; there had been no security risk, and the gossip about the conduct of ministers had no basis in reality.

In the midst of these tribulations the government secured one success. The Prime Minister had devoted much time and perseverance to the negotiation of an international treaty banning atmospheric nuclear tests. At the height of the Profumo affair President Kennedy visited Macmillan to discuss the question. The Russians were less averse to the idea than they had been. Lord Hailsham and Averell Harriman were the British and American negotiators in Moscow who brought about the Test Ban Treaty signed on 5 August. The British contribution was generously recognized by Kennedy.

Macmillan was now nearly seventy. An election was due at the latest in the autumn of 1964. He was determined not to be brought down, as he put it, 'by two tarts'. [1] The Test Ban Treaty revived his morale and he was not certain who ought to be his successor if he resigned. He finally decided on 7 October, after many changes of mind, to solve the problem by not resigning. He would stay on and fight the next election. Within twenty-four hours he was seriously ill with an inflamed prostate gland necessitating an urgent operation. He decided to resign at once. It is far from clear that this was necessary on the eve of the Conservative Conference in Blackpool. The traditional private methods of consultation and 'emergence' were bound to be affected. Nigel Fisher describes his decision as 'a major error of political judgement', but ill people often judge ill.

Much has been written about the discussions which followed. The dust has not yet settled after twenty years. Most people expected that R. A. Butler would be the new Prime Minister. It is clear that Macmillan was determined, for whatever reason, to keep him out. But to the world at large he was the obvious successor, and his younger rivals in the House of Commons – Maudling, Macleod, Heath – cancelled each other out. None was entirely acceptable. By a strange chance, however, the peerage law had been changed that year – ironically, through the efforts of the second Lord Stansgate (Tony Benn) who was determined not to lose his seat in the House of Commons because he was his father's heir. The new Act allowed heirs to peerages to disclaim on inheritance. There was also a temporary provision permitting existing hereditary peers to disclaim if they did so within six months of the Act taking effect. In order to avoid by-elections the government had intended to postpone the operation of this clause till after the next general election, but a last minute Lords amendment made the Act effective from the Royal Assent on 31 July. Lords Hailsham and Home were thus unexpectedly put into the running. Had the crisis occurred a year earlier or a year later, they could not have been candidates, and Macmillan could not have kept Butler out.

Ill though he was, Macmillan was determined to control the succession. The Conservative Party since 1957 when the Cabinet in effect elected the new Prime Minister had agreed on a system of rather wider consultation. Although the choice constitutionally rested with the Queen, she was likely to choose the person most acceptable to the party and to take the advice of the outgoing Prime Minister as to who that person was, if he was willing to give it. Unlike Bonar Law in 1923, Macmillan from his sick bed in the King Edward VII Hospital was more than willing. The first candidate to 'throw his hat in the ring' was Hailsham who on 10 October announced with much panache at Blackpool his intention to disclaim his peerage. Originally Macmillan regarded him as the best bet for blocking Butler, but it soon became clear that Hailsham had overdone things. His exuberant enthusiasm for the premiership was counter-productive. Macmillan now plumped for Home who was a reluctant candidate but after much pressure in Blackpool indicated to Butler on 12 October that he was a potential rival. The Cabinet, junior ministers, Tory MPs and Peers and the National Union were consulted during the next few days though how effectively is not quite clear. The extent of their support for Home has been a subject of dispute ever since. Macmillan, however, was satisfied that at least there was less opposition to him than to anyone else. This may be true but it is now clear that seven or eight members of a Cabinet of twenty would not have chosen him. On 18 October Macmillan advised the Queen to send for Home.

It was not certain that he could form a government. At first Butler refused to serve, and Hailsham, Macleod, Maudling and Powell agreed to follow him. If they had persisted, Home would have had to give up, but later that day Hailsham decided that his own refusal would look too much like personal pique. At the same time Home offered the Foreign Office to Butler who felt that the loss of Hailsham was a sign of evaporating personal support. He accepted next day, and Maudling now saw no point in holding out. Macleod and Powell alone stuck to their guns. Home thus entered office in circumstances anything but propitious – a sullen and divided party disturbed by the blaze of adverse publicity and by charges that an aristocratic 'magic circle' had produced an aristocratic Prime Minister. It was largely nonsense, but nonsense can be more potent in politics than sense.

3

The Conservative Party had been riven by doubts and dissension for many months. The Profumo scandal exacerbated these, and until the leadership question was settled little attention could be paid to the future prospects of the party. The appointment of Home cleared the air, but it was a serious setback to lose Macleod and Powell, two of the cleverest figures in Macmillan's Cabinet. De Gaulle's veto had left the party bereft of policy and purpose. Although there were some Conservatives who welcomed it and were only too glad not to be entangled with Europe, the majority felt rudderless. There was another division in the party – between those who believed in tradition and those who wanted to 'modernize' Britain. Macmillan was a modernizer and in 1960–61 had set up a number of committees to inquire into the state of the nation; they are remembered if at all by the names of their chairmen; Sir Frank Newsam on secondary education, Lord Robbins on the universities, Professor Buchanan on traffic and roads, Lord Beeching on the railways, Lord Pilkington on broadcasting. Most of these reported in 1963 and the general impression they conveyed was of a Britain sadly behind the times. Yet it looked opportunist and slightly unconvincing for the Conservatives to latch on with enthusiasm to their recommendations. Labour, after all, had been saying this sort of thing for years.

Nor did the Conservatives manage the economy with any notable success. Maudling was Macmillan's white hope for an expansionist policy. The problem, as Maudling puts it in his memoirs, was to 'ensure the full use of resources without generating fresh domestic inflation and without diverting resources from exports and thus undermining the balance of payments'.[2] The solution eluded Maudling as it was to elude Callaghan, Jenkins, Barber and all subsequent Chancellors. In a provisional budget in autumn 1962 and in the main budget in 1963 Maudling plunged for expansion with substantial reductions in tax. The idea was that increased demand would lead to a large increase in output from the same equipment thus causing a fall in unit costs of production. The argument presupposed an existing spare capacity in the economy. This seemed to be confirmed by an unusually high (for those times) level of unemployment, but it is not clear that the unemployment was in the 'right' areas of industry. If it was structural unemployment arising from industrial obsolescence it would not easily be absorbed in export industries which might merely be faced, in the absence of an effective incomes policy, with higher labour costs. There was a further problem; exporting industries had to import raw materials and semi-manufactured goods and pay in sterling before receiving the foreign currency for the goods they eventually exported. This was a strain on the balance of payments, no doubt temporary, but – how temporary? There was also the difficulty of sterling being a major and highly sensitive international currency distorted by fixed exchange rates which, many people argued, should have been relaxed much earlier.

In 1964 Maudling produced a neutral budget. At this time the balance of payments was a much publicized political issue. He was advised that it would be even, during the next few months, and he favoured an election in May or June rather than October (the latest date). But the balance went the wrong way with a deficit of £63 million in the second quarter and £192 million in the third quarter of 1964. For other reasons Home had, after much debate, decided on an October election. These figures were inevitably damaging. Maudling was perhaps unfortunate. The deficit soon diminished. If there had not been a new government elected by a whisker and, like all in-coming oppositions, bound to denounce the incompetence of its predecessor, confidence in sterling might have remained, but this can only be a matter for speculation. The Chancellor's 'dash for freedom' did not succeed. Mutual recrimination has gone on ever since.

The Conservative confusion naturally helped Labour. Harold Wilson, a Disraeli-like figure, was a witty and effective leader of the opposition. He never managed to out-match Macmillan, but in the political mood of 1964 he could deal effectively with Home who was not at his best in answering questions in the House – that acid prime ministerial test. The Prime Minister was bad, too, on television. It has never been proved quite how much this mattered – or matters – but Wilson was certainly more plausible and convincing; if votes were to be gained through this medium

417

he was the one to win them. He gave an indefinable impression of being a man of the times, more in touch with 'the modernizing of Britain' whatever that meant, than Home could be expected – or want – to be. The Prime Minister's position was not helped by Randolph Churchill's instant publication of an account of the succession crisis and Iain Macleod's devastating reply early in Janury 1964 in the *Spectator* of which he had become editor after resigning from the Cabinet.

The year that followed Macmillan's resignation was politically one of doubt and uncertainty. Labour had a lead of eight to ten per cent after the leadership crisis, but this soon diminished, and, as the months went by, the upshot of the general election seemed less and less predictable. The Labour Party, faced with the perennial opposition problem of guessing the date, made some serious miscalculations. On the assumption that it would be June 1964 at the latest Wilson engaged in a major tour of the country from January to April. It was not till 9 April that Sir Alec Home announced that there would be no election before the autumn. His decision was partly influenced by the long lead Labour had in the opinion polls, and he must have felt himself fully justified when the disastrous results of the local elections came in. Yet, for reasons not at all easy to explain, the Labour Party's standing declined steadily during the uneasy political pause which ensued. A lead of eight per cent in the Gallup poll on 3 July fell to six and a half per cent on 7 August and to five per cent on 13 September. In the National Opinion Poll the figures were even more startling. A lead of 8·3 per cent on 22 June had been replaced by a 1·6 per cent lead for the Conservatives on 13 September. Two days later Home announced that Parliament would be dissolved on 25 September and the election would be held on 15 October. It had been the longest peacetime parliament since 1911 when the seven year limit was reduced to five.

In the event, after an unexciting election campaign in which neither side greatly distinguished itself Labour won a narrow victory. Wilson had expected to win comfortably though not by a landslide. The Conservative Party chairman Lord Blakenham who had strongly opposed a June election said afterwards that he expected to win by ten or fifteen seats but the general expectation since at least 1962 had been that Labour would win. Most people were surprised that the margin was so narrow. The actual figures were Labour 317, Conservatives 304 (including the Speaker) and Liberals 9. The Labour lead over Conservatives in votes was 0·7 per cent. The electoral turn out was 77·1 per cent, slightly less than in 1959. Labour received 12,205,814 votes, the Conservatives 12,001,396. The Liberals who fought 365 seats received 3,092,878 votes. The result was close but clear. Sir Alec Home decided not to meet Parliament, as some people suggested. At 3.20 P.M. on 16 October he went to Buckingham Palace to resign. At 4 P.M. Harold Wilson became Prime Minister, and the long Conservative reign had come to an end.

EPILOGUE

What sort of Britain was emerging in the early 1960s? The biggest single external difference from the Britain of the 1920s was undoubtedly the disappearance of empire. In 1919 there was a larger area than ever before coloured red on the world map, if one includes the new league mandates for Iraq, Palestine, Transjordan and Tanganyika which were British colonies for all practical purposes. It is of course true that the colour was to some extent delusory. Canada, New Zealand, Australia and South Africa were already independent nations, though owing allegiance to the same crown – a position formalized by the Statute of Westminster in 1931 and remaining the same in 1964, except in the case of South Africa which had by then become an independent republic. This still left a very large area genuinely governed by Britain. Forty-five years later it had vanished, and with it a whole way of life for the middle-class minority which did the governing. In 1964, apart from a few places of no importance, only Hong Kong, Gibraltar, the Falkland Islands, Rhodesia which seized independence in 1965 and Malta which was given it in 1967 remained under British rule.

The process of decolonization was remarkably quick and comparatively peaceful. In the French, Dutch and Portuguese empires there were bitter rearguard actions. The British Empire vanished quietly and almost imperceptibly. Apart from those who had made their careers as colonial or Indian civil servants, most people scarcely noticed the change. It had no particular economic effects, and strategically was, if anything, a relief. There was, however, a legacy of empire which certainly was noticed and which made far more impact on 'the masses', to use Lord Salisbury's language, than 'the classes'. There was no 'colour problem' in the England of the 1920s. By the 1960s there was. Immigrants poured in from the Indian sub-continent, from Africa (largely displaced Asians) and from the Caribbean. Several causes combined to bring this about. The immigrants believed that their common status as subjects of the Crown would make them readily acceptable on equal terms by the British natives. This juridical situation did indeed make it very difficult to restrict immigration without injustice, but it did not lessen the dislike which, for reasons partly xenophobic and partly racialist, was inspired by the newcomers. Another reason was the existence of English as the lingua franca of the Commonwealth. Yet another was the shortage of labour for some types of job during a time of full employment. The difficulty of recruiting at home for transport and the Health Service led to recruitment from the Commonwealth. Above all there was the revolution produced by cheap air travel. It was far easier to get to England than it had been before 1945; unemployment and poverty in the Commonwealth countries provided the inducements to move.

These developments were neither expected nor wanted by most Britons. They became political issues in some places for the first time in the 1964 election and were a major factor in the defeat at Smethwick of Labour's Shadow Foreign Secretary, Patrick Gordon-Walker; Labour was regarded as 'softer' on immigration than the Conservatives, and had opposed the Commonwealth Immigration Act of 1962 which put a drastic curb on new arrivals. By 1964 the immigrant population was 800,000 or about 1·5 per cent of the total. By 1980 it was to be 4·1 per cent. The London and Midland urban working classes were those who most disliked the rivalry and competition of those new and apparently alien visitors.

A corollary of the decline of empire was the loss of Britain's status as a 'great power'. After the end of the First World War there had been only three, the USA, the UK and

France. Italy had an honorary status as one of the countries on the winning side but was not regarded very seriously. Of the pre-1914 great powers, Austria-Hungary had dissolved into a number of small impoverished nation states, likewise Turkey. During the course of 1918 Germany had knocked out Russia and the western Allies had knocked out Germany. This 'vacuum' could not last. By the 1930s Germany and Russia were once again great powers and Japan was in the same class. Thus there were now six, or, if Italy is to be counted, seven. The Second World War transformed the situation. After 1944 there were only two – the USA and the USSR. The UK had palpably lost its co-equal status by the time of Yalta if not earlier, but France, West Germany and Japan, the defeated countries, lagged well behind Britain in terms of wealth and status. By 1964, however, West Germany's gross national product was ahead of that of the UK, France was almost equal and Japan was fast catching up. The USA and USSR still remained far in front of all four. The American GNP was more than twice the Russian, but the greater proportion which Russia, thanks to a totalitarian regime indifferent to consumer interests, could devote to her armed services much reduced the inequality in military strength. Britain was not an unimportant country in 1964, nor is it today, but the power and prestige of the past had gone. This change probably affected the governors more than the governed. Prime Ministers, Foreign Secretaries and their colleagues, most of whom remembered the inter-war years, were conscious of the decline and were disturbed by it. They were personally involved, outfaced from time to time, and occasionally humiliated. The reaction of the 'general public' (if there is such a thing) may have been different.

If on the other hand one compares the domestic economy, the standard of living (that mysterious and largely immeasurable entity) and the general style of existence over the half century between 1914 and 1964, one can see enormous changes which had little to do with imperial or great power decline, and which affected the various elements in society

423

quite differently. It could be summed up by saying that relatively the rich were poorer and the poor were richer, but the adverb is important. There was a sense in which everyone enjoyed amenities which they had not enjoyed before the First World War. Dukes did not have television sets in 1914, and few had central heating. What they did have – and this was true to a level far below the ducal – were servants. People talked about the 'servant shortage' after 1918, but in fact they were plentiful if a bit more expensive. Probably the greatest change after 1945 for the classes defined in Sir William Crawford's famous investigation, *The People's Food*, in 1936–7 as AA (those with incomes of over £1,000) and A (£500 to £1,000) has been the virtual disappearance of domestic servants. In the 1930s it was perfectly normal even for people in Category A to have two servants living in, plus a gardener;[1] of course in the higher AA income brackets the numbers were far more, and the great houses still had a whole retinue of staff elaborately graded from the butler, chef, housekeeper and head gardener downwards. The rich were still very rich, however adversely they compared themselves with their status before 1914. But after 1945 the scene changed. The really wealthy, whether their money came from soaring land values, pop star success, commercial enterprise, or dealings in the City could still preserve a lifestyle not unlike that of the 1930s. But servants were fewer, more prickly and more liable to be crooked. As for the 'middle classes' they were servant-less with a few exceptions – the products of age, loyalty, tradition and habit. This did not necessarily mean that they were less happy.

If the 'classes' were experiencing since 1945 a decline of standards of life in relative terms, the 'masses' enjoyed a notable improvement. In fact despite popular mythology their material welfare was much higher even in 1939 than it had been in 1914. In the second half of our period the rise was still greater. Any statistical comparison that can be made shows this immense change in almost every aspect of life – diet, accommodation, health, warmth, sanitation, leisure, mobility. It is one of the paradoxes of social history that the first two 'total' wars in the annals of the world, despite their vast slaughter and fearful miseries, led to a marked improvement in what used to be called 'the condition of the people'. However, it is unlikely that a third one will repeat the process. Another great contrast was to be seen in the employment situation. There was, it is true, relatively little unemployment in 1914, but by 1921 there were 1·5 million out of work and by 1931 3 million. In 1939 the figure was still over a million. From 1945 to 1964 it was negligible, as it had been, naturally enough, in both wars.

There was an obverse side to this coin. The bargaining power of labour became much stronger and contributed at least in some degree to the inflation which shot upwards in the late 1960s and the 1970s; shortage of labour also had a part in the failure of British industry to compete with that of other countries, and it contributed to the 'take it or leave it' attitude which was in the long run to be so damaging to British export trade. In the first two post-war decades the union leaders who tended to be on the right of the Labour Party used their strength with caution thus masking the shift that had occurred in the balance of industrial power. It was a different story later when the leadership of many of the major unions veered to the left.

The other vast change which took place in this period, though certainly not confined to Britain, was the sexual revolution which affected the whole of the western world – the discovery that intercourse need no longer lead to procreation. Statistics suggest that 'birth control', at least in the middle and upper classes, was being practised as early as the 1880s. There is, however, not much evidence as to how this was done. 'Birth control', as A. J. P. Taylor points out, is a tautology not an explanation. It merely means that conception was being restricted but throws no light on the method.[2] Artificial aids were disapproved of – and not only by the Roman Catholic church. There was little or no mention of such matters in print. Winston Churchill writing in 1905

425

about the Bradlaugh case twenty years earlier refers to 'over-population, its evils and its remedies and other Malthusian topics, which, being among the most tremendous of natural problems, have long been judged unfit for public discussion'.[3] This inhibition, now totally extinct, took many years to disappear. What evidence we have suggests that 'birth control' before the First World War and indeed for much of the inter-war period took the form of either abstinence or the unreliable *coitus interruptus*. The latter remained the practice, so it is believed, of seventy per cent of married couples until 1940.

The situation is the more surprising since millions of young men must have been aware during the war of a safe male contraceptive, the rubber sheath (otherwise known as the 'condom' or 'French letter' – words of obscure etymology[4]). This was an old device first mentioned in the early eighteenth century. Its original purpose was to prevent venereal disease not conception, and that was why it was mass produced for the forces. Whether for reasons of expense or embarrassment – purchase between the wars tended to be a furtive under-the-counter business – the method seems to have been regularly practised by merely one in ten of married couples while the only safe female contraceptive, the diaphragm, invented by a Dutchman in 1919, was used even less. The principal British firm which manufactured sheaths made some 2 million a year in the 1930s. Twenty years later the figure was 100 million, though allowance has to be made for the fact that German imports accounted for the lion's share of the market before 1939.[5] Towards the end of our period an even greater revolution occurred – the invention after thirty years' research of an effective contraceptive pill, but its consequences and implications lie outside the scope of this book.

The extent to which sexual morals changed during the half century is impossible to determine. The silence that prevailed on these matters before 1914 makes it very difficult to find out how people actually behaved. The vast majority was

inarticulate. The minority which could have written about its
experiences was inhibited by powerful conventions of discretion; so the evidence is largely anecdotal and accidental, as it
is for most of the century before 1914. Such Victorian *curiosa*
as *My Secret Life*, or the papers of Wilfred Scawen Blunt may
cast a lurid light on some people's activities. There are many
stories about the care which Edwardian hostesses took in
arranging who should sleep in adjacent bedrooms. Oswald
Mosley's son has revealed the philandering of his father in
the 1920s and there is a sensational book, *White Mischief*,
about 'Happy Valley' in Kenya in the 1930s, which describes
an orgiastic life worthy of the most uninhibited days of
imperial Rome or Restoration London. But what all this
amounts to in terms of generalities no one can say. A further
complication that casts doubt even on the opinion polls and
social inquiries into sex which are now regarded as permiss-
ible, is that there is no subject about which people are less
likely to tell the truth, whether they are claiming vigour or
virtue.

The general impression that by 1960 people were less
'moral' and more promiscuous than they were in 1910 cannot
be substantiated. It may be true but no real proof exists. The
belief itself may be merely an inference from something
which certainly was and is true, viz that from about 1960
onwards people have written about sex, displayed it in the
theatre and on the film with a degree of – according to taste –
candour or indecency never paralleled before. The full
development of this trend which has led to pornography as a
major industry lies outside our period, but its beginning can
be traced to the 1959 Act which replaced the Obscene
Publications Act of 1857 and made 'literary or other merit' a
possible defence. It was tested in the celebrated *Lady Chatter-
ley's Lover* case a year later; D. H. Lawrence's famous novel,
hitherto legally obtainable only in expurgated form, was
acquitted of obscenity and could henceforth be read by
everyone. The stage and cinema were soon to be similarly
'liberated'. By the middle 1960s there were in practice few

427

obstacles to what could be written or displayed. Illustrated sex manuals of the most explicit nature were on sale, and novels contained descriptions of episodes which would have been regarded as unprintable a few years earlier.

Homosexual practices were still illegal but there was strong pressure for change. Ironically this was largely because the police, especially the Metropolitan Police, having for many years been inclined to turn a blind eye, started a spate of prosecutions in the 1950s. Whatever the reason for this change, it was counter-productive, and in 1967 an act was passed legalizing homosexual activities between consenting adults. It gave a new meaning, so jokers said, to 'coming of age'. How much difference it made to what people actually did is anyone's guess.

The changed attitude towards sex may have been connected with a changed attitude towards religion. This was particularly obvious in the case of divorce statistics. Most of the churches frowned on divorce. In 1910 there were in round figures 800 cases, in 1920 3,700 – a rise partly explicable in terms of the break-up of hasty wartime marriages. Ten years later the figure was barely higher. But in 1940 it was 8,400 – war again being perhaps part of the explanation. In 1950 there were 32,500 divorces; in 1960 the figure fell to 25,700, but in the next four years it rose by fifty per cent. By 1970 it was to be over 60,000. Free legal aid and important amendments to the law cannot be the sole reason for a change which reflects a silent revolution in attitudes to marriage and the family. There may be many explanations, but it is hard to doubt that one of them is the decline of religious faith and observance. Indeed a person living in 1964, who had reached maturity before the First World War – born in, say, 1890 – would have found this to be one of the most striking changes in the nation's life. Before 1914 religious and political differences were inextricably intertwined. 'The Church of England is the Tory Party at prayer' – the famous expression whose authorship remains unknown – was an epigrammatic exaggeration of a recognizable phe-

428

nomenon; it made no sense in the 1960s nor does it today, except as a piece of history. The Church of England had long ceased to help Conservativism; its influence was if anything in the opposite direction. Except in Northern Ireland, politics and religion were no longer mixed up with each other in the way that they were and are in much of Europe. The Protestant non-conformist sects, once the prop of Liberalism, declined even faster than the Anglicans in terms of Church attendance. By 1964 sectarianism, one of the most controversial political issues in the century before the First World War, had ceased to matter. The politics of welfare had replaced the politics of theology.

There was of course continuity as well as change. One feature which distinguished this half century from comparable recent periods was war. Anyone who was in his late sixties in 1964 had experienced as an adult two world wars. The great majority of men of that age had served in the armed forces in 1914–18, and a large number had done so in 1939–45 as well. Women had also been deeply involved in both. Everyone who was over forty had as an adult seen, heard or participated in the Second World War. The effect of this experience echoed beyond the age groups concerned. An interesting feature of life since 1945 is the fascination which both wars have exerted in print and through the media over generations which could have had no first-hand knowledge at all of either. It might have been expected that they would close their eyes and write off the two wars as products of the follies of their forebears, but their fascination with battles remains as strong as ever at the time of writing (1984) and shows no sign of diminishing. In the twentieth century war has become a part of life, in a sense that it has never quite been before – at any rate since the Middle Ages. The only comparable experience was the conflict with Napoleon. Yet one could hardly imagine a novelist who wrote after 1914 behaving as Jane Austen did, in making no reference at all to the struggle from which her country so narrowly survived intact.

Another continuity has been the constitution. Of the three component elements of 'the King in Parliament', the House of Commons operated in 1964 much as it did in 1914. There have been changes, but someone who sat in Asquith's House of Commons would not have found himself at sea in Harold Macmillan's. Indeed there were some members who had just this experience or an even longer one. Winston Churchill entered the House in 1900 and, apart from brief breaks in 1908 and 1922–4 was there continuously till 1964. Of course there were some changes in procedure but none of them was fundamental. Nor has the electoral system changed at all radically. The first-past-the-post procedure still remains and there is little sign of it being altered. The franchise was extended in 1918, 1928 and 1949. The first of these extensions may have adversely affected the fortunes of the Liberal Party. Otherwise there were no obvious effects.

After the passing of the Parliament Act of 1911 few people would have expected the House of Lords to remain in much the same condition for over fifty years – in fact over seventy if one speaks of the present day.

Bishops and hereditary peers were still there in 1964 and are still there today. The only important change has been the creation of life peers, but this is hardly a revolutionary step. It was first mooted by Palmerston in 1855. It certainly has affected the style and conduct of the House of Lords but those developments belong to the last twenty years and were not visible in 1964.

The third key component of the constitution is the monarchy. That too has survived unchanged, apart from the brief setback of the reign of Edward VIII. The actual power of the Crown has been perhaps marginally diminished since both the major parties decided to adopt an elective system to choose their leaders whether in power or opposition. But the change is more nominal than real. The last monarch to make a personal choice without reference to party wishes was Queen Victoria when in 1894 she chose Lord Rosebery, who probably would not have headed any poll of the Parliamentary

Liberal Party. When King George V chose Baldwin rather than Curzon in 1923 he was influenced above all by soundings about whom the Conservative Party wanted. A formal intra-party election would have almost certainly produced the same result, likewise in the case of Harold Macmillan in 1957. Whether it would have resulted in Lord Home's election in 1963 is more doubtful. But if the royal choice had existed in 1976 it is most unlikely that the Queen would have sent for anyone other than James Callaghan. The only difference would have been a speedier result and correspondingly less damage in the money markets. However, it is worth remembering that the monarchy still possesses some reserve powers. There could be circumstances in which the Crown could make a real choice of Prime Minister, and apart from that, it still remains, in Sir Ian Gilmour's words, 'The guardian of the constitution' in the event of a real emergency.[6]

The monarchy was highly popular under George V. It was highly popular in 1964 and is still highly popular twenty years later. Republicanism has been virtually non-existent since the 1870s. It cut little ice even then and has shown no sign of reviving in recent years. From time to time an occasional killjoy complains that it costs too much, but the general public, as far as one can judge, is happy to pay the price for a style, splendour and ceremonial which is the secret envy of most of the western world. The concept of a 'king on a bicycle' favoured in Scandinavia has no appeal in Britain.

Britain, as has been said earlier, was the only country to have entered both wars at the beginning and to have remained undefeated to the end in each case. Alone of the European powers Britain, like America, did not suffer from civil strife, revolution or *coups d'état*. Britain in 1914 was as free, tolerant and prosperous a country as any in the world. It was not a bad place to live in. Fifty years later its relative prosperity had markedly declined, but it was still free and tolerant. It was still not a bad place to live in. It used to be customary to personify nations in female classical allegorical

431

form. Perhaps Britannia if asked in 1964 what she had done over the last fifty years would reply as Talleyrand did on a famous occasion *'J'ai survécu,'* or rather since she presumably would not sully her lips with French, 'I am still alive'.

CHRONOLOGY

May 1915–December 1916	Asquith's coalition
1915	
December	Evacuation of Dardanelles
1916	
May	Battle of Jutland
July–November	Battle of the Somme
December 1916–December 1918	Lloyd George war coalition
1917	
April	America enters war
July–November	Battle of Passchendaele
November	Russian Revolution
1918	
February	Representation of the People Act
March	Ludendorff offensive begins
August	Haig's offensive begins
November	Germany capitulates
December	'Coupon' election
December 1918–October 1922	Lloyd George's second coalition
1921	
December	Irish Treaty
1922	
September	Chanak incident
October	Lloyd George resigns
October 1922–January 1924	Bonar Law/Baldwin government
November	General election
1923	
May	Baldwin succeeds Law
December	General election

1924

January–October 1924	MacDonald's first Labour government
October	General election
October 1924–May 1929	Baldwin's second government

1925

April	Return to the gold standard
December	Locarno Treaty

1926

May	General Strike

1927

May	Trades Disputes Act

1928

April	Equal Franchise Act

1929

May	General election
June 1929–August 1931	MacDonald's second Labour government

1931

August 1931–June 1935	MacDonald's national government
December	Statute of Westminster

1932

August	Ottawa agreements

1933

January	Hitler becomes Chancellor
February	Japan leaves League of Nations

1934

October	'Peace Ballot'

1935

June	Anglo-German Naval Agreement
June 1935–May 1937	Baldwin's third government
August	India Act
October	Mussolini invades Abyssinia
November	General election
December	Hoare–Laval Pact; Eden Foreign Secretary

1936

January	Death of George V Accession of Edward VIII

March	Germany occupies Rhineland
July	Spanish Civil War begins
December	Abdication of Edward VIII
	Accession of George VI
May 1937–May 1940	Neville Chamberlain's government
1938	
February	Eden resigns
September	Munich crisis
1939	
March	German occupation of Prague
	British Treaty with Poland
August	Russo-German Pact
September	Second World War begins
1940	
April	Germany occupies Norway
May–June	Battle of France
May 1940–July 1945	Churchill's war coalition
June	Italy enters war
August–September	Battle of Britain
December 1940–February 1941	Wavell defeats Italians in North Africa
1941	
February	Rommel arrives in Tripoli
March–April	Greek campaign
April	Rommel besieges Tobruk
May	Evacuation of Crete
	Defeat of Iraq
June	Syrian campaign
	Germany invades Russia
	Failure of 'Battleaxe'
	Wavell replaced by Auchinleck
November	Operation 'Crusader' relieves Tobruk
December	Pearl Harbor
	Fall of Hong Kong
1942	
February	Fall of Singapore
June	Fall of Tobruk

435

October–November	Montgomery's victory at El Alamein
November	'Torch'
December	Beveridge Report
1943	
January	Casablanca meeting
May	Germans surrender in Tunis
July	Invasion of Sicily
	Fall of Mussolini
September	Italian armistice
	Anglo-American forces cross to Italy
November–December	Cairo and Teheran conferences
1944	
January	Anzio landing
June	Invasion of Normandy – 'Overlord'
	Fall of Rome
July	American breakthrough at Avranches
September	Arnhem
	Second Quebec conference
December	Hitler's Ardennes offensive
1945	
February	Yalta conference
April	Deaths of Roosevelt, Mussolini and Hitler
May	Unconditional surrender by Germany
	Labour leaves coalition; Churchill's 'Caretaker' government formed
July	General election
July 1945–February 1951	Attlee's first government
1945–7	Nationalization measures passed
August 1945	Surrender of Japan
1946	
March	Churchill's 'Iron Curtain' speech
1947	
June	Marshall Plan announced

July	Dollar crisis
August	India and Pakistan given independence
December	Palestine Mandate abandoned
1948	
March	State of Israel proclaimed
July	National Health Service inaugurated
1949	
May	Berlin blockade lifted
September	Sterling devalued
December	Parliament Act
1950	
February	General election
February 1950–October 1951	Attlee's second government
June	Korean War begins
December	Nationalization of Anglo-Iranian Oil Company (BP)
1951	
February	Expanded armament programme announced
April	Gaitskell's budget; resignations of Bevan and Wilson
May	The Burgess–Maclean episode
October	General election
October 1951–April 1955	Churchill's second government
1952	
February	Death of George VI; accession of Queen Elizabeth II
April	Budget and defeat of 'Robot'
July	Fall of King Farouk
1953	
July	Churchill's stroke
August	Return of the Shah of Iran
1955	
April	Churchill resigns
April 1955–January 1957	Eden's government
May	General election
December	Attlee succeeded by Gaitskell

1956
March	Dismissal of General Glubb
	Deportation of Archbishop
	Makarios
April	Visit by Khrushchev
	Macmillan's budget
June	Suez base evacuated
July	Nationalization of Suez Canal
	Company
October	SCUA Conference
November	Invasion of and withdrawal from
	Egypt

1957
January	Resignation of Eden
January 1957–October 1963	Macmillan's government
March	Treaty of Rome
	Ghana receives independence
May	First British hydrogen bomb
	exploded
August	Malay Federation receives
	independence

1958
January	Resignation of Thorneycroft,
	Powell and Birch
	West Indian Federation
	inaugurated
April	Life Peerages Act

1959
February	Cyprus granted independence
June	Singapore granted independence
October	General election won by
	Macmillan

1960
February	Macmillan's 'wind of change'
	speech
May	Collapse of summit conference
July	Cabinet reconstructed
1960–62	Conscription abolished
	Independence for Nigeria,
	Tanzania and Uganda

438

1961
April   Selwyn Lloyd's 'pay pause'
July   Britain applies to accede to
                                   Treaty of Rome
August   Labour takes lead in opinion polls
                                   till 1964

1962
July   Macmillan dismisses a third of
                                   his Cabinet
October–November   Cuba crisis
December   Nuclear agreement with USA at
                                   Nassau

1963
January   De Gaulle's veto
                                   Gaitskell dies; succeeded by
                                   Harold Wilson
June   Victoria Falls Conference to
                                   arrange dissolution of Central
                                   African Federation
                                   Profumo Scandal
                                   Renunciation of Peerages Act
August   Test Ban Treaty
October   Macmillan resigns, succeeded by
                                   Sir Alec Douglas-Home
October 1963–October 1964   Sir Alec Douglas-Home's
                                   government

1964
October   General election; defeat of
                                   Conservatives

NOTES

CHAPTER ONE

1 David Edwards (ed.), *Inside Asquith's Cabinet, From the Diaries of Charles Hobhouse* (1977), 247.
2 Richard Shannon, *The Crisis of Imperialism* (1974), 469–72.
3 See Martin Pugh, 'Asquith, Bonar Law and the First Coalition', *Historical Journal* XVII, 4 (1974), 813–36.
4 Quoted in Roy Jenkins, *Asquith* (1964), 334.
5 Earl of Oxford and Asquith, *Memories and Reflections* II (1928), 93–4.
6 Winston Churchill, *The World Crisis 1911–1918* II (new ed. 1938), 824.
7 Quoted in Robert Rhodes James, *Gallipoli* (1965), 314–15.
8 Ibid., 353.
9 Ibid., 348.
10 The latter was a retrospective reconstruction.
11 Martin Gilbert, *Winston S. Churchill* III (1971), 236.
12 Robert Blake (ed.), *The Private Papers of Douglas Haig 1914–1919* (1952), 102.

CHAPTER TWO

1 Quoted in Martin Gilbert, *Winston S. Churchill* III (1971), 227.
2 See John Keegan, *The Face of Battle* (1976), 237–40.
3 Arthur J. Marder, *From Dreadnought to Scapa Flow* III (2nd ed. 1978).
4 See Marder, ibid II (1965), 436–40 for figures which follow.

CHAPTER THREE

1 Michael Howard, *The Continental Commitment* (1972).
2 The facts were first revealed in 1956 by Lord Beaverbrook who

had acquired the papers of Lloyd George, including his wife's diary. See his *Men and Power* (1956), 262–4.

CHAPTER FOUR

1 Quoted in Martin Pugh, 'Asquith, Bonar Law and the First Coalition', *Historical Journal* XVII, 4 (1974), 144.

CHAPTER FIVE

1 Charles Townshend, *The British Campaign in Ireland 1919–21* (1975).
2 Leland Lyons, *Ireland since the Famine* (1971).
3 Townshend, op. cit., 192.
4 An exception is John Ramsden, *The Age of Balfour and Baldwin* (1978), 159–60.
5 Not to be confused with the 'National Liberal Federation', the sovereign body of the Asquithians or with the 'Liberal Nationals', Sir John Simon's breakaway group formed in June 1931, who became allies of the Conservatives after 1932 and added to the confusion by rechristening themselves as 'National Liberals' in 1948.
6 Ramsden, op. cit., 134 and 162.
7 Martin Gilbert, *Winston S. Churchill* IV (1975), 862.
8 At least, these were the figures given at the time. A debate of the utmost unimportance has later taken place about their accuracy. J. C. C. Davidson's papers show a score of 185 to 88, Austen Chamberlain's 187 to 86 – with 13 abstentions.

CHAPTER SIX

1 Neither Baldwin in 1923, Neville Chamberlain in 1937, Churchill in 1940, Eden in 1955, Macmillan in 1957 nor Home in 1963 felt obliged to secure this ratification in advance. The adoption in 1965 of a formal electoral system within the party has, however, changed the situation.
2 Among them, alas, Robert Blake, *The Unknown Prime Minister* (1955), 492.
3 Ibid., 516–27.

1 David Marquand, *Ramsay MacDonald* (1977), 578.
Much of this chapter is based on this important book.

1 The Conservative and Liberal meetings consisted of MPs, peers and candidates. The Labour meeting contained the two former categories, no candidates, but the National Executive and the General Council of the TUC.
2 Including the author's grandfather who put the proceeds into safe mortgages at five or six per cent or even higher.
3 Robert Skidelsky, *Oswald Mosley* (1975), 288.

1 Frances Donaldson, *King Edward VIII* (1974), 59. This is one of the best royal biographies ever written, despite – perhaps because of – being 'unofficial'.
2 Ibid., 170.

1 The slogan of the Foreign Legion was 'Down with Intelligence. Long Live Death'.
2 Anthony Eden, *Facing the Dictators* (1962), 589.
3 Austen Chamberlain had died unexpectedly on 16 March 1937.
4 Private information.
5 Winston S. Churchill, *The Gathering Storm* (1948), 253.
6 Appreciation by Chiefs of Staff Committee, 20 February 1939, quoted in Michael Howard, *The Continental Commitment* (1972), 127.

CHAPTER TWELVE

1 Angus Calder, *The People's War* (1969), 40.
2 The story that he muttered in an aside 'and beat the buggers over the head with bottles; that's all we've got' is, alas, apocryphal, though *bien trouvé*.
3 See below, Chapter Thirteen.

CHAPTER FOURTEEN

1 See M. R. D. Foot and J. M. Langley, *MI9* (1979).

CHAPTER FIFTEEN

1 Max Hastings, *Overlord* (1984), 186–95.
2 The Russian check outside Warsaw was only partly caused by military factors. The non-communist Polish underground army had risen on 1 August. The evidence strongly suggests that Stalin was not sorry to see it crushed by the Germans.

CHAPTER SIXTEEN

1 Lord Moran, *Winston Churchill: The Struggle for Survival 1940–1965* (1966).
2 Quoted, Michael Foot, *Aneurin Bevan* II (1973), 216.
3 Ibid., 87 n. 2.

CHAPTER SEVENTEEN

1 Lord Butler, *The Art of the Possible* (1971), 135.
2 Michael Foot, *Aneurin Bevan* II (1973), 299.
3 Philip Williams, *Hugh Gaitskell* (1978), 251.
4 See Foot, op. cit., 305–15, 354–8; and Williams, op. cit., 278–83. See also K. O. Morgan, *Labour in Power* (1984), 443–4.
5 Williams, op. cit., 245, quoting evidence of Karel Kaplan in an interview with *The Times*, 6 May 1977.
6 Personal discussion with Lord Cobbold.
7 See Butler, op.cit., 159–60 on Swinton and Lyttelton; Birkenhead, *The Prof in Two Worlds* (1961), 284–9 which exaggerates Cherwell's role; David Carlton, *Anthony Eden* (1981), 296–7.
8 Carlton, op. cit., 300–302.
9 Barry Rubin, *Paved with Good Intentions* (1980), 77–80, based on talks with Kermit Roosevelt and his book *Countercoup* (1979) which was subsequently withdrawn under pressure from British Petroleum, the former AIOC.
10 Rubin, ibid., 89.

CHAPTER EIGHTEEN

1 Quoted in David Carlton, *Anthony Eden* (1981), 382.
2 Herman Finer, *Dulles over Suez* (1964), 48.
3 Christian Pineau, *1956 Suez* (1976), 81.
4 Selwyn Lloyd, *Suez 1956* (1978), 85.
5 Quoted in Kenneth Love, *Suez, the Twice-Fought War* (1969), 370.
6 It is true that a peerage was not regarded as a bar to Lord Halifax in 1940 but then it was a question of wartime emergency.

CHAPTER NINETEEN

1 Quoted in Philip Williams, *Hugh Gaitskell* (1978), 459.
2 Ibid., 471.
3 Nigel Fisher, *Harold Macmillan* (1982), 230.
4 Harold Macmillan, *Pointing the Way* (1972), 118–19.

CHAPTER TWENTY

1 The second was Mandy Rice Davis, who figured frequently with Christine Keeler in the scandal sheets.
2 Reginald Maudling, *Memoirs* (1978) 111.

EPILOGUE

1 This was the position of the author's parents with a joint income of £700 p.a. in the 1930s.
2 A. J. P. Taylor, *English History 1914–1945* (1965), 183 n.2.
3 Winston Churchill, *Lord Randolph Churchill* (new ed. 1951), 107.
4 No one has ever discovered an alleged Dr Condom. As for French letter, it is probably sheer nationalist prejudice at a time when such objects were thought of as improper. The French have retaliated with *capote Anglaise*.
5 Taylor, op. cit., 166 n.1.
6 Ian Gilmour, *The Body Politic* (1969), 320.

FURTHER READING

GENERAL

James Joll, *Europe since 1870* (1973). Useful for a general perspective. Effectively ends in 1953.

T. O. Lloyd, *Empire to Welfare State 1906–76* (2nd ed. 1979). A reliable survey but rather dull.

A. J. P. Taylor, *English History 1914–1945* (1965). Anything but dull, but not always reliable.

C. L. Mowat, *Britain between the Wars* (1955). Still very useful, especially on social history.

SOCIAL AND ECONOMIC

R. S. Sayers, *A History of Economic Change in England 1880–1939* (1967).

Sidney Pollard, *The Development of the British Economy 1914–1967* (1969). Idiosyncratic but important.

J. F. Wright, *Britain in the Age of Economic Management, an Economic History since 1939* (1979). A most perceptive short book.

A. H. Halsey (ed.), *Trends in British Society since 1900* (1972). Much the best on the subject.

Roy Harrod, *John Maynard Keynes* (1951).

POLITICAL AND CONSTITUTIONAL

K. O. Morgan, *Consensus and Disunity 1918–1922* (1979). *Labour in Power 1945–1951* (1984). Excellent accounts of the political situation after each world war.

Robert Blake, *The Conservative Party from Peel to Churchill* (1970). Shortly to be reissued and expanded to 1983.

Trevor Wilson, *The Downfall of the Liberal Party 1914–1935* (1966).

R. I. McKibbin, *The Evolution of the Labour Party 1910–1924* (1975).

Robert Skidelsky, *Politicians and the Slump* (1968). A good account of the Labour government of 1929–31.

Paul Addison, *The Road to 1945* (1975). An interesting analysis of wartime politics.

Ian Gilmour, *The Body Politic* (1969). The best description of the modern British constitution.

Robert Blake, *The Office of Prime Minister* (1974).

S. H. Beer, *Modern British Politics* (1965).

THE FIRST WORLD WAR

C. R. M. F. Cruttwell, *A History of the Great War* (1936). Stands the test of time remarkably well.

B. H. Liddell Hart, *History of the First World War* (reissued 1970, first published in 1934). More controversial.

Cyril Falls, *The First World War* (1960). Takes a different view.

Robert Blake (ed.), *The Private Papers of Douglas Haig* (1952). With an introduction analysing the politics of 1914–18.

A. J. Marder, *From Dreadnought to Scapa Flow* III (2nd ed. 1978). The most authoritative account of Jutland.

John Terraine, *To Win a War, 1918, the Year of Victory* (1978).

Robert Rhodes James, *Gallipoli* (1965).

Paul Fussell, *The Great War and Modern Memory* (1975). A strangely haunting description of the British experience on the western front.

R. H. Mottram, *The Spanish Farm Trilogy* (1927). The best novel about the 'Great War'.

John Keegan, *The Face of Battle* (1976) contains a splendid description of the battle of the Somme.

THE SECOND WORLD WAR

B. H. Liddell Hart, *History of the Second World War* (1970). The best single volume account.

David Fraser, *And We Shall Shock Them, the British Army in the Second World War* (1983).
    Alanbrooke (1982). Chapters 9 to the end give an excellent account of the main British strategic decisions.

Ronald Lewin, *Montgomery as Military Commander* (1971).
    Ultra Goes to War (1978).

Stephen Roskill, *Churchill and the Admirals* (1977).

Max Hastings, *Bomber Command* (1979).
    Overlord (1984).

Robert Wright, *Dowding and the Battle of Britain* (1969).

Dudley Saward, *'Bomber' Harris* (1984).

Evelyn Waugh, *The Sword of Honour* (1962). A brilliant trilogy of war novels issued in one volume.

BIOGRAPHIES

Kenneth Rose, *King George V* (1983).

J. W. Wheeler-Bennett, *King George VI* (1958).

Stephen Koss, *Asquith* (1976).

Thomas Jones, *Lloyd George* (1951).

Robert Blake, *The Unknown Prime Minister, Life and Times of Andrew Bonar Law* (1955).

H. Montgomery Hyde, *Baldwin, the Unexpected Prime Minister* (1973).

David Marquand, *Ramsay MacDonald* (1977).

Keith Feiling, *Neville Chamberlain* (1946).

Henry Pelling, *Winston Churchill* (1974).

Kenneth Harris, *Attlee* (1982).

David Carlton, *Anthony Eden* (1981).

Nigel Fisher, *Harold Macmillan* (1982).
Charles Petrie, *Austen Chamberlain* II (1940).
John Campbell, *F. E. Smith* (1983).
Alan Bullock, *The Life and Times of Ernest Bevin* (2 vols. 1960, 1967).
  Ernest Bevin, Foreign Secretary 1945–1951 (1983).

EMPIRE AND COMMONWEALTH

D. K. Fieldhouse, *The Colonial Empires* (1960).
Correlli Barnett, *The Collapse of British Power* (1972).
Bernard Porter, *The Lion's Share* (1975).
Jan Morris, *Farewell the Trumpets* (1978).
E. J. Hobsbawm, *Industry and Empire* (1968).

FOREIGN POLICY

A. J. P. Taylor, *The Origins of the Second World War* (1961).
  Perverse, paradoxical and provocative.
F. S. Northedge, *The Troubled Giant, Britain among the Great Powers 1916–1939* (1974).
  Descent from Power, British Foreign Policy 1945–1973 (1974).
Paul Kennedy, *The Realities behind Diplomacy* (1981).

BOOKS OF REFERENCE

The Concise Dictionary of National Biography 1901–1970. Useful in itself and a guide to the full entries in the decennial volumes covering 1912–1970.
David Butler and Anne Sloman, *British Political Facts 1900–1979* (5th ed. 1980). An invaluable aid to all historians of the period.
The British General Election Series sponsored by Nuffield College, Oxford, which covers all elections since 1945.

INDEX

INDEX

Strachey, John 206, 315
Strauss, George 317
Strauss, Harry 302
Stresa Conference *1935* 187–8, 189
submarines: in World War I 30–31, 47; in
    World War II 288, 265–6
Sudan, the 250
Sudetenland, the 212–15
Suez Canal 81, 329, 351, 362; in World War
    II 249; *1956* crisis 349, 363–78, 381
Summerskill, Dr Edith 314
Sulva Bay 9, 10
Sweden 230
Swinton, Lord 345, 355 *see also* Cunliffe-
    Lister and Lloyd-Graeme
Sykes-Picot Agreement 75
Syria 74, 75, 387; in World War II 253

Talleyrand, C. M. de 432
Tanganyika 75, 398, 399, 421
tank warfare 49, 58; in World War II 233,
    240, 254, 260–64, 295
tariff truce *1929* 141
tariffs *see* protection
Taylor, A. J. P. 127, 280, 425
Taylor, Vice-Adm. 146
Tebessa 271
Tedder, Air Chief Marshal 288, 303
television 346–7
Templer, Sir Gerald 364
That Was the Week That Was 407
Thirkell, Angela 316
Thomas, H. 368
Thomas, J. H. 112, 135, 139, 162
Thomson, Lord 141
Thorneycroft, Peter 302, 393, 395, 404;
    Chancellor of the Exchequer 381, 383, 384
Times, The 100, 147, 193, 214, 369
Tirpitz 266–7
Tobruk 250, 259, 261, 262, 263, 267
Topping, Sir Robert 147
'Torch' 264, 269–73, 274
Townshend, Gen. 14, 15–18
Townshend, C. 84, 87
trade unions 425; Polish munitions ship and
    77–8; political contributions to 125; post-
    war 318; Communists in 410
Trades Disputes Act *1927* 124–5, 142, 318
Trades Union Congress 77–8, 383, 394;
    General strike and 121–5; *1931* financial
    crisis and 154–5, 442n
Transjordan 74, 421
'Transportation Plan' 291–2
trench warfare 11, 19–24, 48–9
Trenchard, Lord 255
Trevelyan, Sir Charles 113
Trieste 352
Tripoli 250, 261
'Triton' 266
Trondheim 236
Truman, Harry 303; Potsdam conference and
    307; relations with Russia and 310, 311;
    ends 'Lend-lease' 312; Greece and Turkey

supported by 326; Palestine and 329–33;
    Korean War and 338; rearmament and 341
Truman Doctrine 326–7
Tshombe, Moise 401
Tunis 223, 271
Tunisia 269–73, 274–5
Turkey 98–9, 104–5, 221, 423; in World War
    I 12, 15, 17–18, 50–51, 60; post-war
    settlement and 74–6; in World War II 251,
    279; aid to 326; Baghdad Pact 359; Cyprus
    and 362, 389

Uganda 398, 399
Ullswater, Lord 138
Ulster 2, 82, 83
Ulster Unionist Party 86
Ultra 243, 244, 245, 250, 251, 252, 254, 266,
    271, 272, 277–8, 292, 294; importance of
    247–8
unemployment 136; post-war 76, 78, 104;
    1929 elections and 133; in the Depression
    137–42, 169; in the *1950s* 345, 355, 383; in
    the *1960s* 416–17
unemployment benefit 148; May report 150–
    51; cuts in 152–61 *passim*, 169
United Arab Republic 387
United Empire Party 146
United Nations 302; Palestine and 331–2;
    Korean War and 338; Suez crisis and 370,
    371–2, 376
United States of America 128, 136, 209, 226,
    246, 328; in World War I 47, 56–7, 59;
    Treaty of Versailles and 72; Britain in debt
    to 105–6; enters World War II 256–8,
    276–7; in World War II 269–303 *passim*;
    British imperialism and 280; servicemen in
    Britain 281; atomic bomb dropped by
    310–12; Greece and Turkey supported by
    326; Palestine and 329–33; rearmament
    and 340–41; economy 346; Eisenhower
    Presidency 348–51, 359; Suez crisis and
    363–78 *passim*; Bermuda conference *1957*
    381–2; improved relations with 387; joins
    Baghdad Pact 388; reconnaissance plane
    shot down *1960* 395; nuclear weapons
    agreement *1962* 404; power of 422–3
Uthwatt, Mr Justice 305

V1 and V2 rockets 290–91, 299
Vansittart, Sir Robert 167, 185, 190, 192,
    211
Vassal, J. W. C. 410
VE Day 305
Venizelos, E. 14, 76
Verdun, Battle of 22, 25, 30
Versailles, Treaty of 71–4
Victoria, Queen 431
Vietnam *see* Indo-China, French
Vimy Ridge 46
VJ Day 312
von Klüge, Gen. 295
von Rundstedt, Gen. 292
von Schlieffen, Count 233

461

wage restraint 383, 385–6, 393
Wal-Wal incident 186
Wall Street Crash 137
war, experience of 429
Ward, Mrs Dudley 196–7
Ward, Stephen 411
Wardlaw-Milne, Sir John 267
Warren, Sir Herbert 196
Warsaw 296, 442n
Waterhouse, Col. Ronald 108
Waterhouse, Capt. Charles 351
Watkinson, Harold 395
Waugh, Evelyn 205, 231
Wavell, Gen. Sir Archibald 240, 249–50, 251, 253–4, 324
We Can Conquer Unemployment 133
Welensky, Sir Roy 400, 401
welfare state, the 317–18
West Indian Federation 389
Wheatley, John 112, 135
White, Charlie 307
White, Sir Dick 361
Wigg, George 411–12
Williams, Philip 385
Willingdon, Lord 175
Wilson, Sir Henry 45, 46; becomes CIGS 52–3, 55; assassinated 90, 94
Wilson, Harold 336–7, 340, 383; becomes Labour leader 4–5, 408; becomes Prime Minister *1964* 417–19
Wilson, Maitland 288, 289
Wilson, Woodrow 71, 72, 136
Windsor, Duke and Duchess of 195–203
Winterbotham, Grp Capt. 247
women: enfranchized 61, 64, 69
Wood, Sir Kingsley 237
Woolton, Lord 238, 335
Workers' Weekly 115
World War I: shell shortage 1, 5; effect of, on the Liberals 2–3; direction of 4–7; War Council established 5; Dardanelles Committee 6–7; civilian life and 7–8, 24; Cabinet War Committee 10; casualties 10, 14, 25–6, 28, 37; dispute between

'Easterners' and 'Westerners' 11–12, 15, 42, 44–5; *Official History* 12, 28; on the Western Front 19–28; war correspondents 24; artillery bombardment 26–7, 49; naval strength 29–30, 37; War Cabinet 43–4; Imperial War Cabinet 44; convoy system 47; civil-military relationship in 52–3; end of 60; aftermath of 76–9; *see also* trench warfare
World War II: causes of 73; Eastern front *1939* 221; declaration of war 224–5, 230; British Expeditionary Force in France 228, 241; evacuation during 231; the blackout 231–2; army recruitment 232; France occupied 241; British invasion plans 242–5; intelligence in 247–8; in the Mediterranean 249–54; casualties in 254–5; strategic bombing 255–6, 286; Japan and USA enter war 256–8, 276–7; aircraft carriers in 257; allied strategic discussions *1942* 263–4; German defeat in Tunisia 269–73; allied command system changed 272; Italian armistice 278–9; second front discussed at Casablanca 273–5; effect of, on Britain 280–85, 299; British support for second front 282; allied conferences *1943* 286–8; D-Day invasion 288–95; effect of supply shortages 296, 298; allied defeat at Arnhem 297–8; Quebec conference *1944* 298–9; Yalta conference *1945* 301–2; George VI and 348

Yalta conference *1945* 301–2, 310
Yamamoto, Adm. 257–8
Yemen, the 387
Younger, Sir George 66, 91, 93, 96, 104
Ypres 21, 22
Yugoslavia 73, 221, 352; in World War II 251, 300

Zambia 401
Zinoviev letter 116–17
Zionism 329–33